MUTANTS & MYSTICS

MUTANTS

THE UNIVERSITY OF CHICAGO PRESS · CHICAGO AND LONDON

& MYSTICS

SCIENCE FICTION,
SUPERHERO COMICS,
AND THE PARANORMAL

JEFFREY J. KRIPAL

The University of Chicago Press, Chicago 60637
The University of Chicago Press, Ltd., London
© 2011 by Jeffrey J. Kripal
All rights reserved. Published 2011.
Paperback edition 2015
Printed in China

24 23 22 21 20 19 18 17 16 15   2 3 4 5 6

ISBN-13: 978-0-226-45383-5 (cloth)
ISBN-13: 978-0-226-27148-4 (paper)
ISBN-13: 978-0-226-45385-9 (e-book)
10.7208/chicago/9780226453859.001.0001

Library of Congress Cataloging-in-Publication Data

Kripal, Jeffrey J. (Jeffrey John), 1962– author.
    Mutants and mystics : science fiction, superhero
comics, and the paranormal / Jeffrey J. Kripal
        p. cm.
    Includes bibliographical references and index.
    ISBN-13: 978-0-226-45383-5 (cloth : alkaline
paper)
    ISBN-10: 0-226-45383-9 (cloth : alkaline
paper) 1. Comic books, strips, etc.—United
States—History and criticism. 2. Superheroes in
literature. 3. Occultism in literature. 4. Science
fiction, American—History and criticism. 5. Fantasy
fiction, American—History and criticism. 6. Myth in
literature. 7. Literature and myth. I. Title
    PN6725.K75 2011
    741.5'973—dc22
                                                    2011004431

for my brother Jerry,
who collected and lived these fantastic worlds with me

THE SUPER-STORY

MEN DO NOT SUFFICIENTLY REALIZE THAT THEIR
FUTURE IS IN THEIR OWN HANDS. . . . THEIRS [IS] THE
RESPONSIBILITY, THEN, FOR DECIDING IF THEY WANT
MERELY TO LIVE, OR INTEND TO MAKE JUST THE
EXTRA EFFORT REQUIRED FOR FULFILLING, EVEN ON
THEIR REFRACTORY PLANET, THE ESSENTIAL FUNC-
TION OF THE UNIVERSE, WHICH IS A MACHINE FOR
THE MAKING OF GODS.

HENRI BERGSON, *THE TWO SOURCES OF
MORALITY AND RELIGION (1932)*

THE IMAGES
AUTHORING [AND DRAWING] THE IMPOSSIBLE

MAN IS A CREATURE WHO MAKES PICTURES OF
HIMSELF AND THEN COMES TO RESEMBLE THE
PICTURE.
IRIS MURDOCH

THE THING ABOUT COMICS . . . IT'S THE MAGICAL EL-
EMENTS OF IT. THAT'S WHAT I LOVE MOST: THE AR-
TIFACT. . . . THE IDEA THAT THE COMIC FORM ITSELF
IS REALLY BEAUTIFUL BECAUSE IT ENGAGES THE
RIGHT HEMISPHERE AND THE LEFT HEMISPHERE
OF THE BRAIN SIMULTANEOUSLY, SO YOU'RE PROB-
ABLY GETTING INTERESTING HOLOGRAPHIC EFFECTS,
WHICH I THINK IS WHAT ALLOWS COMICS TO COME
TO LIFE IN THE WAY THEY DO.
GRANT MORRISON IN PATRICK MEANEY, **OUR
SENTENCE IS UP**

The mythical themes and paranormal currents of popular culture are generally transmitted through two modes intimately working together: words and images. Here something like the comic-book medium—serialized panels that look more than a little like frames of moving film—is definitely a good share of the message, and it certainly is most of the magic. In the spirit of the conclusion of my last book, where I suggested that we think of an "author of the impossible" as someone who can bring online both sides of the brain, I have transmitted my ideas here through one left-brain-dominant mode (writing) and one right-brain-dominant mode (graphic art). Moreover, in this same two-brained spirit, I have "explained" the illustrations in the body of the text, even as I have "illustrated" my ideas through the images.

I am reminded here of something the French chemical engineer René Warcollier suggested in his 1946 Sorbonne lecture, which became *Mind to Mind* (1948), a seminal text on telepathic drawings (*les dessins télépathiques*) that, along with Betty Edwards's *Drawing on the Right Side of the Brain* (1979), has informed my own impossible thinking about the secret life of popular culture. Warcollier, who was first awakened to the subject by his own telepathic dreams, believed that telepathic communications most likely reveal a form of psychical operation that employs paranormal processes, predates the acquisition of language, and reveals the very "substratum of thought" in what he called "word-pictures." As Warcollier demonstrated through a series of drawings and his own text, condensed, telepathically communicated word-pictures are often creatively expanded on, exaggerated, and added to by the recipient's imagination until they become words and pictures, and finally stories—in essence, minimyths.

Word-pictures. This is simply an initial way to suggest that there is something very special about the double-genres that we are about to encounter, and that it makes no sense at all to encounter them only in their word forms. The pictures are just as important, if not more so. Even if what the images carry cannot be captured by words, and *especially* when what they carry cannot be captured by words, these beautiful images can transmit something directly—"mind to mind," we might say.

0.1 Kali exultant. Photograph by Rachel Fell McDermott, used with permission.

0.2 The Tree of Life. *Promethea* #13 (La Jolla, CA: America's Best Comics, 2001), n.p.

0.3 Sex magic instructions. *Promethea* #10 (La Jolla, CA: America's Best Comics, 2000), cover image.

0.4 Aliens behind the comic. *The Invisibles* #21 (New York: DC Comics/Vertigo, 1996), cover image.

0.5 Nailing the abduction experience. *The Invisibles*, graphic novel edition (New York: DC Comics/Vertigo, 2002), vol. 7, 129.

1.1 The hollow earth strikes back. *The Fantastic Four* #1 (New York: Marvel Comics, 1961), cover image.

1.2 A back-cover sighting. *Amazing Stories* 21, no. 11 (Chicago: Ziff-Davis Publishing Company, 1947), back cover.

1.3 I Am the Man. John Uri Lloyd, with illustrations by J. Augustus Knapp, *Etidorhpa; or, The End of the Earth: The Strange History of a Mysterious Being and the Account of a Remarkable Journey* (Cincinnati: Robert Clarke Company, 1898), frontispiece.

1.4 The gray guide. Lloyd, *Etidorhpa*, 95.

2.1 Dr. Mystic bound for India. "Dr. Mystic: The Occult Detective," *Comics Magazine* #1 (May 1936), reprinted in Greg Sadowski, ed., *Supermen! The First Wave of Comic Book Heroes, 1936–1941* (Seattle: Fantagraphic Books, 2009), 12.

2.2 Superman as insect. *Action Comics* #1 (New York: Detective Comics, 1938), 1, reprinted in *Superman Chronicles* (New York: DC Comics, 2006), 1:4.

2.3 An insectoid alien. Abductee drawing reproduced in John E. Mack, *Passport to the Cosmos: Human Transformation and Alien Encounters* (Largo: Kunati, 2008).

2.4 An insectoid superhero. *Ultimate Spider-Man* #1 (New York: Marvel Comics, 2000), cover image.

All images, unless otherwise noted, are from my private collection. They are reproduced here under the professional practice of fair use for the purposes of historical discussion and scholarly interpretation. All characters and images remain the
property of their respective copyright holders credited above.

ACKNOWLEDGMENTS

LET THE BOY MATURE, BUT DO NOT LET THE MAN
HOLD BACK THE BOY.
PHILIP K. DICK

This is a book about some astonishing artists and authors, some of whom are still living and working among us. These individuals generously answered my insistent queries and read what I had written about them with both grace and helpful criticism. I am grateful, above all, to these practicing artists and authors: Doug Moench, Alvin Schwartz, Whitley Strieber, Roy Thomas, and Barry Windsor-Smith. In this context, I also want to thank Anne Strieber, who did so much to help me with Whitley's work and the Communion letters, and Lawrence Sutin, the pioneering biographer and editor of Philip K. Dick. Larry's two biographies of Dick and Aleister Crowley signal the core idea of the present book, namely, that the roots and effects of sci-fi and superhero fantasy are magical in structure and intent.

I would also like to thank a number of individuals from within the comic-book industry who helped me to understand that professional world. I am especially grateful to: Roy and Dann Thomas and Doug Moench again, for spending a week with a group of us in Big Sur and helping me with so many contacts and personalities; Ramona Fradon, for her own self-described gnostic quest and her teasing laughter at that oh-so-male fantasy that we call the superhero (I can still hear Ramona giggling); historian and archivist Bill Schelly, for his wonderful biography of Otto Binder and for pointing me toward Binder's archives at Texas A&M; historian and artist Christopher Knowles, for his pioneering *Our Gods Wear Spandex* and stunning blog-essays on Jack Kirby and all things pop-gnostic; and graphic artist Arlen Schumer, for his dramatic lectures and insightful writings on the art of the Silver Age (and a really cool Batman drawing/autograph).

There were also a number of individuals who intervened at key points in order to add rich historical and critical perspectives, especially: Victoria Nelson, with her own writings on the modern Gothic in figures like H. P. Lovecraft, Dan Brown, and Guillermo del Toro (none of whom, alas, I could treat here); Elliot Wolfson, with his vision of the Kabbalah and his help here with my reading of Alan Moore's Tree of Life; Rachel Fell McDermott, with her photos of the blue and black Kalis; Joscelyn Godwin, with help with the theosophical, Atlantean, and hollow-earth literature and a last-minute mailing involving Gene Roddenberry and a trance medium; Christopher McIntosh, with help with negotiating the Rosicrucian terrain; Hugh Urban, with help with the history of Scientology; Edwin May, with help with the personal and political complexities of the remote-viewing history; Istvan Csicsery-Ronay, with a cool tip on Julian Huxley; Erik Davis, with a close read in light of his own remarkable scholarship on the gnostic undercurrents of contemporary popular culture; Chip McAuley, with a very close and helpful read-through at the end; Sascha Scatter of the Icarus Project, with her readings of my work on the human potential in the light of her own mad gifts and inspiring zine, *Mutant Superpowers & Lithium Pills*; Dean Nicholas Shumay of the School of the Humanities at Rice University, with some generous financial help that made this book, literally, so colorful; and Hal Hall and Catherine Coker of Texas A&M University. The Moskowitz Collection on pulp and science fiction at that institution was a tremendous help with the Binder materials and a special inspiration for chapter 2.

None of this would have been possible without the support of two men: T. David Brent, my longtime editor at the University of Chicago Press, and Michael Murphy, the cofounder of the Esalen Institute and director of its Center for Theory and Research, which has become a kind of intellectual-spiritual home for me. David patiently guided and encouraged me throughout what proved to be a very long process (and two books instead of one), and Mike and Esalen supported the project by funding a multiyear symposia series on the paranormal and popular culture through which I was able to invite and meet many of the authors and artists treated in the pages that follow. There is really no way to thank, adequately anyway, either man.

The book is dedicated to my brother Jerry, who, along with my cousins Chris and Tim Fiser, collected and lived these fantasies with me when we were all still boys. I am reminded in this context of something the "dead" Philip K. Dick channeled through a medium to his friend and fellow writer, D. Scott Apel: "Let the boy mature, but do not let the man hold back the boy." I have taken Phil's channeled advice to heart in the pages that follow. I remain a man, but I have not held back the boy—at all.

Finally, I would like to thank Wendy Doniger, my Doktormutter and intellectual mentor who once remote viewed an apple corer in Big Sur with Russell Targ. Just nailed the thing. Wendy, this is my myth-book. I hope you find Wonder Woman and the "mental radio" you share with her in its strange pages.

ABBREVIATIONS

have listed below the primary texts of the present work, which I cite in these abbreviated forms in the body of the book. The various superhero story arcs, and many more not listed here, were generally consulted in their archival, omnibus, or graphic-novel editions. The page numbers cited generally refer to these editions and not to the original comics, unless the omnibus edition in question (e.g., *New X-Men*) does not use global page numbers. In that case, I employ an issue/page number sequence.

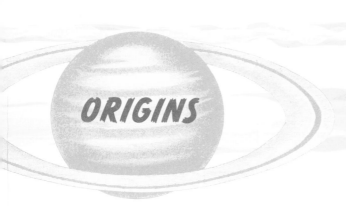

ORIGINS

I am a historian of religions, working in a field that most people would call comparative religion. Basically, I study and compare religions like other people study and
compare political systems, novels, or movies. More especially, I read and interpret
mystical literature, that is, texts from around the world that express some fundamental
but normally hidden connection between divinity and humanity, however these two
natures are conceived. Another way of saying this is that I study how human beings
come to realize that they are gods in disguise. Or superhumans.

In this divine-human spirit, I explore in the pages that follow some of the mythical
themes and paranormal currents of American popular culture. By *mythical themes*, I
mean a set of tropes or story lines about the metamorphosis of the human form that
are deeply indebted to the history of the religious imagination but have now taken on
new scientific or parascientific forms in order to give shape to innumerable works of

pulp fiction, science fiction, superhero comics, and metaphysical film. By *paranormal currents*, I mean the real-life mind-over-matter experiences of artists and authors that often inspire and animate these stories, rendering them both mysteriously plausible and powerfully attractive. Essentially, what I hope to show is that what makes these particular forms of American popular culture so popular is precisely the paranormal, the paranormal here understood as a dramatic *physical* manifestation of the meaning and force of consciousness itself.

No wonder this stuff is so popular. It's us.

In a previous work, *Authors of the Impossible*, I explored the "fantastic" structure of the paranormal, that is, the often frankly paradoxical ways that these kinds of experience express themselves between and beyond the linear, rational, and scientific ways of the left brain and the holistic, symbolic, and image-based ways of the right brain. If that first volume was historical and theoretical, this one is experimental and illustrative (literally), that is, it applies this model of the fantastic to different writers and artists as it traces out the broad narrative or Super-Story that these fusions appear to be forming around us, in us, and as us.

I must stress that this book is not a cultural history of pulp fiction, science fiction, or superhero comics. Those books have already been written, and written well.[1] Nor is this exactly a book about how superhero comics draw deeply on ancient myths and modern occultism in order to reshape them for the contemporary world. That thesis has been most clearly and provocatively stated by comic-book artist Christopher Knowles in *Our Gods Wear Spandex*.[2]

My project is different. Like Knowles, I am interested in what sources my authors and artists draw upon to sketch their stories, but I want to take this project two steps further by showing how these modern mythologies can be fruitfully read as cultural transformations of real-life paranormal experiences, and how there is no way to disentangle the very public pop-cultural products from the very private paranormal experiences. And that, I want to suggest, is precisely what makes them *fantastic*.

ON THE HORROR AND THE HUMOR

There is another way to say all this. It appears that the paranormal often needs the pop-cultural form to appear at all. The truth needs the trick, the fact the fantasy. It is almost as if the left brain will not let the right brain speak (which it can't anyway, since language is generally a left-brain function), so the right brain turns to image and story to say what it has to say (without saying it). Consider how back in the late 1970s the prolific comic-book writer Doug Moench found himself writing out the real in a work of fantasy a few seconds before it became the real, in fact. I sat down with Doug in the spring of 2009. Here is the story he told me.

Moench had just finished writing a scene for a *Planet of the Apes* comic book about a black-hooded gorilla named Brutus. The scene involved Brutus invading the human hero's home, where he grabbed the man's mate by the neck and held a gun to her head in order to manipulate the hero. Just as Doug finished this scene, he heard his wife call for him in an odd sort of way from the living room across the house. He got up, walked the length of the house, and entered the living room only to encounter a man in a black hood with one arm around his wife's neck and the other holding a gun to her head: "It was exactly what I had written. . . . it was so, so immediate in relation to the writing and such an exact duplicate of what I had written, that it became an instant altered state. The air in the room congealed, became almost like fog, and yet, paradoxically, I could see with greater clarity. I could see the individual threads of his black hood." Doug's emotional response to this series of events was a very understandable and natural one. He became obsessed with the black-hooded intruder for months, then years. More immediately, he found it very difficult to write, so terrified was he of that eerie connection between what he might write and what might happen: "It really does make you wonder. Are you seeing the future? Are you creating a reality? Should you give up writing forever after something like that happens? I don't know."[3]

The paranormal, of course, is not always this dark and disturbing. On a lighter note, consider the tongue-in-cheek blockbuster film *Ghostbusters* (1984) that comedian Dan Aykroyd cowrote with Harold Ramis. It would be easy indeed to dismiss all that ectoplasm as pure satire.

Except for fact that the film emerged from four generations of Aykroyd's attending, writing about, and studying séances. Dan Aykroyd's great-grandfather, Samuel August Aykroyd, presided over his own home Spiritualist circle with a medium named Walter Ashurst, whose favorite reading was *The Shadow*, an early and unmistakable precursor of the superhero genre. The actor's paternal grandfather, Maurice, was a Bell Telephone engineer who, Dan Aykroyd recalls, "actually queried his colleagues about the possibility of constructing a high-vibration crystal radio as a mechanical method for contacting the spiritual world."[4] Maurice's son Peter H. Aykroyd, the actor's father, continued the tradition by keeping books on séances he attended and writing a history of psychical research entitled *A History of Ghosts*, which includes such marvels as a discussion of a "German ectoplasm hunter," a wax cast of a materialized hand, and a totally crazy photo of a "teleplasmic mass" emerging from the nose of a medium in which multiple faces appear, including that of Sir Arthur Conan Doyle, the famous detective writer and deeply committed Spiritualist.

Not that Peter Aykroyd buys all this stuff. He clearly does not. But he also, just as clearly, does not dismiss it all. His conclusion is especially relevant to our own approach to the paranormal through the medium of popular culture: "A thought has been in the back of my mind over the years as I've gone through these files and heard these stories: Whether they were believers or skeptics or somewhere in between, those who have experienced psychical phenomena have been entertained. Frightened, amused, touched, moved. And aren't these precisely the emotions we want to experience when we attend a play, or see a movie, or go to a ballet? . . . Performers? Performances? Created characters? Could these phrases be keys to the phenomenon of spirit contact?" By such questions, Peter Aykroyd does not mean to suggest pure stagecraft or simple deceit. He means to suggest what he calls "the existence of layers of unconscious creative potential in the minds of sitters" that create, quite outside any conscious control, an "apparitional drama."[5] If I read him right, he means to suggest that spiritualistic phenomena were a kind of spontaneous, unconscious projection of the psyches present, a quasi-physical projection that needed the premiere entertainment form of the time—live theater—to manifest and enter our public reality.

As for the actor and comedian himself: "My brother Peter and I read [these accounts] avidly and became lifelong supporters of the American Society for Psychical Research, and from all this *Ghostbusters* got made." Actually, there was more to it than this.

Aykroyd was sitting on his family's Canadian property, contemplating tearing down his great-grandfather's house. He asked his departed ancestor if this was okay. It was not. "Suddenly I heard three snaps and everything vibrated like there was electricity around the whole area where I was sitting." He restored the farmhouse. *Ghostbusters*, he believes, was inspired by the same beloved ancestor, "so that I could keep this place as a shrine to a great Canadian spiritualist—my great-grandfather—and to his son and grandson."[6] In short, there is a real-world paranormal context, four generations of context in fact, to what looks at first blush to be a work of pure fantasy and comic pop culture.

And there is more still. Dan Aykroyd, it turns out, is also a serious and eloquent UFO witness and even had what he believes was a brief encounter with some Men in Black, while standing on a street corner and talking to the pop singer Britney Spears on a cell phone about an upcoming *Saturday Night Live* gig, no less.[7] It does not get more pop-paranormal than that!

THE SECRET LIFE OF SUPERPOWERS (AND THIS BOOK)

Drawing on such real-world theater, I want to suggest that the psyche and our social consensus of what reality is somehow "make each other up" within a constant loop of Consciousness and Culture, and that the Culture through which Consciousness often manifests itself most dramatically as the paranormal is that form in which the imagination (and so the image) are given the freest and boldest reign: popular culture. You will find here, then, no proofs *or* debunkings of this or that extraordinary experience. I will make no attempt to prove, say, that what Doug Moench experienced was a terrifying but simple coincidence, or that there is no such thing as a ghost or a UFO. I am neither a denying debunker nor a true believer, and anyone who reads me as either is misreading me.

As a species of the fantastic, of the both-and, what I want to call the secret life of superpowers exists between and beyond these two, equally silly options. There are two distinct but related levels to this secret life—a public mythical level and a personal paranormal level.

On the public mythical level, this secret life reveals itself as a certain metamyth or Super-Story, a deep, often unconscious narrative that underlies and shapes much of contemporary popular culture. This Super-Story with its seven mythemes (explained shortly) is grounded very much in the particulars of American intellectual, literary, scientific, military, commercial, and political history—all those particulars that have made America a "superpower"—but it also participates in the ancient history and universal structures of the human religious imagination and so, in the end, transcends anything solely political or specifically "American." As a whole, this mythical level is certainly speculative, but its basic plots and themes should be familiar to most readers. One can, and should, debate the particular whole that I construct out of these seven parts—for my Super-Story is an imaginative act in itself—but the parts themselves are fairly obvious once they are identified and explained.

On the personal paranormal level, this secret life shows itself to be of an entirely different order. It is its own thing. Accordingly, this level of my argument is much more speculative in its attempt to confront the impossible fact that many of the extraordinary capacities that science fiction stories and superhero comics treat as fantasies (telepathy, precognition, psychokinetic or magical influence, subtle bodies and energies, cosmic unity, and clairvoyance, to name the most common) are well-documented experiences in the history of folklore, religion, and psychical research. These things are real in the simple sense that *they happen*. What they *mean* is an entirely different issue. But whatever they mean, I think it is safe to say that the sci-fi and superhero fantasies reflect, refract, and exaggerate these real-world paranormal capacities. Whether a particular reader finds this aspect of my argument convincing will depend largely on whether or not he or she has experienced such things.

It seems relevant to admit up front what I have already explained in too many other places, namely, that I have experienced such things—in Calcutta, in early November of 1989, to be precise. To employ the mythical language of superhero comics, that encounter is the true "Origins" of the present book.[8] That is when I got bit by my own radioactive spider (who, instead of a many-limbed spider, happened to be a many-limbed Tantric goddess).

It happened like this. For days, I had been participating in the annual Bengali celebration of the goddess Kali in the streets and temples of Calcutta (now Kolkata). One morning I woke up asleep—that is, I woke up, but my body did not. I couldn't move. I was paralyzed, like a corpse, more or less exactly like the Hindu god Shiva as he is traditionally portrayed in Tantric art, lying prostrate beneath Kali's feet. Then those "feet" touched me. An incredibly subtle, immensely pleasurable, and terrifyingly powerful energy entered me, possessed me, completely overwhelmed me. My vibrating body felt as if I had stuck a fork in a wall socket (all sexual innuendos intended . . . and wall sockets in India, by the way, put out far more voltage than American ones). Perhaps more significantly, my brain felt as if it had suddenly hooked up to some sort of occult Internet and that billions of bits of information were being downloaded into its neural net. Or better, it felt as if my entire being was being reprogrammed or rewired. A door in the Night, a portal, had opened.

And this was all before I felt my soul or subtle body (for it still had a shape) being pulled out of my physical body by some sort of invisible Super Magnet. "Electromagnetic" would work extremely well as a descriptor, as long as one understands that this Energy was both obviously conscious and superintelligent.

0.1 KALI EXULTANT

And somehow completely Other or, well, *alien*. In terms of the alien abduction literature, which, as we will see soon enough, bears an unusually intimate connection to the popular cultural materials—which in some sense *is* the experiential core behind the sci-fi and superhero folklore—abductees commonly speak of the "cellular change" they have undergone. Before they are beamed through a wall or ceiling, Star Trek style, it is "as if an intense energy is separating every cell, or even every molecule, of their bodies." After such experiences, moreover, they "feel that powerful residual energies are left in their bodies, as if stored in the cells themselves."[9]

That is *exactly* how it felt, and still feels in my memory. It is almost as if some kind of direct, right-brained, mind-to-mind transmission took place, as if those residual plasmic energies were encoded with ideas or structures that could not be "languaged" but could be stored and later intuited and consciously shaped in the mirror of other resonant or echoing authors until they could appear, now through the prism of the left brain's words, as my books.

In terms of popular cultural images, in this case metaphysical film, my own paranormal experience felt very much like a real-world combination of the scene in *Phenomenon*, during which George Malley (played by real-world Scientologist John Travolta) sees a bright flash in the sky on his thirty-seventh birthday and subsequently finds himself endowed with new intellectual and telekinetic powers, and the classroom scene in *Powder*, during which albino Jeremy Reed is lifted off the floor as his body attracts and then magnifies the electromagnetic energy generated by a classroom teaching device. Even closer to home is Philip K. Dick's late experience of himself as a "homoplasmate," that is, as a human being who has cross-bonded with living knowledge transmitted from a higher Source, in his case the brilliant pink light of Valis, the vast active living intelligence system whom we will encounter in chapter 6.

Such alien abduction scenes and sci-fi notions are hardly fictions for me, although, of course, they are *also* fictions. I am not claiming an alien abduction here, much less superpowers or a sci-fi divinization.[10] What I am claiming is a very real experience that I have absolutely no doubt vibrates at the energetic core of this book. The reader needs to know that. The damned thing is radioactive.

CORRESPONDENCES: ALAN MOORE AND GRANT MORRISON

I am hardly alone in my altered states of energy and subsequent authorial convictions. Indeed, it is precisely these kinds of paranormal experience that help inspire the work of some of the very best contemporary comic-book writers. Two in particular, Alan Moore and Grant Morrison, are very much worth dwelling on for a moment here in order to show just how central, how complex, and how sophisticated the paranormal currents of popular culture can become. It would certainly be difficult to name two more prominent and accomplished comic-book writers. It would also be difficult to name two other writers more committed to magical practices. Each man, it turns out, is a modern magus—literally.

British writer Alan Moore understands the arts to be deeply intertwined with occultism, by which he means a particular worldview that asserts that the physical world accessible to the senses is surrounded by and infused with another invisible world (occultus is Latin for "hidden") seemingly inhabited by a whole host of subtle beings and daimonic creatures.[11] Hence his mind-blowing Promethea series (1999–2005), an elaborate compendium of occult philosophy, Jewish mysticism, the Tarot, Tantric yoga, psychedelia, countercultural history, and sex magic, all expressed—and gorgeously illustrated by J. H. Williams III and colleagues—in the form of a superhero comic book.

The thirty-two books of the series are organized around Moore's own unique vision of the Kabbalah and its ten sefirot, the luminous "spheres," sapphire-like "reflections," or "numbers" of the divine nature in Jewish mysticism. Rendered as an abstract diagram sometimes referred to as the Tree of Life, there are twenty-two pathways connecting these ten spheres, hence the thirty-two books of Promethea.

A bit of historical background. In the third chapter of Genesis, the fruit of the Tree of Life is said to divinize the eater, but Adam and Eve are banished by God before they can partake of it. Kabbalah, in some sense, redeems this story by recreating that Tree of Life, rendered now as a mystical diagram, and teaching its adepts how to use it as a kind of supermap for the interpretation of the Torah or sacred scriptures and—this is the really shocking part—the actualization of God and the human soul. To put the matter most bluntly: deep reading and the esoteric interpretation of scripture through the ten spheres are understood to be cosmic acts that bring into being both divinity and humanity. Reality, if you will, comes to be in the space between the properly trained reader and the revealed text. Reading is mysticism.

These are not simply technical observations on my part. They impinge directly on the writing practices of Alan Moore and the core plot of Promethea. Hence the series advances through the adventures of college student Sophie Bangs, a young feminist

0.2   THE TREE OF LIFE

who discovers through a college writing assignment that she has slipped through into the Immateria (a kind of astral plane of the Imagination that is self-existent and accessible to every individual) and become the subject of her term paper, the ancient warrior-wisdom goddess Promethea. The message is clear enough: be careful what you write about. Or as Barbara, the previous human vessel of Promethea, tells Sophie in the first issue: "Listen, kid, you take my *advice*. You don't wanna go looking for *folklore*. And you *especially* don't want *folklore* to come looking for *you*."

The goddess Promethea, then, incarnates the most basic magical convictions that there is something fundamentally mystical about writing, and that words, stories, and symbols *can become real*. As a self-conscious occult comic, *Promethea* is also meant to portray magic as beautiful and bright instead of as dark and dangerous. Moore explains the origins of the idea: "Utilizing my occult experiences, I could see a way that it would be possible to do a new kind of occult comic, that was more psychedelic, that was more sophisticated, more experimental, more ecstatic and exuberant." So the figure of Promethea, who, Moore observes, looks a bit like Wonder Woman, "is about as perfect an expression of the occult as I could imagine doing in a mainstream super-hero comic book."[12]

And, by *expression* Moore means something very specific. In order to recreate the sefirot or spheres of consciousness in his art, he first attempted to actualize each sphere in himself through a magical practice, an actualization that he then recreated *as* the comic. It was in this way that the pages of *Promethea* became "meditational tools" and potential "triggers for altered states of consciousness," and the comic itself has become a "spiritual tool."[13] Reading *is* magic.

Like the Kabbalah, it is impossible to summarize *Promethea*, but three metathemes seem worth flagging here, since they will all enter my own goddess-inspired *Promethea* book. These are: (1) Moore's occult evolutionary vision of the cosmos; (2) the mystical cipher or central symbol that is Promethea's caduceus staff; and (3) Moore's erotic mysticism or sexual magic.

As we have it in *Promethea*, Moore's worldview is an occult evolutionary vision that is deeply informed by modern science, but that also goes well beyond science in its insistence that mind and matter are two manifestations of a deeper intelligence or cosmic being. Everything emerges from "the pure essential working that is God" (P 7); explodes from the "immense male spurt of energy" that was the Big Bang (P 12, 22); develops through the vast, fetal, womblike darkness of cosmic history; and eventually takes on the forms of planetary, biological, cultural, and now occult or spiritual evolution.

This latest occult "leap" from our materialist assumptions into the mystical realms of the Immateria will signal a new evolutionary moment for humanity. Consider, Promethea asks, what would happen if enough people followed her into the magical realms of the Imagination. "It would be like the great *Devonian* leap, from *sea* to *land*. Humanity slithering up the beach, from one element into another. From *matter . . .* to *mind*" (P 5). The present human being, then, is basically an amphibian for Moore, a being who can live in two different worlds at once (P 5). We are now swimming, and more or less stuck, in matter, but we are also crawling, ever so slowly, up onto the beach of Mind.

One of Moore's most consistent metaphors for this evolutionary vision is the caduceus, the two entwined snakes (humorously named Mike and Mack in the comic) that one still sees on medical buildings. The caduceus is central to the *Promethea* series. It is Promethea's glowing magical weapon. It is at once the double-helix scepter of the DNA molecule, the phallic serpent who brought sex and death into the world in the myth of the Garden of Eden, and a sign of the kundalini, the two-spiraled currents of energy that are likened to a serpent as they spark and spike up, down, and around the central channel of the spinal column in Tantric yoga. Most of all, though, the caduceus is the staff of Hermes, the ancient Greek god of language and, later, occult philosophy, alchemy, and Western magic. Moore explains: "Magic, after all, is ruled by Hermes, his symbol, this caduceus, its double-helix serpents representing mankind's evolution. They wind apart, then recombine, progressing towards their ultimate synthesis. Towards winged blazing Godhead" (P 32).

One of the keys to Moore's caduceus symbol is Jeremy Narby's *The Cosmic Serpent*, in which the anthropologist argues that, by ritually ingesting mind-altering plant mixtures, Peruvian Amazon shamans "take their consciousness down to the molecular level and gain access to biomolecular information."[14] Most remarkably, what they gain access to is the DNA strand itself, which appears to be conscious and capable of bestowing real knowledge about botany, medicine, culture, and life itself. Nature is *minded*. Hence the ladders and snakes seen in the shamanic visions and the cosmic serpent creation myths found around the world. In Moore's terms now, the double-snake helix, wherever it is found—from ancient Greece's Hermes to India's kundalini to his own *Promethea*—is "an icon projected by our double-spiral DNA, as conscious entity" (P 32). In another place, Moore suggests that all earthly things arise from a dance between the universal Imagination and her masculine servant, "our snaking spiraled DNA" (P 13). Nature is *imagined*.

Which brings us directly to Moore's sexual magic, itself no doubt secretly driven by the Imagination and that same double-helix phallic snake god. There are two key issues here: one being what we might call the deeper mystical nature of sex; the other being the techniques of putting this deeper nature into practice.

Moore treats the ultimate nature of sex in issue 22, where—just below the pure golden Consciousness that is identification with God in the first sphere of *kether*, or Crown—he locates the pure Energy of the second sphere of *chokhmah*, or Wisdom. Here is the source of all existence in a "so pure" and "so dirty" "Godsex." Here is the highest male principle, of "all wands, all spirit, all fire," and all "initiating energy." Here finally is the sphere, near the very top of the Tree of Life, from which emerges, in one immense orgasm, all that exists, captured in a single ecstatic word: *"I."* "I just came," a naked Sophie confesses after she participates in this vision of divine eros and cosmic Self. *"Everything* just came." The Big Bang.

So Moore understands his sexual magic as something that participates in and expresses the deepest, most subtle, most primordial energies of the universe. But how is it practiced? Moore treats the techniques in issue 10, where he explores the subject through an encounter of an old and sagging Jack Faust with a young Sophie Bangs, who, at Faust's request and to Sophie's great relief, has been temporarily possessed or pushed aside by Promethea.

Moore's treatment in this issue is a synthesis of Aleister Crowley's Western sexual magic and Indian Tantric yoga. "I practice a *Tantric* discipline, so there's no *emission*," Faust tells Promethea, who would have much preferred that he just use a condom. After Promethea slowly strips over four full pages, Faust, awed and aroused now, drinks deeply of the female principle from the sacred receptacle, that is, the "the Holy Grail" of her blue glowing loins. Then comes the male principle. Over and over, Faust immerses his "magical wand" into her "cup" as he teaches Promethea/ Sophie the principles of Western sex magic. Promethea moans back: "Aohh. . . Yes. But explain again."

So he does, this time in the spinal and breathing terms of Tantric yoga. Now amid visions of pink lotus blossoms, Promethea experiences something "all tensed and coiled" in her spine as Faust tries to explain, between breathless ellipses, the place

and nature of the different chakras or energy centers of the subtle body: "Think of ahh ... your *caduceus*. The *snakes* ... winding ... up the shaft ..." Finally, the still united couple is transformed into glistening beings of golden light as the energy rushes out the final chakra at the top of the head and takes them "out of time" and then "outside everything." Transcendence.

After all of this magical and sexual gravitas, the issue ends on a humorous note. Sophie's girlfriend is waiting for her outside in the rain. Pissed off, she pesters Sophie about what she has been doing in there for the last two hours. Once she realizes that Sophie has indeed "humped the hippie," she asks in disgust: "So, how far did you *go*?" Sophie answers, "Only to just above the crown of my *head*. Jeez, what do you think I *am*?"

 Moore, it should be noted, was not always a self-confessed magus penning light-filled occult comics. He was an atheist and a rationalist, and his writing could be very dark. His widely acclaimed deconstruction of the superhero genre, *Watchmen* (1986–87), represented for him the symbolic end of this period of his creativity, a "coming to a limit to what I could further understand about my writing rationally." This was no longer enough. "I felt I had to take a step beyond the rational, and magic was the only area that offered floorboards after that step." This was hardly a rational step, though. It was a life-changing Origins event, "a full blown magical experience that I could not really account for."[15] And it had a precise date: January 7, 1994.

Moore speaks openly about his use of psychedelics, especially magic mushrooms, and describes a number of scenes in conjunction with the 1994 occult opening, including spending part of an evening talking to an entity who claimed to be a Goetic demon first mentioned in the *Apocrypha* (Moore would later weave Goetic demons into *Promethea*). He struggled over whether the demon was purely internal, that is, a projection of his psyche, or whether it was external and more or less what it claimed to be. In the fantastic paradoxical pattern that will structure all that follows, Moore confesses that the most satisfying answer is that it was *both*: "That doesn't make any logical sense but that satisfied me most emotionally. It *feels* truest."

"These are gnostic experiences," the writer declares. "You've either had them or you haven't." By *gnostic*, Moore means a particular kind of direct and immediate experiential knowledge of one's own divinity that cannot be reduced to reason or faith and stands very much opposed to the consensus reality of society and religion: "Faith is for sissies who daren't go and look for themselves. That's my basic position. Magic is based upon gnosis. Direct knowledge."[16]

Enter the serpent (again). With a close friend, Moore experienced the occult presence of what seemed to be the second-century Roman snake god Glycon, who, Moore tells us, was believed to be the reincarnation of Asclepius, the god of healing who holds (like Promethea) the caduceus. As Moore's history has it, Glycon was essentially a hand puppet that a scam artist or false prophet named Alexander used to dupe the faithful. Moore, a writer who delights in expressing profound truths through obvious fictions, loves this little tidbit. He did not, after all, encounter the glove puppet. He encountered the IDEA of Glycon, a kind of "serpent current" or a "certain sort of consciousness" that was once expressed through a fake snake (or "as Asclepius, or Glycon or Kundalini or whatever"), but that is none of these things, really.[17]

Among other things, what this serpent current revealed to Moore was a stunning vision of the true nature of Time:

> AT LEAST PART OF THIS EXPERIENCE SEEMED TO BE COMPLETELY OUTSIDE OF TIME. THERE WAS A PERCEPTION THAT ALL OF TIME WAS HAPPENING AT ONCE. LINEAR TIME WAS PURELY A CONSTRUCTION OF THE CONSCIOUS MIND, AND IN FACT TIME IS MUCH MORE THE WAY THAT PEOPLE LIKE STEPHEN HAWKING SEEM TO DESCRIBE IT, WHERE SPACE-TIME IS ALMOST LIKE SOME BIG FOOTBALL, AND YOU'VE GOT THE BIG BANG AT ONE END OF IT AND THE BIG CRUNCH AT THE OTHER, BUT ALL OF THE MOMENTS ARE ALL EXISTING AT ONCE, IN THIS HUGE HOLE AT THE MOMENT. IT'S ONLY OUR CONSCIOUSNESS THAT'S MOVING THROUGH, FROM A TO B TO C TO D.[18]

This is an idea, really a gnosis, that we will encounter repeatedly in the pages that follow, particularly through the very similar occult openings of figures like the fantasy artist Barry Windsor-Smith and the sci-fi writer Philip K. Dick (in whose obsessively recorded experiences Moore was stunned to see eerily accurate reflections of his own).

 Similar, very explicit magical patterns can be seen in Scottish rock musician and writer Grant Morrison. Morrison, who has penned any number of superhero series, from *All Star Superman*, *Batman*, and *Justice League of America* to *Doom Patrol* and *The New X-Men*, has written and spoken explicitly of his own authorial intentions as a sexual magus, complete with explicit sexual instructions for the willing reader of his work.[19]

Much of this pop magic, as he calls it, works through something called the *sigil*. A sigil is an abstract swiggle or design created by a practicing magician as the visual embodiment of a particular desire or wish. The sigil is then empowered through dramatized intentional acts, like bungee jumping or engaging in magical masturbation. In terms of the latter, "the idea is that, at the height of orgasm, basically there's this kind of empty moment, there's a kind of gap in consciousness, and the sigil can be projected into that."[20]

Morrison's interest in sexual magic goes back to the age of nineteen and an eerily successful experiment with the techniques of Aleister Crowley (the guy just never goes away). But his more recent speculations around mystical forms of eroticism and the reality-generating potentials of reading and writing are linked more directly to a contact experience that he underwent in 1994 in a Kathmandu hotel room overlooking a Buddhist temple, where, he explains, he had traveled to find enlightenment. He found it. Well, he found *something*.

Whatever he found (or whatever found him), it was this contact event that formed the paranormal template for what is probably Morrison's most celebrated comic-book epic, *The Invisibles* (1994–2000).

Like Moore's magical conversion event earlier that same year, Morrison's Kathmandu contact experience was richly multidimensional and so is capable of multiple readings. In one recent version of the story, we are told that the writer "was visited by shiny silver anti-bodies from the 5th dimension, an experience he described as 'being electrocuted by god,' and something that 'no drugs could ever recreate.'" Morrison found the relationship between these fifth-dimensional beings and our normal three-dimensional consciousness particularly significant and creatively applied it to his comic-book writing on the two-dimensional page: "I thought I could just interact with the 2nd dimension the way they relate to the 3rd dimension."[21] Hence lines like this one: "If our words are circles, theirs are bubbles" (I 5.192).

In a long and rich interview with comic-book critic Patrick Meaney, Morrison puts this same Kathmandu event in a broader context. There he relates these "mercurial creatures" to the sex magic of Crowley, the language mysticism and hyperspace machine elves of psychedelic bard Terence McKenna, the visitors of Whitley Strieber's *Communion*, and the Valis experience of Philip K. Dick. Although they are clearly visualized in the comic-book series as classic almond-eyed aliens, Morrison, much like Strieber, generally resists the language of "aliens." He prefers to call them

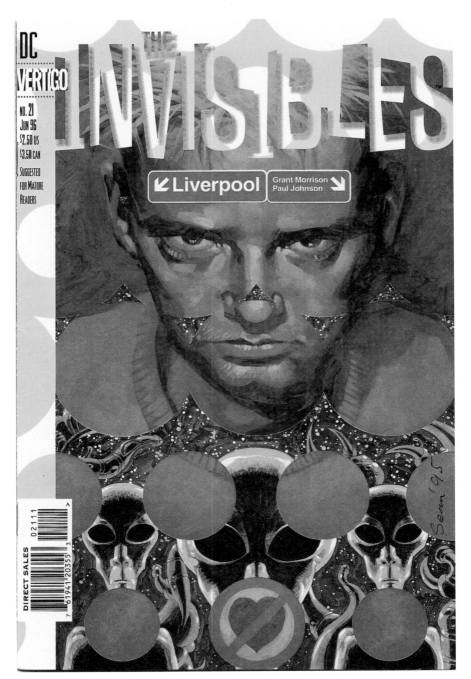

0.4   ALIENS BEHIND THE COMIC

"anti-bodies" (I 5.38), another complex expression that can be interpreted in either microbiological or spiritual ways—or both.

The anti-bodies certainly lived up to their name. Morrison describes how the creatures effected a "collapsing stargate effect" that took him outside his body. "I was in a super-realistic space. There were three suns," and "there was a planet that was kind of blue and green." Those went right into *The Invisibles*. And there was "a kind of communication with fanlike creatures made out of neon tubes . . . which worked on sound frequencies and light." Those went into *All Star Superman*. The same creatures peeled him off the four dimensions of space and time and showed him "things as they were, from the outside."[22] Not unlike Alan Moore, he saw Time as a single whole—the "AllNow" or "Supercontext," as he calls it, which is a kind of "higher unfolding reality," a perspective above space-time through which one identifies "with everything in the universe that is *not-self*" (I 7.271) and sees "all of history and all our tomorrows as the single object I believe it is" (I 5.22).

Morrison saw that "we were all just this one object, like a huge anemone on the planet, and it was kind of the idea that we were devouring the environment," rather like a larval caterpillar on a leaf, he notes, in order to "fuel its metamporphosis into something bigger."[23] Hence that most striking representation toward the very end of *The Invisibles* of what a human being, really a human process, looks like *spread through time*. Like a vast Hindu super-deity, it turns out: "the body decades long, billion-eyed and billion-limbed, the worm-cast that you leave in time. This is your *complete* body, not its *section*" (I 7.253–54).

In terms of a basic plot, the graphic novel (the first comic series to allow full-blown swearing) orbits around a secret society of occult subversives battling a vast cosmic conspiracy run by extradimensional aliens or anti-beings called "Archons." The plot, in other words, is a Manichean one (and Morrison explicitly invokes Manichean-ism throughout the story), with two opposing forces battling for the soul of humanity: the forces of total control and the powers of radical freedom and thought. Morrison even imagines two interpenetrating universes, a good universe A and a bad universe B, with our own little world the result of a kind of interference pattern or hologram between the two.[24]

Kathmandu, of course, is in Nepal, and, very much like Calcutta, the city is famous for its elaborate Tantric temples, art, and rituals, here in both Hindu and Bud-dhist forms. Little wonder, then, that explicit Tantric themes appear throughout *The*

Invisibles. The Invisibles, for example, are led by King Mob (clearly modeled on Morrison himself), who was taught by an "ascended master" in a cathedral academy called the Invisible College until he was "versed in all things occult and Tantric" (I 3.84, 2.5). In a series of dream sequences induced by torture and drug, King Mob is seen engaging in a sexual ritual among Buddhist Tantric icons with a woman, under whom he experiences the awakening of his own serpent current or kundalini, a "fire snake ripping up through the spinal channels" (I 3.51–52). In a later scene, the same woman "interfaces with super-dimensional libraries," fuses with a suit of antimaterial, and manifests as an extradimensional, four-armed, insect version of "Kali unbound" (I 3.80).

At different points later in the story, we learn the source of the sexual ritual memory. The memory, it turns out, is an accurate one from *both* the future *and* the past. We learn that the original scene took place in 1924 London with a woman named Edith Manning. Edie has kept a "lifetime's tantric journals" (I 7.104) after being initiated into the Tantra by a certain Mr. Reddy. As Edie tells the story, this latter tantric teacher, while having sex with her in an Indian hotel, ejaculated in reverse, ignited her kundalini, and stripped off his human "suit" to reveal his true energetic form within a bolt of plasmic electricity (I 7.142–43, 184).

As if that were not enough, in another scene, we witness Edie giving King Mob some sort of strengthening potion from a Tantric skull cup and explaining to him how in India she once learned, no doubt from Mr. Reddy, "how one has sex with a thought form" (what the Tibetans call a *tulpa*). This is significant because King Mob has already told her that *he* is such a thought form, a ghostlike psychical projection from the future, where, a few issues back, we saw him lying in trance, in San Francisco in 1998, to be precise. After the time-warping ritual sex, still back in 1924, the couple anoint an occult left hand, called the Hand of Glory, with their sexual fluids: "and everything was made ready" (I 5.146–47). It is through this green, glowing left hand that an interdimensional door opens in the fabric of reality and the Archons enter our world (I 7.140). Perhaps it is significant, perhaps it is not, that radical Hindu Tantra is called "left-handed."

The tantric allusions continue throughout the story. In one scene, for example, a burning sensation up and down the back (the kundalini again) signals the appearance of a flying saucer and a classic alien abduction on a dark highway that initiates the invisible career of future New Age billionaire Mason Lang (I 4.14, 5.64, 96). In another, the Brit punk character of Dane McGowan enters a deep Buddhist meditative state in which he becomes a Buddha, knows all things, and psychically enters a classical

Tantric *yantra* or meditative diagram: "I was home. I was God, looking at myself in the mirror. I was perfect in eternity" (I 3.179).

These are not throwaway lines. The writer expects his readers to go and research the historical and philosophical background of such "fictional" allusions. Indeed, by Morrison's own description, *The Invisibles* is one immense *hypersigil* of his multidimensional contact experience in Tantric Nepal, and the novel was consciously designed to conjure and effect that which it explores in the form of fiction. Words here are power-substances, literal spell-ings in their own right. But only if they can be activated by knowing readers. As Morrison puts it: "*The Invisibles* is the ritual, is the spell, and the collaboration of the readership in that spell is important too."[25]

And he *does* mean participation. At one point, on November 25, 1995, when sales of *The Invisibles* was dipping, he encouraged his readers to empower the series with their own masturbatory magical rituals—"a gigantic global wank," as he jokingly puts it.[26] The sales went back up.

The Invisibles was not just about a Tantric-contact experience in Nepal, though. Throughout those six years of writing and living, "the comic was the diary."[27] It was about Morrison's love of the Beatles and the 1960s. It was about his psychedelic trips on LSD, magic mushrooms, ecstasy, and DMT in the 1990s. It was about his reading of H. P. Lovecraft and all those space monsters.

And a near-death vision of Jesus. In December of 1995, Morrison lay dying of an advanced, undiagnosed staph infection that had collapsed a lung. A "Gnostic Jesus," "a kind of slightly savage, bearded firebrand," appeared to him in a giant column of light and said this: "I am not the god of your fathers, I am the hidden stone that breaks all hearts." The writer put that line in *The Invisibles* (I 3.189, 5.144). This fiery Jesus then told Morrison a number of beautiful things about how the world works, none of which he can remember. He also told him something that he did remember: that he didn't have to die, that he could return, if he was willing "to work for us" and "spread the light."[28] He returned.

Like Edie's Tantra, Jesus's firebrand Gnosticism is everywhere in *The Invisibles*. The Archons and demiurges (lower creator gods) whom the Invisibles battle throughout the narrative, for example, are taken, at least in name, directly from ancient gnostic texts. As is the raging spirit of lines like this one: "The greatest lunacy is to believe in a creator. . . . By doing so, we deny our *own* divinity. Broken to the yoke of religion, we forget who made our burden and set it upon us" (I 1.128).

Then there is Mason Lang's childhood UFO abduction, which culminated in the boy drinking something called the "ultramenstruum" from a chalice identified as the Holy Grail. After explaining this detail of the visionary experience to King Mob, an adult Mason mumbles: "Ultramenstruum? Where the hell did that one come from . . . ?" (I 6.204). Well, from ancient rumors surrounding the Christian Gnostics, who were accused of consuming sexual fluids in their secret rituals. They may have.

As a fantastic practice, Morrison's approach to religion is at once radically critical and deeply sensitive. Put most simply, organized religion for Morrison is an alienating, often intolerant and violent power structure built around a mistaken reading of what was originally a real paranormal experience—like Jesus's, like the Buddha's, like his own: "And people just confuse it. They think they've heard the voice of god, or they think they've heard the voice of angels, or the voice of aliens, or the voice of devils, or if they grew up particularly fearful and the experience frightens them, they think they've heard the voice of Buddha or Allah, but they haven't. They've just heard their own next room up, talking down to them. . . . It's just the next rung up the ladder."[29] Morrison's near-death encounter with the gnostic Jesus, then, is not finally about Christianity, or even ancient Gnosticism, for that matter. It's about each of us realizing the divine-human or Christ within. It's about recognizing "the gnostic error" of hating the material world and not seeing it from within the Supercontext as "the part of heaven we can touch" (I 7.276). It's about knowing that "the divine has descended through mind into matter," that "matter is the divine in its most condensed form" (I 6.122–23). It's about our next developmental stage, as the larval forms of our consciousness morph into "the next rung up the ladder." It's about our own evolution.

I would not presume to draw from a book like *The Invisibles* the precise details of Morrison's Kathmandu contact experience or his near-death encounter with the gnostic Christ. Nor would I be so naïve as to conflate a work of fantasy and a particular sex-magical practice, as we have them performed in an astonishing work like Moore's *Promethea*. That is not what I am about here.

What I can say, though, is that I recognize in both *Promethea* and *The Invisibles* the lineaments and occult energies of my own contact-experience in Calcutta and the subsequent, essentially magical understandings of writing and reading that they eventually produced in me. The Godsex and initiating energies of Moore's Kabbalah and the Calcutta/Kathmandu correspondences are particularly striking to me. Indeed,

0.5   NAILING THE ABDUCTION EXPERIENCE

Morrison's words on this single page (see fig. 0.5) could well be my own (I 7.129). And why not? We were both "electrocuted by god" in Tantric Asia.

THE THREE AGES AND THE SUPER-STORY

Mutants and Mystics is about the prehistory of such magical writing practices. It is about how we got here and why it is so important for the deep reader of science fiction and superhero comics to think, rigorously, about the mind-blowing terrain of gnostic, esoteric, and mystical literature. If we can do this deeply enough, we are going to end up reading out of science fiction and superhero comics a very different story.

Take the history of superhero comics. It is usually organized into three descending "ages" that are in turn complicated by sundry crisis and transformation points. There are, of course, numerous variants of this standard history, but most of them follow some version of the following timeline:

- NURTURED BY ALMOST TWO DECADES OF PULP MAGAZINES, NEWSPAPER STRIPS, AND EARLY HEROIC FIGURES LIKE TARZAN, PRINCE VALIANT, THE PHANTOM, AND THE SHADOW, THE GOLDEN AGE IS DEFINITIVELY INITIATED BY THE APPEARANCE OF SUPERMAN IN *ACTION COMICS* #1, ERUPTS IN THE SUMMER OF 1938, ROLLS THROUGH WORLD WAR II WITH CHARACTERS LIKE BATMAN, CAPTAIN AMERICA, CAPTAIN MARVEL, AND WONDER WOMAN, AND THEN PETERS OUT AFTER THE WAR, WHEN AMERICA NO LONGER NEEDS ITS HEROES

- MULTIPLE GENRES OF COMICS AND STRIPS CONTINUE TO BE PRODUCED IN EXTRAORDINARY QUANTITIES; A CRISIS PERIOD FOLLOWS IN THE 1950S WITH A CONGRESSIONAL CAMPAIGN DIRECTED AGAINST THE INDUSTRY CATALYZED BY A PSYCHOANALYST BY THE NAME OF FREDERIC WERTHAM; MUCH OF THE INDUSTRY COLLAPSES, THE REST SELF-CENSORS IN ORDER TO SURVIVE, AND THE INDUSTRY ENTERS A FLAT, ULTRACONSERVATIVE ERA; A NEW TECHNOLOGY ALSO DEVELOPS THAT WILL EVENTUALLY SPELL THE END OF THE MASS APPEAL OF COMICS—TELEVISION

- THE SUPERHERO GENRE SENSES A RENAISSANCE OF SORTS WHEN THE SILVER AGE IS INITIATED BY JULIUS SCHWARTZ AND CARMINE INFANTINO IN 1956 AT DC COMICS WITH THE RECREATION OF A GOLDEN AGE SUPERHERO, THE FLASH; A SUPERHERO EXPLOSION SOON FOLLOWS, LED MOSTLY THIS TIME BY STAN LEE AND JACK KIRBY AT MARVEL COMICS IN THE EARLY 1960S WITH A WHOLE STRING OF SUCCESSES, BEGINNING WITH *THE FANTASTIC FOUR* #1 IN NOVEMBER OF 1961; THE SPACE RACE, THE COLD WAR, THE AMERICAN COUNTERCULTURE, AND THE VIETNAM WAR SUPPLY MUCH OF THE YOUTHFUL ENERGY—COSMIC, ATOMIC, SEXUAL,

MUSICAL, PSYCHEDELIC, AND TRAUMATIC—FOR THIS SECOND SUPERHERO EXPLOSION

- AS THE COUNTERCULTURE WINDS DOWN AND ITS SOCIAL EFFECTS ARE INTEGRATED INTO (OR REJECTED BY) THE LARGER CULTURE, THE BRONZE AGE IS INITIATED IN 1975 WITH THE RE-CREATION OF THE X-MEN TEAM IN *GIANT-SIZE X-MEN* #1 TO REFLECT THE NEW ETHNIC, RELIGIOUS, AND CULTURAL DIVERSITY OF AMERICAN CULTURE; A NEW SOPHISTICATION IN THE WRITING BEGINS AS A GENERATION OF FANS, FIRST HERALDED BY ROY THOMAS AT MARVEL, ENTERS THE INDUSTRY AND BEGINS TO TRANSFORM IT FROM WITHIN

- AFTER THE SUCCESS OF VARIOUS GRIM-AND-GRITTY SUPERHEROES IN THE LATE 1970S (LIKE MARVEL'S THE PUNISHER), A KIND OF POSTMODERN DECONSTRUCTION OF THE SUPERHERO BEGINS IN THE EARLY 1980S AND EXTENDS WELL INTO THE 1990S THROUGH BOOKS LIKE FRANK MILLER'S *DAREDEVIL* AND *THE DARK NIGHT RETURNS* (THE LATTER EFFECTIVELY TRANS-LATED TO THE SCREEN IN TIM BURTON'S 1989 *BATMAN*) AND ALAN MOORE'S *THE WATCHMEN*

- THE INDUSTRY ALMOST COLLAPSES AGAIN IN THE EARLY 1990S, THIS TIME BECAUSE OF MARKETING AND DISTRIBUTION PROBLEMS AND THE SHEER IRRELEVANCE OF THE COMIC-BOOK GENRE BEFORE THE OVERWHELMING FORCES OF TELEVISION, FILM, AND SOON THE INTERNET; STILL, BY THE END OF THE CENTURY, THE INDUSTRY BEGINS TO WITNESS A THIRD DRAMATIC RENAISSANCE OF THE SUPERHERO, THIS TIME THROUGH THE CGI TECHNOLOGIES OF HOLLYWOOD AND THE VIDEO GAMING INDUSTRY

This chronology certainly works well enough as a straight history, but there are numerous problems with it. None perhaps are more telling than the fact that the overarching symbolism of this history, adopted from the Five Ages of the Greek poet Hesiod (c. 700 BCE), strongly suggests, like most premodern mythical systems, that the really good stuff, the revealed truth, lies in the deep past, in "the Golden Age."[30] There is certainly some really good stuff in the past, "in the beginning," as the ancient myths have it, but such a traditional idea belies the fact that at no time have superheroes been more popular, more influential, and more financially lucrative than in the present. If there is a Golden Age of superheroes, we're living in it.

There is also a deeper problem here, though: as modern mythologies indebted to science and technology, the superhero stories generally (not always) place the best stuff *in the future*. In these new mythologies of science, the past is precisely what one wants to leave. The basic thrust of the sci-fi and superhero mythologies, in other words, generally works in the *opposite* direction of the descending-ages model. We may be returning, but we are also evolving.

Finally, there is also the related, and more practical, issue of whether the Three Ages system itself has a future. I mean, just where are we supposed to go now? If we follow Hesiod, we would move into the Heroic Age, when humans co-exist with the gods and heroes, which seems accurate enough in light of our present pages on real-world supernormal powers. Okay, but then what? Into an Iron Age? And then what? Into a Stone Age? Are we going to end up, like William Hurt as Dr. Jessup in the movie *Altered States*, regressing further and further back into evolutionary time until we end up as a sperm and ovum or, worst yet, in the Big Bang? Obviously, although it will no doubt continue to be used by collectors and dealers (for whom the past really *is* more valuable), the Three Ages system has run its course and exhausted its usefulness. It is time for another way of reading this story.

Enter the Super-Story.

I call it a Super-Story because I think its seven basic tropes or "mythemes" lie at the base of a vast array of American popular culture. This, if you will, is the Story above (*super-*) the stories. Not that there is any single plot, cast of characters, or definite ending. Quite the contrary. These seven mythemes have been repeated endlessly in a mind-boggling array of combinations, variations, and conclusions—in essence, a centuries-long thought experiment that is still in process, still being told.

I also call it a Super-Story for spiritual reasons. I call it a Super-Story because the mythical themes and paranormal currents that give it life are commonly experienced by artists, writers, and readers as realities entirely above and beyond (*super-*) the material histories of plot design, character development, artistic layout, material production, distribution, marketing, even history and time itself. Despite the fact that the mythemes are clearly historical products, this is a story that often ends—like the time-transcending experiences of Moore and Morrison—*outside* the story, a story whose very purpose is to project the reader beyond his or her constructed, relative, written world.

As a set of separable or independent mythemes, the Super-Story looks something like this:

1. DIVINIZATION/DEMONIZATION. WESTERN CULTURE HAS BEEN INFLUENCED FOR MILLENNIA BY FORMS OF INTELLIGENCE THAT HAVE APPEARED UNDER THE DIVINE AND DEMONIC MASKS OF LOCAL MYTHOLOGIES AND RELIGIONS. TRADITIONALLY, THESE INTELLIGENCES HAVE TAUGHT, GUIDED, WARNED, SAVED, AWED, AND TERRIFIED INDIVIDUALS BY APPEARING IN THE INNER WORLDS OF DREAMS AND VISIONS; IN THE FORCES, PLANTS, AND ANIMALS OF

THE NATURAL WORLD; AND "IN THE HEAVENS," THAT IS, IN THE SKY. HUMAN BEINGS HAVE LONG SOUGHT COMMUNION WITH THESE SUPERBEINGS AND THEIR TRANSFORMATIVE ENERGIES. THEY HAVE ALSO SOUGHT PRACTICAL CONTROL OVER OR PROTECTION FROM THESE SACRED POWERS THROUGH THE TECHNIQUES OF MAGIC, RITUAL, TEMPLE-BUILDING, PRAYER, SACRIFICE, AND WORSHIP.

2. ORIENTATION. FOR MUCH OF WESTERN HISTORY, THIS SACRED SOURCE OF POWER AND WISDOM WAS TRADITIONALLY LOCATED "FAR AWAY," "LONG, LONG AGO," AND, MORE OFTEN THAN NOT, "IN THE EAST." BUT THERE WERE OTHER STRATEGIES AS WELL. AFRICA AND THE NEW WORLD, FOR EXAMPLE, ALSO FULFILLED A SIMILAR SYMBOLIC FUNCTION, AS DID MYTHICAL LANDS, LIKE ATLANTIS, LEMURIA, THE CENTER OF THE EARTH, THE UNREACHABLE PRIMORDIAL PAST, THE HYPERBOREAN AGE, AND SO ON. EACH OF THESE IMAGINATIVE CONSTRUCTS "ORIENTED" THE WESTERN RELIGIOUS IMAGINATION TO THE SACRED AS SOMEWHERE ELSE.

Eventually, however, as Western civilization colonized the world and the blank spots on the map became smaller and smaller, there was a felt need to locate the Somewhere Else, well, *somewhere else*. Modern science unwittingly provided the language and metaphors for this relocation of the sacred through three major discoveries.

3. ALIENATION. THE FIRST DISCOVERY, WHICH EMERGED GRADUALLY FROM MODERN COSMOLOGY, INVOLVED THE MIND-BOGGLING REALIZATION THAT THE AGE, SCOPE, AND WORKINGS OF THE PHYSICAL UNIVERSE ARE NOT WHAT OUR ANCIENT STORIES CLAIMED. ACCORDINGLY, THE GODS AND THEIR WISDOM NO LONGER COME FROM THE EAST, FROM THE PRIMORDIAL PAST, OR EVEN FROM OUR SMALL STELLAR NEIGHBORHOOD (THE SUN, MOON, AND PLANETS OF TRADITIONAL ASTROLOGY). THEY COME FROM THE VAST REACHES OF *OUTER SPACE*. THEY NOW WATCH US. THEY GUIDE THE DEVELOPMENT OF HUMAN CIVILIZATIONS. THEY MANIPULATE OUR RELIGIOUS BELIEFS AND MYTHOLOGIES. THEY VISIT US, SPY ON US, SOMETIMES EVEN ABDUCT US USING THEIR MYSTERIOUS PHANTOM SHIPS. HAVING ONCE COLONIZED THE EARTH, WE NOW REALIZE THAT WE ARE OURSELVES A COLONY.

4. RADIATION. THE SECOND DISCOVERY INVOLVED THE EQUALLY STUNNING REALIZATION THAT MATTER ITSELF IS NOT MATERIAL BUT ENERGETIC AND POTENTIAL, THAT THE FURTHER ONE GOES DOWN INTO THE SECRET LIFE OF MATTER, THE STRANGER THINGS APPEAR UNTIL ONE ENCOUNTERS A KIND OF PURE POTENCY, A POWER THAT IS LITERALLY EVERYTHING. EVENTUALLY, WE FIGURED OUT HOW TO RELEASE THIS POWER, HOW TO ACTUALIZE THE COSMIC POTENTIAL OF MATTER ITSELF. THUS FREED, THIS FORCE CAN SERVE US, TRANSFORM US, MAYBE EVEN SAVE US. IT CAN ALSO UTTERLY DESTROY US.

5. MUTATION. THE THIRD DISCOVERY OF SCIENCE THAT CHANGED THE SACRED YET AGAIN INVOLVED THE REALIZATION THAT SENTIENT LIFE HAS EVOLVED OVER BILLIONS OF YEARS. LIKE EVERY OTHER SPECIES, HUMANITY IS A TRANSITIONAL OR TEMPORARY FORM, ONLY ONE OF COUNTLESS POSSIBILITIES THAT LIFE CAN, HAS, AND WILL TAKE ON THIS PLANET AND, NO DOUBT, ON COUNTLESS OTHER PLANETS. IN SHORT, LIFE IS NOT HUMAN, AND IT IS CONSTANTLY CHANGING, CONSTANTLY EVOLVING.

While playing with these mythemes, the creators eventually intuited the insight that lies at the very base of modern critical thought, namely, that human beings are not as free as they imagine, that through the intimate, often invisible influences of family, language, culture, and religion they are being constructed—*they are being written*. We might locate at least two stages in this difficult, ongoing awakening.

6. REALIZATION. IN THE FIRST STAGE, AN AUTHOR, ARTIST, OR READER BEGINS TO REALIZE THAT PARANORMAL EVENTS ARE REAL, AND, MOREOVER, THAT THEY REVEAL A DIMENSION OF THE WORLD THAT WORKS REMARKABLY LIKE A TEXT OR A STORY. THROUGH THE UNCANNY PRACTICES OF WRITING, READING, AND ARTISTIC PRODUCTION, THESE INDIVIDUALS COME TO REALIZE THAT WE ARE ALL FIGMENTS OF OUR OWN IMAGINATION, THAT WE ARE CAUGHT IN A STORY (OR STORIES) THAT WE DID NOT WRITE AND THAT WE MAY NOT EVEN LIKE.

7. AUTHORIZATION. IN THE SECOND STAGE, THIS INSIGHT INTO THE REALIZATION THAT WE ARE BEING WRITTEN MATURES INTO THE EVEN MORE STUNNING IDEA THAT WE CAN DO SOMETHING ABOUT THIS, THAT WE CAN WRITE OURSELVES ANEW. THE FINAL SECRET OF THE SUPER-STORY, THEN, IS THAT IF WE ARE INDEED "ABOVE" (*SUPER-*) IT, THEN IN SOME WAY THAT WE DO NOT YET UNDERSTAND, *WE* ARE AUTHORIZING IT. WE DO NOT NEED TO BE PUP-PETS AT THE MERCY OF SOME NEUROLOGICAL PROGRAMMER, OR FOR THAT MATTER SOME FAITHFUL BELIEVER IN THE DICTATES OF SOME AUTHORITARIAN SKY-GOD. WE CAN BECOME OUR OWN AUTHORS. WE CAN RECOGNIZE THAT WE ARE PULLING OUR OWN STRINGS, THAT THE ANGELS AND ALIENS, GODS AND DEMONS *ARE US*.

THE MATTER OF MYTH AND THE MYTH OF MATTER

As the Origins of Moore, Morrison, and myself make clear, beginnings are particularly important for writers of all sorts. So too in the superhero comics. Often the superhero acquires his or her powers from some sort of accident or trauma: the alien Superman crashes onto planet earth from Krypton; Batman, struggling with the horrible memory of the murder of his parents, learns the martial arts and dedicates his life to fighting crime; scientist Bruce Banner is radiated by an atomic bomb test—that sort of thing. Every superhero, it turns out, needs a story about how he or she came to be different, how he or she became *super*.

But I am not the potential superhero here. You are. It is my hope anyway that this book might function as a crash landing or radioactive blast for at least some of its more imaginative superreaders. In any case, this particular book possesses its own Origins story. It goes like this.

In the fall of 1962, two Stanford graduates, Michael Murphy and Richard Price, founded a little visionary community on a remote cliff in Big Sur, California. It would come to be known as the Esalen Institute. The intentions of the two founders were multiple, but on Murphy's side all of the deepest ones boiled down to an evolutionary vision that understands psychical and paranormal experiences to be "evolutionary buds" witnessing to the future occult form of the species, what Murphy calls "the future of the body."

We will get into some of the details of this particular story later on. For now, it is enough to note that I spent the first seven years of the new millennium researching and writing a history of Esalen and, while doing so, found myself, with no little embarrassment, becoming more or less obsessed with the comic-book mythologies of my adolescence. At first, this simply puzzled me. But the obsession would not go away, so I began to quiz it, ask it questions, talk to it (yes, I do this sort of thing). Eventually, the obsession turned into an intuition, an idea-in-the-making. I began to realize how eerily similar Murphy's evolutionary mysticism is to the mythology of the X-Men. Indeed, the similarities border on the uncanny. I would go even further. Murphy's evolutionary mysticism not only looks very much like the X-Men. It *is* the X-Men. To add insult to injury, the evolutionary mystical school that would become Esalen was founded in Big Sur in the fall of 1962, that is, one year before Stan Lee and Jack Kirby dreamed up a similar occult school in Westchester, New York, for their X-Men. This strange resonance between East Coast mythology and West Coast mysticism, between mutants and mystics, I decided, was the probable source of my embarrassing midlife obsession with superhero comics.

Then, like all things paranormal, these mythical musings literally entered my physical world in the summer of 2006. I was walking out of the cave of a cool dark movie theater after watching *X-Men 3: The Last Stand* and feeling especially perplexed, again, about how close this popular mythology was to Murphy's evolutionary mystical system, about which I had been writing and thinking all that same summer. As I watched these strange ideas appear and disappear "in here" and approached my minivan in the hot parking lot after the movie, something suddenly appeared "out there," something golden and shining in the painfully bright sun. I couldn't possibly miss it, as it was lying immediately below the van door, as if it were waiting just for me. At first, I thought it was a Christian cross (I live in pious Texas, after all). It turned out on closer inspection to be a cheap piece of costume jewelry in the perfect and unmistakable shape not of a cross, but of an *X*.

That was the final straw that broke this rational camel's back. That was the moment I decided to write this book. The pages that follow are an imperfect record of what happened when I picked up that *X*, decided to trust whatever it was that it represented, and write the present seven meditations on what Chris Knowles has so aptly called "the x-factor" of superhero comics. I found that x-factor—literally.

I am not, of course, asking the reader to be particularly impressed by that cheap piece of costume jewelry in that extraordinarily ordinary parking lot picked up by this particular dingbat. I certainly would not be if its sudden appearance did not correspond perfectly with my internal hypercreative state. I recognize, fully, that the force and meaning of such a minor event can be appreciated only by the person experiencing it. I am not, then, asking the reader to experience my experience. I am asking only that the reader know that what follows is a creative expression of *both* the bright movie screen *and* the hot parking lot. Put a bit paradoxically but not at all inaccurately, the Super-Story I am about to tell you is unquestionably a myth, but it is a myth made of matter.

Or a piece of matter made of myth. I'm not really sure.

In any case, you're holding it.

Good luck with that.

ORIENTATION

FROM INDIA TO THE PLANET MARS

JANMAUSHADHIMANTRATAPAHSAMADHIJAH
SIDDHAYAH.

PARANORMAL POWERS ARISE FROM BIRTH AND
FAMILY, PSYCHOTROPIC PLANTS, THE RECITING OF
MAGICAL FORMULAS, ASCETIC PRACTICE, AND YO-
GIC UNION.
YOGA-SUTRAS 4.1 (FIFTH TO FIRST CENTURY
BCE, INDIA)

The notion of an Orientation is a somewhat paradoxical concept, witnessing at once to a sense of place or perspective *and* to a sense of lack, loss, or need. Every place, after all, needs a Somewhere Else, an Other in relation to (or, alas, more often, against which) one can define oneself and one's community. It is a sad truth, but the true believer *needs* the unbeliever. The righteous patriot *needs* the foreign enemy.

That Other, however, is not simply alien, foreign, and scary, but is also, by defini-tion, what one is not. Hence, if the seeker or hero is spiritually mature (that is, neither a true believer nor a righteous patriot), the Other can also complete one, function as the source of new knowledge or wisdom, even offer a kind of real transcendence from one's own, always relative and limited lifeworld. This is why "the truth is out there," as *The X-Files* had it in the 1990s, and why the truth—like the sacred itself—can be so terrifying and so alluring at the same time. The key for now, though, is that the awe-full truth of things is almost always out there *somewhere else*.

SIX WAYS TO BE SOMEWHERE ELSE

To be clear, there have been innumerable Somewhere Elses in the Western imagina-tion. For the sake of conciseness, we might briefly explore six: (1) worlds above; (2)

worlds below; (3) speculative prehistoric worlds or lost lands; (4) geographically distant civilizations and tribal cultures; and, most recently, (5) outer space. This latter strategy quickly brought a sixth to the fore: (6) future worlds or, what often amounts to the same thing, other dimensions or parallel universes.

In this latter sci-fi motif of multiple dimensions, which we will encounter over and over again, the Somewhere Else intriguingly also becomes a Somewhen Else . . . or, paradoxically, a *right here, right now*. The pilgrim, spiritual seeker, or adventuring hero comes back home.

WORLDS ABOVE. The gods, of course, have long come from the sky, "from the heavens," as we say in an English phrase that neatly captures the way that the human religious imagination has almost universally equated the sacred with the sky, sun, and stars. The original heroes of Western civilization were connected to this world of the gods above. In the ancient world of Greek religion, for example, a hero might be a mortal man who was immortalized after death and worshipped as such. He might also be a divine-human hybrid, the product of a sexual union between a horny deity and a human being. The very archetype of the Western hero, Herakles or Hercules, for example, was the son of the god Zeus and the human woman Alcmene (and Zeus's wife, Hera, was not at all happy about this).

Later, this notion of the Greek hero or divine-human hybrid would be taken up by Christianity and transformed into something quite different. Now the pagan hero and his labors became the Christian saint endowed with miraculous powers and a message that conformed to the teachings of the Church, or, in Eastern Orthodoxy, the Christian mystic rendered immortal through the divine energies of grace and a transformative process called "divinization," literally a "god-making" (*theosis*). And, of course, whether in the Latin West or the Greek East, the ultimate and singular Christian hybrid-hero was the god-man himself, the Christ, the Son of God who had descended from the world above to take on human flesh in Jesus of Nazareth through a virginal divine-human conception.

WORLDS BELOW. The depths of the earth, of course, have long been a central feature of the Western religious imagination as well, where they have often functioned as the place of a darkly and mistily conceived afterlife, as in the Hebrew Sheol or the Greek Hades, or as a place of torture and punishment, as in the medieval Christian

Hell. Such notions were given a new life in the fantasy life of the modern West after the rise of modern science through some most unusual occult tropes. These included the hollow earth, the polar holes, and, much later, the notion of underground alien bases. Since such ideas have played a major role in the fantasy materials that we will encounter below, it is worth digging in a bit here, as it were.

Although there were certainly precedents to the notion of a hollow earth, it was the English astronomer Edmund Halley (the man we know through his predicted comet) who got the ball rolling in 1691, and in three lectures to the Royal Society of London no less, by suggesting that the inner earth consisted of a series of three concentric spheres magnetically spinning about in a sort of life-giving luminosity. Oddly, Halley was not so far from the geological truth of things as we know it today, since, as David Standish points out in his wonderful history of the hollow earth, the planet does consist of "separate spheres of sort: the outer crust; the mantle, which accounts for two-thirds of the planet's mass; a dense liquid layer of magma consisting chiefly of molten iron that's about half the earth's radius in extent; and a solid inner core inside that. The layer of molten metal is circulating—like Halley's internal Sphere—which creates electrical currents, which in turn create magnetic fields. The earth can be thought of as a great electromagnet."[1] The earth as a "great electromagnet." Hold on to that idea. It will come back to us.

The man, though, who did the most to promote the idea of the hollow earth was an American eccentric and army captain named John Cleves Symmes. On April 10, 1818, Symmes self-published and distributed what has come to be called Circular 1. It partly reads thus:

TO ALL THE WORLD:

I DECLARE THE EARTH IS HOLLOW AND HABITABLE WITHIN; CONTAINING A NUMBER OF SOLID CONCENTRIC SPHERES, ONE WITHIN THE OTHER, AND THAT IT IS OPEN AT THE POLES TWELVE OR SIXTEEN DEGREES. I PLEDGE MY LIFE IN SUPPORT OF THIS TRUTH, AND AM READY TO EXPLORE THE HOLLOW, IF THE WORLD WILL SUPPORT AND AID ME IN THIS UNDERTAKING.

JNO. CLEVES SYMMES OF OHIO, LATE CAPTAIN OF INFANTRY[2]

No one knows where Symmes got such a fantastic idea (I suspect some sort of visionary experience), but he clearly believed it. The circular goes on to ask for "one hundred brave companions, well equipped, to start from Siberia, in the fall season, with reindeer and sleighs, on the ice of the frozen sea." He promised that they would find "a warm and rich land, stocked with thrifty vegetables and animals, if not men," and that they would return in the spring.

Symmes spent the rest of his life trying to get to what came to be called, appropriately enough, Symmes's Holes. He never got to them. He did, however, manage to write, under a pseudonym, one of the first American utopian novels, entitled *Symzonia: Voyage of Discovery* (1820). *Symzonia* (so named "out of gratitude to Capt. Symmes for his sublime theory") established what would become the standard structure of such adventure stories and much of later science fiction.[3] Standish sums up that structure this way: "the trip to the pole, discovery of a land and people/creatures inside, adventures and revelations while there, and a return home, usually to ridicule and disbelief."[4] A memorial statue to Captain Symmes and his hollow globe, erected by his son Americus, can still be seen in a public park in Hamilton, Ohio.

The advances of geology and polar exploration made the captain's holes look increasingly dubious, however. Undeterred, fiction writers continued to play with what was basically an irresistible idea. Edgar Allen Poe, for example, was a fan of Symmes through the lectures and writings of J. N. Reynolds (who, among other things, heard a story about a monstrous white whale off the coast of Chile that reached, via a magazine article he wrote entitled "Mocha Dick; or, the White Whale of the Pacific," a certain Mr. Melville).[5] Poe wrote his only book-length novel based on Symmes's idea, *The Narrative of Arthur Gordon Pym*, which ends with the protagonist and his long-suffering crew being sucked down a huge polar chasm, in essence, a Symmes Hole, where they finally encounter "a shrouded human figure, very far larger in its proportions than any dweller among men. And the hue of the skin of the figure was of the perfect whiteness of snow." In a weird and slightly eerie twist, Poe's last words on his poisoned deathbed—"Reynolds . . . Reynolds . . . Reynolds"—remain completely unexplained. Perhaps, like the crew of his only novel, he was being sucked into another kind of polar hole toward a different kind of human figure, this one of the spirit.

Through the translations of the French poet Charles Baudelaire, another Frenchman came to know of Captain Symmes's polar holes: Jules Verne. With Verne's classic *Journey to the Center of the Earth* (1864), the hidden underground regions, now reachable through an ancient Icelandic volcano crater, hit the big time and in the process began to take on new meanings, mostly of a Darwinian and paleontological sort. As Verne's scientific team ventures further and further into the earth, it encounters more and more ancient creatures, including the first dinosaur fight in literature, this one between a plesiosaur and an ichthyosaurus in the Central Sea.

Then there was the enigmatic figure of Cyrus Teed. In October of 1869, at the age of thirty, Teed was working in his "electro-alchemical" laboratory near Utica, New York. He was seeking what he called a "victory over death . . . the key of which I knew to be in the mystic hand of the alchemico-vietist." Standish, whose lively account I am relying on here, jokes about Teed's big "nine-dollar words," but he probably translates Teed's "alchemico-vietist" just right: "an alchemist working on the mysteries of the life force." Put a bit differently, Teed was after immortality, and probably physical immortality through some kind of spiritual chemistry.

But there was more. It seems Cyrus was also trying to materialize a magical female being, his "highest ideal of creative beauty" or "creative principle." There are vague sexual connotations and gender-bending complexities here, like the fact that Teed describes "her" as constituting "the environing form of the masculinity and Fatherhood of Being." And then there was all that magnetic and spiritual ecstasy, which Teed rather remarkably linked, like a modern neuroscientist, to the anatomy of the brain:

> I BENT MYSELF TO THE TASK OF PROJECTING INTO TANGIBILITY THE CREATIVE PRIN-
> CIPLE. SUDDENLY, I EXPERIENCED A RELAXATION AT THE OCCIPUT OR BACK PART
> OF THE BRAIN, AND A PECULIAR BUZZING TENSION AT THE FOREHEAD OR SINCIPUT;
> SUCCEEDING THIS WAS A SENSATION AS OF A FARADIC BATTERY OF THE SOFTEST
> TENSION, ABOUT THE ORGANS OF THE BRAIN CALLED THE LYRA, CRURA PINEALIS, AND
> CONARIUM. THERE GRADUALLY SPREAD FROM THE CENTER OF MY BRAIN TO THE
> EXTREMITIES OF MY BODY, AND APPARENTLY TO ME, INTO THE AURIC SPHERE OF MY
> BEING, MILES OUTSIDE OF MY BODY, A VIBRATION SO GENTLE, SOFT, AND DULCIFER-
> OUS THAT I WAS IMPRESSED TO LAY MYSELF UPON THE BOSOM OF THIS GENTLY
> OSCILLATING OCEAN OF MAGNETIC AND SPIRITUAL ECSTASY.[6]

This "vibratory sea" that extended *miles* outside his physical body was his "newly-found delight." Standish glosses it as "this ocean of electro-magneto-spiritual energy," but we might just as well read it as Teed's discovery of a larger body, a cosmic human form, as it were. In any case, we will see such language return with our mytheme of Radiation, of which Teed is a textbook protoexample.

A voice, channeled through his own, then reveals to Mr. Teed that "the Mother" has nurtured him through "countless embodiments" or reincarnations. She appears to him as a woman of exquisite beauty holding a caduceus staff and describes herself as "thy Mother and Bride" (more of that sexual complexity again, and oh so oedipal). She tells him that through Teed's (again, vaguely sexual) "quickening," "the Sons of God shall spring into visible creation." She also reveals to him "the law of transmutation," that is, "the correlation of force and matter . . . that matter and energy are two qualities or states of the same substance, and that they are each transposable to the other." Standish does not look away from the obvious here. It is, after all, 1899 looking back to an occult encounter of 1869: "What's eerie about this is that through the most occult, electro-alchemical path, Teed has arrived at an idea—matter is energy, energy matter, simply different forms of the same thing—that would shortly became an essential scientific truth."[7] Einstein's famous papers would begin to appear in 1905.

Teed's full illumination and religious message, which he came to call Koreshanity (Koresh is Hebrew for Cyrus), is not so scientific, though, for much of it revolves around the notion that the universe is a single cell or hollow globe, and all life lives on its inner concave surface. The sky we see, in other words, is actually *inside* this cosmic womb, and we live on its inner surface. Teed called this his "cellular cosmology."[8]

The hollow-earth theme would play a major role in subsequent fantasy writing. The inexhaustible Edgar Rice Burroughs, for example, staged many a novel, including some of his Tarzan stories, "at the earth's core." Similarly, the very first feature-length Superman film, *Superman and the Mole Men* (1951), starring George Reeves, returned to the hollow-earth theme again, as did the opening salvo of Marvel Comics' superhero renaissance in *Fantastic Four* #1 (November 1961). Indeed, the cover of the latter classic features an immense mole monster attacking New York City from below, and the story itself is pure hollow-earth stuff.

SPECULATIVE PREHISTORIC WORLDS OR LOST LANDS. Then there were all those lost lands of myth and speculative prehistory. Greek mythology, for example, knew a land called Hyperborea, the earthly paradise of perpetual sunshine and warmth in the Far North, beyond (*hyper-*) the North Wind (*Boreas*), which was thought to be the primordial home of humanity. But, as Joscelyn Godwin has demonstrated, the Far North and the legend of the shifting poles have birthed many a myth, mystical movement, and spiritual center, including the Asian subterranean land of Agarttha, which was invented in the nineteenth century by European occultists.

1.1   THE HOLLOW EARTH STRIKES BACK

Agarttha appears to have been created by Saint-Yves d'Alveydre (1842–1909), who had a mysterious Sanskrit tutor by the name of Hardjji Scharipf, who went by the title of "Guru Pandit of the Great Agartthian School."[9] According to Saint-Yves, Agarttha is a subterranean kingdom of millions of beings and advanced technology located somewhere in the East, protected by the "Master of the Universe" and ruled by an Ethiopian pontiff. This school and underground kingdom, which Saint-Yves claimed to have visited through astral travel, is allegedly still in existence and in possession of the original human language and its twenty-two-lettered alphabet, called Vattan or Vattanian. Remember that too. It will come back to us soon enough.

Then there is the Tibetan spiritual utopia of Shambhala. This is a very different sort of story. This hidden realm, after all, has long been considered a "pure land," a place of favored rebirth in the *Kalachakra Tantra* (literally, "the Teaching of the Wheel of Time"), a major initiatory text and transmission tradition within Tibetan Buddhism that is still very much alive. The key point here is that the status of Shambhala cannot be slotted into any simplistic Western categories of "real" or "imaginary." Joscelyn Godwin is well worth quoting on this subtle idea, as his observations bear directly on some of our later figures, including Superman and Batman writer Alvin Schwartz, who has engaged these very same Tibetan materials:

THE MEDITATOR MAY SUMMON UP SUCH PLACES IN ALL THEIR DETAIL, AND ENDOW THEM WITH A SENSE OF REALITY THAT MAY EVEN BECOME PALPABLE TO OTHERS. THE KALACHAKRA TANTRA IS A VERY COMPLEX MEDITATION OF THIS KIND. BUT THE PRACTITIONER ALSO KNOWS THAT, HOWEVER REALISTIC THE VISIONARY EXPERIENCE, IT IS NOT ULTIMATELY REAL. IF SUCCESS IS REACHED IN THE MEDITATIVE CREATION OF CITIES AND LANDSCAPES, GODS AND DEMONS, THEN THE PRACTITIONER GAINS THE CORRESPONDING CAPACITY FOR THE "DE-CREATION" OF THE MATERIAL, EVERYDAY WORLD, THAT IS, FOR THE AWARENESS THAT EARTHLY CITIES, LIKE SHAMBHALA, ARE MIND-CREATED ILLUSIONS.[10]

In short, if one can realize that visionary landscapes and paranormal realities, however convincing, are ultimately authored by oneself and one's culture, then one can also realize that things like "society," "religion," "self," and "other," even physical reality itself, are equally authored, and so also illusory. In short, the fantastic, handled properly, might help us to realize the true nature of the real, which is fantastic.

Among other mythical lands we might also list the ancient land of Thule. A man by the name of Pytheas tried to sail north in the fourth century BCE. He managed to sail for six days past what we know as England to the Arctic Circle, a place he called Thule. This term would wind its way through European history and much later enjoy a bizarre resurrection in Nazi mythology about an Aryan homeland in the north peopled by supermen possessing a high technology.[11]

Lost lands, usually sunk beneath some ocean, were also becoming increasingly popular in the imagination of the late nineteenth and early twentieth centuries. There were, of course, Plato's famous references in the *Timaeus* and the *Critias* to Atlantis, that lost island culture dedicated to Poseidon located somewhere in the Mediterranean Ocean or, in some later versions, in the aptly named Atlantic Ocean (hence the Golden Age superhero the Sub-Mariner, lordly king of the underwater realm of Atlantis). In the nineteenth and early twentieth centuries, however, other lost continents were proposed, from a place called Lemuria to James Churchward's Mu. More on Lemuria in a moment.

Finally, it is worth noting that the UFO would play a later role in both the hollow-earth and the submarine mythologies, this time through the notion of alien underground or underwater bases. These are sometimes put in the polar regions, as with the Nazi survival mythologies that have Hitler escaping to Antarctica, armed with UFOs or UFO planes as examples of Nazi superwar technology (Godwin notes, insightfully as always, that the North Pole, which is "up," is imagined positively and the South Pole, which is "down," is imagined negatively, hence Hitler's escape to the South Pole).[12] At other times, the underground bases become underwater bases and are connected to the USO, that is, the Unidentified Submersible Object.

On the baffling side, UFOs are often in fact—as in "actual experience"—seen emerging from and diving down into large bodies of water, especially seas and oceans, but also occasionally rivers and lakes.[13] The underwater lost continent, or in this case the underwater alien base, lives on in such bizarre encounters. Hence movies like James Cameron's *The Abyss* (which features an immense UFO emerging from the ocean) and pulp fiction back covers like this one from the November 1947 issue of *Amazing Stories*. If you open this particular magazine and read the story that the back cover illustrates, you will discover that it is taken from a historical report, which was located and flagged by the American writer Charles Fort. In other words, you will discover that the pulp fiction cover is not exactly fiction.

IMPOSSIBLE BUT TRUE

On Nov. 12, 1887, the British steamer *Siberian* saw an enormous ball of fire rise from the sea off Cape Race, move against the wind toward the ship, then move away to be lost from sight in five minutes. What was it? Fire does not rise from the sea, it does not move against the wind. Was it really a submersible-aircraft-spaceship the *Siberian* saw?

1.2   A BACK-COVER SIGHTING

DISTANT CIVILIZATIONS OR TRIBAL WORLDS. Another extremely common strategy of Orientation was to place the Other in a contemporary civilization more or less distant or foreign to Europe: Egypt, China, Africa, India, and "the New World" of the Americas have all played central roles at different times. By the time we get to the late nineteenth century and the origins of modern fantasy literature, however, it is India and, a bit later, Tibet that have taken central stage, primarily through British colonialism, but also through major earlier European intellectuals like Voltaire, the great French Enlightenment philosopher who believed that everything came ultimately from the banks of the Ganges, or the great German philosopher Immanuel Kant, who identified Tibet as the primordial home of the human.[14]

The truth is that much of this early European fascination with India and Tibet was largely a function of these intellectuals' utter contempt for the intolerance and blatant fictions of Jewish and Christian monotheism. "India" and "Tibet," in other words, functioned as idealized Others through which they could condemn, and hopefully transcend, their own religious cultures.

OUTER SPACE AND FUTURE WORLDS. The Orientations that ultimately came to define modern science fiction and fantasy literature, however, were outer space and the idea of future worlds. Think Edgar Rice Burroughs's John Carter of Mars (1912), Alex Raymond's Flash Gordon (1928), and Philip Francis Nowlan's Buck Rogers (1934). Other dimensions (a staple of nineteenth-century Spiritualism and occultism) would also soon be entertained, as would, most recently, parallel universes, multiple dimensions, and now entire universes being born like soap bubbles from the interaction of immense cosmic waves that modern cosmologists call "branes" interacting within a higher-dimensional superspace called the "bulk." Enter the multiverse.

CONSCIOUS MYTHMAKING: THE ROSY CROSS AND THE SECRET DOCTRINE

There were two esoteric or "secret" traditions that played an especially important role in the occult origins and historical development of fantasy literature and science fiction: Rosicrucianism and Theosophy. A grasp, however slight, of each of these very complex (and very confusing) traditions is crucial if one wants to understand some of the innermost workings of the Super-Story that follows.

Complexities and confusions aside, the key to understanding both forms of

Western esotericism is really quite simple, and it is this: both Rosicrucianism and Theosophy are modern mystical movements based largely on conscious fictions that nevertheless emphasize the real existence of "secret knowledge" and latent "powers." Put a bit more boldly, both forms of esotericism use religious fantasy to express, explore, and transmit paranormal experiences.

Here are the basics. The Rosicrucian tradition or "Fraternity of the Rosy Cross" is difficult to define, mostly because it has always been a loosely based movement of individuals dedicated to radical spiritual independence, private study, and secret truths. Central to the tradition in almost any form, however, is what historian Christopher McIntosh calls "the idea of the mysterious adept commanding secret knowledge and strange powers."[15] Often this figure of the Rosicrucian adept fuses occult or mystical interests and scientific pursuits in eerie and provocative ways, as we find, for example, in the iconic figure of Victor Frankenstein of Mary Shelley's famous novel. Dr. Frankenstein is a scientist, an alchemist, and a hermeticist—that is, a magician-scientist akin to the Rosicrucian adept—and it is precisely this fusion of the scientific and the occult that drives the narrative of the novel.[16]

Other recurring key themes of Rosicrucianism include: the existence of a secret society of initiates moving incognito among the normal lot of humanity; the model of the seeker of hidden wisdom or secret knowledge; a reading of history that sees distinct ages or eras moving inevitably toward a "new age," which the secret fraternity will help catalyze; the existence of a hidden shrine or sacred base in the form of an underground vault (a mini hollow earth, perhaps); and the practical stratagem of adopting whatever religious tradition is at play in one's own place or time, but never confusing the external forms or literal beliefs of this (or any other) religion with the universal mystical truths that these local forms both reveal and conceal. Significantly, particularly for later occult movements that claimed other sorts of "hidden masters" in underground kingdoms and realms, usually in Tantric Tibet, there was also the repeated rumor that after the Thirty Years' War, in 1648, the Rosicrucians left Europe and regrouped in Asia.[17]

McIntosh sums up the Rosicrucian worldview by describing it as gnostic, by which he means "the view that the human spirit is trapped, as it were, under water, living a kind of half-life, ignorant of the fact that the sunlight and air of the true spirit are overhead. If knowledge (or *gnosis*) can make people aware of this, they will make the effort to swim upward and be reunited with their real element."[18] Such an observation is profoundly relevant to our present pop-cultural materials, for, as we have already had occasion to see, comic book writers and artists commonly invoke the category of Gnosticism to describe their work and worldview. In earlier centuries, they may well have described themselves as Rosicrucians.

Historically speaking now, the Rosicrucian tradition began in 1614 with the publication of a German pamphlet, known in its Latin main title as the *Fama Fraternitatis* or "Legend of the Fraternity." The *Fama* claimed to tell the story of a certain Father Christian Rosenkreuz (literally, "Father Christian Rosy Cross"), who lived in the fourteenth and fifteenth centuries, founded a mystical brotherhood in Germany after traveling to the Middle East (Damascus and Fez) where he acquired a mysterious *Book M* and learned various occult teachings, and died at the ripe old age of 106. In short, the mytheme of Orientation. According to the legend, his body, which did not deteriorate, was preserved in a magical vault for 120 years until it was discovered in 1604 by his followers, an event that is believed to signal the dawn of a new age of spirit beyond the corrupt and violent reaches of "emperor" and "pope," or what we would today call "state" and "religion." The *Fama* pamphlet also assured any of its readers who were interested in joining that their intentions, once expressed in writing or speech, would become known by the Order, and that they would be subsequently contacted.

What this mysterious order had to offer was so attractive that many a later reader and admirer, including intellectual giants like Descartes and Leibniz (Francis Bacon also clearly knew about and engaged the tradition in his utopian novel *New Atlantis*), would attempt to associate with it in some way. Such men were inevitably disappointed, however, for they could find no such order.

There was a good reason for this. It didn't exist. By the repeated insistence of the likely author of the Rosicrucian myth, a man by the name of Johann Valentin Andreae, it was all a *ludibrium*, a playful hoax, a teaching trick. McIntosh suggests that Andreae had hoped that his works would be interpreted symbolically. When the public insisted, quite to the contrary, on taking it all literally, he was bitterly disappointed, even openly disgusted. Thus in a later work, he writes: "Listen ye mortals, in vain do you wait for the coming of the Brotherhood, the Comedy is at an end."[19]

Well, sort of. Later readers, literary figures, scholars, Masons, and private occultists would take up the Rosicrucian spirit and its dream of a New Age of the Spirit and develop these into a hundred different forms, from the most erudite and esoteric to the most crass and commercial.

One nineteenth-century author who carried on this rich Rosicrucian mix of fiction writing and private occultism was the English aristocrat and ex-cabinet minister Edward Bulwer-Lytton. Bulwer-Lytton's novel *Zanoni* (1842), the inspiration for which came to him in a dream, demonstrates a real grasp of the historical literature on Rosicrucianism.[20] Bulwer-Lytton purports to be the mere editor of the text, which he claims to have received from an old man who instructed him in wisdom and gave him the key to his book after meeting Bulwer-Lytton in an antique bookstore in Covent Garden that specialized in esoteric subjects. McIntosh, who did research in Bulwer-Lytton's library, notes that the bookstore, owned by a man named John Denley, actually existed between 1790 to 1840, and that there are good reasons, including private correspondence, to think that *"Zanoni* is based on an actual encounter with a member of some highly secret Rosicrucian group who either initiated him or revealed a certain amount and then enjoined him to silence."[21]

Initiation or no initiation, what Bulwer-Lytton really became famous for was his hollow-earth novel, *The Coming Race* (1871), which is widely considered to be one of the first examples of a genre that would eventually morph into science fiction. The story is set in an underground kingdom of Egyptian columns and super-evolved beings, the Vril-ya, the coming race that is destined to supplant the human species on the surface. It features two protagonists: an Englishman, who has fallen into the underground world while exploring a mine, and his female Vril-ya savior and guide, a superwoman named Zee.

The novel orbits around a mysterious electromagnetic-spiritual energy called *vril* (likely a contraction of *virile*), which is most potent in the feminine members of the Vril-ya. As with contemporary uses of the paranormal, vril is employed in the novel to both mystical and technological ends. It is used to cut out rock and build cities, power vehicles, control "automaton figures," power mechanical wings, light lamps, direct engineering projects, and end all war (since its absolute destructive power renders all war absurd and suicidal). Likened explicitly to electricity or magnetism, it is also compared to the mysterious forces at work in "mesmeric clairvoyance" and is used to zap the body and render it superconductive to its own natural healing energies. Vril can even induce various altered states of consciousness, like trance and vision, through which thoughts can be transferred from one brain to another "and knowledge be thus rapidly interchanged."[22] In short, psychical powers.

The vril also carries patently erotic overtones, particularly in the females, whose "command over the mystic agencies of vril" are "pretty sure to run down [the male's] neck into what we call 'the fatal noose.'"[23] Even more so around the neck of a hapless human. When the Englishman is considering yielding to Zee's advances, he is warned what might well happen in "her amorous flame": "if you yield, you will become a cinder."[24] Such dangers are mollified somewhat when the Englishman imagines how humanity might still be saved from certain extermination if the Vril-ya decide finally to emerge on the surface: through "intermixture of race," that is, through a hybrid breeding program.[25]

The Coming Race, then, combines in quite obvious and explicit ways the my-themes of Orientation (the subterranean world, the Egyptian architecture, and the "silent forms" of the Vril-ya seated "in the gravity and quietude of Orientals"[26]), Radia-tion (the vril), and Mutation (the coming race and the constant reflections on Darwinian themes). This particular author's Orientation was also clearly a colonialist's anxiety, since as a former secretary of state for the colonies (1858–59) he could write of "Chris-tendom . . . this glorious Europe, with all its offshoots in yet vaster regions, that may each be a Europe hereafter."[27] What The Coming Race seems to signal, on one level at least, is that those "vaster regions" might well resist this Europeanization and assert their own identities over the colonizer. They might arise.

We are also quickly approaching Alienation, in passages like those on the "inter-mixture of race," on the skulls of the Vril-ya, which are "far loftier in the apex"[28] (thus suggesting the oblong, tall skulls of what would become the classic Gray), and on an evil subterranean race of reptoids or lizard men. Clearly, we're already off and running.

And in a distinctly paranormal direction. In his own words, Bulwer-Lytton sought to "embrace all the modern learning of mysticism."[29] He also clearly thought in that third realm of what would become the paranormal—that is, he rejected both "the materialism of one sect of reasoners" and the believing "enthusiasm of many sects of visionaries" for what he calls "the principle of soul." "Soul," for this author anyway, was the mediating Third between and beyond "mind" and "matter."[30] Similarly, "the Marvellous" (or what I have called the fantastic) was that "perpetual struggle" between "the creed of his reason" and "the question his experience [of the occult] puts to his reason."[31] Accordingly, he found the rejections of "the reasoners," captured in their cry of "imposture and conjuring," a bit silly and superficial.

In short, Bulwer-Lytton believed in "the substance of what used to be called Magic," namely, that "there are persons of a peculiar temperament who can effect very extraordinary things not accounted for satisfactorily by any *existent* philosophy."[32] Which, of course, suggests that we might still work toward one that will be satisfactory, if we can only get beyond the reasoner's "Imposture!" and the believer's "It's all the work of God!" Hence Bulwer-Lytton's fierce independence from all religious creeds and churches, his definition of prayer as "the release of all imaginative sensibilities,"[33] and his fundamental insistence that the supernatural is the natural not yet fully understood. Hardly your typical believer, but very Rosicrucian of him.

Finally, we are getting ahead of ourselves here, but I cannot help pointing out that the core themes of *The Coming Race* continue to influence modern writers, whether consciously or not. Consider, as a single stunning example, the following passage from Whitley Strieber, the talented horror writer become visitor-mystic whom we will meet in chapter 7. Here is Strieber correcting his interviewers on their use of an all too familiar word: "No," Strieber jumps in, "I didn't say aliens. I never said that. I don't use the word aliens because I don't know what they are. My impression is that the physical beings that are involved are from the Earth. They are an evolutionary leap of some kind, but that they are primarily Earth-oriented. That's my impression. We are not looking at aliens. We are looking at our replacements."[34] The coming race.

Significantly, for our own purposes at least, much of the most recent Rosicrucian action has taken place in the U.S. According to McIntosh, the first man to openly promote Rosicrucian ideas in the States was Paschal Beverly Randolph, a fascinating figure well known to historians of Western esotericism through the definitive study of John Patrick Deveney, whose subtitle sums up the man nicely: "A Nineteenth-Century Black American Spiritualist, Rosicrucian, and Sex Magician."[35]

Randolph was born of mixed race in 1825 and grew up in an orphanage. He led a contingent of Northern black soldiers in the Civil War and after the war taught emancipated slaves in Louisiana at the request of none other than President Abraham Lincoln. Randolph, in short, was an abolitionist and an early civil rights activist. He aligned his teachings with Rosicrucianism, but he was crystal clear that he bore no official connection to any Rosicrucian brotherhood: "Very nearly *all* that I have given as Rosicrucianism originated in my soul," he honestly confessed. And what originated in his soul nearly all had to do with the metaphysical and magical dimensions of human sexual energies. In short, Randolph taught a form of sex magic.

Which got him into a whole lot of trouble. In 1872, a judge in Boston described the writer as "beyond all reasonable doubts *the* most *dangerous* man and author on the soil of America if not of the entire globe." Randolph had been put up on charges of teaching free love. He probably was. He was acquitted.

It was not the free love part that stunned Randolph, though. It was the mystery of sexuality itself—it was the erotic as the mystical. According to Randolph, much like Father Christian Rosenkreuz, "subsequent to his return from oriental lands, whither, like myself, and hundreds of others, he went for initiation," he claimed that his erotic gnosis was obtained in a spiritual pilgrimage to the Middle East. Orientation again.

In his own words: "One night . . . I made love to, and was loved by, a dusky maiden of Arabic blood. I of her, and that experience, learned—not directly, but by suggestion—the fundamental principle of the White Magic of Love." This white sexual magic involved both the correct use of sexuality and the conductivity of the spirit through the polarization of the two genders, but also a very special sexual secretion, "which is only present under the most fierce and intense amative passion in either man or woman." This was a magical fluid that constitutes "the union of magnetism, electricity and nerve-aura."[36]

Many Rosicrucian groups would appear after Randolph, including one with explicit connections to the sexual magician, but the most influential was a group called the Ancient and Mystical Order Rosae Crucis (the latter two words are Latin for "of the Rosy Cross"), otherwise known simply as AMORC. This group was founded by a man named H. Spencer Lewis. It eventually established headquarters in San Jose, California, where it still resides on its own campus featuring recreations of Egyptian architecture and artifacts. As the architecture might suggest, the "Orient" for AMORC is more or less equivalent to a reimagined and rebuilt ancient Egypt. Orientation yet again.

AMORC is especially relevant to our present project because it occupies a strong and obvious presence in the pulp fiction magazines, a presence that, as far as I can tell, has yet to be adequately noticed, much less studied and interpreted. Nowhere is this more obvious than in AMORC's pulp advertising campaigns, which fantastically blurred the line between fact and fiction by publishing countless ads for the development of "psychic powers" in pulp magazines filled with fictional stories about psychical powers.

Summing up the Rosy Cross for our own purposes now, we might say that the origins of Rosicrucianism lie in the conscious allegorizing of a few independent Protestant writers, who fused fantasy, religious devotion, and their own spiritual experiences to create a bold new form of Western esotericism coded in a kind of Christian fiction, a fiction that was later taken up and developed into a spectrum of mystical movements that eventually went far beyond anything that the original writers had in mind. This, I might observe, is not as strange as it sounds, particularly if one holds, as Rosicrucians generally do, that the external or literal forms of *all* religions are in fact fictions that hide deep experiential truths. If all religions are fictions, why not use fiction to express one's mystical experiences? Indeed, what else *could* one do?

Also important to our own Super-Story is a once-popular movement called Theosophy, literally, the "Wisdom" (*sophia*) of "God" (*theos*). The term itself is much older than the modern occult tradition and generally referred to Christian mystical traditions that emphasized personal and direct experiences of the divine, often of an unorthodox or even heretical nature—think gnosis again. Modern Theosophy continues this unorthodox tradition, and then some.

The Theosophical Society was founded in 1875 in New York City by an eccentric Russian woman named Helena P. Blavatsky, an American journalist who had been reporting on Spiritualism under the name of Henry Steel Olcott, and the Irish American lawyer and occultist William Quan Judge. Through its many sectarian splits and cultural transformations, Theosophy played a key historical role in garnering public enthusiasm for the comparative study of religion, promoting the early study of "the powers latent in man," and opening Western culture up to an early appreciation of "Eastern" religions. In short, Theosophy was a major, maybe *the* major promoter of the mytheme of Orientation.

Like Rosicrucianism, Theosophy is extremely complex, and even more confusing. This is partly because one of its central texts, Blavatsky's two-volume, fifteen-hundred-page tome, *The Secret Doctrine* (1888), sets out its teachings in highly symbolic, abstract, and largely mythical terms. Read literally, the book is baffling. Read as a work that advances its claims "hidden under glyph and symbol," that is, as a creative act of religious liberalism, modern mythmaking, and an attempted subversion of Western religion and science, *The Secret Doctrine* remains a difficult, often frustrating, but also rich read.[37] There is also much in *The Secret Doctrine* that displays a certain "automatic" quality, as in "automatic writing" or what is today called "channeling."[38] In short, the book appears from and appeals to something other than reason and the conscious ego.

Blavatsky appears to have drawn on Bulwer-Lytton's *The Coming Race* to express her own secret doctrine of a coming race of spiritually evolved superhumans. Little wonder, then, that one interviewer described meeting her in 1884 as an encounter with an incarnation of *Zanoni* and *The Coming Race*.[39] Her system, however, was much more complex and certainly cannot be explained by any single source.

To put things much too simply, we might summarize the secret doctrine as an anti-Darwinian, evolutionary vision in which the entire universe is seen as emerging from a single divine Monad or One, whose various life forms then evolve through huge stretches of time until they can become fully conscious of the divinity from which everything first emerged. Basically, the cosmos is seen as an organic conscious Being that emerged from pure Spirit and is now evolving toward the realization of pure Spirit. The present human form is seen as a moment in this cosmic cycle of awakening, as one chapter in the larger story of seven "Root-Races," four of which have already passed, one of which we are in now (the fifth Root-Race), and two of which are yet to come.

The first Root-Race, which lived on "The Imperishable Sacred Land" at the North Pole, was invisible and ethereal, an "astral" or "shadow" but also colossal form of the gods who created it. The second, which lived on Hyperborea, again in the North, was a slightly more material form of the first. They were androgynous, monsterlike beings and only semihuman. It is only with the third Root-Race, the Lemurians, that the evolving species abandoned its original androgynous nature and began to reproduce sexually. The fourth Root-Race, the Atlanteans, were a surviving remnant of Lemurian civilization, after the latter was destroyed by a natural cataclysm and sank below the oceans. We are the sixth subrace of the fifth Root-Race (I warned you that it's complicated), which will soon be replaced by the sixth Root-Race in a familiar place: "Occult philosophy teaches that even now, under our very eyes, the new Race and Races are preparing to be formed, and that it is in America that the transformation will take place, and has already silently commenced."[40]

Other common tropes in theosophical literature include: the existence of *auras*, shifting patterns of colored light that are said to radiate from living things, especially human bodies; the *astral body*, literally a "star body" that survives the death of the physical form and that one can use on the "astral plane" to travel from place to place, even to other realms and planets; the *chakras*, subtle energy "wheels" or centers of consciousness that are said to be located along the spinal channel within Tantric forms of yoga; the use of the term *super-human* (to designate the Superior Being from whom humanity is said to be born); the likely coinage of the expression "the New Age" as it is used today; and the *Mahatmas* (literally, "Great Souls") or *ascended masters*, enlightened beings who are believed to secretly rule the world, often, it is implied, from the mountainous regions of Tibet. Alongside these major tropes we also encounter some most delightful minor ones, like the Lemurian hunter with his pet dinosaur, the gigantic stature of the Atlanteans, and the Atlantean libraries, which featured manuscripts written on the tanned hides of ancient monsters.[41] Well, the Theosophists were anything but boring.

All of these fantastic themes have entered, usually in highly idiosyncratic forms, the pop-cultural materials that we will encounter below. But it is the third Root-Race and the lost land of Lemuria that probably need the most explaining, particularly since they will shortly play a rather major role in our mytheme of Alienation.

Sumathi Ramaswamy has given us a wonderful study of Lemuria in its scientific origins, Theosophical revisionings, and cultural aftermaths among freelance scholars both in America and India.[42] She asks not whether such a place existed or not (okay, it did not), but what is invested in describing it now as "lost." In essence, Lemuria for Ramaswamy is a "labor of loss," a modern utopia (literally, a "no-place") or cultural dream of what humanity might become through the bold reimagining of what it once was, that is, of *what we have lost*.

And we have lost a lot. The universe, "once perceived as alive and as cognizant of its own goals and purposes, is now an inert entity, hurtling about neverendingly, an immense machine of matter and motion blindly obeying mathematical laws."[43] If we are to believe our own science, mystery and magic are no more, and we ourselves are so many organic robots, foolishly imagining that we possess free will and an independent spirit, when in fact we are nothing more than the elaborate froth of neurological loops, selfish genes, and firing brain cells completely conditioned by social learning and the cultural environment. Like Data on *Star Trek: The Next Generation*, we are so many machines that desperately want to be a human spirit, but never will be. There is, after all, only one thing: matter.[44]

Lemuria is a profoundly eccentric and oppositional dream posed against this sort of scientific materialism that began, oddly enough, in the heart of science. Lemuria, it turns out, was first born in a scientific journal, in an 1864 essay entitled "The Mammals of Madagascar" by the English zoologist Philip Lutley Sclater. Sclater was puzzled by the existence of some thirty species of the lemur on the island, in contrast to Africa (which, he noted, possesses only eleven or twelve) and India (which sports just three). He quite rationally posited an ancient land connection between the island and the two large landmasses. Because the lemur is closer to the monkeys of the New World than it is to those of the Old World, Sclater also posited that this hypothetical land mass extended into the Atlantic Ocean and, at some point, joined up with the New World. His name for this sunken land mass? "I should propose the name of Lemuria!"[45]And so it began, with a drowned continent named after some little monkeys.

The scientific community did not yet have the German meteorologist Alfred Wegener's theory of continental drift, which would not begin to be articulated until 1912, much less the very recent "raft theory" (which has select animals during four migration events floating to the island from the African continent on dead trees after major storms), so Sclater's theory held, more or less, for awhile.

Lemuria withered away in science after the continental drift model and its notion of a super landmass called Pangaea (literally, "All [the] Earth") took hold, but not before it was reborn in a very different form in Theosophy and Rosicrucianism. For our own purposes here, there were three stages in this process: (1) Lemuria as the lost land of Blavatsky's Third Root-Race in the 1880s, where protohumans took on a physical form and higher beings incarnated as human egos through a kind of alien evolutionary intervention; (2) Lemuria's "move" to the Pacific Ocean off the American Northwest in the 1920s, from which it would pass into American occult movements around Mount Shasta; and (3) the pulp fiction magazine *Amazing Stories* in the late 1940s and something called "the Shaver Mystery." We will return to the Shaver Mystery in the next chapter. For now, it is enough to treat the occult prehistories of Lemuria.

Theosophist writer K. Browning sums up the matter most succinctly:

THE STORY OF MAN, AS DISCOVERED BY OCCULT INVESTIGATION, CAN BE BRIEFLY TOLD. HE IS DEVELOPED IN SEVEN CLEARLY MARKED STAGES CALLED ROOT-RACES. THE FIRST THREE WERE OCCUPIED IN THE WORK OF BUILDING A SERVICEABLE PHYSICAL BODY AND DEVELOPING THE SENSES OF HEARING, TOUCH, AND SIGHT. NO PHYSICAL TRACES WILL EVER BE FOUND OF THE FIRST TWO, FOR THEIR BODIES WERE MADE OF SUCH FINE MATTER THAT NO FOSSILS COULD BE LEFT, AND THEY DID NOT BUILD CITIES OR TEMPLES. THE THIRD RACE HAS MORE IN COMMON WITH OUR OWN. IT INHABITED THE CONTINENT OF LEMURIA IN THE SECONDARY PERIOD, AND IT WAS THEREFORE A CONTEMPORARY OF THE GIGANTIC SAURIANS.[46]

That last line is especially revealing, as it suggests that the constant tendency of science fiction novels and superhero comics to stage their stories in prehistoric settings, with human protagonists and those supercool dinosaurs sharing the same space, may be bad science, but it is good Theosophy. Hence the Lemurian and his pet dinosaur.

Through clairvoyant, telepathic, and other occult channels (a stock staple of human-alien communication in the later UFO accounts), Theosophy claimed further to offer an account of "the ascent of man" that was really more of a "descent of man," that is, a descent or emanation from the Divine Mind.[47] In this vision, we are all avatars, literally "descents" of the divine. And Lemuria played a key role here. It, after all, was the land of the first civilization, which the Lemurians developed with the help of some divine teachers from the planet Venus, the Lords of the Flame who arrived in the chariot of the Sons of the Fire in order to breed the next Root Race, the Atlanteans, from the stock of the Lemurians.[48]

The notion of alien intervention in human evolution was in fact a staple of the theosophical imagination, and it worked on many levels. As Theosophist Alfred P. Sinnett—one of the first to popularize the terms "occultism" and "occult" for the English-speaking world—put it: "The evolution of man is not a process carried out on this planet alone. It is a result to which many worlds in different positions of material and spiritual development have contributed."[49] This notion of a Venusian-Earth hybrid civilization would come to play a major role in science fiction, pulp fiction, and the UFO contactee cults of the 1950s and '60s, as would Theosophy's central assertions around some "occult dimensions to human evolution of which material sciences were barely cognizant."[50] In short, before there was science fiction, there was Theosophy.

For the Theosophists, when Lemuria sank, Atlantis survived as a kind of Lemurian remnant, and it was the Atlanteans that finally bestowed full humanity and full human civilization on the future, that is, the Fourth and Fifth Root-Races, the latter of which are most commonly represented by light-skinned peoples. Alas, although Theosophy worked to relativize the primacy of a colonizing West through its privileging of Asian wisdom traditions and became a major force for both the Indian independence movement and Buddhist reform and renaissance in Ceylon (now Sri Lanka), it did not entirely escape the racial theories of the time.

Lemuria, though, will rise again—literally, through the cataclysms of volcanoes and geographical shifts—and reunite scientific knowledge with ancient wisdom, that is, it will usher in a New Age of the Secret Doctrine. Ramaswamy suggests that one of the most original and important contributions Blavatsky and her disciples made to later occult thought was their moving of Lemuria to the Pacific Ocean, where it is supposed to resurface, as we have already seen, in America and the sixth Root-Race. It was not Theosophists who did the real heavy work here, though. It was West Coast American Rosicrucians, who located the sunken continent somewhere off the coast of the American Northwest, where it in turn became identified as the ancient mother of California and became associated with Mount Shasta and a whole bevy of American occult traditions.

Particularly important here was H. Spencer Lewis, the founder and Grand Master of AMORC, the same San Jose Rosicrucian group that we encountered above in their pulp fiction advertising campaign. Lewis, under the pen name of Wishar S. Cervé, published *Lemuria: The Lost Continent of the Pacific* (1931), which soon became an occult and later New Age classic. In this book, which the publishers claim is based on some secret archives of Tibet and China and features on its cover a vaguely looking Asian goddess seated on a lotus (classic Orientation moves), Lewis not only identified America as the original home of the Garden of Eden, but he also imagined a submerged Lemuria that geographically, literally, links East Asia and America (no need for the Orient anymore). He also insisted that the original beings of Eden now live in the depths of Mount Shasta, which he claimed is a geographical remnant of Lemuria. This is how he explained all those "stories whispered in Northern California about the occasional strange-looking persons seen to emerge from the dense growth of trees in that region."[51] In a final chapter, charmingly entitled "Present-Day Mystic Lemurians in California," Lewis discusses what he claims are hundreds of reports of silent, silver, boat-shaped airships drifting about the mountains and ocean coasts of California. He also describes a most unusual effect that Mount Shasta is said to have on automobiles that get too close: after a flash of light, their electrical systems fail.[52] What to do? Godwin, with his typical genius for finding the glowing nugget amid the dross, correctly points out that this little detail anticipates by several decades a central feature of later UFO encounters.[53]

So we already have protohumans amid the dinosaurs, alien genetic intervention, occult evolution, and now forest humanoids and silent, silver airships. Well, we can see where this is all going. We can also begin to see why California became one of the most active zones of American occultism: the place butts up against the lost land of Lemuria (or *is* Lemuria). Weirdly, the very first UFO sighting, near Mount Rainier,

Washington, in 1947, occurred in the same mountain range, about five hundred miles north of Mount Shasta, as did some of the earliest and most famous Sasquatch sightings. But, as the American collector of anomalies Charles Fort used to say, that is just a little too interesting.

THE RISE OF THE IMAGINAL: THE PSYCHICAL RESEARCH TRADITION

Rosicrucian authors like Bulwer-Lytton portrayed magical powers in their stories as real forces of Nature that we do not yet understand but will someday, after which we will be able to work true wonders. The paranormal will become normal. This was also the basic understanding of the British and American psychical research traditions, our third protochapter, alongside Rosicrucianism and Theosophy, in our emerging Super-Story.

The key writer here was a man named Frederic Myers. Myers was trained as a classicist at Trinity College, Cambridge, before he dedicated himself to over two decades of intense psychical research, which included the collection and analysis of thousands of written accounts from Europe and America on unusual experiences that occurred around the death of a loved one and literally hundreds of séance sessions with dozens of mediums. Myers died in Rome in 1901, fully convinced that the human spirit survives the disintegration of the body.

For Myers, however, this spirit or soul cannot be equated with the conscious subject or social self. "Below the threshold or *limen*" (*sub-liminal*) of this conscious self exists another Self, a secret identity endowed with what Myers called "supernormal" powers of sensation and cognition, including something he named, for the first time in 1882, *telepathy*, literally, a "profound feeling (*pathos*) at a distance (*tele*)." It was this *subliminal Self* beneath the threshold of normal awareness that Myers believed is the true subject of psychical perceptions, the possessor of supernormal powers, and the survivor of death's grisly decay.

Perhaps most pertinent to our present concerns involving the paranormal and popular culture, however, was Myers's understanding of the imagination and its intimate connection to deeper metaphysical energies. Basically, Myers became convinced that the imagination can become empowered and make contact with what appears to be a real spiritual world or, at the very least, an entirely different order of Mind. He wanted to use a new adjective for this superpowered version of the human imagination. It clearly was not a matter of the "imaginary." He thus called it the *imaginal*. In the opening pages of his masterwork, *Human Personality and Its Survival of Bodily Death* (1903), Myers defined the adjective this way: "A word used of characteristics belonging to the perfect insect or *imago*;—and thus opposed to *larval*;—metaphorically applied to transcendental faculties shown in rudiment in ordinary life."[54]

What Myers intended to communicate by this difficult phrase was the idea that the human imagination under certain very specific conditions—often involving the trauma of death, or near-death, and what he called "the influx" of spiritual energies—can take on extraordinary capacities that represent hints of a more highly evolved human nature. In his more technical terms, such states were "preversions" that represented "a tendency to characteristics assumed to lie at a further point of the evolutionary progress of a species than has yet been reached."[55] In short, an occult radiation triggering a spiritual evolution, a zapping effecting a mutation.

In his choice of expression, he was probably thinking of entomology or the scientific study of insects. Hence just as the larval stage of an insect looks nothing like the *imago* or mature image of its adult form (which indeed appears "bizarre" or alien-like in comparison to the larval slug), so too the images of the human imagination can mature into extremely strange but nevertheless accurate evolutionary forms as imaginal visions.

The classic case Myers and his colleagues studied involved what they called "veridical hallucinations." They collected thousands of these. Here's one from our own era: "I had a dream that [my grandpa Gogueon] was on our property, walking down to the lake, waving good-bye to me. When I woke up, there was a telegram saying that he had died." The visionary? Dan Aykroyd.[56] Such a dream remains a dream, that is, a product of the imagination, but it also appears to know things that no normal channels of sense can explain. In the terms of Myers, Aykroyd's dream is a clear example of the "supernormal" capacities of the human personality and a "preversion" or sign of its future "imaginal" powers.

Myers constructed an allegory—perhaps from the classical tidbit that the word for "soul" in Greek, *psyche*, can also mean "butterfly" or "moth"—to explain why so many insist on thinking in only larval terms, that is, why it is so difficult for us to accept our own emerging supernormal natures and their evolutionary futures and why we want to discount our most extraordinary experiences as simply "imaginary." Here is how he put it:

LET US SUPPOSE THAT SOME HUMBLE LARVAE ARE DISSECTING EACH OTHER, AND SPECULATING AS TO THEIR DESTINIES. AT FIRST THEY FIND THEMSELVES PRECISELY SUITED TO LIFE AND DEATH ON A CABBAGE-LEAF. THEN THEY BEGIN TO OBSERVE CERTAIN POINTS IN THEIR CONSTRUCTION WHICH ARE USELESS TO LARVAL LIFE. THESE ARE, IN FACT, WHAT ARE CALLED "IMAGINAL CHARACTERS"--POINTS OF STRUCTURE WHICH INDICATE THAT THE LARVA HAS DESCENDED FROM AN IMAGO, OR PERFECT INSECT, AND IS DESTINED IN HIS TURN TO BECOME ONE HIMSELF. THESE CHARACTERS ARE MUCH OVERLAID BY THE SECONDARY OR LARVAL CHARACTERS, WHICH SUBSERVE LARVAL, AND NOT IMAGINAL LIFE, AND THEY CONSEQUENTLY MAY EASILY BE OVERLOOKED OR IGNORED. BUT OUR SUPPOSED CATERPILLAR STICKS TO HIS POINT; HE MAINTAINS THAT THESE CHARACTERISTICS INDICATE AN AERIAL ORIGIN. AND NOW A BUTTERFLY SETTLES FOR A MOMENT ON THE CABBAGE-LEAF. THE CATERPILLAR POINTS TRIUMPHANTLY TO THE MORPHOLOGICAL IDENTITY OF SOME OF THE BUTTERFLY'S CONSPICUOUS CHARACTERS WITH SOME OF HIS OWN LATENT CHARACTERS; AND WHILE HE IS TRYING TO PERSUADE HIS FELLOW-CATERPILLARS OF THIS, THE BUTTERFLY FLIES AWAY.

"This," Myers explains, "is exactly what I hold to have happened in the history of human evolution."[57] We are all future butterflies who think, wrongly, that we are just slugs. And we are evolving, whether we admit it or not, into something else. Something with wings.

TURN OF THE CENTURY TRANSITIONS: A WAR OF THE WORLDS, A GRAY GUIDE, AND A PRINCESS ON MARS

Our quick trip through the different ways that the Western religious imagination has oriented itself already suggests how the mytheme of Orientation slid into that of Alienation. Basically, a colonizing Western civilization ran out of "other lands" until it eventually found itself floating, metaphorically and eventually literally, in outer space. Little wonder, then, that the base story of much science fiction—that of the alien invasion—was first imagined as a critical response to British colonialism, whose primary object was the East, as in India. Enter H. G. Wells and his *War of the Worlds* (1898), easily one of the most important and influential English novels of the modern era.

According to the literary critic Brian Stableford, the novel had its creative origins in Wells's private reflections on Western colonialism and in his study of Darwinian biology. Wells had studied biology with none other than T. H. Huxley, "Darwin's bulldog" who fearlessly championed the biologist's shocking ideas before an offended church and a deeply skeptical public. Such a training would have likely given Wells the idea of alternate species and alternate evolutionary pathways on other planets. In other words, we have hints of Mutation here as well.

But it was European colonialism that affected the author most directly. Indeed, his most famous story came to him when he was walking with his brother and discussing the fate of the Tasmanians, who had recently been decimated by the British colonialists, whose technology far surpassed that of the defenseless islanders. Wells proposed to his brother a scenario in which the tables were turned and the British colonizers became the colonized. And so Wells's colonizers become Martians who arrive in southern England in overwhelming force.

The result was as electrifying as it was terrifying. As Stableford points out, this story of an alien invasion, of an imperialistic force far superior to anything any human civilization has ever known, "became one of the central myths of twentieth-century Anglo-American science fiction."[58] It would also, as we shall see soon enough, become the central myth, and central fear, of the UFO phenomenon.

There were other historical moments, however, in which one can detect the gradual (or sudden) shift from Orientation to Alienation. One of the more intriguing involves a Russian occultist named Nicholas Roerich. Roerich was a painter, theatrical set designer, and peace activist. His wife, Helena, was a channel for Master Morya, one of Theosophy's Mahatmas or ascended masters. Nicholas wrote a book on Shambhala in which he associated the secret city with the hidden realm of the Mahatmas, and the couple would later write a book together entitled *Agni Yoga*, on the "Agni" or "Fire" of Shambhala, the "great eternal energy, this fine imponderable matter which is scattered everywhere and which is within our use at any moment." Godwin notes the similarities with Bulwer-Lytton's vril here and even shows us how this same "Practice of the Fire" would find a new life in the pulp fiction visions of a man we will meet soon enough, Richard Shaver.

Pulp fiction aside for the moment, the Roerich family was traveling through China in the summer of 1927. On August 5, the party witnessed the following: "We all saw, in a direction from north to south, something big and shiny reflecting the sun, like a huge oval moving at great speed. Crossing our camp this thing changed in its direction from south to southwest. And we saw how it disappeared in the intense blue sky. We even had time to take our field glasses and saw quite distinctly an oval form

with shiny surface, one side of which was brilliant from the sun."[59] In short, the Roerich family and their party witnessed a flying saucer, but twenty years before there
was a "flying saucer" (the term and the phenomena were not named as such until the
summer of 1947).

Another symbolic transition from Orientation to Alienation was John Uri Lloyd's
remarkable 1895 hollow-earth novel *Etidorhpa*. The odd title is "Aphrodite" spelled
backward—*eros* reversed. It is also the name of a cosmic goddess who appears toward
the end of the novel in order to reveal to the central protagonist that everything in the
universe, from the atoms, suns, and stars, to the passions, arts, sciences, and evils
of human society, are so many manifestations of the same force used for good or for
ill: "love." Love, Etidorhpa teaches, "may guide a tyrant or actuate a saint, may make
man torture his fellow, or strive to ease his pain."[60] Freud, who was just coming on the
scene, could not have put it any better.

It is difficult to know where to begin with this one. The novel is set (and published)
in Cincinnati, that is, in the neighborhood of Captain Symmes. Rife with references to
secret brotherhoods and fraternities, savants and adepts endowed with secret knowledge and astonishing "superhuman" powers moving unknown among society as they
work for the good of mankind, "true esoteric psychologists," "Esoteric philosophy,"
"Christian mysticism," the "occult Wisdom possessions of Oriental sages," even a
traitorous Alchemistic Letter poised to reveal the shattering truths of a "Secret Society," the text reads like a Rosicrucian novel, despite the fact that the Rosicrucians are
never mentioned (which, I suppose, is very Rosicrucian).

In an alleged handwritten letter (patriotically dated July 4, 1895) appended to
the back of the book, the author states clearly his intentions for publishing the work:
to share with the public material that has discredited in his own mind the scientific
dogma of materialism, and to suggest that future science will one day confirm the
truths of occultism, particularly the doctrine "that force and spirit are neither less real
one than the other and that matter is not more substantial than either." In short, the
author seeks to suggest that "the study of matter may finally bring man to question if
the very attributes of matter are not qualities of force." So John Uri Lloyd appears to
have been influenced by the preaching and writing of Cyrus Teed.[61]

Both the narrative and the illustrations make it likely, which is not at all to say
certain, that the novel was deeply influenced by the author's ingestion of mind-altering
plants, particularly magical mushrooms, which appear, in immense treelike forms, in

the illustrations. Lloyd certainly would have had access to such things. By profession, he was a pharmacist; he was president of the American Pharmaceutical Association in 1887–88; and his knowledge of various narcotics was extensive. In Standish's terms, "Lloyd appears to have been the Carlos Castaneda of the hollow earth." Lloyd's biographer Michael A. Flannery sternly rejects this psychedelic reading, partly because of Lloyd's own stated concerns about drug abuse, partly because of this reading's speculative excesses in countercultural authors.[62]

I'm not so sure. We know, after all, that authors often code real experiences in fictional texts, sometimes even inserting standard warnings as literary devices toward a kind of plausible deniability.

Drugs or no drugs, as a simple narrative, *Etidorhpa* involves four major protagonists and what amounts to a book within a book, that is, a revealed occult manuscript: (1) the historical author and publisher John Uri Lloyd, who claims to have discovered in a library the thirty-year-old manuscript of (2) a man named Llewelyn Drury, who is the main narrator of the book and the original owner of the library (and who I suspect is a stand-in for Lloyd himself); (3) the telepathic "mysterious being" of the subtitle, named simply "I Am the Man" or "I Am the Man Who Did It," who allegedly visited Drury in his library one night, and many nights thereafter, as a kind of physical ghost or spectral double in order to read aloud a manuscript that narrated his terrifying journey into the bizarre and bright mysteries of the hollow earth;[63] and, finally, (4) the nameless, eyeless, telepathic guide who met I Am the Man at the mouth of a Kentucky cavern and guided him on his journey deep below the surface of things. This eyeless guide—who is really the star of the book—is alternately described as "this mystic Brother," "the mysterious being" (like I Am the Man), a "mysterious earth-being," "a cavern-born monstrosity," "a sage," and "a scientific expert, a naturalist, a metaphysical reasoner, a critic of religion, and a prophet" who "clothed his language intentionally in mysticism."[64]

Drury was instructed by I Am the Man to wait thirty years to publish the manuscript that the latter gave to him before he disappeared for good. Drury failed to do this, but Lloyd stepped in and accomplished the sacred duty, which amounted to a revealing of carefully guarded occult secrets.[65] Hence the appearance of *Etidorhpa*, first as a privately distributed publication and later as a widely published and successful illustrated book in multiple editions and languages.

I must confess that this particular text freaks me out a bit, mostly be-

I am the man

1.3   I AM THE MAN

cause of the historical fact that, already in 1895, it is consciously dramatizing virtually all of our mythemes, even as it is signaling striking iconic features (like huge foreheads and weird, naked, genital-less, short gray humanoids) that would be recombined, in different but similar ways, in the future. Whatever Lloyd was reading or ingesting (or reading after ingesting), it took him directly into the heart of our Super-Story and allowed him to see things that were still over the horizon of the next century's fantastic future.

Consider, for example, the astonishing illustrations of the later editions of the book, which included this one of the narrator's eyeless spirit-guide who looks, in Standish's terms now, "like a cross between E.T. and a cave fish."[66] What Standish does not tell us is that, if you crossed that cave fish E.T. with the forehead of I Am the Man (see fig. 1.3 again), you would have something that looks remarkably like a modern Gray. Indeed, the eyeless guide is described as shorter than an adult human, and his skin is explicitly described as the color of "light blue putty," that is, as gray.[67] All we are missing is the eyes, and we are *literally* missing those, almost as if they were intentionally left out so that they could be added later—which, of course, they were.

Me projecting? Hardly. Early in the novel, Lloyd describes the forehead of I Am the Man as "so vast, so high, that it was almost a deformity, and yet it did not impress me unpleasantly; it was the forehead of a scholar, a profound thinker, a deep student." Oddly, he could not tell the age of the mysterious being. He might just have been twenty-five as ninety, "and for an instant there was a faint suggestion to my mind that he was not of this earth, but belonged to some other planet."[68] This "expected visitor," by the way, is also called "the gray head."[69] It's 1895, folks.

As if that were not enough, the text is filled with explicit references to the mythemes of Radiation and Mutation. And I mean *explicit*. Indeed, the central revelation of the revealed manuscript is that force and matter are interchangeable, that what materialists mistake on the surface to be hard and stable is in fact moving and minded. Moreover, all known forces, from magnetism and electricity to heat and light, are so many manifestations "of something that lies behind them all, perhaps creates them all, but yet is in essence unknown to men. . . . something with which we are not acquainted, and yet in which we are submerged and permeated. . . . an unknown spirit, which, by certain influences, may be ruffled into the exhibition of an expression, which exhibition of temper we call a force."[70] This is "the spirit that saturates the universe," "a medium

"CONFRONTED BY A SINGULAR LOOKING BEING."

in which the earth, submerged, floats as a speck of dust in a flood of space."[71] This is "the all-pervading spirit of space."[72]

The mytheme of Mutation is just as clear and conscious. Consider, for example, the eyeless guide's teaching about "latent faculties" yet to be actualized by the processes of evolution that will allow human beings to understand the identity of matter and energy and communicate beyond culture through "mind language," that is, telepathically:

> IN TIME TO COME, MEN WILL GAIN CONTROL OF OUTLYING SENSES WHICH WILL ENABLE THEM TO STEP FROM THE SEEN INTO THE CONSIDERATION OF MATTER OR FORCE THAT IS NOW SUBTLE AND EVASIVE, WHICH MUST BE ACCOMPLISHED BY MEANS OF THE LATENT FACULTIES THAT I HAVE INDICATED. . . . STEP BY STEP, AS THE AGES PASS, THE FACULTIES OF MEN WILL, UNDER PROGRESSIVE SERIES OF EVOLUTIONS, IMPERCEPTIBLY PASS INTO HIGHER PHASES UNTIL THAT WHICH IS EVEN NOW POSSIBLE WITH SOME INDIVIDUALS OF THE PURIFIED ESOTERIC SCHOOL, BUT WHICH WOULD SEEM MIRACULOUS IF PRACTICED OPENLY AT THIS DAY, WILL PROVE FEASIBLE TO HUMANITY GENERALLY AND BE FOUND IN EXACT ACCORD WITH NATURAL LAWS. . . . PHENOMENA THAT ARE FAMILIAR TO THE COMING MULTITUDE, AND AT LAST, AS BY DEGREES, CLEARER KNOWLEDGE IS EVOLVED, THE VOCAL LANGUAGE OF MEN WILL DISAPPEAR, AND HUMANITY, REGARDLESS OF NATIONALITY, WILL, IN SCIENCE AND EVEN IN DARKNESS, CONVERSE ELOQUENTLY TOGETHER IN MIND LANGUAGE. THAT WHICH IS NOW ESOTERIC WILL BECOME EXOTERIC.[73]

Other *Etidorhpa* teachings that suggest that the text was inspired by Lloyd's own mystical experiences, with or without the mushrooms, include: (1) the notion that time is merely "a conception of the human intellect," and that eternity, which is "everlasting to the soul" and realized as such when the soul is liberated from the body, is not an infinite time, but a kind of ever-present now "outside of all things," where "time and space are annihilated"; (2) the conviction that "there is consciousness behind consciousness; there are grades and depths of consciousness"; (3) the claim that the spinal column is the physiological locus of occult revelation ("I quivered from head to foot, not with cold, but with a strange nervous chill that found intensest expression in my spinal column, and seemed to flash up and down my back vibrating like a feverous pulse"); and (4) the teaching that "matter is an illusion, spirit is the reality."[74] Finally, there is also (5) a most striking vision of what we would call today a kind of interdimensional multiverse or alien occultism that transcends the normal limitations of space-time:

> WILL THE BRIGHTER THOUGHTS OF MORE GIFTED MEN, UNDER SUCH FURTHERINGS AS THE FUTURE MAY BRING, PERCHANCE COMMUNE WITH BEINGS WHO PEOPLE IM-MENSITY, DISTANCE DISAPPEARING BEFORE THY EVER-REACHING SPIRIT? . . . MAY NOT BEINGS, PERHAPS LIKE OURSELVES BUT HIGHER IN THE SCALE OF INTELLIGENCE, THOSE WHO PEOPLE SOME OF THE PLANETS ABOUT US, EVEN NOW BECKON AND TRY TO CONVERSE WITH US THROUGH THY SUBTLE, EVER-PRESENT SELF? AND MAY NOT THEIR EFFORTS AT COMMUNICATION FAIL BECAUSE OF OUR IGNORANCE OF A LANGUAGE THEY CAN READ?[75]

"Our ignorance of a language they can read." We are back to the paranormal as mean-ing, as a kind of alien language, as a series of signs to read (or, more likely, not read).

Our last example of a transition from Orientation to Alienation was one that ap-peared four years after *Etidorhpa* and just a year after *The War of the Worlds*, that is, at the very end of 1899, that is, *right* at the cusp of the turn of the century. The timing could not have been more perfect.

Nor the title. The book was by a French psychologist named Théodore Flournoy, and it was entitled—it does not get much better than this—*From India to the Planet Mars*. The book, about a Swiss medium and silk shop worker named Élise Müller (known as "Hélene Smith" in the book) and her spontaneous creations of "Sanskrit" and "Martian" languages, is a masterwork of simultaneous suspicion and sympathy, both working together to understand and analyze a series of what Flournoy calls "sub-liminal romances."

For Flournoy, a subliminal romance is a story that spontaneously emerges, of-ten complete and perfectly formed, from the subliminal or unconscious depths of a medium, who is suspended in an altered state or hypnotic trance (Flournoy, like con-temporary alien abduction researchers, used hypnosis to access Müller's "memories"). Remarkably, such a subliminal romance tries to pull individuals into its drama and plot. Multiple personalities (or characters), for example, may appear—sometimes through the mechanism of automatic writing, sometimes through the voice of the medium—and interact with whomever is present, including and especially the researcher, who often plays a central role in catalyzing the appearance of the romance itself. In essence, the reader becomes part of the story here. Flournoy was very aware of all of this. He literally entered this story, and it in turn developed with him in mind. A subliminal romance, then, is a kind of living occult novel into which a research-reader can enter in a most unusual and direct way. As such, it is very similar to what we saw Peter Aykroyd calling an "apparitional drama." Here, though, the chosen form of paranormal expression is the novel, not the theater.

In the case of Müller, there were three distinct subliminal romances, which Flournoy dubbed "the Martian Cycle," "the Hindoo Cycle," and "the Royal Cycle." These developed serially and in parallel over the course of several years (more or less exactly like monthly or bimonthly pulp fiction magazines or superhero comic books). Sonu Shamdasani, a historian of depth psychology, sums up the basic plotline of the drama that unfolds: "She was Élise Müller, shop girl, Marie Antoinette, the princess Simandini, and a regular visitor to Mars: under his gaze, she became Hélène Smith, immortalized as a psychological case history of multiple personality. He was Théodore Flournoy, psychologist, professor, and scientist: under her gaze he became her former love, the [Hindu] prince Sivrouka."[76] (For what it is worth, a psychiatrist in Flournoy's time was called an *alieniste*.) To complicate things further (as if that were possible), there was also a special spirit-guide or protector of the medium, who went by the name of Léopold, but who was "actually" Cagliostro, the alter ego of the eighteenth-century Italian occultist Joseph Balsamo. Flournoy added to all this high drama by doing things like calling Hélène Smith "the heroine of this book."[77] It worked. Shamdasani points out that the book was a sensation when it came out, with some reading it as a work of critical psychology and others reading it as a novel.

It all started in December of 1894, when Flournoy was invited by another professor to attend some séances with a medium of "whose extraordinary gifts and apparently supernormal faculties I had frequently heard." He was very impressed with what he witnessed, and he left the event "with renewed hope of finding myself some day face to face with the 'supernormal'—a true and genuine supernormal—telepathy, clairvoyance, spiritistic manifestations, it matters not what name it be called, provided only that it is wholly out of the ordinary, and that it succeed in utterly demolishing the entire frame-work of established present-day science."[78]

Behind such lines was Flournoy's disgust with the laboratory academic psychology of the day that had no room for the deeper dimensions of the human psyche. Flournoy sought to create something very different, a "subliminal psychology" that engaged human lives in great detail and depth. As his uses of the expressions "subliminal" and "supernormal" suggest, he was deeply influenced by Frederic Myers, whose system he describes as at times reaching "the mysticism of true metaphysics."[79]

Using Myers's central notion of the *limen* or "threshold" of consciousness, Flournoy employed the techniques of hypnotic trance and approached the medium as someone whose threshold was very thin and unusually permeable. This permeability made the medium a very special figure through whom the workings of the unconscious and the subliminal imagination might be witnessed, analyzed, and understood in an especially clear way.

In a pattern that will become increasingly clearer as we proceed through our own subliminal romance, our Super-Story, all of the data Flournoy could collect about Élise Müller's early life suggested that her mediumistic gifts clustered around her fifteenth year, and all made their first appearances between the ages of nine and twenty. This connection between psychical phenomena and what Flournoy very carefully calls "a phase of development of major importance" is a classic one, which we can restate today with more clarity and less prudery: the paranormal and the sexual often appear together. Even the ghostly Léopold seemed to agree. He put the general date of his own appearances to the young girl at thirteen, that is, at puberty. Flournoy explains that Léopold could not appear much before that, "because the 'physiological conditions' necessary to his appearance were not yet realized."[80] Well, it does not get much clearer than that—at least not in 1899.

Contrary to what Flournoy suggested in his opening pages, it *did* matter what one calls these psychical phenomena, and his researches hardly ended up demolishing the framework of science. Flournoy employed something called cryptomnesia (the remembrance of hidden or forgotten memories, often of astonishing detail) to demolish the pious claim that mediums were contacting real spirits. For Flournoy, what a medium like Müller was really doing was remembering and refashioning details about historical figures and living people in the room that she had picked up from various textual and personal sources in the past, and perhaps—and this is where it gets very tricky and really interesting—through telepathic rapport.

It is no accident, then, that the Spiritualists were very upset with Flournoy and published a brochure against him and his work. Or that Müller was more or less furious with the psychologist, feeling betrayed by the scientist and what she experienced as his horribly demeaning theories. Perhaps most of all, she also felt hurt by all the public ridicule that came her way via the book's popularity.

The popularity not only came with a price, though. It also brought one. Shamdasani explains how all that fame also attracted a wealthy American benefactress, whose financial help allowed the medium to leave her day job and devote herself full time to her psychical vocation. Later in life, the medium would transmute her psychical gifts into a career as a religious painter. She renounced her earlier belief in her Hindu and Martian incarnations (in other words, Flournoy was right about that), but she remained adamant about her earlier existence as Marie Antoinette, and she never left the fold of Spiritualism or its general worldview.[81]

Flournoy's final conclusions are quite complex and nuanced. Basically, Flournoy read the spirits and Müller's memories of other lives on another planet and in another land as subliminal romances that encoded fantasies, life memories, and emotional complexes of the medium herself. He rejected the external existence of any of the personalities that appeared, but he also recognized and accepted that they were indeed personalities, that is, presences with a certain degree of autonomy.

In a fascinating final chapter entitled "Supernormal Appearances," he also stated very clearly his conviction that both telepathy and telekinesis were real. The medium, he explains in some detail, had produced both telekinetic phenomena and apports (objects that were believed to be produced out of thin air by a medium), the latter in 1892–93, before he came on the scene: "in midwinter roses showered upon the table, handfuls of violets, pinks, white lilacs . . . seashells were obtained that were still shining and covered with sand."[82] In terms of telekinesis, he speculates that, "certain abnormal and emotional states set at liberty in the organism latent forces capable of acting at a distance."[83]

On the rest, he remained agnostic, that is, he refused "to ascertain whether these facts are messengers of a superior economy or forerunners of a future evolution [which is exactly what Myers thought] rather than the survival of a condition of things which has disappeared, or whether they are purely accidental, . . . denuded of signification."[84] "Unless," he adds in a stunning passage that witnesses to his own implicit Gnosticism, "it is the cosmic power itself, the amoral and stupid demiurge."[85] For his part, Flournoy, exactly like Bulwer-Lytton, much preferred a classic middle way that bowed to neither the "ostrich philosophy" of the materialists nor the embarrassingly silly beliefs of the Spiritualists. As he himself put it, he found the assumed choice between spiritism and materialism frankly "puerile."[86]

Before we leave this little chapter of our story, it is worth suggesting where these patterns will eventually take us. Élise Müller would become a religious painter. Today we would be tempted to call her a fantasy artist. Both the psychologist and the medium, moreover, became virtual patrons of the surrealist movement. Flournoy's *From India to the Planet Mars* would deeply impress and influence a younger Swiss psychologist by the name of C. G. Jung, who confided in the older psychologist, particularly after his own break with Freud and his growing awareness that Freud's rationalism could not account for the full scope of the human psyche, especially its parapsychological and transcendent dimensions.[87]

There was also, of course, John Carter of Mars, the cosmic hero of Edgar Rice Burroughs. I have no idea if Burroughs ever read Flournoy (I somehow doubt it), but the resonances are nevertheless there, perhaps just part of the cultural air. John Carter, for example, is an immortal Virginian who practices a form of astral projection in order to travel to Mars (which was very theosophical of him), where he battles various monsters and foes on behalf of the planet's people. Some of the monsters, like those in one of his most famous tales, *The Princess of Mars*, vaguely resemble Hindu deities through the motif of many arms.[88] In other words, if Flournoy had identified a Martian Cycle and a Hindoo Cycle in the Martian-visiting Hindu princess who was Élise Müller, Burroughs chose to combine them—Orientation and Alienation combining and recombining yet again in a Super-Story that was just beginning.

 So what are we to make of all of this? Well, nothing yet. It is only the first chapter. Nevertheless, a few thoughts can be offered as humble signposts of where we are headed.

For my own part, I think that Joscelyn Godwin had it just right when he approached the history of the polar myths with "whatever the tools the study of comparative religion and esoteric practice has provided."[89] In short, Godwin approaches the myths as expressions of real mystical experiences or channeling events that were then often misread by the visionaries themselves as relating to literal places on a map or, worse yet, to points inside a globe or in an actual historical past. Basically, they misread their own experiences as literal truths instead of as paranormal experiences.

Like Goldilocks's third bed, this feels just right to me. It certainly helps us to understand and even appreciate the obviously sincere convictions of individuals like Captain Symmes, Cyrus Teed, Madame Blavatsky, and Élise Müller. Visionary experience and occult revelations they no doubt had, but they mistook, or at least seem to have mistaken, the visionary forms of these mystical experiences for historical facts and geographical places. They had not yet realized, like the Tibetan Tantric meditator mentioned above, that, "however realistic the visionary experience, it is not ultimately real."

But the message is not simply a negative one. There is a positive pole as well. If, after all, you can learn that your visions and religious projections are finally unreal, you can also begin to see the hard lines of the material world shimmer and dissolve into a liberating and finally mysterious depth, out of which you can then create other worlds and other fictions. In short, if you can understand how you have been written (Realization), you have also begun to learn how you might write yourself anew (Authorization).

Framed thus, we might suggest that, however naïve some of these occult movements and literary works about leaving "the surface of things" and traveling into "the core of things" were, they did in fact sometimes function as a kind of spiritual pilgrimage and as a sharp critique of the official world's superficial understanding of things. Here is how the gray guide puts it just before he departs the scene at the end of *Etidorhpa*:

> IT HAS BEEN MY DUTY TO CRUSH, TO OVERCOME BY SUCCESSIVE LESSONS YOUR OBEDIENCE TO YOUR DOGMATIC, MATERIALISTIC EARTH PHILOSOPHY, AND BRING YOUR MIND TO COMPREHEND THAT LIFE ON EARTH'S SURFACE IS ONLY A STEP TOWARDS A BRIGHTER EXISTENCE, WHICH MAY, WHEN SELFISHNESS IS CONQUERED, IN A TIME TO COME, BE GAINED BY MORTAL MAN, AND WHILE HE IS IN THE FLESH. THE VICISSITUDES THROUGH WHICH YOU HAVE RECENTLY PASSED SHOULD BE TO YOU AN IMPRESSIVE LESSON, BUT THE FUTURE HOLDS FOR YOU A LESSON FAR MORE IMPORTANT, THE KNOWLEDGE OF SPIRITUAL, OR MENTAL EVOLUTION WHICH MEN MAY YET APPROACH; BUT THAT I WOULD NOT PRESUME TO INDICATE NOW, EVEN TO YOU.[90]

I hope that this chapter has not felt like a series of vicissitudes. If so, I can at least promise you a different sort of future in the chapters ahead. But like the eyeless spirit-guide, I will not presume, not yet anyway, to indicate what that future mental evolution might hold. I'm a better storyteller than that.

ALIENATION

SUPERMAN IS A CRASHED ALIEN

"I TEACH YOU," CRIES ZARATHUSTRA, "THE SUPER-MAN! MAN IS SOMETHING THAT SHALL BE SUR-PASSED. WHAT, TO MAN, IS THE APE? A JOKE OR A SHAME. MAN SHALL BE THE SAME TO THE SU-PERMAN: A JOKE OR SHAME. . . . MAN IS A BRIDGE CONNECTING APE AND SUPERMAN."
FRIEDRICH NIETZSCHE, *THUS SPOKE ZARATHUSTRA*

MAN HIMSELF MAY WELL BE A THINKING AND LIV-ING LABORATORY IN WHOM AND WITH WHOSE CON-SCIOUS CO-OPERATION [NATURE] WILLS TO WORK OUT THE SUPERMAN, THE GOD. . . . THUS THE ETER-NAL PARADOX AND ETERNAL TRUTH OF A DIVINE LIFE IN AN ANIMAL BODY . . . A SINGLE AND UNIVERSAL CONSCIOUSNESS REPRESENTING ITSELF IN LIMITED MINDS AND DIVIDED EGOS, A TRANSCENDENT, IN-DEFINABLE, TIMELESS AND SPACELESS BEING WHO ALONE RENDERS TIME AND SPACE AND COSMOS POSSIBLE.
SRI AUROBINDO, *THE LIFE DIVINE*

By the turn of the twentieth century, the universe was not what it used to be. For one thing, it was getting embarrassingly big. In the early fifteenth century, the Europeans who would colonize what they mistakenly called the New World were still living in a medieval cosmos of profound meaning but relatively comfy pro-portions, with the sun, moon, stars, and planets all revolving around the earth, that is, around them. Already in the early twentieth century, the human being no longer lived in the center of the universe, but on a minor planet orbiting a minor (gulp, dying) star somewhere on the outer arm of an average galaxy, of which we would soon learn that there are billions.

The cosmos was now so unspeakably vast, its physics so utterly mindbending, that individuals were simply no longer capable of processing everything. A few elite astronomers and astrophysicists may have understood a portion of the math, but no one, *no one*, could now fathom the total vision, much less what it all meant. Hence the famous quip of J. B. S. Haldane that "the universe is not only queerer than we suppose, but queerer than we can suppose." There was more to it than queerness, though. The human being had, in a very profound sense, lost a home and, with it, a sense of belonging. Everything, literally everything, had become fundamentally alien.

SECRET ICONS: SUPERMAN'S OCCULT ROOTS AND SPIDER-MAN'S ALIEN EYES

Superman, created by writer Jerome Siegel and artist Joseph Shuster, first appeared in June of 1938 in *Action Comics* #1. The two young Cleveland men, both avid science fiction fans, had created the figure back in 1933, but it was not until 1938 that they finally had a taker in National Comics (later DC Comics). The immediate success was breathtaking, with each issue selling upward of a million copies until, in effect, a new genre, a new industry, and a new subculture were all established. It was thus Superman who "literally created the comic book industry as an important publishing business."[1] It was also Superman who gave the superhero comic its archetypal form, that is, a costumed man or woman with a secret identity and superpowers.

The occult and sci-fi backgrounds of the Man of Tomorrow are well worth teasing out. Before Siegel and Shuster created Superman, for example, the same two young men created "Dr. Mystic: The Occult Detective." As we have it in this single two-page strip, Mystic, as he was called for short, joins his ally Zator, and together they flash along through the spirit world "at a speed greater than that of light itself" toward India and "the Seven." Dr. Mystic's face and build look more or less exactly like the later Superman. These same two pages also contain what Greg Sadowski has described as "comic books' first flying caped figure," that is, Zator.[2] These, then, are some of the roots of the superhero genre: a mystic flying to India in the astral plane to do occult work.

This earlier explicit occultism was gently suppressed by Siegel and Shuster until it could only be gleaned from coded details like the notion that Superman was eventu-

ally said be an exile from another planet called Krypton (first introduced on January 16, 1939), which translates, if it were Greek (which it is), as the Hidden or the Occult. Put simply, Superman is a crashed Alien from the Occult.[3] The accent, though, had clearly shifted *from* the Occult *to* the Alien, that is, from the mysticism to the science fiction, which is all to say from the mytheme of Orientation to that of Alienation.

Superman has attracted a great deal of criticism, some of it quite thoughtful, some of it grossly exaggerated. It is often claimed, for example, that the trope of the Superman was originally Nietzschean. It is then pointed out, correctly, that the Nazis loved Nietzsche's dream of the Übermensch—the Overman, Superman or, perhaps most literally, the Superhuman. This assumed conflation of the Superman and Nazism is then extended to the entire genre of superheroes, as if being a superhero is the same thing as being a fascist. The psychoanalyst Frederic Wertham, for example, consistently conflated Superman and fascism in his famous 1950s rant against comics, *The Seduction of the Innocent*. Numerous writers—from Frank Miller's *The Dark Night Returns* to Alan Moore's *Watchmen*—have since exposed the genre to similar withering critiques from within.

But equating the Superman, much less the superhero, in toto with fascism or any other political ideology is, at best, a half truth and, at worst, a gross misrepresentation. To begin with, Nietzsche was not a Nazi, and he despised the anti-Semitism, racism, and nationalism that he saw around him: he would have hated Hitler. It was his sister who later misrepresented him to the Führer and the Nazis. His concept of the Superman, moreover, is complex, undeveloped, and by no means clear. What is clear is that the men who created Superman were Jews, as were most of the movers and shakers in the early comic-book industry. And key superheroes, like Captain America, were explicitly and consciously created to *fight* Hitler, not sing his praises. Finally, the roaring success of the earliest American superhero comics is intimately connected to the GIs who fought the Nazis on the European front and took their comics, Superman and all, with them, too often to their own gruesome deaths. When the moral courage of World War II was no longer needed on the European front, the superheroes simply went away. To equate Superman and the superheroes with fascism, then, is a precise reversal of the truth.

There is also the deeper historical fact that the idea of a superhuman is finally an ancient religious trope, not a political, American, or even especially Western one. Indeed, we could easily trace the notion back to what many believe to be the "first" and most primordial figure of the history of religions: the shaman. The shaman's mystical calling through an initiatory crisis, often around puberty (mental illness, anomalous sexuality, near-death experience via visionary dismemberment or descent into the underworld, lightning strike), and subsequent magical powers (clairvoyance, soul flight, luminous energies, the acquisition of animal languages, magical battle with demons and black magicians) look *a lot* like our modern superhero myths. Numerous other examples, moreover, could easily be found in the history of Western mystical literature, where notions of the Divine Man abound, from Christianity's famous man-god and the Divine Intellect (*nous*) of the philosopher-mystic Plotinus through Goethe's figure of Faust to Ralph Waldo Emerson's Oversoul and hymn to humanity as "a god in ruins."

Similar notions of humanity's secret identity can easily be found in Asia as well. In ancient and medieval India, for example, we encounter the lore around the Siddhas or "perfected ones" of the Hindu, Buddhist, and Jain traditions and the literally towering figures of Jainism (portrayed still today in immense multistory-tall standing stone figures), whose supercosmic conception of the human form and its *siddhis* or "perfected powers" make almost anything in the superhero comics look downright banal. Indeed, one such founding Jain teacher is known as Mahavira, literally, the "Great Hero," or, with just a little spinning, the "Superhero."

Closer to the present, an Indian freedom fighter turned spiritual teacher by the name of Aurobindo Ghose taught an "integral yoga" that combined evolution and Indian philosophy. Aurobindo believed that such a yoga would eventually conjure a superconsciousness that would "descend" into this world in order to integrate the upper and lower worlds and finally enable humanity to realize its own inherent divinity. He named this the Supermind and suggested that it would descend to help evolve a new "supernormal" species of "gnostic beings" that he collectively called the Superman. Yes, that's right: the Superman. Aurobindo, of course, was well aware of Nietzsche's earlier expression, and he meant something entirely different by his own: he meant a humanity that has taken full possession of its spiritual nature, a supernature that includes all sorts of psychical powers (the *siddhis* again), with which Aurobindo personally experimented and then classified and cataloged with incredible precision in his yoga journals. Aurobindo, in short, was writing out and *practicing* the Superman a good two decades before Siegel and Shuster came on the scene in 1938.

And on and on we could go through culture after culture. So, no, the general idea of a superman is not new, and no, it has no necessary connection to Nazism, or any other political or religious system. Of course, the American Superman displays his own nationalist dimensions. All that red, white, and blue works on many levels, including the obvious and repeatedly stated one of representing "truth, justice, and the American way." I am not denying the obvious. I am simply suggesting that there is also a "secret life" to Superman that extends far, far beyond his latest incarnation and "descent" (or crash landing) into American pop culture.

And there is more. In a pattern that is seldom fully appreciated, Siegel and Schuster's Superman is closely linked to the mytheme of Mutation. Hence Superman's early epithet as "The Man of Tomorrow," which, of course, suggests that Superman is functioning as a model for the future evolution of human nature: basically, Superman is us from the future. Hence on the very first page of *Action Comics* #1, we read that the alien child's "physical structure was millions of years advanced." We are also treated to "A Scientific Explanation of Clark Kent's Amazing Strength." The latter two frames employ the examples of the ant, which "can support weights hundreds of times its own," and the grasshopper, which "leaps what to man would be the space of several city blocks," to make its case (the early Superman could not literally fly; he leapt, like a grasshopper). To extend our reading now, we might say that the genre of the modern superhero begins with the trope of the Alien from the Occult, who is compared to a super-evolved Mutant Insect as a sign of the Future Human.

I am highlighting such themes because they are weirdly resonant with the phenomenon of the alien in twentieth-century America. As the ufologist knows, the alien experience is suffused with an insectoid pattern that is in turn linked to an evolutionary schema. Hence the spaceships or the aliens themselves are often described as "buzzing" like bees or large flies, and they often appear to share a hivelike communal mind, two features emphasized as early as 1950 by British American writer Gerald Heard, who also, by the way, wrote extensively about psychical powers, was inspired by Indian philosophy, and was committed to an evolutionary mysticism.[4]

Moreover, in countless cases, the aliens are described as either super-evolved humanoids or as instectoid, or, combining these two themes now, as humanlike insects. Hence the last century's most famous and eloquent abductee, Whitley Streiber, who consistently described the "visitors" whom he encountered as insectlike, hivelike, or, in one scene, a "terrible insect" that "rose up beside the bed like some huge, predatory spider" (T 181). When another abductee, this one interviewed by Harvard psychiatrist John E. Mack, drew what she had encountered, she sketched what amounted to a humanoid bug (see figure 2.3).

SUPERMAN

JEROME SIEGEL & JOE SHUSTER

As a distant planet was destroyed by old age, a scientist placed his infant son within a hastily devised space-ship, launching it toward Earth!

When the vehicle landed on Earth, a passing motorist, discovering the sleeping babe within, turned the child over to an orphanage

Attendants, unaware the child's physical structure was millions of years advanced of their own, were astounded at his feats of strength.

When maturity was reached, he discovered he could easily:

Leap ⅛th of a mile; hurdle a twenty-story building . . . .

Raise tremendous weights . . .

. . Run faster than an express train . . .

. . And that nothing less than a bursting shell could penetrate his skin!

Early, Clark decided he must turn his titanic strength into channels that would benefit mankind

•

And so was created . . .

SUPERMAN!

CHAMPION OF THE OPPRESSED, the physical marvel who had sworn to devote his existence to helping those in need!

A SCIENTIFIC EXPLANATION OF CLARK KENT'S AMAZING STRENGTH

Kent had come from a planet whose inhabitants' physical structure was millions of years advanced of our own.

Upon reaching maturity, the people of his race became gifted with titanic strength!

-- Incredible? No! For even today on our world exist creatures with SUPER-STRENGTH!

The lowly ant can support weights hundreds of times its own

The grasshopper leaps what to man would be the space of several city blocks

Z.Z   SUPERMAN AS INSECT

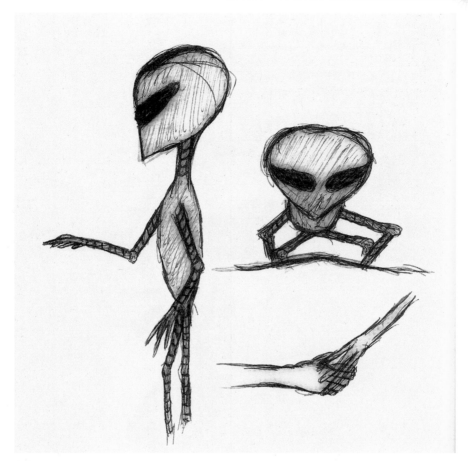

2.3   AN INSECTOID ALIEN

Or an alien Spider-Man. This is where things get a bit uncanny. Spider-Man, after all, is the humanoid insect par excellence. Moreover, his iconic wraparound eyes—created in 1962 by Marvel monster artist Steve Ditko in *Amazing Fantasy* #15— reproduce, almost perfectly, the classic almond eyes of the alien. With the exception of Superman's *S*, there is no superhero symbol more beloved and more iconic than Spidey's eyes.

Is it possible that Ditko's Spidey eyes informed the later abduction accounts of the mid-1960s, '70s, and '80s? The dates certainly make this possible. The first major

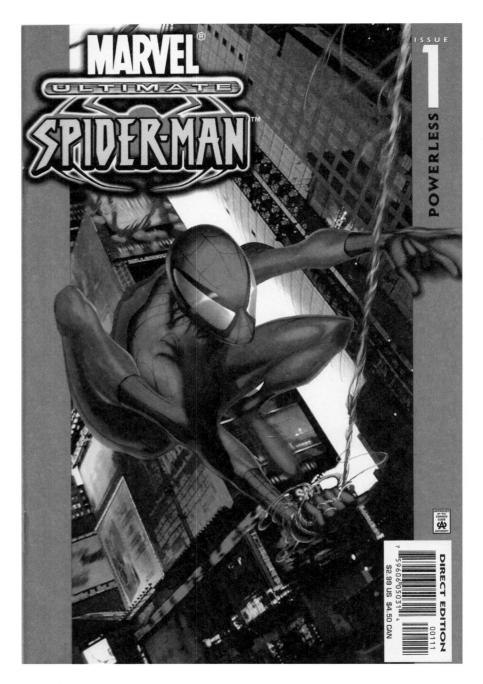

Z.4   AN INSECTOID SUPERHERO

published study of an alien abduction, *Saturday Review* columnist John G. Fuller's classic *The Interrupted Journey* (1966), recounts the September 1961 abduction of Barney and Betty Hill, complete with multiple descriptions of the aliens as possessing large foreheads, slits for mouths, and bluish gray or metallic skin. Most of all, though, especially for Barney, there were the awed descriptions of those haunting, vaguely Oriental or Asiatic "slanted" eyes.

Barney drew these eyes from within a hypnotic trance state: the sketch looks like a child's drawing of Spider-Man's head (with pupils now). In another passage, he describes how everything disappeared *except* a single eye, like, he points out, the Cheshire cat in *Alice in Wonderland*: "this growing, one-beam eye, staring at me, or rather not staring at me, but being a part of me." These eyes did strange things too. They "spoke" to him telepathically and told him not to be afraid. They carried a subtle smile. They "pushed" into his eyes as they came closer and closer. And they "burned" into his senses and left "an indelible imprint."[5] Such descriptions were drawn from hypnosis and therapeutic sessions that took place the first six months of 1964, well after Spider-Man's first appearances, month after month, on the magazine racks of America. So the door of influence is left open here.

There are other likely pop-cultural sources. In "Gauche Encounters: Bad Films and the UFO Mythos," Martin Kottmeyer traces the specifics of Betty's dream-vision (big alien noses, examination tables, needles, and star maps) back to the imagery of the B-movie *Invaders from Mars* (1953) and Barney's wraparound eyes to an episode of the PBS series *The Outer Limits* entitled "The Bellero Shield" (February 10, 1964). The latter episode, it turns out, aired just twelve days before the hypnosis session that produced this key iconic feature.[6] And this is just the beginning: in case after case, Kottmeyer shows how this or that detail of this or that famous abduction looks a lot like this or that movie scene. In the end, his claim that it is "the badfilm buff" who has the privileged perspective on all things alien and abducted is difficult to counter. He has effectively reduced the paranormal to popular culture.

But is it really that simple? We have already seen Barney invoking *Alice in Wonderland*. Similarly, Betty herself reports asking Barney, after he has looked in astonishment at the thing in the sky through a pair of binoculars and realizes that the occupants of the craft have seen them and are coming after them, if he had watched a *Twilight Zone* episode recently. He doesn't answer.[7] My point is this: Barney and Betty's experiences on the road clearly rendered any such simple explanations patently inadequate

2.5 DITKO'S SPIDEY EYES

for them. They were perfectly aware of the possible pop-cultural influences, but these could not possibly explain the full contact experience.

This historian of religions can only agree. Many traditional religious encounters, after all, are equally "gauche" in their use of gaudy art. But just because something is encountered *through* the imagery of bad movies or sappy religious art does not mean that what is being encountered *is* a bad movie or a pious painting; it might simply mean that all religious experience is culturally conditioned, and that the human imagination often draws on the most immediate, not to mention the most colorful, to paint and frame an encounter with the sacred. It is a lesson well worth learning early in our Super-Story: trauma and Technicolor, God and the gauche, are *not* mutually exclusive.

Whatever we make of the ultimate iconic origins of the alien's eyes, we can well posit that the influence eventually went the other way, that is, from the alien abduction experiences to the representations of Spider-Man, since some of the later artistic renditions of Spider-Man (including fig. 2.4) look more and more like an alien. This later "Ultimate Spider-Man" (created by artist Mark Bagley at the turn of the millennium, in 2000) approaches an almost archetypal or spiritualized form, as it moves further and further away from the human body of Peter Parker to the lithe, thin, huge-eyed, "subtle body" of the classic alien Gray.

Or Black. Consider also Spidey's famous black suit, which first appears in 1984 in *Secret Wars* #8. Not only does this black suit appear at the height of the abduction narratives, and not only does it make the wall-crawler look even more like an alien, but we quickly learn that the black suit *is* an alien, that is, a sentient alien symbiote that can take on and exaggerate, inevitably in violent and aggressive ways, the personality features of anyone with whom it bonds (read: abducts). In the film *Spider-Man 3*, the alien symbiote even bonds to Peter in a manner eerily similar to the classic alien abduction experience, that is, in bed while Peter is sleeping on his back. This, I must add, is the classic physical posture and scenario of what folklorist David Hufford has called the "old hag" or "supernatural assault" tradition and tracked around the world, including through the modern American folklore of the alien and the physiology of "sleep paralysis." Such universal experiences coded in local forms, Hufford shows, are usually terrifying experiences but also, strangely, sometimes possess ecstatic or spiritual dimensions.[8] Rather like the blue and black Spideys.

There is also the further complication that there is one more very solid historical precedent for the modern almond eyes of the alien and the blue and black Spider-Man,

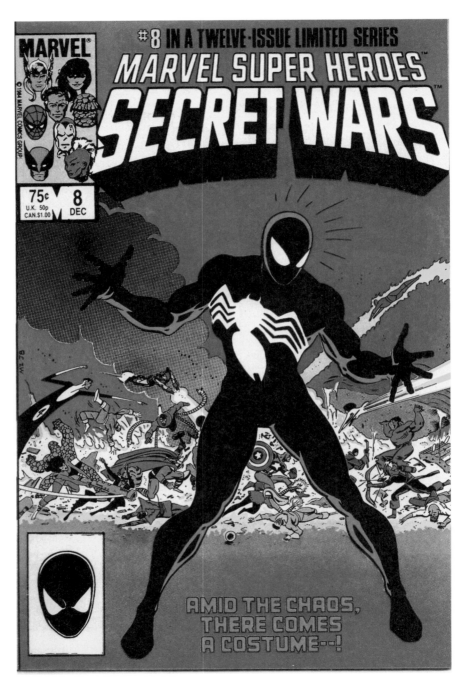

Z.6   THE ALIEN SUIT

2.7   KALI IN HER TWO FORMS

and it has nothing to do with bad B-movies. That precedent is South Asian Tantric art. We are back, already, to Orientation. The slanted "alien" eye, after all, has been a standard feature of sacred art in South Asia for centuries, where it can easily be traced in any number of goddesses, including the sexually aggressive Tantric goddess Kali, one of whose classic poses (standing on her prostrate husband, Shiva, who is variously portrayed as a corpse, in ecstasy, sexually aroused, or asleep, but always on his back) renders her a remarkably apt South Asian embodiment of Hufford's sleep paralysis traditions. The black almond-eyed Kali—known for her violent *and* redemptive ways, mounting a sleeping Shiva, and "bonding" with her devotees through mystical union— more than resembles the black alien suit taking on the physical form of a sleeping Peter Parker.

And it gets weirder still. That Kali is usually portrayed with six limbs makes her look more than a little like a spider (okay, which has eight). Moreover, in West Bengal, where the Kali traditions are especially active, there are actually two major forms of Kali: a blue, gentle, motherly form and a black, aggressive, "sinister" form. Sound familiar?

Certainly there are numerous historical reference points here that render my speculations—really, personal confusions—more than simply suggestive. Aliens, after all, have often been described as "Oriental." Flying discs have also been called "mandala machines," and at least one very famous Western intellectual, C. G. Jung, even speculated that the flying saucers *are* mandalas—that is, Tantric circular diagrams designed to aid meditation and engender psychical wholeness—in the sky.

It is probably also relevant here that the origins of the UFO contactee cults in the 1950s were clearly linked to Theosophy and its "ascended masters," indeed so much so that Christopher Partridge has suggested that in the UFO religions the "ascended masters" of Theosophy have been transformed into the "descended masters" of the UFO religions.[9] Hence the first and most famous contactee, George Adamski, founded the Royal Order of Tibet in the Los Angeles of the 1930s before he claimed a sighting, on October 9, 1946, of an immense cigar-shaped UFO on Mount Palomar and became a spokesman for Orthon of Venus, appropriately (or inappropriately) just below one of America's most famous telescopes.[10] Which is all to say that Alienation easily slides back into Orientation, just as Orientation once easily slid into Alienation.

Superman and Spider-Man are by no means the only coded aliens among the superheroes. The simple truth is that, of all of my proposed mythemes, Alienation is probably the most central to both the science fiction and superhero genres. Even a series that seemingly has nothing to do with aliens, like Roy Thomas and Barry Windsor-Smith's *Conan the Barbarian*, set between the sinking of Atlantis and Lemuria and the dawn of human history, is filled with things like a magical star-stone (C 1.25), a Hindu-looking space-being mistakenly worshipped as a deity (C 1.93), a star-gate (C 2.64, 69), and a space-toad that manifests through a portal set up by two black monoliths (C 2.176). Indeed, I would go so far as to say that without the mytheme of Alienation, there could be no science fiction and no superhero comics. It is that foundational. This mytheme, however, is also extremely complex—historically, conceptually, and spiritually.

We might identify at least six layers here. First, there is the New Age literature of the 1980s and '90s, filled as it is with notions of extraterrestrial contact and channeled wisdom (layer 1). This literature, however, was itself a popularizing and increasingly commercialized outgrowth of the occult "magical revival" of the American, British, and French countercultures of the 1960s and '70s (layer 2). The origin point of the alien theme in both the countercultural and New Age literatures in turn lies partly in the much-maligned but nevertheless important early UFO contactee cults and UFO magazines of the 1950s (layer 3). These in turn were "predicted" in the pulp and fantasy literature of 1920s, '30s, and '40s (layer 4), which were in turn deeply indebted to the weird books of a single astonishing American author, Charles Fort, who was writing in the late teens, '20s, and early '30s (layer 5). Fort, however, was himself clearly influenced by the earlier novels or "scientific romances" of authors like Jules Verne and H. G. Wells (layer 6). So we have an immense literature here spanning over a century that looks something like this: New Age literature (1980s and '90s) < countercultural occultism (1960s and '70s) < contactee cults and UFO magazines (1950s) < pulp fiction (1920s, '30s, and '40s) < Charles Fort (1919–32) < scientific romance (1870s, '80s, and '90s). Obviously, we cannot treat all of this literature in a single little chapter. How, then, to proceed?

If I had to vote for the single most influential modern author of the paranormal as it relates to the mytheme of Alienation, I would not hesitate to choose Charles Fort. My second vote would go to the editor-author who did so much to translate various paranormal and alien themes into the garish covers and fantastic plots of the pulp fiction and paranormal magazines of the late 1940s and 1950s: Ray Palmer. Finally, if I were to pick a date around which the mytheme of Alienation orbits in the twentieth century, I would not hesitate to pick the summer of 1947. Together, these two men, immeasurably helped along by those few hot weeks, spawned an entire mythical universe in which many people are still living. It is to these two men and the events surrounding the middle of the last century that we now turn. In later chapters, I will treat some of the later contactee, countercultural, and New Age literatures that erupted in the decades that followed. In truth, we will never really leave the mytheme of Alienation.

BOOKS OF THE DAMNED: CHARLES FORT AND THE BIRTH OF THE SUPER-STORY

Charles Fort (1874–1932) was an odd, funny man who looked a lot like Teddy Roosevelt. He published a single novel and four really weird books: *The Book of the Damned* (1919), *New Lands* (1923), *Lo!* (1931), and *Wild Talents* (1932).[11] It is difficult to categorize these volumes, partly because Fort completely rejected the distinction between fiction and nonfiction. "I cannot say that truth is stranger than fiction, because I have never had acquaintance with either," he wrote. There is only "the hyphenated state of truth-fiction" (WT 864). This is what he called his "philosophy of the hyphen."

Nor—and this is key—did Fort believe in any stable distinction between the imagined and the physical (WT 1010). Indeed, the imagination, properly understood in its true scope, is nearly omnipotent in Fort's worldview. Indeed, it is so powerful (and potentially perverse) that Fort suggested in more than one context that we are all living in someone else's novel, which was not a particularly good one (BD 79). He even speculated about something called "transmediumization," which basically boiled down to the idea that imagined things could become real, physical things.

He was quite serious about all of this (in a humorous sort of way), and he was out to prove it. His main occult method of proving that we are caught in someone else's writing and that the world is a physical-mythical quasi-thing was a rather unique form of—what else?—reading and writing. There is a certain logic here, which is also the logic of the present book. It goes like this: if we are being written, the best way to realize this and eventually free ourselves from this writing is to read our situation more deeply, more critically, and then begin to write ourselves anew. If we do not want to be written and read this way, we must learn to read and write our lives differently.

So Charles Fort sat at a table in the New York Public Library (or, for a while, the British Museum in London), spending more or less every working afternoon for a quarter century reading the entire runs of every scientific journal and newspaper he could find, in English or French. "A search for the unexplained," he explained, "became an obsession" (WT 918).

And he found quite a bit. In his quite ordinary newspapers and journals he found reports of frogs, fish, crabs, periwinkles, and other unidentified biological matter that fell from the sky and piled up in the ditches for anyone to see. Or smell. He found reports of rocks that fell slowly from the ceiling of a farmhouse or from the sky as if materializing out of nowhere just a few feet up. He found orphaned boys and servant girls who had the curious habit of psychically setting thing on fire, seemingly unconsciously and almost always in broad daylight (so no one, he reasoned, would get hurt). He found objects, animals, even human beings appearing out of nowhere on a cold city street or in the room of a house, apparently "teleported," as he put it, from somewhere else.

That word that he coined, "teleport," would have a long history in later science fiction. Any story that now employs it—from the "beam me up" of *Star Trek*, through the teleporting X-Men character of Nightcrawler, to the 2008 movie *Jumper*—is indebted to Charles Fort, whether he's acknowledged or not. Indeed, *Jumper* is based on a serialized 1950s sci-fi novel called *The Stars My Destination* by Alfred Bester, which features a power called "Jaunting." In the novel, Bester attributes the discovery of this strange ability to a man named Charles Fort Jaunte. In the recent movie, one of the teleporting or "jumping" protagonists is a fan of Marvel superhero comics. And on and on we weave.

Like Frederic Myers, Charles Fort very much liked the prefix *super-*. Only more so. As in the later superhero comics, almost anything could become super in the world of Charles Fort. To cite only a partial list, Fort writes of a super-bat, super-biology, super-chemistry, super-constructions, a super-dragon, super-embryology, super-evil, super-geography, a super-imagination, super-magnets, a super-mind, Super-Niagaras, a super-ocean, super-religion, the Super-Sargasso Sea, super-scientific attempts, super-sociology, super-sight, super-vehicles, super-voyagers, super-whiskeys (with ultra-bibles, no less), and super-wolves. In most of these cases, the expression carries a distinct but expansive meaning, one somewhere between and beyond our own present concepts of the paranormal and the extraterrestrial. In other words, he meant more or less what superhero comics mean by the prefix.

Fort's total system was organized around the number three. Indeed, his entire system works through the neat dialectical progression of three Dominants or Eras. A Dominant or Era is a totalizing system of thought that defines reality for a particular culture or period. The three Dominants are important to set out here, since they also structure the Super-Story that I am trying to tell. Indeed, the Super-Story is basically a variant of Fort's third Dominant. His three Eras or Dominants are: (1) the Old Dominant of religion, which he associates with the way of knowing called *belief* and the professionalism of priests; (2) the present Dominant of materialistic science, which he associates with the way of knowing called *explanation* and the professionalism of scientists; and (3) the New Dominant of what he calls Intermediatism, which he associates with the way of knowing called *expression* or *acceptance* and the professionalism of a new brand of individuating wizards and witches with various "wild talents"—in essence, superpowers.[12]

Whereas the first two Dominants work from what Fort called the systemic principle of Exclusionism, that is, they must exclude data to survive as stable systems (he called this "damning" a datum), the New Dominant works from the systemic principle of Inclusionism, that is, it builds an open-ended system and preserves it through the confusing inclusion of data, theoretically *all* data, however bizarre and offending, toward some future awakening. His *The Book of the Damned*, then, was so named because it contained and celebrated all those things the present Dominant of science and the previous Dominant of religion have excluded or damned.

He does not imagine, of course, that his particular expressions of the New Dominant are absolute, only that they include more and exclude less and so better approximate the Truth of things. This is why he also calls his New Dominant a species of Intermediatism. It is a humble term that announces its own demise. It is an open-ended system "intermediate," in between, on its way to the Truth, but it is *not* the Truth, and it too "must some day be displaced by a more advanced quasi-delusion." It is this sense of being intermediate, of thinking in-between, that constitutes Fort's central insight.

Fort did not become famous for his three Dominants, however. He became famous for his many reports of what he called "super-constructions" in the sky. These were essentially spaceships, floating over cities around the world, shining searchlights, baffling witnesses, and otherwise making a mess of the rational order of things: "one of them about the size of Brooklyn, I should say, offhand. And one or more of them wheel-shaped things a goodly number of square miles in area" (BD 136). These super-constructions float through all of Fort's texts, giving his implied narrative, which he seldom makes explicit, a certain ominous quality.

The possible implications of all of this hardly escapes Fort. He invokes the night of October 12, 1492, and the image of Native Americans gazing out over the ocean waters at lights they had never seen before. For Fort, what the newspaper stories imply is that we are *all* natives now, and we can no more fathom the intentions and powers of the airships than the American natives could fathom the intentions and powers of the colonial waterships. He thus speculates about a certain galactic colonialism going on, with the entire earth now as the colony.

But there are darker possibilities still. Earth may not be a colony at all. It may be a farm:

WOULD WE, IF WE COULD, EDUCATE AND SOPHISTICATE PIGS, GEESE, CATTLE?
WOULD IT BE WISE TO ESTABLISH DIPLOMATIC RELATION WITH THE HEN THAT NOW FUNC-
TIONS, SATISFIED WITH MERE SENSE OF ACHIEVEMENT BY WAY OF COMPENSATION?
I THINK WE'RE PROPERTY. (BD 163)

Fort apparently wrote two earlier and now lost (or self-destroyed) book manuscripts, *X* and *Y* (1915–16). In Jim Steinmeyer's reconstruction of the lost manuscript of *X*, largely through Fort's correspondence with the American novelist Theodore Dreiser in a three-page letter dated May 1, 1915, it appears that *X* was a more confessional version of the worldview that later would be more agnostically presented in *The Book of the Damned*. Dreiser (who was an avid reader of Fort and helped him get his books published) was stunned by its thesis, which involved the idea that all of earthly biological and social reality is a kind of movie (we would now say "virtual world") from the rays of some unknown alien super-consciousness (from Mars, Fort initially speculated). Dreiser, who then had a dream that seemed to confirm the thesis, summed up Fort's *X* this way: "The whole thing may have been originated, somehow, somewhere else, worked out beforehand, as it were, in the brain of something or somebody and is now being orthogenetically or chemically directed from somewhere; being thrown on a screen, as it were, like a moving-picture, and we mere dot pictures, mere cell-built-up pictures, like the movies, only we are telegraphed or teleautographed from somewhere else."[13] But if the world can be thought of as a Martian movie, it is a movie out of which we can, conceivably at least, awaken and "step out of the screen."

The acts of reading, collecting, and comparing all those damned stories, then, constituted a kind of occult metapractice for Fort that could lead, at any moment, to a sudden awakening. Hence Fort's obscure but telling claim that "systematization of pseudo-data is approximation to realness or final awakening" (BD 22). He at least collected, classified, and compared in order to wake up, to become more fully conscious of reality as truth-fiction. He was not just reading the paranormal writing us (Realization), although he was certainly doing that as well with his notions of the earth as a galactic colony or farm. He also wanted now to share in the writing of the paranormal writing us (Authorization). He was ready to step out of the dream or movie screen and *wake up*. That's what makes Charles Fort one of the premiere authors of the Super-Story I am writing (to not be written) here.

It is of some note that Fort was writing during a time in which the terms and rules of the science fiction genre had not yet been established, and that he wrote at least one early short story, "A Radical Corpuscle" (about a conversation between blood cells suspecting that they may be part of a larger cosmic body) that can be classed as early science fiction.[14] Put a bit more to my point, Fort was writing during the *exact* period in which the genre was coming into clear focus. The stories of writers like Jules Verne and H. G. Wells had been marketed as "Voyages extraordinaires" or as "scientific romances." It was the American pulp magazines of the 1920s—so named after the thick, cheap, and quickly yellowing paper on which they were published—that science fiction came into its own and was first named as such. The first pulp appeared in 1919, the very same year as *The Book of the Damned*, but it was not until editor Hugo Gernsback's *Amazing Stories*, which began publication in 1926, that the industry really got off the ground. And it was Gernsback, by his own account at least, who first coined the expression "science fiction" out of an earlier, not so successful attempt—"scientifiction."

As a perfect illustration (literally) of Fort's fantasy future, consider the fact that in 1934, just two years after he died, parts of Fort's *Lo!* were serialized in the pulp fiction magazine *Astounding Stories*. At the back of each issue, we come across Fort's *Lo!*, described in some of the issues as "The greatest collation of factual data on superscience in existence."[15] There is that prefix again: *super-*.

This is how Fort's career in science fiction began: as fiction and fact wrapped up in fantasy. By 1952, his reputation in the world of pulp fiction was considerable enough (and controversial enough) for the editor of another pulp magazine, *Fantastic Story*, to feel he must address it for his readers. The editorial begins with the apparently common assumption of the time that "no truly complete understanding of science-fiction is possible without at least a nodding acquaintance with the works of Charles Fort."[16] And the cover? A shapely woman in shorts stands behind some kind of astro-man sporting a long oblong oxygen tank on his back, which points to her breasts. The couple watches—she shields her eyes, he doesn't—an explosive "eruption" in the distance that originates from the detonator poised between the man's legs.

Now Fort was not being quite *this* fantastic (or this Freudian). But it is nevertheless very easy to see how he helped inspire the pulps. It is also easy to see why his first biographer was a well-known science fiction author, Damon Knight. Or why a later run of *Amazing Stories* would feature a series of quirky back-cover paintings illustrating Fortean scenes, from the USO we witnessed in chapter 1 (November 1947) to "The Rain of Fish" (December 1947) and "Spaceship Seen over Idaho!" (January 1948). Or, jumping closer to the present now, it is also fascinating to see how "Seed of Destruction" (1994), the opening story of Mike Mignola's remarkable *Hellboy* series, begins with a reference to "the British Paranormal Society," a clear allusion to the London Society for Psychical Research, and introduces us to the American paranormal expert Professor Malcolm Frost, who looks more than a little like Charles Fort. A few pages later, frogs fall out of nowhere in order to signal both a supernatural assault with the next page turn and, for the knowing at least, a grateful debt to Fort's *The Book of the Damned*.

But it was not Fort who would finally fuse science and fiction into a potent For-

tean potion of truth-fiction that would confirm the paranormal experiences of many a reader and confuse the hell out of the rest of them. That man was Ray Palmer.

THE PARANORMAL PULPS: THE AMAZING STORIES OF RAY PALMER

Even the man's name alludes to paranormal powers and superhero comics. When a comic writer by the name of Gardner Fox re-visioned a Golden Age superhero called the Atom for DC Comics in 1961, he chose to give his hero an alter ego whose fantasy lineage was unmistakable: Ray Palmer. There was probably a bit of good-intentioned humor here, as Ray Palmer (the alter ego now) had the unique, and rather dubious, superpower of becoming really, really small (hence the early covers featured scenes like the Atom being picked up by a pair of tweezers and flushed down a drain), whereas Ray Palmer (the pulp fiction editor now) was really, really small in real life. The man stood a mere 4' 8".

There is a story here. Lots of them, actually. Palmer's own real-life Origins story has him hit by a butcher truck at the age of seven, leaving him with a damaged spine that prevented further growth and a subsequent passion for pouring himself into pursuits, like pulp fiction, that did not require a normal body. One also wonders, though, if the broken back did more than make him a midget. One wonders whether it also opened something up, as Palmer's life was riddled, really defined, by a whole host of precognitive and telepathic experiences, many of them connected to the imaginal band of dreams. "Ray Palmer," then, as both the Atom and the psychically gifted pulp fiction editor, is an almost perfect cipher for my present musings on the fantastic fusions and mutual creations of superhero fiction and paranormal experience.

Palmer clearly deserves a biography of his own. We do not possess such a biography, although the writer left numerous autobiographical pieces and personal musings on everything from the nature of flying saucers and the hollow earth to the possibility of sex in heaven. In terms of the latter, he was especially interested in "the spiritually useful part of sex," that is, "the fun part" (F 1.15.22), as opposed to the procreative part (and perhaps it is relevant that Palmer was a friend of Hugh Hefner and claimed that he was once offered a quarter share in *Playboy* [F 5.66.32]). Of particular note to the biographer are the first volume (the only one to appear) of a massive projected autobiography, *The Secret World*, and a chatty fanzine series featuring letters from his readers called "The Forum," named after that part of ancient Rome where, as the cover had it, "any man could speak his mind." Palmer certainly spoke his.

Z.9   RAY PALMER AS THE ATOM

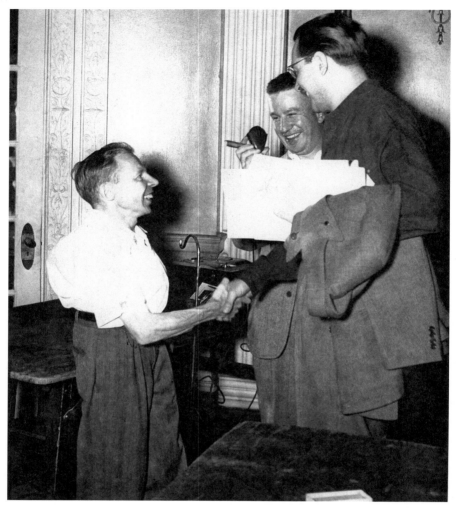

2.10   RAY PALMER AS HIMSELF

The Secret World, which appeared just two years before his death, was one of
Palmer's last publications. It opens with what I have called Realization and Authorization: again, the uncanny experience that one is being written (Realization) and the
decision to take a more active role in this paranormal process (Authorization). As he
begins, Palmer claims that a book like this one "just 'happens' by some mysterious

on-going process that sometimes seems to be the whim of chance Fate, but in an awe-some number of instances, seems manipulated by a Deliberate Manipulator—some super Intelligence beyond normal comprehension." The conclusion dawns on one that "there is a Plan," which, alas, sometimes feels more like a "Plot." It is precisely this tension between the Plan and the Plot that fascinates Palmer so, particularly when he realizes that these different readings of a life are not "out there" somewhere, but rather express a basic duality within the person. Both the Plan and the Plot, it turns out, are *in here*.

The Human is Two for Palmer. This twoness spins out into numerous seeming paradoxes that are not really paradoxes, including this one: "It is as though Life is a blueprint, but a design that you manufacture yourself!" Everything, of course, depends on how one defines that "you." Palmer, at least, was convinced that he was not who he thought he was, that his deepest self was not a "normal man," that there was another being or "dream-maker" at work in his life. Given the nature of his reported experi-ences, it is easy to see why he thought this.

In terms of its own history, *The Secret World* is based on Palmer's lifelong prac-tice of writing a "Martian Diary," which he tried to publish, without apparent success, late in life (F 5.66.27–32). He began such a diary when he was a young man as a creative way of stepping out of his culture in order to analyze it, "as though I were a visitor from Mars, researching Earth and its life forms, and was now making my report back to the home planet." It seems to have worked, as some later readers would insist that he really was from Mars, and the women working in his office teasingly called him "the Martian" (F 1.22.24). Martian or Earthling, Ray Palmer came to realize that he had long been living "with the reality, the existence of a great Secret." A secret life.

There are four Palmer fascinations that merit our special attention: (1) Palmer's memory practice and his subsequent convictions in a kind of universal record or store-house of meaning; (2) something called "the Shaver mystery"; (3) Palmer's central role in the development of the flying saucer craze of the late 1940s and '50s; and (4) his religious commitments to the *Oahspe* Bible. Here, then, are the barest outlines of Palmer's secret life, with a special focus on these four metathemes.

If we begin at the beginning, the matter of the author's earliest memories already lands us in some familiar Freudian territory and some unfamiliar spiritual spaces. In the course of *The Secret World*, Palmer explains how when he was spread out in his "torture-bed" (an orthopedic contraption called a Bradford frame) to straighten his broken back, he used to do two things: he would read voraciously, and he would practice remembering (SW 29).

In terms of the latter discipline, he would begin with what happened yesterday, then a week ago, a month ago, and so on, until he believed that he could remember very precise things about his childhood, his infancy, and beyond. One of the things he came to remember intensely was suckling at his mother's breast. He could also remember "peering through the bars of my cradle at her, sitting naked on a chair in the sunlight beside the window, combing her long red hair, which was so long it touched the floor as she sat." He especially remembered this beautiful naked mother crying and talking to her infant son about her own unspeakable sufferings. The infant could not understand her words, but the remembering boy could, and "it was then that I learned for the first time in my life how to hate." This is the traumatic memory, which he refuses to explain to us, to which Palmer attributes his later vocation and his keen sense of justice. "These memories are not for this book, or any other," he explains. "But they did influence my entire life. Coupled with the accident that crippled me, made me a hunchback, I became a lone-wolf, a bitterly determined, stubborn man dedicated to defying injustice and meanness wherever I found it" (SW 16). In a mother's trauma, revealed to an infant boy at the breast of a beautiful naked woman, a real-life hero was born.

But Palmer's memories did not stop there. He reports remembering back before he was born to the very moment he was conceived, "that moment when sperm mated with ovum and a single fertile cell was created." Obviously, "we've left memory far behind now," for "this has nothing to do with memory cells in a brain, because they do not yet exist. And yet I *know*!" (SW 17). He liked to italicize that kind of knowing. No doubt about it: Ray Palmer was a pulp fiction gnostic, a man who claimed to know things directly and immediately.

Impossible things like the possibility that "somewhere, somehow, the total sum of all knowledge exists" (SW 18). This, in fact, is an ancient idea to which we will repeatedly return in our journey through the Super-Story. Plato, for example, believed that any profound knowledge is not really learned but "remembered" from a preexistent source and life. Palmer, who shows few signs of having read Plato (Theosophy's "Akashic Record" was probably the nearer influence), appears to have believed the same. Palmer's most direct source of confirmation here was clearly his own occult

experiences, particularly his dreams in which he would find himself present at historical events or in some sort of astral world.

Like the time he found himself "floating at some weird vantage point" where he
could see all the details of a World War II naval battle as it took place. "As each ship
was sunk, I would hear the name of it, and was aware of the number of men who died
on each ship." He decided to use this one as a test. Here, after all, was something
he could verify. So he asked a coworker at Ziff-Davis (the publishing house where
he worked at the time) to take out a piece of paper and record what he was about
to say. Palmer gave him a list of names of ships together with a list of the men lost
(their number, I presume). He then asked his colleague to put this information in an
envelope and seal it. Eight months later, the details of the battle of Savo Island were
finally released. Palmer asked his colleague to open the envelope: "I was correct to
the last detail." Palmer's takeaway? That "somehow I was able to *know* something
by a means that I am not able to identify."[17] When, through a kind of waking dream
involving a spirit-guide, Palmer later learned the details of his brother's death in a
military hospital from injuries suffered after his leg was blown off in the same war,
Palmer goes further still: "It is possible to gain information of any kind, if you want to
get it earnestly enough" (SW 23).

Palmer's first published story, "The Time Ray of Jandra" in *Science Wonder
Stories*, was a classic example of the mytheme of Orientation, that is, it was a time-
travel story that involved a lost civilization. He based the details of the landscape he
wrote about on one of his many dreams (he claimed he dreamed every night and could
remember his dreams in great detail), only to get a letter from a field guide in Africa
who had just read the published story and was certain the writer was one of the few
people whom he had personally guided up the mouth of a river on the Atlantic coast
of southwest Africa: the details were all precise. The guide simply did not believe
Palmer when the teenager wrote back and confessed that he had never been to Africa, much less to that particular river and secret city, which had been destroyed by a
volcano exactly as Palmer had narrated. "His letters were a disaster," Palmer writes.
"They destroyed any complacency I might have had about being a normal person. . .
. I dreamed true! How could this be, and what could it be?" And "if the dreaming was
true, why not the imagining?" (SW 11–12). Palmer would write hundreds of stories in
the future, and into each of them he would weave some little "dream-truth" from his

secret life with the hope that some future readers might recognize them and write with their own confirmations, like the African guide.

In 1930, at the age of twenty, Palmer developed Pott's Disease, a form of tuberculosis in the spine. He was admitted into Muirdale Sanatorium in Wauwatosa, Wisconsin, for one purpose: to die. The doctors told him that the spine graft that had earlier saved his life was being eaten away by the disease, along with six of his vertebrae. He had a mere six months to live. Palmer responded by betting his doctor $5.00 that he was wrong. According to his own account, he then literally willed new bone into place: "For six months I held a mental picture of bone forming around that damaged series of vertebrae, first as cartilage, then slowly hardening and fusing into a solid mass" (SW 27). After those six months, that is, after the lapse of time in which he was supposed to die, Ray Palmer was taken into a conference room filled with a dozen flabbergasted doctors. The vertebrae had been encased by a solid mass of new bone and new cartilage.

In May of this same year, Palmer helped create with Walter Dennis the first fanzine in the pulp fiction world, a mimeographed bulletin called *The Comet* (later renamed *Cosmology*). He would then advance through the ranks of the pulp subculture as he held down a solid day job with a sheet-metal company on the South Side of Milwaukee. Then, in 1938, he hit it big: he became editor of one of the industry's flagship magazines, *Amazing Stories*.

Palmer claims that he literally willed this position into being, like his bone. As he tells the story, he simply quit his sheet-metal job, sat in his apartment, and waited for the phone call that he wanted to come, and all of this despite the fact that *Amazing Stories* was published in New York City. Through a complicated series of events, the magazine was bought out by Ziff-Davis, a Chicago firm whose offices were just eighty miles away, and Palmer was offered the job (SW 26–27). He subsequently edited the magazine, and eventually all eight of its related pulp adventure titles, for Ziff-Davis from 1938 to 1949.

It was probably in the office building of Ziff-Davis in downtown Chicago that Palmer saw his first flying saucer shortly after he began working there, in 1939. It was "a brilliant silvery disk, apparently at an elevation of some 5,000 feet, directly west of Chicago's Loop," he writes. "It hung in the sky for more than forty-five minutes and was witnessed by more than a hundred people in the office building where [I] was located."[18] We are back to Fort's truth-fiction: an office publishing pulp fiction on alien invasions stops its work to watch a flying saucer hover over the city. Palmer would see another flying saucer on February 4, 1952, near Amherst, Wisconsin, just after he copublished *The Coming of the Saucers* with Kenneth Arnold. Of course.

It was at the Ziff-Davis office building that the Shaver mystery began. This chapter in our story involved a specific sort of underground occultism. And I do mean *underground*, as in "under the ground." The earlier Orientation strategies involving claims about a hollow earth took on a bizarre new life from December of 1943 to June of 1947, when Ray Palmer began obsessively publishing, really cowriting, a string of stories in *Amazing Stories* inspired by the occult (and probably schizophrenic) experiences of another man.[19]

In the course of his editorship at Ziff-Davis, Palmer would receive letters from enthusiastic readers. One day, in September of 1943, he received such a letter from a welder in Barto, Pennsylvania, by the name of Richard Shaver, which he then published in the first *Amazing Stories* issue of 1944. Actually, it was not a letter. It was more of a little treatise on an alleged twenty-six-lettered "ancient alphabet," which readers would later learn was called Mantong (probably a bad pun for "Man's Tongue"). Shaver believed that this language-key was "definite proof of the Atlantean legend."[20] Palmer wrote back to ask about the source of the alphabet. Mr. Shaver responded with a ten-thousand-word story typed, Palmer explains with more than a little grace, "with what was certainly the ultimate in non-ability at the typewriter" (SW 36).

The garbled thing was entitled "A Warning to Future Man." It set out an elaborate, deeply paranoid cosmology that Shaver claimed had been revealed to him by voices he heard emanating from the ground. Actually, he had originally picked the voices up around 1933 through his arc welder in a Ford plant in Detroit, Michigan: "I began to notice something very strange about one of the guns. Whenever I held it, I heard voices, faroff voices, of endless complexity. . . . right away I knew what was in Bill's lunch box; which girl Bunny was going to take out that night; what Hank's mother was planning for his wife. . . . That welding gun was, by some freak of its coils' field attunements *not* a radio, but a *teleradio*: a thought augmentor of some power."[21] Shaver would come to understand these experiences through the prism of an elaborate and completely unbelievable sci-fi scenario: such "unseen rays," he claimed, were beamed at him and other human beings by sinister machines below the surface of the earth.

According to Palmer's reconstruction, the original story was about how the earth's earlier inhabitants fled the surface when the sun's radiation became too extreme about twelve thousand years ago. The lucky ones, the immortal ones called Titans or Atlans, fled their underground civilization and left in spaceships. They now live in the blackness of outer space, where they need no longer fear a star's radiation. The not so lucky ones, the abandoned ones (called abandonderos), fled into the bowels of the earth, where they developed into two distinct races: the insane and largely sinister deros (for "detrimental robots") and the good and noble teros (for "integrative robots").[22] Alas, the former soon outnumbered the latter and have been haunting and using the abandoned technology of the Titans and Atlans to zap the poor fools who could not escape into space or the underworld ever since—that is, us. We don't remember any of this any longer, of course. All we have left are vague folk memories of "Atlantis" and "Lemuria" and weird stories about various species of giants, ogres, little people, gremlins, and devils, which, according to Shaver, are really all deros . . . that, or fake projections beamed up by the deros.

Much of this is, well, too much. Shaver's ancient alphabet, for example, is clearly no such thing. It is nothing more than the English alphabet related to a series of Shaver's own embarrassingly literalistic puns and free associations ("A—Animal [used AN for short]," "B—Be [to exist—often command]," "C—See," and so on), which are then used to imagine a series of fake English etymologies: a handy tool perhaps for creating a fictional world, but definitely, most definitely, not an ancient alphabet. In terms of our earlier discussions, Shaver's Mantong bears a very distant similarity to Élise Müller's imaginary Martian and Sanskrit languages, and its claim to be the original language of the human race recalls Saint-Yves's Vattan or Vattanian language of the subterranean kingdom of Agarttha.

No doubt relevant here is the fact that during the period Shaver claimed he was suffering in the hollow earth, he was actually, according to Palmer himself, suffering in a mental hospital. This certainly helps explain the embarrassing "Montang" alphabet episode, Shaver's ultraparanoid fantasy of the underground deros, and his complete inability to distinguish between his visions and basic geology (which we have already seen with other hollow-earth visionaries). It does not, however, explain away the real-world weirdness that surrounded these fantasies, including Palmer's own paranormal responses to them. This is a difficult but key point to our secret life: psychopathology and the paranormal go just fine together, as do mushrooms and religious revelation, or madness and holiness, or car wrecks and near-death experiences, or mystics and sexual trauma; once the ego is dissolved, *however* it is dissolved, the imaginal, the supernormal, and the spiritual can come rushing in. And when they do, they almost always rush in *together*. Hence the Shaver mystery.

Which was also something of an erotic mystery. Shaver, for example, likes to focus on the letter *V*, which he tells us stands for "vital (used as 'vi')" and refers to "the stuff Mesmer calls animal magnetism."[23] When Palmer published an essay on Mantong, a single phrase was added after "animal magnetism": "sex appeal."[24] Shaver's *V* probably alludes back to Bulwer-Lytton's vril. Hence his elaborate explanations of how the deros possessed machines for rejuvenating the libido called "stim" machines (for "stimulation"). Indeed, an elaborate and explicit sexuality ran throughout the Shaver mystery stories. It is hard to miss the graphic erotic covers that advertised the Shaver issues of *Amazing Stories*. Or Shaver's claims, in Jim Wentworth's words now, that he "was given sex stim that augmented every cell impulse to a power untold, thereby producing joy and pleasure beyond description."[25]

Palmer's own response to Shaver's "A Warning to Future Man" was not too surprising. "I put a clean piece of paper into my typewriter, and using Mr. Shaver's strange letter-manuscript as a basis, I wrote a 31,000 word story which I entitled 'I remember Lemuria!'" It appeared in *Amazing Stories* in the March 1945 issue, with a preface by Shaver, who identified himself as "the racial memory receptacle of a man (or should I say a being?) named Mutant Mion, who lived many thousands of years ago in Sub Atlan, one of the great cities of ancient Lemuria! I myself cannot explain it. I know only that I remember Lemuria!" He then goes on to claim *both* that "What I tell you is not fiction!" and that "it is tragic that the only way I can tell my story is in the guise of fiction." [26]

The early Shaver stories sold like mad. A magazine that normally ran a circulation of 50,000 quickly now ran to 185,000. The Shaver mystery was an immediate sellout. Then came the letters. And more letters. And more letters. Over fifty thousand of them, Palmer claims, before it was all over (the usual number was forty-five to fifty per issue). Stranger still was what the letters contained. Many of them recounted elaborate stories of the authors' personal experiences with the caves, with the deros, and with the flying spaceships. "Actually," paranormal investigator John A. Keel notes, "many of them were expressing the recognizable symptoms of paranoid-schizophrenia, while others were recounting the classic manifestations of demonology."[27]

Perhaps the most significant chapter of the Shaver mystery, though, is one that is not sufficiently emphasized, namely, the very real differences that existed between Palmer and Shaver. Shaver's worldview was a deeply paranoid one in which pretty

ICE CITY of the GORGON
by RICHARD S. SHAVER and CHESTER S. GEIER

Z.11   A TYPICAL SHAVER COVER

much everything of importance was traced back to evil deros and sinister machines in the hollow earth. He did not believe in God, an afterlife, a spiritual world, or paranormal powers: all such things were the purely physical and totally illusory effects of the ray machines of the deros. We have all been duped, and we are constantly being zapped in our dreams, diseases, and disasters. "The unseen world beneath our feet, malignant and horrible, is complete in its mastery of Earth,"[28] he declared with not a doubt or qualification in sight. So, too, there is no such thing as astral travel or spirits. The spirits seen in séances are in fact projections of the machines controlled again by entirely physical creatures seething and scheming below us. Like other hollow earthers before him, Richard Shaver was what Palmer called "an extreme materialist."[29] He knew nothing of the psychology of projection, and he seemed completely incapable of thinking symbolically or metaphorically, which I take as a fairly clear symptom of whatever psychological condition he suffered.

Not so Ray Palmer. He believed in God, an afterlife, a spiritual world, and paranormal powers: all such things were perfectly real for him. His worldview may have been equally eccentric, but it was deeply spiritual and profoundly hopeful. Not to mention occasionally practical and down to earth: in a typical issue of *Forum*, for example, he could express his well-known opposition to the war in Vietnam, reject the principles of reincarnation and "Eastern philosophy," refer to Shaver's theories as "ridiculous," and flatly reject all the conspiracy theories that had floated through his magazine pages for the real controller of modern life: money (F 1.4.4, 11, 13–14, 32, 4).[30] He also clearly recognized and constantly emphasized the metaphorical and symbolic nature of religious language.

An important exception here is his dual understanding of dreams. Palmer distinguishes between two kinds: (1) the "meaningless mumbo-jumbo" of the conscious and unconscious mind during sleep created by "juggled memories and imagined inventions," which are usually seen in black and white and whose interpretation is pointless (since they possess no meaning); and (2) "the kind that seem to be actually occurring events," which are always seen in color and should not be interpreted, since they are precisely what they seem to be (F 1.8.17, 32). In short, Palmer appears to have rejected dream interpretation in toto, even as he insisted that his astral color dreams were real experiences in real places. Hence those dream-inspired stories that turned out to be true.[31]

It was not just through astral travel and dream that one can fly, however. Palmer was also clear that the "me" or the "you" (he resisted the categories of "soul" or "spirit" as too confused and contested [F 1.16.31; 1.21.15]) is a personality that can also be dislodged from the body via those two famous acronyms: LSD and the UFO. Not that anyone should attempt such a thing. On the contrary, he pled with his readers not to trust either "opening of the door," that is, not to take the psychedelic drug or to accept a ride on a flying saucer.[32]

Indeed, Palmer (who explains that he has not taken LSD, but that he was given another drug in a hospital that had the same effect [F 5.67.22]) stated flatly that "I think LSD is an 'open doorway'" into a real "area of existence," but then goes on to compare the experience to "a fish out of water" discovering that there really are birds. Like the gasping fish, few individuals are truly ready for this, and such a realm should be approached only "with utmost care." Here Palmer also objects to other common modes of surrendering one's individuality, including automatic writing (F B.2.31–32), séances, the Ouija board, self-hypnosis, and "certain yoga practices" (F 1.15.11–18). As the latter phrase, his constant jabs at reincarnation, and his description of Madame David-Neel (a famous Western explorer and popularizer of Tibet) as "a fantastic garble of mysticism . . . containing a quite extensive weird cake-batter of pure fantasy and imagination" (F B.2.23) make more than a little clear, Orientation was a mytheme to which Ray Palmer was not the least bit attracted.

Much like Charles Fort, however, Palmer believed in intelligent civilizations in the upper atmosphere—four to one hundred miles up, he noted with an odd matter of factness. He routinely writes of these upper worlds as the true source of flying sau-cers, which are at once spiritual and physical. Indeed, Palmer insisted that ultimately "matter" and "Spirit" are two expressions of a single transcendent reality.[33] The flying saucer was a kind of symbol and sign of this deeper supersource.

In a similar spirit, Palmer suggests that flying saucers are "Earthly some-things."[34] But by "Earth," he does not mean what the geologists mean. He means the round rock for sure, but also the atmosphere and the magnetic fields that extend, he believes, for tens of thousands of miles into space. Like fish in water, flying saucers exist in both the outer and inner worlds of such an "Earth." It was in this way that Ray Palmer could accept the visions of Richard Shaver but reject what he calls their "literal sense" (F 1.8.28). Palmer, for example, firmly denied the visionary's location of the visions in the literal underworld of a physical hollow earth.[35] Quite the contrary, their true source is in the upperworld, in what he called the "atmospherea."[36]

Put a bit differently, for Palmer, Shaver's "hollow earth" equals his own "atmospherea," and since that atmospherea is as much a magnetic and spiritual reality as a physical one, it can penetrate our physical earth and be "underground" as well. The atmospherea, then, is a kind of alternate dimension not normally accessible to our senses in which our own understanding of "earth" and "sky," or "up" and "down," for that matter, mean nothing. Invoking a theosophical language, Palmer presents the atmospherea as a kind of astral plane and insists that "the planet Earth in its larger aspect, which includes its atmosphere, is more extensive than our meager science has dreamed it can be."

Such an idea, by the way, was not original with Palmer. A West Coast psychologist by the name of Meade Layne, after making spirit contact with some aliens through a medium, published *The Ether Ship Mystery and Its Solution* (1950), which explained that flying saucers do not come from another planet but from another dimension.[37] This interdimensional reading, moreover, long a staple of Spiritualism through the famous "fourth dimension," would have a very long life within ufology and is still very much with us today.

Palmer applied his atmospherea metaphysics to his friend's visions and stated his "suspicion that between Shaver and the spiritualists there exists no real difference of opinion, only interpretation." As already noted, Palmer was even more attracted to another, by now familiar nineteenth-century tradition: that of Theosophy and its key terms "astral" and "astral powers."[38] Hence, in his mind at least, Shaver's deros were degraded human spirits in the afterlife, his travels to the caves misinterpreted astral travels, and his "voices" the products of an unrecognized clairvoyance. He also pointed out, with some refreshing common sense, the reason no one could find any physical proof for Shaver's caves: they don't exist. [39]

Palmer also adamantly rejected Shaver's claims that he was ever in any caves, "and he knows it!" He was not in some underground world those eight years. He was in an insane asylum.[40] Indeed, even in the famous "Shaver issue," Palmer calmly states that he never believed that Shaver got his original story "from the caves." That is precisely why Palmer retitled it according to his own psychical lights "I Remember Lemuria!" (recall that the original, more paranoid title was "A Warning to Man").[41] By "remembering," Palmer seems to have in mind his own early experiences and some kind of access to Theosophy's Akashic Records, or what he prefers to call "Thought Records." In an issue of *Forum*, for example, he flatly explains how he and Shaver combined "fiction" and Shaver's perception of these Thought Records (which Shaver misunderstood as literal messages) to create the entertaining pulp fiction that was demanded by the science fiction fans who read *Amazing Stories*. "Fiction was used as the vehicle" of the "facts," he explains (F B.2.26).

Then there were perhaps the ultimate authorities: the wives, Marjorie Palmer and Dorothy Shaver. In November of 1950, the Palmers moved into a cabin near Amherst, Wisconsin, partly no doubt to be near the Shavers, who lived nearby. So the Shavers and the Palmers were neighbors. Both wives had some serious reservations about their husbands' wild theories. As Wentworth describes the scene, Marjorie was well aware that Ray was considered a "nut" in the area, and Dorothy would just emphatically shake her head no whenever Richard brought up the deros and those damn rays.[42]

Whatever one thinks of such a duo, it is difficult to deny that it was a productive one. Palmer edited and cowrote Shaver mystery stories from the December 1943 issue to the June 1947 issue. *Amazing Stories* could have easily been renamed *The Shaver Mystery Magazine* during this time, for that is what it was. Not everyone was happy about this. Many of the faithful readers of *Amazing Stories* eventually grew weary with the Shaver mystery and became particularly upset about the blurring of alleged fact and indubitable fantasy in the stories and Palmer's constant enthusiastic editorializing on them. They mounted a letter-writing campaign against the team. It didn't help that one particularly upset letter writer wrote William B. Ziff directly and explained to him that the Shaver mystery contradicted Einstein (SW 40). And that was probably a gross understatement.

In support of Shaver, Palmer resigned from the magazine and left Ziff-Davis in order to publish a new magazine with one of his former office colleagues, Curtis Fuller. Numerous titles would follow, in a very confusing but sincere series of publishing ventures, most from the Amherst cabin. Among these were *Fate*, *Mystic*, *The Hidden World*, *Search*, *Flying Saucers*, and *Forum*.

Palmer chose for his first new publishing venture with Fuller the title *Fate*, which was rather odd, since he did not believe in the concept. Indeed, he despised it. Hence his amazing stories about things like willing his spine graft back into place and magically acquiring the editorial job at Ziff-Davis, or his rejection of automatic writing and the ingestion of LSD. *Anything* that compromised a person's freedom, self-determination, or conscious control, Ray Palmer rejected.

Fate or no fate, Fuller and Palmer hit the ball out of the park with their first issue. *Fate* #1 featured a cover story by a businessman and small-engine pilot by the name of Kenneth Arnold, who had recently witnessed nine silvery boomerang-like shapes

FATE

SPRING
1948
25c

VOLUME 1   NUMBER 1

THE TRUTH ABOUT THE FLYING SAUCERS
By KENNETH ARNOLD

MARK TWAIN AND HALLEY'S COMET
By HAROLD M. SHERMAN

INVISIBLE BEINGS WALK THE EARTH
By R. J. CRESCENZI

TWENTY MILLION MANIACS
By G. H. IRWIN

Many Other Startling Articles And Features

The FLYING DISKS

Z.12   THE FLYING SAUCER DEBUTS

zip in perfect formation near Mount Rainier in Washington state. It was this sighting, on June 24, 1947, that initiated the modern flying-saucer era and gave us the modern expression "flying saucer" (a reporter by the name of Bill Bequette coined it in a newspaper article after interviewing Arnold that same day). It helped that, just a few weeks later, the papers reported on a crashed flying disc that was supposedly recovered in Roswell, New Mexico. It helped even more that this second story was denied the very next day and replaced by what looked like a lame "weather-balloon" yarn. Now we had more than a story about crashed aliens. We had a story about crashed aliens wrapped in a government cover-up.

Superman of Krypton had crashed nine years earlier, in the summer of 1938. Now, in the summer of 1947, he had *really* crashed. Or so it seemed. An entire mythology had been developed in the pulps and the superhero comics all those years. It was waiting in the wings. Now it entered American history and the front pages of newspapers across the land. And Ray Palmer would not let go. He knew when he had a good thing. So he just kept publishing stories, and more stories, on flying saucers.

In 1952, Palmer teamed up with Arnold again and cowrote *The Coming of the Saucers* (1952). The title sounds like a bad B-movie. Except that they were being serious. Sort of. On the acknowledgment page, the authors thank J. Edgar Hoover "for the many nice chats we had with his operatives"; *Fate* magazine, "for the facts"; *Amazing Stories* magazine, "more truth than fiction"; the *Saturday Evening Post*, "not so true"; and the Little Men from Venus, "who weren't there at all."

But really, why stop at these stories about flying saucers? Why not just name a magazine *Flying Saucers*? And so that is what Ray Palmer did. The October 1959 issue featured on its cover the essay title "Superman—Does He Really Exist?" It was a rhetorical question, of course. He does. As do the "cosmic men" or "'Federation' of super beings," who are watching our crude technology and doing things like raining fish and frogs down on us. Clearly, the author had read both his Superman comics and his Charles Fort. He saw the connection.

Finally, there was yet another paranormal dimension to Palmer's late publishing ventures that is well worth mentioning. As Palmer became more and more involved with the Shaver mystery, he began to ask his readers for help. They gave him help. One such letter was from a woman who sent him a book entitled *Oahspe*, which she somehow felt had something to say to the Shaver mystery. Richard Shaver had never heard of this strange book, but to Ray Palmer it was a literal godsend: "The book proved itself. To me, it could not be a fake. It had to be authentic—because it proved the key to all the vast amount of material I had collected in my lifetime, and especially of that amazing adventure, the Shaver Mystery. *Oahspe* proved Shaver, and Shaver proved *Oahspe*. Somewhere between both, the actual truth lies. I don't believe the literal 'truth' can ever be known—we can only approximate truth in the framework of our capability of understanding" (SW 32). There was a deeply personal side to this double attraction. Basically, when Palmer read the book, he recognized numerous details that were more or less exactly like the dream-vision he had three years earlier when he had seen his dead brother and determined the cause of his death in the war: "It was this 'dream' experience," he explains, "which gave me such a tremendous jolt when I found so much of it corroborated in a book written [in] 1881" (SW 23).

What was this *Oahspe*? It was an "American Bible" channeled to a New York dentist by the name of John Ballou Newbrough (1828–91). In his own memoirs, Palmer explains that after years of spiritual searching, which included interviewing and host-ing numerous mediums in his home, Newbrough began receiving his own revelation at 4:30 a.m. on January 1, 1881. Every morning hence he would sit down at his Sholes typewriter and watch his fingers type out, as if possessed, a revelation. If mediums before him had practiced automatic writing, Newbrough had invented a new one: au-tomatic typing. This occult writing practice continued apace until December 15, 1881, when the revelation was complete. The book was published the following year.

Newbrough's only biographer, Daniel Simundson, describes the visionary as a romantic, a reformer (concerned especially about orphans), as rabidly anticlerical, and as deeply invested in Spiritualism and the occult.[43] He would eventually lead a small pacifist and vegetarian community to the deserts of New Mexico, where they hoped to found a utopia modeled after the wisdom of *Oahspe*. That utopia, like all utopias, failed. But the book lived on in some unexpected places, including the warm heart and yellowing pages of Ray Palmer's pulp magazines.

When Palmer came upon this strange book, he discovered that its publisher, a man by the name of Wing Anderson, was deceased. But he also discovered that Wing had a mailing list of forty thousand people who had purchased *Oahspe*. Ever the savvy businessman, Palmer commandeered the mailing list for the launching of his new magazine venture, *Fate*, and so joined the future of *Fate* to the future of *Oahspe*.

Palmer eventually located a copy of the original edition and republished it in his "Green edition" of 1960 (SW 34). The book, like many channeled theologies, is a complex and often frankly frustrating read. There are some real nuggets here, though. *Oahspe*, for example, is often claimed to be the first text to use the word "starship." It also includes a section called the Book of Thor and develops a complex theology about how gods and goddesses are advanced angels and how every angel was once a mortal, either from earth or from some other planet. The *Oahspe* Bible, in other words, echoes some of the more radical strands of Mormonism, which also claim, in their own specific ways of course, an eventual divinization of the elected human being (and it is probably no accident that Palmer had read *The Book of Mormon* [F 5.67.24]). The Divine Superman again.

I do not want to make too much of these observations, mostly because I am working from secondary sources and can claim no expertise in any of these texts. Still, it is worth at least mentioning that many aspects of Palmer's comparative vision were thoroughly gnostic both in the sense of emphasizing direct mystical knowledge and in the deeper and more difficult sense of advancing a sharp critique of orthodox religion. Palmer described his whole life, for example, as an outcry against the concept of faith, "this unthinking, illogical, unreasoning waste of the mind!" (F 1.17.32). He accepted "all bibles, but only as books, to be analyzed and questioned" (F 1.4.22). He insisted that scriptural texts contain errors, pointed out the common mistake of calling people who believe differently "heathen," and observed that the intolerant followers of the world religions have helped catalyze untold violence (F 5.67.25). Similarly, he understood all religions as "really only way-stations along the line"; suggested that the religious founders people often met in their afterlife visions were really "false gods" or "pretenders" of the real founders out to recruit for their own selfish kingdoms; and read scriptural texts, including the *Oahspe* Bible, as largely allegorical. He even encouraged his readers not to read *him* literally, that is, he suggested that his writings may be "allegory in the same sense" (F 1.9.8–11, 22–24).

Like the early Christian and Jewish Gnostics, moreover, Palmer often sharply distinguished between the creator god and the true God. Whereas God is "the Entirety," completely beyond all conception and human attributes, the Creator, for Palmer, is very much like a man. Indeed, he *is* or *was* a man who has advanced to a higher role in the cosmos, for "there is no such thing as a 'spirit' in my dictionary—There is nobody but REAL people, living in different ways, in different localities" (F 1.9.10, 19). Such an extraordinary claim, we might observe, echoes Blavatsky's theosophical notion that humanity was created by a Superior Being who was not supernatural but super-human.

And things got wilder and more super still. In at least one version of Palmer's

Oahspe-inspired world, humanoid beings evolve into creator-gods over hundreds of thousands of years on other planets and then employ some of that already existing matter to chemically engineer their own planets. When a planet is sufficiently developed, the creator-man creates a physical container for immortal spirits from other planets, who are invited to take on these new bodies. These spirits then engage in sexual intercourse in order to create "reconstituted human beings," who, like them, are immortal. Such a process is eventually refined through selective breeding and natural selection until an individual human being appears who is capable of fashioning, in Palmer's own words now, "a WHOLE WORLD, and after that a Solar System, and even an Island Universe." Indeed, "why not eventually a Cosmos?" (F 1.15.20–23).[44] Talk about superpowers!

However we interpret Ray Palmer or decide on his final views, clearly, this little big man did far more than read, write, and edit pulp fiction. With the help of Richard Shaver, Kenneth Arnold, and the *Oahspe* Bible, he created an entire occult world in the mirror of pulp fiction and his own paranormal experiences. And by "in the mirror," I mean both "in the mirror" and "*through* the mirror," since, in Palmer's mind at least, he had stepped through the mirror of fantasy and encountered something very real on the other side. The pulp fiction had become psychical fact. He was now living inside one of those fantastic cover paintings and doing what he had long been doing—writing himself in the bright colors of those astral-traveling dreams. Basically, Ray Palmer had become his own *Amazing Stories*.

ANCIENT ASTRONAUTS IN THE COMICS

Charles Fort, Ray Palmer, and Ken Arnold had a tremendous influence on the fantasy worlds that followed them. We have already had occasion to note the role of Alienation in the creation of the superhero genre via the iconic figure of Superman, the crashed alien. We have also briefly mentioned the precedents, including John Carter of Mars, Buck Rogers, and Flash Gordon. But all of this was still in the realm of pure fantasy. All of that changed, and changed overnight, with Kenneth Arnold's sightings of those nine silvery shapes; the Roswell cover-up (*whatever* was covered up); the various secret or pseudo-secret military projects designed to study, shoot down, mimic, or dismiss UFOs; and the widely reported UFO waves of the late 1940s and '50s. Now the mytheme of Alienation took center stage. Now it became *real*. Or real-unreal.

Consider, as one of a thousand possible pop-cultural examples, EC Comics' *Weird Science* #13. *Weird Science* was a boldly imaginative series that employed scien-

Z.13   SAUCERS OVER WASHINGTON

tific ideas to write about traditional occult themes. The series also showed a remark-able ability to respond to the surrounding culture and times. In July of 1952, on two consecutive weekends, newspapers reported that seven UFOs buzzed Washington, D.C. The military certainly considered the objects real enough. The things showed up on radar, and F-94 fighter jets were scrambled in the sky to try to shoot them down.[45] The comic writers and artists at EC responded with *Weird Science* #13. What were strange darting lights in the sky in the original historical events now became very distinct discs in broad daylight on the comic cover. In short, the popular paranormal expression exaggerated and reshaped the original event around the stock motif of the flying saucer, but—and this is where things get tricky—there *was* an original event behind the popular paranormal expression.

John Keel notes that "concurrent with the 1952 flap, Hollywood entered a fly-ing saucer cycle," which included the classic *The Day the Earth Stood Still.* Keel also reminds us that science fiction writer Arthur C. Clarke turned to the same phenomena in the 1950s and concluded that the behavior of the things in the sky (with impossible speeds and turns that would instantly kill any human occupant) suggested that they were not physical at all. "So he looked deeper, into psychic phenomena, philosophy and theology," Keel tells us, "and published his findings in *Childhood's End* (1953)."[46] This was a sci-fi classic that would come to have a major influence on the counterculture of the 1960s and future readings of UFOs, like those of Keel. The novel underlines the profound religious challenge the immense ships and the Overlords pose to the world religions below.

Clarke would also later sponsor three volumes of Fortean anomalies and write a number of critical essays on the subject of contactees and flying saucers.[47] He would also co-write, with Stanley Kubrick, what would become one the great alien interven-tion films of the twentieth century—*2001: A Space Odyssey* (1968). Significantly, the film employs Richard Strauss's tone poem *Also sprach Zarathustra* (*Thus Spoke Zarathustra*, the title of Nietzsche's famous text in which he introduced his notion of the Superman) to mark the evolutionary leaps from ape to man (via tool use early in the film) and from man to Star-Child (via astronaut Bowman's visionary encounter with the black monolith at the very end of the film).[48] The mythemes of Alienation and Mutation have probably never seen a more powerful and more beautiful artistic expression.

We could list comic-book story arcs involving flying saucers and aliens for hun-dreds of pages (and by "we" I don't mean "me"; I mean someone else). Just about all of them, however, would rely in some way on the four weird books of Charles Fort, the amazing stories of Ray Palmer, and the aftermath of those still unexplained events that swirled around pilot Ken Arnold that fateful summer of 1947.

When America entered the space race in the early 1960s, such themes became even more potent. A superhero team of astronauts was quickly introduced in Marvel's *The Fantastic Four* #1, in the fall of 1961. The series both launched the superhero renaissance at Marvel and quickly became one of the premiere places to explore the motifs of the UFO and the alien. The historical context of the series, of course, was an American-Soviet space race featuring the *Apollo* space program heading, like the four astronauts in a later issue, to the moon. Hence the "Red Ghost" hinted at on the cover of *The Fantastic Four* #13 will turn out to be no ghost at all, but a communist or "red" mad scientist, battling the Fantastic Four for the control of the moon's surface. The heroes also discover—as in many later NASA conspiracy theories—that the moon is already inhabited, that there is an alien base there, and that we are being watched from the moon's surface by a benevolent, large-headed humanoid named, appropriately enough, the Watcher.

One of the most famous story arcs of the Fantastic Four series appeared in issues #48–50 (1966), a three-part series that has come to be known as the Galactus Trilogy. One version has it that the plot originated with four words from writer Stan Lee to artist Jack Kirby: "Have them fight God."[49] Kirby's story is different, but not that different: "I went to the Bible, and I came up with Galactus."

Kirby, it turns out, had been reading popular science literature on the possibility of human beings encountering an alien species someday in order to exchange technology. But what if the aliens do not want our primitive technology? What if they want us, as in to eat us? This was Kirby's worry. In *The Fantastic Four* #48, he created the Silver Surfer as a way of expressing this concern. He rendered the cosmic being humanoid, basically naked, with Spidey-like alien eyes (there they are again), and glowing silver skin, as if he were made of mercury. Painfully, he rode around on what was essentially a California surfboard, which was all the rage in 1966. Happily, the later movie version altered this: in a number of scenes, the angle is handled in such a way so that the "surfboard" looks more or less exactly like a small UFO. Issue #48 also reintroduced the Watcher, who now appears in order to warn the planet of an approaching supergod named Galactus. Galactus is a cosmic being who feeds off the life energies of entire planets, and the Silver Surfer is a kind of cosmic scout for this hungry deity.

Z.15 THE COMING OF GALACTUS

As has often been noted, the Galactus Trilogy is a profoundly gnostic tale: "Have them fight God." Even Stan Lee, who usually wanted to emphasize the brighter and more positive aspects of his mythologies, wrote of the Silver Surfer as a kind of semidivine being "trapped" on the planet as a punishment for nobly refusing to do Galactus's will, much as the soul is trapped in matter in the ancient Jewish and Christian gnostic systems. In any case, "fighting God" and "being a Gnostic" are more or less the same thing. What the Gnostic is really fighting, of course, is a lower god *pretending* to be the real God. What he seeks is the God beyond god, the cosmic truth of things beyond all the religious bullshit.

These same gnostic sensibilities can be detected again in one of the most popular subthemes of the mytheme of Alienation, something called the ancient-astronaut theory. This is the idea that UFOs are not recent appearances, but have been interacting with humans for millennia, if not actually millions of years, guiding and shaping our biological and cultural evolution. Some versions of this theory are very abstract and leave things largely unexplained, as we have it, for example, in Kubrick and Clarke's mysterious black monolith. Some versions of this theory have it that the human species is a literal biological hybrid of early primates and visiting aliens (a theme, already present in the theosophical literature, that was given a dramatic new life in the abduction narratives and hybridization theory of the late 1980s and '90s). Other forms function as popular theories of religion, focusing on how such ancient visitations were recorded in myth and legend and the ancient visitors thus became our "gods." Sometimes this is read in a fascinated, positive light. Other times—and this is when it gets really gnostic—it is read in a very negative light, that is, as a millennia-long deception or control mechanism.

We will have occasion to return to this ancient-astronaut theme many times in subsequent chapters. We will have to. It is everywhere. One very obvious example will suffice for now. This is *Marvel Preview* #1 and its cover story, "Man-Gods from beyond the Stars," written by Doug Moench, the same writer with whom we began this book.

The cover of *Marvel Preview* certainly suggests that the ancient-astronaut theory is more than a theory. "Impossible—or true?" is ambiguous enough, but the question mark is effectively rendered null in the next lines: "Photos, fantasy, and facts about the starmen who walked the earth before time began." The Moench story is followed by, among other things, a bibliographic essay that correctly identifies Charles Fort as "the Great-Grandaddy of all the modern flying saucer broo-ha-ha"[50] and a number

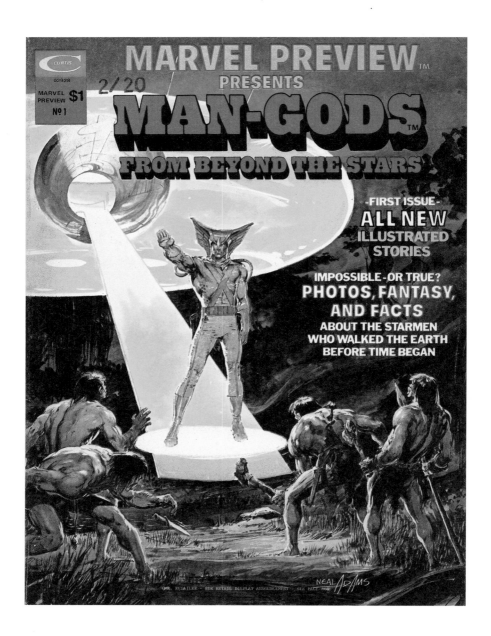

of supporting essays about the cultural phenomenon of Erich von Däniken's *Chariot of the Gods,* which was clearly the real catalyst for this particular issue. Von Däniken, previously a hotelier by profession, is a Swiss enthusiast of ancient history. His mega-bestseller, which argued that much of the ancient history of religion was really a history of human contact with spacefaring aliens, was originally published in Germany in 1968, a year later in English in Britain, then in America in 1970.

It is easy, and all too common, to dismiss popularizers and so miss entirely the important, and often very subtle, roles that they play in the history of ideas.[51] It is also all too easy to dismiss an idea by naïvely equating it with an easily dismissible popularizer, as if the popularizer was not popularizing a complex and nuanced idea that was already there in the culture. This is precisely the case with the ancient-astronaut idea. There were certainly earlier, more nuanced, and more elite versions of the same thesis.[52]

To take a single example, von Däniken's comparison of a photograph of an American *Apollo* astronaut and an ancient drawing from the Sahara, which could be construed as a one-eyed alien in a spacesuit, was almost certainly inspired by Carl Sagan's earlier discussion of the ancient-astronaut theory, which appeared in 1966 (and there were many other authors, in England, France, and the U.S., who preceded and followed Sagan in these provocative waters[53]). Sagan had imagined "colonies of colonies of colonies" in outer space (which echoes his signature line, "billions and billions"), and—much like Charles Fort—he deftly used the mythical memories of contact with European colonizers from North America and sub-Saharan Africa in order to suggest that other "contact myths" may encode ancient encounters with galactic astronauts, who "would probably be portrayed as having godlike characteristics and possessing supernatural powers."

After teasing his readers with the aforementioned ancient fresco from central Sahara depicting, in the words of a French archaeologist, "the great Martian god," Sagan zeroed in on a series of Sumerian myths as particularly suggestive of extraterrestrial contact. "Sumerian civilization is depicted by the descendents of the Sumerians themselves to be of non-human origin," he wrote. "A succession of strange creatures appears over the course of several generations. Their only apparent purpose is to instruct mankind. Each knows of the mission and accomplishments of his predecessors. When a great inundation threatens the survival of the newly introduced knowledge among men, steps are taken to ensure its preservation." As for the gods themselves, they were associated with individual stars, the cuneiform symbols for "god" and "star" being identical.

Sagan, of course, is offering this as a thought experiment, not as the truth of things, although it is also clear that he considers such scenarios to be real historical possibilities. He even speculates about a possible interstellar base on the far side of the moon (remember *The Fantastic Four* #13?) and suggests one possible reason for intervening in another planet's evolution: "to head off a nuclear annihilation."[54] These, of course, are all standard tropes in the contactee and ufological literatures, not to mention science fiction and the later alien abduction literature. In short, the mytheme of Alienation.

RADIATION

METAPHYSICAL ENERGIES AND SUPER SEXUALITIES

AS I HAVE EXPLORED THE ABDUCTION PHENOM-
ENON, IT HAS BECOME INCREASINGLY CLEAR THAT
VIRTUALLY NONE OF ITS ELEMENTS CAN BE APPRECI-
ATED WITHOUT A CONSIDERATION OF THE EXTRAOR-
DINARY ENERGIES INVOLVED. THESE INCLUDE LIGHT
OR HEAT FROM UFOS THEMSELVES OR TRANSPORT
TO THEM, THE MEANS BY WHICH UFOS MOVE AND
THE POWERFUL VIBRATORY SENSATIONS EXPERI-
ENCED BY THE ABDUCTEES. . . . EXPERIENCERS
REPORT VARIOUS FORMS OF INTERFERENCE WITH
APPLIANCES IN THEIR VICINITY (I HAVE SEEN THIS
FREQUENTLY MYSELF), WHETHER OR NOT AN AB-
DUCTION EXPERIENCE IS TAKING PLACE, AS IF THEY
WERE THEMSELVES EMANATING SOME SORT OF
STRANGE ENERGY.

JOHN E. MACK, **PASSPORT TO THE COSMOS**

lthough Orientation and Alienation were the first major mythical tropes of both
early science fiction and the superhero comic, the later development of the two
genres took place in what came to be known as the Atomic Age, that era of global
anxiety, terror, and metaphysical awe initiated by the detonation of two atomic bombs
over Hiroshima and Nagasaki in August of 1945. If cosmology had taught us that planet
Earth floats in an unimaginably vast sea of space and time, the Einsteinian physics
behind the bomb now suggested, rather paradoxically, that everything is connected,
that everything is One. Matter is frozen energy, the same energy, the same cosmic force

that once issued from some unspeakable explosion that scientists wanted to call—in what must count as history's greatest and dumbest understatement—"the Big Bang." Enter the trope of the Atom and the mytheme of Radiation.

ALIENATION TO RADIATION: COLD WAR SCARES AND SUBTLE BODIES

The transition from Alienation to Radiation was not so much a transition as it was a series of fusions of the two mythemes. The very first UFO scares, for example, were essentially Cold War scares, and as the sightings continued into the 1950s and '60s, numerous interpreters would note how the craft often appeared around atomic bomb installations or above military bases, as if the purported aliens had become aware of and concerned about our very recent nuclear technology. Moreover, the core message of "the Space Brothers" of the early contactee movement of the 1950s involved an attempt, however silly at times, to raise awareness around the very real issues of nuclear apocalypse and environmental collapse.

There is also the still-unexplained fact that reports of the mysterious objects often included elaborate descriptions of electromagnetic effects. Cars and tractors— really anything that runs on a battery or electricity—were reported to stop or go haywire in the presence of a UFO. Betty Hill, for example, originally contacted the air force after she and Barney "lost" two hours on a New Hampshire road because her car trunk had strange polished circles on it that made a compass go crazy and she was deeply concerned that they had been exposed to radioactivity. Witnesses have also developed strange skin rashes, eye infections, even alleged radioactive burns and cancers. Alienation sometimes *is* Radiation, it turns out.

And things are more complex still. Such energetic effects, after all, do not stop with the unidentified objects or alien presence. They extend to *the bodies of the witnesses themselves*, as if these bodies had been rendered super and become living UFOs. Perhaps one could speak more accurately here of the subtle bodies of the witnesses, as many of the reported experiences lie well outside anything conceivable with the physical body. We often hear, for example, of incredibly intense "vibrations," sometimes connected to sexual intercourse with the interdimensional beings. We read of the individual cells of the body being transformed and transmuted, even of the very atoms of the radiated body vibrating at unimaginable speeds, speeds that allow the witnesses to float and fly, pass through walls, enter other dimensions, even sometimes realize a profound unity with the entire universe. Although couched, and no doubt experienced, in an astonishing sci-fi register, such reports are often indistinguishable from countless examples of extreme religious experience recorded in mystical literature from around the world.

In the more extreme cases, such spiritualized superbodies even appear to have real effects in the physical world. Hence the bodies of witnesses—once radiated, empowered, or otherwise zapped by an alien encounter—do things like stop appliances, turn out street lights, and play havoc with electronic and computer equipment, as the late Harvard psychiatrist John Mack notes in our opening epigraph. Mack even recounts one reported case in which an entire neighborhood was blacked out during a visitation to two abductees.[1]

Weirder still, human encounters with UFOs often display a very clear, and very dramatic, psychical component. That is to say, the human being, once radiated, begins to display paranormal powers. This is one of the clearest and strongest links between the mytheme of Radiation and "superpowers." Such psychical components range from telepathic transmissions, overwhelming states of creativity, and realizations of immortality, through mind-to-matter phenomena like telekinesis, implants, or symbolic scars, to completely fantastic scenes involving teleportation and storm-raising. We might say, then, that whereas Alienation is the privileged mytheme of *altered states of consciousness*, Radiation is the privileged mytheme of *altered states of energy*.

It was not Kenneth Arnold's flying discs, much less the later abduction reports, however, that ushered in the mythology of Radiation. It was the bomb. The bomb changed everything, including American literature, film, fantasy, and popular culture. John Canaday has thus written of "the nuclear muse" in modern literature, and David Seed has explored the role the Cold War and the constant threat of nuclear annihilation played in the development of American science fiction.[2]

The impact, of course, was just as profound in Japan, where an entire industry was built up around the monstrous transformations the bomb effected there, both literally and culturally. Godzilla, who made his first debut as a sleeping dinosaur awakened and transmogrified by an exploding atomic bomb in Tana Tomoyuki's *Gojira* (1954), was in his origins a serious meditation on the horrors of the bomb and environmental degradation. Here is how William Tsutsui describes his beloved "radioactive saurian": "Well before the series degenerated into big-time wrestling in seedy latex suits, well before Godzilla had a laughably unlikely son, well before a giant technicolor moth was passed off as a gruesome monster, well before Tokyo was besieged by rapacious aliens or vengeful undersea civilizations (all fluent in Japanese, of course), *Gojira* was a solemn affair, an earnest attempt to grapple with compelling and timely issues, more meditative and elegiac than block busting and spine chilling."[3]

We all grappled. Tsutsui and I are more or less the same age. In 1972, he was nine and living in Bryan, Texas. I was ten and living in Nebraska. As I approached and passed puberty, I realized that my home state was lined with nuclear missile silos, and that Omaha was home to the Strategic Air Command (SAC) air force base where, or so we were told on a grade school field trip, the president would be brought in case of a nuclear exchange with the Soviet Union. We were also told that if we approached a particular plane parked on the runway and ignored the warnings of the guard on duty, we would be shot.

I never saw that plane or that guard, but those underground missile silos and that air force base marked the End of Days for me. I was absolutely terrified, and I was certain that I would not live to see forty. It is indeed difficult to communicate the fear we felt then. Okay, the fear that *I* felt. We were not, after all, talking about a "dirty bomb" that would tragically kill a few hundred people and radiate a few thousand with what amounts to a bad dentist X-ray. We were talking about *tens of thousands* of nuclear missiles vaporizing every major city in the States, Europe, *and* the Soviet Union, pretty much the entire Northern Hemisphere, and taking hundreds of millions of people, not to mention the entire global ecosystem, down with them. We were talking about the end of life as we know it. And—and this is the truly scary part—this was no fantasy or sci-fi film. It was entirely, horrifyingly possible. We really had (and still have) the technological means to do it. *This* was the historical background that made all that talk of radioactive this and radioactive that in the science fiction and superhero comics so gripping, so compelling, so disturbingly familiar.

But this wasn't the only story in town. There was also something else going on in the Silver Age myths I grew up with in the late 1960s and early '70s, something ultimately positive and redeeming. These, after all, were energies that did not just blow things up. They also illuminated, inspired, awakened, and empowered people. Indeed, they transformed these individuals into superhumans or demigods. The radiation, then, was not simply radiation. It was also a kind of spiritual power or mystical energy. In the end, these guys didn't get cancer. They got superpowers.

FROM THE OD TO THE ID: THE POWERS THAT (CANNOT) BE

The Silver Age radioactive myths that expressed this secret life were new, but the idea behind the myths was at least two centuries old, and probably then some. I want to capture and condense that idea here in a single two-word phrase: *metaphysical energies*. By metaphysical energies I mean all those human experiences of a palpable, overwhelming power, force, energy, vibration, frequency, beaming, or zapping that is obviously real (in the simple sense that it is experienced as such), but nevertheless cannot be fit into any known naturalist model. Whatever these energies are, they spike from somewhere "beyond the physical" (*meta-physical*), that is, beyond the physical dimensions that are normally accessible to the senses and its respectable science. They may turn out, of course, to be entirely natural, but for now they remain literally metaphysical, that is, outside or "beyond" (*meta-*) our present models of the physical world.

Such energies are extremely common in the history of religions, where their constant presence, at once alluring and terrifying, is coded in myth and symbol, and their incredible powers are domesticated through ritual, taboo, and temple. This all began to change in early modern Europe, however, when a few brave individuals realized that these metaphysical energies could be separated from their traditional cultural contexts, that they could be experienced in the natural world, and, most radically of all, that they could be empirically tested. It was no longer enough to experience the sacred. They now wanted, in Eric Wilson's terms, to *evidence* their spiritual intuitions.[4] Wilson is writing here of the American Transcendentalist Ralph Waldo Emerson and his core fascination with electromagnetism, which he considered to be empirical proof that matter was really force or energy (an idea that would resurface later in Cyrus Teed and John Uri Lloyd). To invoke the ancient alchemical notion, Emerson was out to demonstrate that *matter was really spirit*.

There were other, earlier versions of this idea. The Austrian wizard-healer Anton Mesmer (1734–1815), for example, had dramatically demonstrated a mysterious current of healing force that he called "animal magnetism." This was a subtle fluid or current that he claimed permeated the entire universe, including and especially the human body. When the current flowed freely in the body, health, happiness, altered states of consciousness, and strange powers were the result. When it was blocked, disease and suffering followed. Here, Mesmer thought, was the real secret behind all those traditional "miraculous" healings.

Animal magnetism eventually merged with Spiritualism, a broad-based popular movement that began in America in 1848, but quickly hopped the pond and spread throughout Europe as well. Spiritualists sought to make contact with dead loved ones through (mostly female) mediums working out of their own homes. The Spiritualists also sought to unite a scientific worldview with a religious one. Hence, with the invention of the telegraph and the discovery of electricity, the Spiritualist world was all abuzz with talk of "vibrations," "frequencies," the "spectrum" of consciousness, a "fourth dimension," even a "spiritual telegraph" connecting the living and the dead. The supernatural wanted to become scientific.

Nor were the earlier Magnetists and later Spiritualists alone in their metaphysical energies. In 1845, right in between them, the German scientist Karl von Reichenbach began publishing essays on the results of his own journey into mystery: a blue polarized force that permeated the natural world but could only be picked up by sensitives. He named this blue force "od" or the "Odic force," after the Norse god Odin. Reichenbach believed that such metaphysical energies could not be stopped, that they could penetrate *anything anywhere* in the universe. Reichenbach, in other words, considered od to be the ultimate superpower. He also believed that, were we more endowed with such an od, "we should be something like angels," half human and half divine.[5] In essence, we would be so many divine-human hybrids.

It was not Mesmer's animal magnetism or Reichenbach's od, though, that would capture Western culture. It was Freud's id. By the "id," Freud meant, literally, the It, that is, the instinctual base of human nature that seethes with both aggressive and sexual energies and that needs to be controlled by both the internalized voice of society, the superego (literally the "over-I"), and the ego or conscious sense of self.

The id was also closely aligned with what Freud called the libido. The libido is a mysterious, morphing energy that courses through the human body and takes on different forms at different stages of life according to differently prescribed cultural practices and family dynamics. So each culture produces a different "libidinal organization," a different energetic body, we might say. This same energetic body is profoundly linked to the cultural mysteries of what Freud, drawing on earlier alchemical and chemical uses (signaling the transformation of a solid directly into a gas), came to call "sublimation," a kind of "making sublime" of the libidinal energies that results in acceptable "gaslike" or spiritlike cultural products, such as philosophy, literature, and art. Or, we might add, not so acceptable cultural products, like adolescent comic books filled with radioactive superheroes.

Later psychoanalysis would downplay and largely deny the literal reality of both the id and the libido. It would choose to reread them as metaphors. Such a move was certainly faithful to the public Freud, but not to what we might call the secret life of Freud: the Freud who told occult stories late into the night; who accepted the core truth behind reports of telepathic dreams and wrote six papers on telepathy; and the Freud who wrote a mind-blowing essay on the German psychotic mystic, Daniel Paul Schreber, who believed himself miraculously transformed into a woman and impregnated by the spermlike "rays of God" so that he could mother a new race of men (remember Mr. Tweed?). Schreber also sought to live in a permanent state of "spiritual voluptuousness," which he linked directly to sexual pleasure and identified as a foretaste or fragment of the heavenly bliss enjoyed by departed spirits and God himself. Now *that's* a libido.

It was not the orthodox Freudians, however, who ultimately carried these energies into the metaphysical movements of the twentieth century. It was a Freudian heretic by the name of Wilhelm Reich. Reich began in Freud's circle, but he was soon kicked out, according to Reich anyway, for actually believing in the libido as a real energy or force. He renamed it the orgone. For Reich, the orgone was the basic energy behind the stars, the weather, the miracles of Christ, and that most intimate and most healing of all human expressions—the orgasm. For Reich, the orgone was the secret life of everything. Interestingly, a few renegade ufologists, like Trevor James Constable, would extend this everything to UFOs, seeing at least some of them as invisible alien life forms or "critters" that give witness to a "revolutionary biological power"—a Reichian "cosmic pulse of life."[6]

For his part, Reich thought he was resurrecting Freud's id with his orgone. What he was really doing was resurrecting Reichenbach's od. Exactly like the od, Reich's orgone permeated nature, and its color was said to be blue (I am also reminded here of the blue mystico-erotic plasma of Alan Moore's *Promethea*).

Much like the early Magnetists, Reich believed that a freely flowing orgone resulted in health and happiness, whereas a blocked, repressed, or stunted orgone resulted in sickness and mental suffering. The conclusion was obvious: the goal of therapy for Reich was to produce a psychophysical state in which what he called "the body armor" was sufficiently dissolved and a full orgasm was possible. And by full, Reich meant *really, really full*. He meant cosmic. He was not exaggerating. He was confessing. This was a conviction that went back to a sexual encounter he had had as a soldier with an Italian teenage girl during World War I, during which he first experienced the true cosmic nature of the sexual energies. Echoes of Paschal Beverly Randolph and his initiation into the deeper magical nature of sexuality, into "the union of magnetism, electricity and nerve-aura," with his Arab lover.

The Super-Story with respect to Radiation hardly ends with Reichenbach's od, Freud's id, and Reich's orgone. The twentieth century gave us another frame of reference that has proved immensely productive of new mystical literature: that issuing from the new field of quantum physics. Such mystical readings of physics are often read as some kind of New Age invention. It is simply not true. Emerson, as we have seen, engaged the early theories of electromagnetism to create his own identification of spirit and matter, as did the alchemical eccentrics Cyrus Tweed and John Uri Lloyd later in the same nineteenth century. Even more strikingly, Charles Fort was already jokingly, but seriously calling the teleporting behavior of subatomic quanta a matter of "witchcraft" in the early 1930s.

But perhaps no chapter in the history of physics is more relevant here than that involving the pioneering quantum physicist Wolfgang Pauli and his deep friendship with the Swiss depth psychologist Carl Jung. Jung came to his key notion of "synchronicity"—by which he meant to signal those magical moments in our lives when "coincidental" events appear to be connected through networks of meaning and metaphor rather than mechanism and causality—through a long correspondence and friendship with Pauli. Pauli had originally sought Jung out for help with his emotional and sexual problems, which were by all accounts volcanic.

Or explosive. Pauli was famous among his physicist colleagues for a most unusual and somewhat humorous ability: when he would walk into a lab, a piece of equipment would often break, fizzle, fry, or just plain blow up. This bizarre, poltergeist-like (not to mention expensive) ability was so common and so well known that his colleagues even gave it an official, scientific-sounding name—the Pauli Effect. And they were serious. One physicist, Otto Stern, actually forbade Pauli from coming anywhere near his laboratory, and I was recently told about a physics conference in Jerusalem at which the organizers made Pauli sit on the side of the room opposite the air conditioner. On a more ominous note, although Pauli was in residence at the Institute for Advanced

Study in Princeton during the Manhattan Project, he was not invited onto the project. Some seriously believe that this was because Oppenheimer and his colleagues were well aware of the Pauli Effect and simply could not take the risk.[7] Now *that's* a libido.

So, no, there is nothing superficial or particularly recent about noting the profound connections between quantum physics and mystical and magical forms of thought. Even the comparison between quantum physics (Radiation) and Asian religions (Orientation) possesses an elite lineage. Niels Bohr, for example, was so impressed with the analogies between the double nature of light (at once particle and wave) and Chinese Taoist philosophy that he chose the *yin-yang* symbol for his coat of arms. Erwin Schrödinger studied Hindu idealist philosophy and its central doctrine of *brahman* or cosmic consciousness just before his breakthroughs in quantum mechanics. And J. Robert Oppenheimer chose a verse from the Hindu mystical classic the *Bhagavad-Gita* to mark his viewing of the detonation of the first atomic bomb, which, by the way, was called "the Trinity test." God had become a bomb.

Such comparisons were developed yet further when quantum theorist David Bohm and the Indian philosopher and radical mystic Krishnamurti struck up a decades-long conversation in the early 1960s, but they did not really take off until Fritjof Capra's *The Tao of Physics* (1975) and Gary Zukav's *The Dancing Wu Li Masters* (1979) made two very popular, and very eloquent, cases for the parallels between quantum physics and Asian forms of mysticism.[8] As with Sagan's ancient astronaut theory, here we have another elite idea that became a popular one. Now the notion is pretty much everywhere, including and especially in science fiction and superhero comics.

Consider the character of Dr. Manhattan of Alan Moore's *The Watchmen*. Dr. Manhattan is a naked blue man who embodies the subatomic principles and perspectives of quantum physics. His full frontal nudity is not simply titillating or accidental. It is an expression of his utter rejection of the Newtonian social world and its arbitrary customs and illusions, all of which appear silly and superficial to his deep subatomic perspective of cosmic unity and total indifference. Accordingly, Dr. Manhattan likes to do things like build a crystal getaway on Mars and sit in the lotus posture of Indian yoga, which makes him look more or less exactly like the Hindu god Shiva, who also, by the way, is often represented as blue, is associated with his *lingam* or divine phallus, and some of whose followers practice ritual nudity as a form of social transcendence. Orientation (the blue god sitting in the lotus posture and practicing ritual nudity), Alienation (Mars), and Radiation (quantum physics) again.

If one, then, takes a broad historical perspective, it becomes patently obvious that the mytheme of Radiation had precious little to do with the historical reality of the atom bomb, which, after all, did absolutely nothing good to the populations it vaporized, melted, murdered, or otherwise tortured with tumors, and everything to do with the history of animal magnetism, Mesmerism, Spiritualism, psychical research, psychoanalysis, and now the mystical implications of quantum physics.

The origins of the Silver Age are relevant here. Those origins are commonly located, as we have already noted, in the re-creation of a single Golden Age superhero: the Flash. Julius Schwartz explains how the Silver Age began in the physics of light: "The Golden Age Flash, as I recall, had his superspeed by inhaling some hard water that fell on the floor. I thought it might be better if the chemicals had splashed on Barry Allen, the Flash-to-be, and were hit by a bolt of lightning, which travels one hundred eight-six thousand miles a second. That would be a reasonable explanation."[9] The Silver Age began, in other words, with the fantastic speed of light. Which is all to say that it began with the mytheme of Radiation.

Not so the Golden Age, which of course began before the bomb and so is better situated within the mytheme of Alienation. But note the differences with respect to Radiation. In the Superman story arc, the mytheme of Radiation, refigured here as Kryptonite, is precisely *what takes away* Superman's powers. In the later Silver Age stories, however, Radiation in various forms is precisely what *bestows* the powers. This, I would suggest, is a basic mythical pattern—by no means absolute—that distinguishes the superbody of the Golden Age from that of the Silver Age.

THE ATOMYTHOLOGIES OF STAN LEE AND THE KIRBY KABBALAH

No two men had a greater role in the development of the mytheme of Radiation within superhero comics than Stan Lee (born Stanley Martin Lieber) and Jack Kirby (born Jacob Kutzberg).

Stan Lee was born to Romanian immigrants in 1922 and grew up in poverty. The young boy escaped into literature of various sorts, from the early science fiction of Verne, Wells, and Burroughs, through mystery novels and the pulps, to classics like Shakespeare. He began working at Timely Comics in 1939, just after graduating from high school. Martin Goodman, who ran the company, was the husband of one of his cousins.

Jacob Kutzberg (1917–94) grew up in Manhattan like Stanley Lieber, that is, poor.

He loved the movies, and he adored pulp fiction and newspaper strips like Hal Foster's exquisitely drawn *Prince Valiant*. By nineteen, he was an aspiring artist without a high school diploma. Jacob experimented with various pen names, but finally landed on Jack Kirby as both catchy and close enough to his birth name. It sounded right.

In 1938, Kirby began working on the new upstart genre of the comic book, moving from this to that studio looking for work and an adequate paycheck. The first superhero he drew, the Blue Beetle, went nowhere, as did most everything else to which he put his pencil. But then in 1941, working now with fellow artist Joe Simon (with whom he would collaborate closely for the next sixteen years), he broke out of the box with a real smash-hit that the two men created together for Timely Comics: Captain America. The first issue sold over a million copies. Goodman now had a hero that could compete with DC's two megahits, Superman and Batman. Mark Evanier, Kirby's former assistant, friend, and biographer, notes the almost perfect timing: "The first issue reached newsstands on December 20, 1940. Just nine days later in a fireside chat, President Franklin Delano Roosevelt told the U.S. of A. that war was imminent and that America must be 'the great arsenal of democracy.' If ever there was the moment for a patriotic super hero, that was the week."[10]

This first success was not without a price, though. Kirby and Simon angered the German American Bund (a Nazi youth group that, among other things, dressed like Hitler to show their support for the Führer and the Fatherland) by depicting Captain America punching out Adolf Hitler on the cover of the very first issue. Then there was the story of issue #5, entitled "Killers of the Bund." The Bund was not pleased. The American Nazis flooded the office of Timely, which was mostly Jewish, with hate mail and called in various and sundry death threats. One wrote Kirby and told him to pick a lamppost in Times Square: he would be hanged on that post when Hitler arrived. The staff did not take all of this too seriously until threatening men began appearing outside their office building. But then so too did the police. The staff found this as confusing as comforting, until Mayor La Guardia called Joe Simon and personally promised police protection for Timely's "good work."[11]

Simon and Kirby did not stay long at Timely, but not because of the Nazis. They left because they were convinced that Goodman was cheating them out of the very significant profits Captain America was making. So off they went to DC, and with a handsome deal for the time. Kirby would not return to Timely for sixteen years.

Kirby was drafted on June 7, 1943. After a disastrous stint as an attempted mechanic (the man couldn't even really drive), he was reclassified as a rifleman and sent off to the front with Company F of the Eleventh Infantry. His commander was General George S. Patton.[12] When his superiors found out that he could draw and was the co-creator of Captain America, they made him an advance scout and ordered him to sketch what he saw behind enemy lines. There were few more dangerous assignments.

The young artist witnessed horrific suffering and unspeakable violence during his military service on the front lines. Biographer Ronin Ro, for example, tells the story of how Kirby once took emotional shelter in a foxhole by taking up a pencil and paper to draw. While he drew, a German shell blew the head of one of his friends clean off, and a piece of it landed on his drawing.[13] Kirby often told these stories of noble heroism and mindless carnage later in life to fans and colleagues. The same memories were no doubt one of the main sources for the extreme bodies and excessive postures of his dynamic art, which he repeated endlessly, as if he were trying to work through the traumatic memories over and over again.[14]

Simon and Kirby returned to comics after the war. When 1954 saw the virtual ruin of the industry via the censorship campaigns of Frederic Wertham (whom we will meet below), Joe and Jack split up. After bouncing around the industry for years, Kirby returned to Timely, now called Atlas (and soon to be called Marvel). It was a significant demotion, as Atlas did not pay what DC did. "Shipwrecked at Marvel" is how Kirby remembered it.[15] But it was there that he would work closely with Stan Lee on a number of new titles, books that would revolutionize the industry.

Goodman at this time was having Lee write a number of horror and occult comics, with titles like *Strange Tales*, *Amazing Fantasy*, *Journey into Mystery*, and *Tales to Astonish*. This was the pop occultism and monthly whacky eeriness out of which a new breed of superheroes would soon arise. Spider-Man, for example, was a single-issue experiment in the very last issue of *Amazing Fantasy* #15 (August 1962), Thor originally appeared in *Journey into Mystery* #83 (August 1962), Doctor Strange in *Strange Tales* #110 (July 1963), and so on.

Of course, there were other major artistic talents at Marvel in the 1960s, including Neal Adams, John Buscema, Gene Colan, Steve Ditko, Don Heck, Gil Kane, Herb Trimpe, and John Romita Sr. Ditko, as we have already noted, envisioned the costume and basic "alien" look of what would come to be Marvel's signature character, Spider-Man. Ditko was also responsible for some of the most mind-bending visions in the business, including the quasi-psychedelic scenes of Doctor Strange, the "Master of the Mystic Arts." Doctor Strange, who gained his magical powers through a desperate pilgrimage to Tibet, came to function as the Marvel icon of Orientation and the East/West mystical fusions that we traced with respect to Theosophy in chapter 1. Bradford W. Wright puts the situation this way: "Dr. Strange's adventures take place in bizarre worlds and twisting dimensions that resembled Salvador Dali paintings. They involve mystical spells, trances, astral travel, and occult lore. Inspired by the pulp-fiction magicians of Stan Lee's childhood as well as by contemporary Beat culture, Dr. Strange remarkably predicted the youth counterculture's fascination with Eastern mysticism and psychedelia."[16]

But it was some combination (the precise details of which constitute an immensely contested subject) between the talents of Lee and Kirby that would become the major creative force at Marvel in the early and mid-1960s. Whereas Lee was generally optimistic, modern, and bright in his outlook, Kirby was pessimistic, premodern, and essentially pagan, even literally alien in his sensibilities. They made a brilliant team, and the hits followed fast and furious: the Fantastic Four, the Incredible Hulk, the X-Men, and Thor, to name the most obvious, all appeared during a three-year span, 1961–63, just before the counterculture began to break things open in 1964.

What fascinates me about Kirby is what I suspect fascinated most young boys who witnessed his cosmic visions explode on the page. Writer Neil Gaiman speaks for many when he sums up the effects the artist had on him in two words: *raw power*.[17] Gaiman is hardly alone in his admiration. Michael Chabon dedicated his Pulitzer Prize–winning novel, *The Amazing Adventures of Kavalier & Clay*, to Kirby. He has also gone on record as saying that "I don't think it's any accident that at this point in their history the entire Marvel universe and the entire DC universe are now all pinned or rooted on Kirby's concepts."[18] That may be an exaggeration, but it is a perfectly understandable one. Mark Evanier has also written about "the Lee-Kirby superstructure" that underlies and gives life to the Marvel universe.[19] And even the Smithsonian requested to be sent Kirby's drawing desk.[20] Which is all to say that the raw power Jack Kirby managed to transmit through his pencil strokes also vibrated and pulsed at the very core of the superhero comic. It was as if Kirby split the atom of the genre.

We now have numerous historical and autobiographical accounts of the details behind the creation of the Marvel superheroes in the early 1960s. I need not repeat these here. What I want to do instead is draw out some of the different ways in which our present mytheme of Radiation played itself out in these radiating atomythologies.

This is not very difficult to do. Indeed, it is something of an industry joke that virtually every Marvel Comics character created in the early 1960s achieved his or her powers from some kind of radioactive accident. Okay, in the case of the Fantastic Four, it was "cosmic rays," but that amounted to the same thing in an adolescent brain. Lightning, atomic bomb, radioactive spider, cosmic rays—it really didn't matter. What mattered was the implicit theme of *metaphysical energy*. What mattered was the mytheme of Radiation.

The Fantastic Four came first (November 1961). Hence their Origins story is a kind of fusion of the earlier Alienation mytheme and the later Radiation mytheme: the Fantastic Four are American astronauts accidentally radiated by "cosmic rays" (Radiation) in space (Alienation). Shortly after they arrive back on earth, they discover that they have superpowers.

Then came the Hulk (May 1962). Here was a pure expression of the mytheme of Radiation. When a young man named Rick Jones drives his convertible into a gamma-ray bomb site just before detonation, atomic scientist and missile expert Dr. Bruce Banner runs out to save him, but alas, not in time. Banner is radiated by the blast as he pushes the teenager out of harm's way. Later that night, he morphs into a gray monster (almost immediately changed to green because of technical difficulties with the gray reproduction process) that, as has often been observed, looked more than a little like Boris Karloff's Frankenstein monster with a Beatles haircut. The Hulk's obvious literary precedents lay in the Frankenstein story and in Dr. Jekyll and Mr. Hyde, but, much in line with our present meditations, this particular Kirby creation had a secret life of its own. The artist, it turns out, had just read about a woman who had literally lifted a car to rescue her trapped child.[21] This gave him the idea that trauma and powerful emotions can transform a human being into a superbeing.

By August of the same year, the Kirby-Lee team came up with the idea of mining Norse mythology for a new superhero: Thor. Not that the story arc is really about Norse anything. The story begins with a landed spaceship and stone men from Saturn, described as "aliens," attacking a slightly crippled American named Dr. Don Blake, who happens to be vacationing in Norway. Chased by the stony aliens, Dr. Blake hides in a cave, where he soon discovers a secret chamber and what looks like a stick. When he strikes the scraggly thing against a boulder in frustration, the cave fills with blinding light and Blake finds himself transformed into the ancient Norse thunder god with long, hip blond hair and a mighty hammer. Later, in the same issue, the stone

3.3   RADIATION TRANSFORMATION

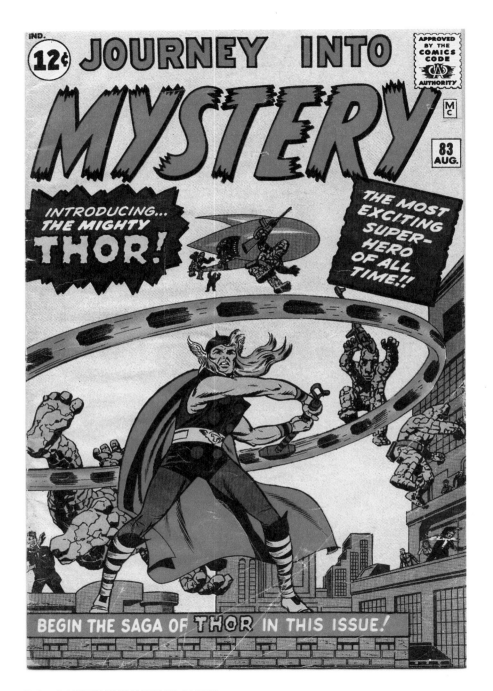

3.4   A NORSE GOD BATTLES ALIENS

men are caught on NATO radar as one of Kirby's favorite themes: unidentified flying objects. Divinization (Dr. Blake into Thor), Orientation (the frame of Norse mythology), and Alienation (UFOs) again.

Thor would become Kirby's signature character through whom he would bestow some of his own deepest cosmic and frankly gnostic sensibilities. Later issues, for example, would explore antimatter and hypnosis, time travel into the future and multiple dimensions, earth as a living being, and, on one powerful cover, the human being as a fallen or "trapped" god.

Then, of course, there was Spider-Man, aka Peter Parker, the conflicted teenager bitten by a radioactive spider (fall of 1962). As we have already seen, this was a Ditko creation, not a Kirby one. I mention him here because of the Radiation mytheme. The radioactive spider, of course, was stock Radiation stuff. The transforming agent of an earlier version of this hero was a much older and prescientific trope: a magical ring.

The X-Men (September 1963), a joking band of mutant teenagers led by a wheelchair-bound telepathic professor, were another Lee-Kirby creation. We'll treat this Marvel mythos at length in our next chapter.

Then there was Daredevil, another classic radioactive hero working well within the mytheme of Radiation, at least in his origins (April 1964). When lawyer Matt Murdock pushed an elderly man out of the way of a truck, the people in the truck, humorously labeled "Ajax Atomic Labs Radio-Active Material," threw an isotope out of the burning vehicle, which struck Murdock's eyes. He could now read by touching pages (which, by the way, was a classic superpower in the nineteenth-century magnetic and psychical traditions) and possessed a certain "Radar Sense." Bill Everrett drew the series, but at least one story has him getting the original sketches from Jack Kirby at a dinner at the latter's home.[22]

Passover of 1969. Carmine Infantino, one of DC's most talented artist-editors, came to visit Jack and his wife, Rosalind, or Roz as she was affectionately called. Jack showed Carmine covers for three new books that he had dreamed up: *The Forever People*, *Orion of the New Gods*, and *Mister Miracle*. He also told him that he wanted to come over to DC. This is eventually what he did, after, according to Kirby, he was sent a very poor contract by the Marvel lawyers in 1970 and told to sign it or get out.[23] He got out. He went to work for Infantino at DC, but on one condition: that he would now write the script that appeared in the narrative balloons. Jack Kirby was now an artist-writer. The odd situation that this defection to DC created in the comic book world

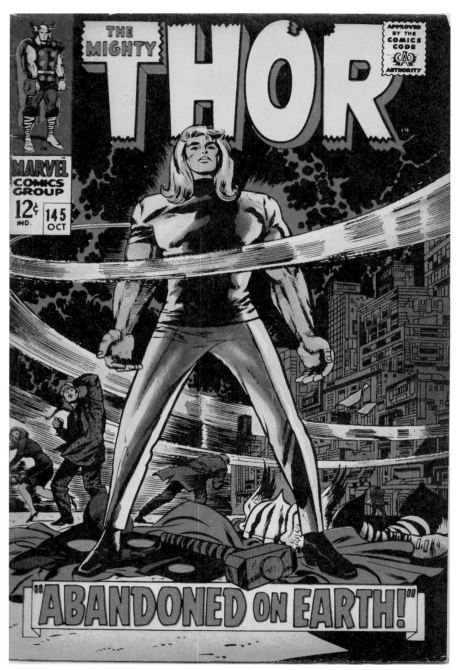

3.5   THE HUMAN HERO AS FALLEN GOD

hardly escaped him. He once told Mark Evanier and Steve Sherman over at DC that, since he had co-created the Marvel Universe with Lee, now "I'm basically competing against myself."[24]

Kirby would compete with himself through four different titles, which ran consecutively in rotation for about two years without ever concluding: *New Gods* carried the main plotline from the perspective of the gods; *The Forever People* aligned itself with the counterculture that was at that point opposing President Nixon and the horrors of the Vietnam War in order to tell the story from the perspective of the youth culture and its vibrant but often naïve idealism; *Mister Miracle* featured a former orphan become escape artist appropriately named Scott Free (as in, "he got away scot-free"); and *Superman's Pal, Jimmy Olsen*, which told some of the most bizarre chapters of the story from the perspective of the mortals or human beings. Kirby wanted DC to present all the titles under the title *The New Gods*, but they eventually called them *The Fourth World*.[25] No one seems to know why. Sort of like the fourth dimension, I suppose.

Now freed from another's scripting, Kirby set out to express what amounts to a new modern mythology—his own. *The Fourth World* is thus often read as a kind of coded autobiography reflective of Kirby's deepest convictions. Hence the Fourth World mythology begins where the artist's beloved Thor story arc left off, that is, with the epic battle of Ragnarok, the death and demise of the old gods, and a planet torn in half.

Literally. Two new divine worlds were created out of this battle: the peaceful planet called New Genesis and the violent planet called Apokolips. New Genesis is a kind of ecological utopia uncluttered by human constructions, with an ultramodern "orbital city" named Super Town floating harmoniously above the lush green Mother Planet. Apokolips, on the other hand, is an ominous thing pitted with spewing lava-holes, darkness, and monstrous technologies. Paradoxically, both worlds exist "in eternal partnership" (FW 1.199). They, after all, are both expressions of what Kirby calls simply "the Source." The Source is the deepest mystery of the cosmos that lies beyond not only good and evil, but beyond every god, every perspective, and every natural law (FW 2.136–37). The Source is the ultimate secret of the Fourth World epic. It is the name for the nameless in Jack Kirby's personal mysticism.

The story itself involves a secret war over earth being waged between the gods of New Genesis and Apokolips. The former world is led by a peaceful and paternal figure named Highfather, whose staff acts as a kind of beacon for the wisdom of the Source. The latter world is led by the ruthless Darkseid, who is after "the anti-life equation," a kind of mythical stand-in for fascism that will deprive every living creature in the universe of free will and result in "the outside control of all living thought" (FW 1.114). This is no simple battle between good and evil, though. Given Kirby's paradoxical notion of the Source, such an either-or simplicity is impossible. And so Kirby often hints that Darkseid may be the embodiment of evil and total control, but he is also "the other face" of humanity itself. He is us. Or at least half of us.

The partnered planets of New Genesis and Apokolips, in other words, are matched by the double-sidedness of humanity itself and, of course, its divine and demonic gods. This is the sacred mystery, or what Kirby calls the "cosmic joke" that escapes our normally bright, but false half-assessments of human nature (FW 2.26). Hence Kirby can dream up a bizarre amusement park called Happyland that is, in actual fact, the Kingdom of the Damned, a place of torture and violence for those who are trapped behind its mirrors and fakery. But such a dual nature is perhaps most fully expressed in Orion, the possessor of the "astro-force." "I am two worlds," Orion notes early on in dismay (FW 1.111). More so than he realizes, for, although he fights for good, he is in fact the son of Darkseid.

It is quite beyond my purposes here to relate the details, or occasional pure wackiness, of Kirby's elaborate storyline (witness the appearance of Don Rickles). Some of the paranormal currents Kirby plays with in the course of telling the story, however, deserve mention, since they almost certainly reflect, through the safe prism and freedom of fantasy, Kirby's own deepest convictions. These include: (1) the obvious countercultural allusions of the epic; (2) the related roles of UFOs, evolved aliens, and the ancient-astronaut thesis; (3) the figure of Metron and the ultimate mystery of the Source as expressions of a kind of pop-Kabbalah; and (4) the models of what we might call transcendent Consciousness and metaphysical Energy.

1. *A HYMN TO THE COUNTERCULTURE.* The countercultural resonances are everywhere. Although Kirby probably never took a psychedelic substance in his life, you would never know it by looking at his art. Indeed, I would go further. I have often suspected that the visionary imaginations of Kirby and Ditko in particular deeply influenced the psychedelic aesthetics of the counterculture. This is more than a guess. "He sits for hours on end reading comic books, absorbed in the plunging purple Steve Ditko shadows of Dr. Strange," wrote Tom Wolfe in *The Electric Kool-Aid Acid Test*, describing Merry Prankster Ken Kesey on his 1964 Magic Bus psychedelic

tour across America.[26] Similarly, as Arlen Schumer has pointed out in his stunning graphic re-creation of Silver Age comic art, Ditko's Doctor Strange appeared regularly on underground rock concert posters in the Bay Area of the 1960s and '70s. The simple truth is that "American counterculture" and "Silver Age superhero renaissance" are more or less (mostly more) the same thing.

And all of this comes to something of a head in *The Fourth World*, published in the months of 1970 and 1971, this time by DC as it tried to catch up to a much hipper Marvel. As Kirby himself put it in the voice of a taunting hipster in a disco scene panel: Superman is "a charter member of the establishment" (FW 2.300). A square, indeed *a steel square*. It doesn't get much squarer than that. But not Jack Kirby. Hence he could create the Forever People, basically a team of hipsters as superheroes. Then there are "the Hairies," who ride motorcycles and share a dropout society in a place called "the Wild Area." Kirby explains that the Hairies are part of something called "the Project," a massive genetic experiment designed to produce evolutionary "step-ups" and eventually "aliens" (FW 1.171). In short, the hippies as mutants. In another scene, Serafin, one of the superhip Forever People, pulls a "cosmic cartridge" from his cowboy hat and tells a young boy named Donnie to swallow it. The cartridge looks exactly like a bullet (hence the cowboy hat) or a pill (hence its effects): the cosmic cartridge grants Donnie a mystical experience of universal harmony and omnipresence, of "All there is!" (FW 1.186).

2. ALIENATION AS MUTATION.   Then there is Kirby's fascination with the alien, the UFO, and the ancient-astronaut thesis (FW 2.38–39, 2.149). Here we encounter abduction scenes, operating rooms, and genetic experiments on people (FW 1.123, 2.364), much talk of dimensional bridges and space-time portals, including something called "the Boom Tube," a variant of which had already appeared in Kirby's beloved Thor series as a "dimension door."[27]

3. THE KIRBY KABBALAH.   It is fascinating how gods, not machines, are called UFOs in the epic (FW 1.182, 302, 2.149). It is difficult to say why this is so, but part of it seems to be an expression of what I would like to call the Kirby Kabbalah. Kirby's technical knowledge of Jewish mysticism may have been very slight, but the resonances between the mystical tradition, the UFO theme, and the comic art are very obvious. There are numerous reasons for such a fusion, and all are very much worth dwelling on for a moment.

On the popular front, the idea that the prophet Ezekiel's vision of a rainbow-wrapped humanoid seated on a throne above four weird animal-angels and their accompanying "wheels" was really a kind of ancient UFO encounter is a widely held view in the UFO literature. It is not difficult to see why. Although the thing is called a chariot in two other biblical contexts and in later Jewish tradition, it barely resembles a chariot, and nowhere in the prophetic book is it actually called one.[28] Moreover, if we were honest, we would have to admit that, well, there *are* elements of the ancient vision that do look a lot like a modern UFO encounter.

The immense wheels, whose simultaneous (multidimensional?) movements inside one another make no clear sense, have numerous "eyes" on their rims, and they move with the four angelic hybrids very much as UFOs are reported to move—essentially, they float. We could also read back into the ancient text the roar of some kind of propulsion system (the "rushing water" or "thunder" described in the text) and detect a classic saucer dome in the crystal-like vault that is described as arching above the heads of the angelic creatures. We even witness a kind of traumatic "abduction"—after the glowing glory of God that was the chariot-throne lifts off the ground, the prophet is carried by the spirit of God to another location, after which he was in a stunned stupor for seven days.

Most of all, though, there is what the literary critic Michael Lieb has beautifully called "the mysterium of *hashmal*."[29] The latter term is an exceedingly rare ancient Hebrew word in the scriptural texts that is used in Ezekiel to describe the "amber," "polished brass," "glowing metal," or *electrum*-like qualities of the bodies of both the hybrid angels and the fiery humanoid. Translated in the ancient world by the Greek *elektron* and the Latin *electrum*, the same word now means "electricity" in modern Hebrew.

This is all eerily significant for our present purposes, and for at least three reasons. First, "electro-," "electricity," and the "electron" all enter the language of Spiritualism and occultism in the modern period, hence our mytheme of Radiation can be seen as another instance of "the mysterium of *hashmal*." Second, this same Hebrew hashmal or *electrum* was and is surrounded by a whole host of traditional warnings and restrictions, as if its presence in the prophetic book posed serious dangers (and wondrous holiness) to any who dare engage it. One early rabbinic tale, for example, has a child reading the first chapter of Ezekiel in the home of his teacher, understanding the truth of hashmal, and immediately being consumed by the same fiery mystery. From then on, we are told, the rabbis sought to restrict access to this most dangerous, and most holy, of biblical books. Only serious scholars, who understood the text on their own, were allowed to expound on it, and then only to qualified disciples.

Given this deep background, one could well suggest—I am anyway—that what Jack Kirby was doing was presenting his own understanding of "the mysterium of *hashmal*" to his readers, who, of course, happened to be mostly adolescents, that is, children. I doubt very much that any of them were consumed by a divine fire, but I am quite certain that many were zapped in other ways. I am also certain, with Lieb, that the "wheels" of Ezekiel's original vision have escaped, entirely and completely now, all of those traditional prohibitions and carefully guarded secrets, and that they are to this day appearing in the dreams, visions, roads, and skies of countless ordinary people. These are Lieb's "children of Ezekiel," the UFO visionaries of the New Age, the new riders of the chariot who turn to the language of science fiction, space travel, and the machine to experience and express something of what the ancient Hebrew prophet knew in his own priestly terms of throne, angel, temple, and glory.

And what to do with Ezekiel's apparent mental illness, including one modern diagnosis of him as a paranoid schizophrenic? After all, he did things like cook his bread over cow dung (after he complained to God, who first commanded him to cook it over human feces) and lie on his right side for 390 days. The paranoid reading would suggest weird, centuries-long links between the original prophetic vision and the oft-noted paranoid quality of so many contemporary UFO cults.[30] What to do?

Then there is the throne. There are many forms of Kabbalah, but one that stands out in the literature is now called by two names: "throne mysticism" and "chariot mysticism," each dedicated to different aspects of Ezekiel's vision. This is significant for our own present purposes, because Kirby's figure of Metron is a fusion of both. Metron, after all, rides what amounts to a *flying throne*. Called the Mobius Chair, the thing can bend space and time. In the very last scene of the unfinished epic, Metron sits on Mobius, like Ray Palmer's *Oahspe* god-man, to tow his own personal planet, which vaguely resembles our own early earth.

The Jewish mystical resonances continue. The weird symbols on Metron's chest and forehead, for example, invoke the ten sefirot or spheres of classic Kabbalah. Moreover, much like the Source, God in the kabbalistic tradition possesses both "good" and "evil" aspects. We might also mention that Kirby's character of Serafin is an obvious play on "seraph" or "seraphim," one of the highest classes of angels in Jewish mys-

3.6   METRON TOWS A PLANET

ticism, and that Metron is very close to the name of the ancient Jewish superangel Metatron, who was so exalted that in some (heretical) contexts he was considered a second God. Finally, it is worth pointing out that in Kirby's mythology, Metron is the figure who most longs to know "the knowledge of the Source" (FW 1.113). He is "the seeker and wielder of cosmic knowledge" (2.237). In short, Metron is a Jewish mystic, a kind of cosmic pop-kabbalist.

4. CONSCIOUSNESS AND THE BODY ELECTRIC. Reading Kirby, it is clear that he thought of consciousness as something irreducible, as a mystery that cannot be explained by the body or the brain. Hence he can write of weird things like the Mind-Force, which he describes as "a living, thinking being that exists as pure energy," as "a personality without a body," as an "unseen personality" that "must manifest itself in the physical world" via something called "animates" (FW 1.365). Or of "a wandering, god-like being" who deposits his power and personality in a hospitalized paraplegic (FW 2.45).

For Kirby, the human body is a manifestation or crystallization of finally inexplicable energies—a superbody. He can thus write in one scene of "body electricity." This is a force that human beings "store and generate," and it is uniquely obvious in a superhuman like Superman (FW 1.302). What Mesmer called animal magnetism, Reichenbach knew as the blue od, and Reich saw as a radiating blue cosmic orgone becomes in Jack Kirby a trademark energetics signaled by "burst lines" and a unique energy field of black, blobby dots that has come to be affectionately known as "Kirby Krackle" (probably inspired by Kirby viewing the first quasar photographs published around 1965).[31] The final result was a vision of the human being as a body of frozen energy that, like an atomic bomb, could be released with stunning effects, for good or for evil. These metaphysical energies, I want to suggest, constitute the secret Source of Kirby's art.

After his DC contract expired, Kirby went back to Marvel and worked on, among other things, a series called *The Eternals* (1976–78). This storyline was based, once again, on the ancient-astronaut theory. If Kirby's beloved Thor story arc was the privileged place of his core idea that ancient aliens would have been perceived as gods, and if *The Fourth World* was the place where he was first given free rein to develop this notion as a writer-artist, *The Eternals* was the consummation and perhaps clearest statement of this same personal mythos.

This self-described "cosmic series" employs strikingly obvious allusions to both Richard Shaver's hollow earth mythology and von Däniken's ancient astronaut specula-tions toward a rereading of traditional mythology as a coded, but shockingly real history of space gods and their interaction with humanity. The first few issues, for example, feature: a race of "Deviants" (basically Deros) who live in the inner earth, possess terrifying z-ray guns, and clash with humans in battles that are recorded in myth and legend as encounters with devils and demons; illustrations that strongly resemble the images in von Däniken's *Chariot of the Gods*, including an initial cover image of an Incan god with a kind of breathing device; an underwater USO base that turns out to be sunken Lemuria; and ancient genetic manipulations of apes by "space gods" or Celestials who created the three races of the Deviants, the humans, and the super-evolved Eternals (basically Teros). The latter godlike beings are described as "the race of mystics" who, through "ages of development," have required "great mental powers," including the ability to levitate or fly—"mind and matter working in perfect harmony."

Friends and historians of the genre differ on how much Kirby believed the an-cient-astronaut story. Evanier, who worked as his assistant in the early 1970s and became a lifelong friend, leaves the issue open with a quote from Kirby himself: "Can you prove it couldn't have happened that way?"[32] Roy Thomas, by the way, framed the issue in an almost identical way when introducing Doug Moench's ancient-astronaut story in *Marvel Preview* #1. We seem to have a kind of consensus here, at least among some key figures at Marvel in the mid-1970s.

If the Kirby mythos of a cosmic battle between good and evil acted out by a host of interdimensional aliens who are all manifestations of the same mysterious Source sounds familiar, that's because it is. Kirby almost certainly influenced other creators of popular culture. Consider, as an example, the *Star Wars* trilogy of George Lucas (who was himself an avid comic-book reader). The parallels are espe-cially striking. Ro lays some of them out:

JACK HIMSELF FELT THE NAME LUKE SKYWALKER SOUNDED SUSPICIOUSLY LIKE MARK MOONRIDER FROM ***THE FOREVER PEOPLE***, AND THAT LUCAS'S THE FORCE WAS SIMILAR TO THE NEW GODS' VAGUE COSMIC ESSENCE THE SOURCE. IN ***STAR WARS***, A KIND, GRAY-HAIRED MENTOR [OBI WAN-KENOBI] URGED LUKE TO JOIN A GALACTIC BATTLE AND RETURNED FROM THE DEAD, JUST THE WAY HIMON RECRUITED SCOTT

3.7 THE SPACE GODS RETURN

FREE IN *MISTER MIRACLE* AND ALSO OVERCAME DEATH. LIKE DARKSEID, DARTH VADER

RULED STORMTROOPERS AND LIVED ON A PLANET THAT HAD A HUGE CIRCLE CARVED

INTO ITS SIDE (LIKE THE FLAMING FIRE PIT HE'D ALWAYS DRAWN ON APOKOLIPS). AND

DARTH VADER SERVED THE DARK SIDE. LATER, ACTOR MARK HAMILL, WHO PLAYED LUKE

SKYWALKER IN THE FILM AND HAD READ AND ENJOYED HIS FOURTH WORLD BOOKS,

TOLD JACK THAT UPON ARRIVING ON THE SET AND FIRST SEEING DARTH VADER, HE'D

THOUGHT, OH, IT'S DR. DOOM.[33]

And Ro goes on for another full paragraph, laying out more details. They are difficult to deny, particularly the obvious resonances between Darkseid and the Dark Side, as well as those between Orion, possessor of the astroforce and secret son of Darkseid, and Luke Skywalker, possessor of the Force and secret son of Darth Vader. According to Ro, Kirby was not overly upset by these obvious resonances. He simply wished that Lucas would have admitted the influence.

Kirby appears to have been more upset with another director and his pop-cultural staple, Steven Spielberg and his *Close Encounters of the Third Kind*. The artist-writer was not upset because Spielberg had borrowed anything from him, but because he believed that the film presented a false utopian picture. Kirby may have believed in aliens, but certainly not the gentle, beneficent kind that land at the end of the film at the base of Devil's Tower. The alien gods were not beneficent deities for Kirby. They are not here to help or save us. They are here to use us. Or eat us.

Finally, it is also important to point out that part of Kirby's reception has also been explicitly mystical, that is, select readers have approached him as a gifted metaphysical figure in his own right. Nowhere is this more apparent than in comic artist Christopher Knowles and his remarkable *Secret Sun* blogs. Knowles sees Kirby as an "astrognostic" possessing an "astronaut theology" that emerged from a mélange of "psychics, saucers, and supermen." This Kirby mysticism was signaled in earlier work like the artist's beloved Thor story arc until it gradually took over the very core of his output from the early 1970s on. Hence books like *The New Gods* and *The Eternals*.

And *Spirit World* #1. Here, or so it seems, Kirby wore his deepest convictions on his proverbial sleeve. Or the cover. This magazine—which saw only a single issue and accepted no subscriptions—is well worth dwelling on for a moment, as it highlights in an especially clear fashion my central claim with respect to Jack Kirby, namely, that his Silver Age pop art is suffused with paranormal currents. Indeed, in an almost

ridiculously exact demonstration of this thesis, the opening story of *Spirit World* is entitled "Premonition: Black Art—or—Mass Art?"

Most of the stories inside feature a classic Kirby-drawn hero—square jaw, immense body, an archetypal muscular frame. But this time the hero wears no costume and punches no villain. He is parapsychologist Dr. E. Leopold Maas. Dressed in a suit and tie, he speaks directly to the reader in order to teach us about the reality of psychical phenomena and how such things have been distorted in history by associations with religious belief, the "ridiculous excess" of demonology, and modern mediums. Through four different stories, Dr. Maas tells the tale of an ordinary housewife who is overwhelmed by a premonition of President Kennedy's assassination; relates his investigation of a haunted house; explores some hypnosis sessions with a young female college student, who in a previous incarnation was burned at the stake during the Spanish Inquisition; and teaches the reader about the historical figure of Nostradamus and what his poetic prophecies suggest about the true nature of time and mind. Kirby's rhetorical questions with respect to the last story are likely his own answers: "Or, is the mind another sort of instrument—a probe, perhaps! With still unrecognized capacities!!? . . . Does man have neglected faculties he has always been trying to use?"

The only story that does not feature the parapsychologist is "The Children of the Flaming Wheel," a brief tale exploring one of Kirby's favorite topics: contact with an alien race through psychic means. Here contact is achieved through a young female hippie, who goes into trance to form a "mind-link" with a UFO orbiting around a distant planet. This is the "secret California cult" promised on the cover.

What strikes me most about this *Spirit World* is how easily the classic Kirby techniques and superhero motifs have merged with the paranormal experiences depicted in the magazine, as if that is what the techniques and motifs were really gesturing toward all along. With a little imagination, one can easily detect a series of superhero allusions—the energetic transformation, the Kirby Krackle, a ghostly golem figure, a portrayal of a female psychic's astral body that looks exactly like the invisible Sue Storm of the Fantastic Four, a Thor-like hammer, and (okay, this is a stretch) a flying plate that vaguely resembles Captain America's shield.[34] Sue Storm has become an ordinary housewife. Thor's hammer has become a murderer's club. Captain America's shield has become a poltergeist-launched plate. And the hero's energetic transformation has become the ghost hunter's encounter with a cold blast in a haunted house. In effect, the superpower has become the paranormal event, *and the aesthetic is seamless.*

"Something very, very powerful hit [Kirby] around '65 or '66, and transformed him from an already imaginative man into a psychedelic shaman disguised as a free-lance pencil pusher," Knowles observes. Hence Kirby's *synchromysticism*, by which Knowles means the uncanny ways Kirby's art appears to have prefigured actual historical events: Kirby as unconscious prophet, if you will, with his own "Mass Art" as "Premonition," exactly as he had it in that opening story of *Spirit World.*

Two of Knowles's most impressive examples here are "the face on Mars" phenomenon and what looks very much like Kirby's precognition of the Gulf War in his mid-1970s DC series *OMAC: One Man Army Corps.* In terms of the former, Kirby drew, in 1959, a story about a face on Mars seventeen years before the NASA *Viking* probe took a photograph in 1976 of what many took to be a face on Mars. In terms of the latter, in his *OMAC: One Man Army Corps* series (1974–75), Kirby drew and named a nonexistent technology called "smart bombs," drew an evil dictator named Kafka who looks remarkably like Saddam Hussein, and even had the dictator arrested in a ground bunker and put on trial for a series of crimes that replicate those of the Iraqi leader.[35]

I am reminded here of Doug Moench's unconscious precognition of the black-hooded intruder through his *Planet of the Apes* storytelling. Or of Philip K. Dick meeting a woman named Kathy at the end of 1970 who fit, in fantastic detail, a character named Kathy whom he had "invented" a few months earlier in *Flow My Tears, the Policeman Said.* "It is an eerie experience to write something into a novel, believing it is pure fiction, and to learn later on—perhaps years later—that it is true," Dick mused (SR 266).

One wonders what Morgan Robertson thought when the *Titanic*, the largest ship on the planet and considered unsinkable at 880 feet long, crashed into an iceberg in the north Atlantic on April 14, 1912, just before midnight with far too few lifeboats. Robertson, after all, had published a novel in 1898 entitled *Futility*, about the *Titan*, the largest ship on the planet and considered unsinkable at 800 feet long, which crashed into an iceberg in the north Atlantic on an April night carrying far too few lifeboats. In both cases, the disaster happened because the ship captain, pressured by his company, was trying to break a speed record in clear violation of the safety regulations.

At least the two ships had the decency to travel in exact opposite directions: the fictional *Titan* from New York City to England, the real-world *Titanic* from England to

New York City.[36] And at least it was the second journey for the *Titan* and the first for the *Titanic*. Well, thank goodness we don't have to think about *that* one anymore.

*O*N THE MOTHMAN, GOD, AND OTHER MONSTERS: JOHN A. KEEL AND THE SUPERSPECTRUM OF THE OCCULT

I suspect that Jack Kirby was reading John Keel.[37] If he wasn't, he should have been. If Jack Kirby was the quintessential artist of the mytheme of Radiation, John Keel was its most radical theorist.

By profession, John Alva Keel was a writer and journalist. By avocation, he was a kind of *X-Files* Agent Mulder of the real world. As a young man, he was a stage magician and did a stint in the army as a propaganda writer, which is to say that he was something of an expert on the dynamics and practice of illusion, trickery, and psychological warfare. This was a man who could not be easily fooled.

Keel spent much of his adult life tramping around the Middle East, Asia, Europe, and the Americas looking for anything that was bizarre, absurd, or fantastic. He found quite a bit of it. Remarkably, the path of his writing career follows more or less precisely the same chronological development of our first three mythemes: Orientation, Alienation, and Radiation. That is to say, Keel began his journey in "the East," moved on to write extensively about UFOs, and landed squarely in a worldview dominated by the occult reaches of what he came to call the superspectrum.

His first major book, on "black magic in the Orient," was entitled simply *Jadoo* (1957). Part adventure story, part travelogue, Keel presents himself here as a kind of Indiana Jones figure out to expose—that is, not be fooled by—many of the apparent mysteries that have made the fakirs, wizards, witches, and holy men of the Middle East, India, Nepal, Tibet, and East Asia so famous, and so infamous, throughout the centuries. He even goes looking for the Abominable Snowman of the Himalayas in these pages. And spots him. Two of them, actually.

Thirteen years later, after multiple men's magazine articles, some 150 newspaper pieces, and extensive interviews with over two hundred silent contactees (that is, individuals who sought no publicity for their UFO encounters), Keel's *UFOs: Operation Trojan Horse* appeared.[38] It was here that he formalized the notion of "windows" (geographical areas that witness occult weirdness century after century) and advanced the startling thesis that UFOs are neither truly extraterrestrial nor particularly trustworthy. With respect to all things paranormal, Keel had moved, in his own terms now, from

(a) a position of professional skepticism (as in *Jadoo*); to (b) astonished belief, since it became patently obvious to Keel that the contactees were not lying about their experiences, as they kept reporting, independently of one another, the same stories, even the same details; to (c) disbelief, since many of these same experiences were patently absurd and clearly made no sense within the standard UFO frame of reference.[39]

This latter disbelief, it should be stressed, was not at all the same thing as his earlier debunking. I am tempted to call it an "astonished disbelief." It was in fact a quite subtle and sophisticated position poised well beyond *both* reason *and* belief. What Keel had really done was shift registers. As he had it now, UFOs were not "hard" stable objects, much less high-tech spaceships. Rather, they were "soft" paraphysical manifestations, "transmogrifications of energy," as he put it, very much akin to the apparitions of traditional demonology and angelology. Put differently, the secret of the contactee experience is not in the light shows in the sky or in some secret government file or paranoid conspiracy theory. The secret of the contactee experience is in the contactees themselves, that is, in the deepest structures of consciousness and its astonishing, essentially mystical relationship to the cosmos.

It was also here that Keel noted the UFO phenomenon's "reflective" quality, that is, its tendency to reflect back to the witnesses whatever cultural assumption, religious beliefs, or frames of reference that they brought to the events: the demons and angels of medieval Catholicism and the elves, fauns, and fairies of early modern European folklore thus became the sci-fi aliens and beneficent Venusians and warring Martians of Cold War America. It was in this way that Keel rejected the ancient-astronaut thesis so dear to Jack Kirby and many others. Human beings did not mistake ancient astronauts for gods. Modern aliens *are* ancient gods, or better, *both* modern aliens *and* ancient gods are equally illusory forms of some deeper superintelligence that is a kind of "cosmic joker."[40]

"Beware," Keel tells his readers in so many words. "The demons and deities of the ancient world are still with us, and they deal, as they have always dealt, in tricks, illusions, and distractions." If the motto of *The X-Files* was "I want to believe," the motto of John Keel was: "Don't."

The same year that *UFOs* appeared, Keel also published *Strange Creatures from Time and Space* (1970). Much of this third book, including its title, reads like the sci-fi, monster, and horror tales that Stan Lee was telling in the 1950s and early '60s in the pop-occult series from which the superheroes would soon emerge, series like *Strange Tales*, *Journey into Mystery*, and *Amazing Fantasy*, many of which featured UFOs before

3.10 FLYING SAUCER MYSTERIES

they featured superheroes. There was one big difference: Keel was suggesting that such monsters had a kind of intermediate or subtle reality of their own. This was not quite hard fact. But it was certainly not fiction either. We are back, once again, to Fort's truth-fiction (and Keel was a big fan of Charles Fort).

Significantly, the first edition of *Strange Creatures* featured a striking Frank Frazetta painting. For the comic-book fan, this linked the Keel paperback on the paranormal directly to the pulp fiction and comic-book worlds, since Frazetta was already a legend in the latter worlds for his super-realistic (and hypererotic) paintings of barbarians, monsters, dinosaurs, and barely dressed damsels in distress. Even more significantly, Keel dedicated this same book to the memory of his recently deceased friend Otto Binder, a major superhero comic-book writer who became a ufologist. Much more on Binder in chapter 5.

Strange Creatures can be fruitfully read as part of a Keel monster trilogy, which also includes his next book, *Our Haunted Planet* (1971), and his last book, *Disneyland of the Gods* (1988). All three popular works develop the same basic idea, namely, that the aliens and monsters of traditional and contemporary folklore (demons, jinn, faeries, the Abominable Snowman and Sasquatch, the UFO alien, Martian apparitions—you name it) are so many manifestations of "our haunted planet." Again, they are not quite real, but they are not quite unreal either. As far back as we can see into human history, they have been here with us, taking on a variety of guises and a host of names as human cultures developed various religious ideologies and ritual systems in response to their presence and shenanigans. Basically, they've been screwing with us.

Probably the closest Keel ever came to articulating a full theory of the paranormal-as-screwing-with-us was in his two 1975 books, *The Eighth Tower* and *The Mothman Prophecies*. Whereas the former book sets out the theory in its boldest form, the latter book represents Keel's longest and most detailed case study, which screwed with him.

The subtitle of *The Eighth Tower* announces *The Cosmic Force behind All Religious, Occult and UFO Phenomena*. That pretty much sums it up. For Keel, all religious and occult phenomena are manifestations of a single metaphysical energy, which he now calls the superspectrum and relates, more or less directly, to the electromagnetic spectrum of modern physics. He had already suggested as much in *UFOs*, showing, for example, how many UFOs "appear" and "disappear" as they move up or down the electromagnetic spectrum, appearing, for example, as purplish blobs as they manifest out of the

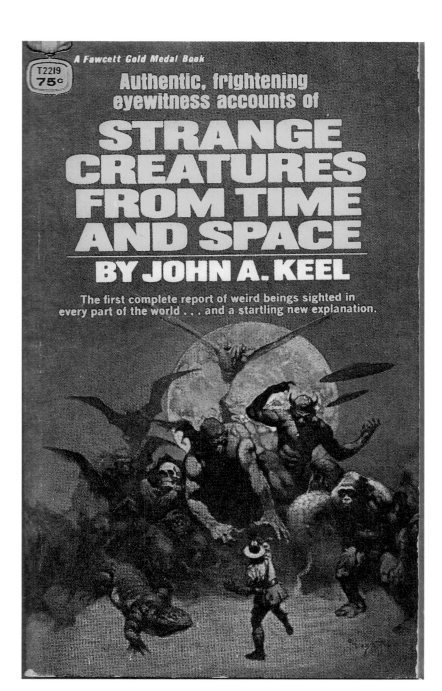

A Fawcett Gold Medal Book

T2219
75c

Authentic, frightening eyewitness accounts of

STRANGE CREATURES FROM TIME AND SPACE

BY JOHN A. KEEL

The first complete report of weird beings sighted in every part of the world . . . and a startling new explanation.

ultraviolet end of the visual spectrum and disappearing with a burst of red in the lower infrared end. Now he develops this idea in full color, as it were.

It would be difficult, if not actually impossible, to find a clearer expression of the mytheme of Radiation: for Keel, the world's mythologies are *literally* vibrations or frequencies along the electromagnetic spectrum (EM) interacting with the vision-generating, mythmaking organ of the human brain. We see what our cultures and religions have conditioned us to see as we interact with these energies, but—and this is the subtle part—there may well be something "out there" interacting with us. Though he often framed the issue in the form of a rhetorical question, Keel clearly believed that there exists in the environment "a mysterious exterior force that has the ability to manipulate us."[41] We are being written, and zapped, and screwed with.

By what? By the superspectrum, a spectrum of energies that, at least at its higher reaches, cannot yet be measured with our present technology and science. Why can't we measure these higher reaches of the superspectrum? Because "it is extradimensional, meaning that it exists outside our own space-time continuum yet influences *everything* within our reality." In a word, it is *occult*. Occult or not, the superspectrum's effects on sensitive biological organs (read: the human brain) are especially obvious. Here is "the source of all paranormal manifestations from extrasensory perception (ESP) to flying saucers, little green men and tall, hairy monsters."[42]

Keel's most famous case of how the superspectrum works was the Mothman of Point Pleasant, West Virginia. In *UFOs*, he had already noted that great winged beings, often headless, haunt the modern contactee experience, very much like medieval demons and angels, and he told tantalizing stories of his traumatic research experiences in West Virginia.[43] Now, in *The Mothman Prophecies* (1975), he tells his readers the full story.

For thirteen months in 1966 and 1967, a seven-foot humanlike brown figure with huge batlike wings, no visible head, and glowing red eyes on its upper chest terrorized the little community of Point Pleasant, West Virginia. The residents at first called it a "birdlike creature," "Birdman," and "Bird-Monster," likened it to an immense Man-Bat, and then landed on the name "the Monster Moth Man" and eventually simply "Mothman," probably because Batman was all the rage on TV then, and this seemed like a real world supervillain to the residents of Point Pleasant (and, besides, "Batman" was already taken). Is it at all relevant here that, again, the Greek for "soul" can also mean "moth"?

Men in Black, UFOs, scary synchronistic experiences with phone lines—the place went more or less nuts for thirteen months. Indeed, the "window" area where the UFOs were appearing—an old ammunition dump ominously called the TNT area with God-only-knows-what buried below—became a veritable parking lot, as the roads filled up with hundreds of cars driving out to watch the strange lights dart about in the sky and men armed with shotguns went monster hunting in the night.

But close readers of Keel already knew how it would all end, since he had given away the final chapter in *UFOs: Operation Trojan Horse*. There Keel reported that in October of 1966 he had a "lengthy long-distance call from a being who was allegedly a UFO entity." He told Keel two things: that many people would die in an Ohio River disaster, and that there would be a huge blackout when President Johnson turned on the Christmas lights in the White House.

On November 3, Keel wrote his journalistic colleague, Mrs. Mary Hyre, in Point Pleasant about the possible river calamity. When he returned to Point Pleasant for Thanksgiving, things got more ominous still. He learned that Mrs. Virginia Thomas, who was living in the very epicenter of the apparitions, was having horrible dreams. She was dreaming "of pleading faces and brightly wrapped Christmas packages floating on the dark water of the Ohio." Then, on December 11, Keel was awakened by another mysterious caller who informed him of an upcoming plane crash in Tucson. The next day, an air force jet careened into a shopping mall in the city.

On December 15, President Johnson hosted the annual tree-lighting ceremony. Keel watched the event on his television in New York City, waiting for the worst. Nothing happened. The tree lit up, and the East Coast stayed lit up. Then, just thirty seconds after the twinkling Christmas tree, an announcer broke into the broadcast: "A bridge between Gallipolis, Ohio, and West Virginia has just collapsed. It was heavily laden with rush-hour traffic. There are no further details as yet."

"I was stunned," Keel writes. "There was only one bridge on that section of the river. The Silver Bridge between Point Pleasant, West Virginia, and Ohio. Christmas packages were floating in the dark waters of the Ohio."[44] There were more than Christmas presents floating in those waters. There were bodies. Thirty-nine individuals died that evening, crushed and drowned in what was, by one account, the worst bridge disaster in American history.[45]

Keel was extremely upset by what happened around Point Pleasant. His editor convinced him that he had to write about it, which is what he eventually did. *The Moth-*

man Prophecies was a commercial success. The book was eventually made into a Hollywood movie starring Richard Gere, which, except for a poignant shot of those floating Christmas presents, captured almost nothing significant about the book. The book, in a later edition, also garnered another Frazetta cover, this one beautifully linking the Mothman directly to the UFO, which was accurate enough. But, alas, the painting also misses the actual appearance of the Mothman, which looked nothing like the image Frazetta painted. Clearly, the artist never read the author.

Frazetta or no Frazetta, the Mothman appeared right alongside television's Batman, and one of the first newspaper articles on the phenomenon clearly linked it with a famous line from the Superman serials: "It's a bird . . . It's a plane . . . It's Superman!" The Mothman article began by humorously cutting things short: "Is it a plane? No, it's a bird."[46]

Not quite. According to different witnesses, the thing stood around seven feet tall and boasted immense shoulders, that is, its physique reproduced the standard he-man frame of the superhero. Reports described clawed hands, a running speed of up to a hundred miles per hour, a flight speed that could do circles around a speeding vehicle, an unnerving scream that blew up a television set, and a strange ability to control people, like a magnet. Weirder still (if that's possible), it seemed to provoke a kind of sacred "sixth sense" of intense fear in many, as if they could "feel" the thing before they could see it.[47] Most of all, though, people spoke, in awed terror, about its haunting, mesmerizing red eyes.

The pop-cultural frames of reference have only become more and more iconic over the decades, as can easily be seen in Jeff Wamsley's *Mothman: Behind the Red Eyes*. Wamsley, a citizen of Point Pleasant and inveterate researcher of all things Mothman, includes in one his books multiple drawings from different artists. Some of the most striking, those of Gary Gibeaut, are absolutely indistinguishable from comic-book art. Stunningly, Gibeaut's Mothman looks very much like a cross between a winged alien and Spider-Man, suggesting once again the "alien Spidey" theme.

The Mothman Prophecies is a weird, scary book. One does not know whether one is reading fiction or reporting or, most likely, reporting mixed in with fiction. I suppose that that is precisely Keel's Fortean point, namely, that reality participates in fiction and fiction in reality. What I find most interesting, though, about Keel is not "whether it all really happened," but the astonished disbelief that he brings to his materials and colleagues in Point Pleasant. Simply put, John Keel gets the sacred, which is

The
MOTHMAN PROPHECIES

JOHN A. KEEL

3.12 FRAZETTA ON THE MOTHMAN

also the scared. We clearly have yet another modern Gnostic on our hands here who *knows* that the world is basically illusory, a sinister sham set up by a stupid deity, who is messing with us.

It is easy to dismiss the exaggerated forms in which an author like John Keel chooses to express his ideas. It is more difficult to dismiss the obvious moral concerns that animate his prose. It is all too easy to find historical errors with respect to the history of religions in Keel's books. They abound. But it is impossible to miss his rage against the destructive demigods and devil theories that are so often "religion." And *whatever* one thinks of such writings, it is simply impossible to miss the profound ways that they resonate with, even as they sharpen and focus, the basic atomythologies of Stan Lee and Jack Kirby and all those gnostic superheroes and battling gods born of this or that radioactive accident, that is, this or that frequency hop along the superspectrum.

GOLDEN CELIBACY, SILVER SUBLIMATIONS, AND SUPER SEXUALITIES

From Plato to Freud, Western culture has long claimed that erotic energies express themselves along what we can well call, following Keel, a superspectrum, which encompasses everything from the humblest sexual obsession or the most vile act of sexual violence to the highest reaches of philosophical revelation, mystical union, and divinization. Remember *Etidorhpa*? The same patterns can easily be seen in the popcultural materials. On the crude end of the spectrum, it seems almost ridiculous to point out the role that male sexual fantasies play in the pulps and some of the more daring comics. Why, there is hardly a single pulp cover that does not sport some barely dressed babe, usually in a seductive pose or compromising position.

It was precisely this sort of sexual humor and explicit display that got the comic-book industry into so much trouble, primarily through the psychoanalyst turned social reformer Frederic Wertham and his *Seduction of the Innocent* (1954). As already noted, this was the book that almost sunk the comic-book industry in the 1950s and led, immediately, to the Comic Book Code Authority of 1954.[48] Wertham's role in all of this has been richly narrated and variously analyzed by Bradford W. Wright, Bart Beaty, and David Hajdu.[49] I need not repeat their work here, only make a few fairly basic observations toward my own ideas about why the radioactive superhero exploded on the scene exactly when he did.

The first thing that needs to be said about Wertham is that his observations were often correct, and that it was primarily the violence and sadism of the comics that so appalled him. As one of dozens of examples, consider the 1952 comic that features on its first page, in Wertham's words now, "a horrible picture of a man shot in the stomach, with a face of agonized pain, and such dialogue as: 'You know as well as I do that any water he'd drink'd pour right out his gut! It'd be MURDER!'" Here it wasn't just the violence that irked Wertham so. It was the audience to whom this gruesome scene was consciously marketed and sold. The name of the publisher of the above scene? Tiny Tots Comics, Inc.[50] This is not a subtle point.

Granted, the sex is a problem for Wertham too, a big problem, but it tends to play second fiddle in his criticisms. When it is invoked, moreover, it is usually because the sex was an adult eroticism being sold to children, or, more often, because it was being linked to graphic violence, grossly sexist attitudes toward women, and various sorts of prejudices toward blacks and Asians (who were, of course, often portrayed as sexual violators of white, blond women).

The difficult truth is that Wertham is a complex and often frankly convincing read. One can easily question his argument that there is a clear causal link between violence in comics and juvenile violence in the real world. Clinical observations that boiled down to "I have never treated a juvenile delinquent who did not read comics" mean almost nothing in an era in which just about every kid in the country read dozens, if not hundreds, of comics each year. One can also object to his notion that reading comics reduces children's vocabularies and leads to illiteracy (the exact opposite is almost certainly the case). It is impossible, however, to deny Wertham's demonstrations of "race hatred" and "race prejudice," that is, the manner in which the comics of the 1940s and '50s were filled with grossly racist, xenophobic, ethnocentric or blindly "patriotic," anti-Semitic, sadistic, and misogynistic tropes. These latter critiques were essentially unanswerable.[51]

What interests me most about Wertham is not these well-known critiques, but their historical and, above all, *erotic* effects. Put more precisely, I am interested in how these critiques played a central role in changing the libidinal organization of the superhero mythologies. By "libidinal organization," I mean something equally precise, that is, how the hero's sexuality is understood by the myths to be related to the hero's superpowers. And here it was Wertham's over-the-top sexual criticisms—crystallized in two consecutive chapters deliciously entitled "I Want to Be a Sex Maniac!" and

"Bumps and Bulges"—that played the key role in what was essentially a massive public process of repression and sublimation. By "repression" and "sublimation" I mean more or less what Wertham's own psychoanalytic training meant, that is, a "pushing down" of libidinal or sexual energies into the unconscious (here a kind of cultural unconscious) until they transform themselves and manifest again on a higher "sublime" plane as something else, something more culturally acceptable, more symbolic and safer. Like radioactive superheroes.

"Comic books stimulate children sexually," Wertham bluntly explained in a key passage. And this "is a sexual arousal which amounts to a seduction."[52] What he meant by this was that comic books play an active, *causal* role in juvenile delinquency and sexual pathology. They are not simply fantasies that become problems when children with problems pick them up, which is what his critics were suggesting (Wertham bluntly calls this denial of direct causality "pseudo-scientific drivel"[53]). Comic books actually *cause* children to be problems: they are *temptations* and *seductions* into real-world violence and inappropriate sexual fantasies and acts, including and especially homosexuality.[54]

Hence his two most famous case studies took on Wonder Woman and Batman. In Wonder Woman's Amazonian pact with her fellow female warriors and their constant battles against "those wicked men," Wertham sees clear and unmistakable signs of a glorified lesbianism. He is particularly upset with the argument that an "advanced femininity" is being explored in the comic books, that young women are breaking out of their usual roles through the fantasy of the Amazonians. Wertham complains bitterly of such awful "anti-feminine" role models: "They do not work. They are not homemakers. They do not bring up a family. Mother-love is entirely absent. Even when Wonder Woman adopts a girl, there are Lesbian overtones." Wertham misses, completely, what a young girl might see in a strong female figure like Wonder Woman.

It is at this point that Wertham invokes, in complete disdain, fellow psychologist William Mouton Marston. Marston invented Wonder Woman in *All-Star Comics* #8 (1941) after his experiments with the first lie detector, which he invented at the tender age of twenty-two, led him to conclude that women were more honest, efficient, and reliable. "An early champion of women's rights," historian of the genre Mike Conroy observes, "he conceived the Amazon Princess as a counter to what he considered to be an overly masculine-dominated culture."[55] Wertham quotes Marston's reasoning only to reject it: "Who wants to be a girl? And that's the point. Not even girls want to be girls. . . . The obvious remedy is to create a feminine character with all the strength of Superman." Wertham probably agreed with Marston, though, on why the decked-out Amazonian also attracted the boys: "Give (men) an alluring woman stronger than themselves to submit to and they'll be proud to become her willing slaves."[56]

But Wonder Woman plays a minor role in Wertham's text compared to "Batman and his boy," that is, Bruce Wayne and "Dick" Grayson (the suggestive scare quotes are Wertham's).[57] Following an earlier California psychiatrist whom he does not name, Wertham detects "a subtle atmosphere of homoeroticism" pervading the adventures of the Dynamic Duo.

Okay, not so subtle. He notes that Robin's legs are bare and often discreetly spread, that the couple enacts "a wish dream of two homosexuals living together," and that female characters like the Catwoman are portrayed as threats to the intimacy and safety of the male duo.[58]

Wertham had a point, and even Batman listened. After Wertham's book appeared, Batman soon found a new, if rather cool, love interest in Batwoman (in 1956). Things were straighter now, and presumably safer. That is, until ABC got a hold of things and in 1966 aired its first episode of the wildly popular *Batman* television series, thereby transforming the Dynamic Duo into what would become the veritable archetype of gay camp.[59] Not that it was only the homoerotic that returned from repression in ABC's *Batman*. The series also included any number of memorable heterosexual episodes and lines, like those uttered by the gorgeous and leathered Catwoman to a sexually naïve Robin, that Boy Wonder: "Hi, Robin, my name is Pussycat, but you can call me Cat!"[60] Cat indeed.

I am certainly not denying the sex that Wertham saw in the comics. It's there. My point is a very different one. The sexual energies carried by all those breasts, buttocks, and bumps did not just go away when Wertham went public and Congress got involved. In effect, all that sex went underground, morphed into something else, and reappeared above the surface in a sublimated form, in this case, in the idealized body and powers of the radioactive superhero. Put most succinctly, we might say that whereas the libidinal organization of the Golden Age superhero generally separated sex *from* the superpower, the libidinal organization of the Silver Age superhero tended to sublimate sex *into* the superpower. Hence what took superpowers away in the Golden Age bestowed superpowers in the Silver Age. This is the secret life of the mytheme of Radiation. It is also why the mytheme did not take off immediately after 1945, which is what one would expect if these creative processes were entirely conscious and simply cultural. The historical truth is that the superhero genre effectively *died* when the bomb was dropped and did not reappear with any real force until the late 1950s and early '60s, that is, shortly after Wertham's censorship campaign.

There was sex enough, of course, in the Golden Age (we're all here, aren't we?). But the sex tended to be separated from the metaphysical energies of the superpowers. Thus Superman is partly a fantasy to get the girls, and Joe Shuster drew erotic bondage art as he drew the flying impenetrable man in the red and blue suit, but he did not bring the two together, not at least in any obvious, public way.[61] This Golden Age separation of sex from the superhero finds further support in the observations of Umberto Eco, who has noticed "the platonic dimensions of his affections, the implicit vow of chastity" that define the character of Superman.[62]

Echoing Eco, I would also point out that the major superhero with the most active sex life, that is, Batman or playboy Bruce Wayne, also possesses the fewest superpowers. Indeed, *he has none*. The metaphysical implications of the erotics of Superman and Batman, then, are fairly obvious: the superpowers and the sex draw on the exact same superspectrum. In the Golden Age, these metaphysical energies can be used for superpowers or for sexual expression, but not both, not at least at the same time. Like many forms of conservative religion and asceticism, the Golden Age effectively *separates* the two energies (even as this very separation implies, indeed demands, that the two energies are really the same energy in two different forms).

In a very similar spirit, some have speculated that the superpowers of a comic-book hero and the sexual powers of its creator (or most devoted readers) are inversely related: the more superpowers, the less sex; the less superpowers, the more sex. This rule again holds for the earliest and most archetypal figures of the American comic-book genre: Superman and Batman. Whereas the two young Jewish Cleveland men, Jerry Siegel and Joe Shuster, who created the almost invincible Superman were nerdy, shy, and confessedly awkward around the opposite sex, Bob Kane, who dreamed up a Batman without any supernatural powers whatsoever, was tall, handsome, and dashing.[63] Who needs X-ray vision when one lives in what is basically a playboy mansion? The correlations and their implications are almost ridiculously obvious.

The history of the American superhero comic book, then, is also a coded erotics. Little wonder that much of the inspiration for the earliest superheroes came from sexualized pulp magazines, or that the earliest publishers and distributors of the genre also dealt in soft porn.[64] Little wonder that the comic book has always been hounded by accusations of "obscenity." Or that Jack Cole, the 1940s creator of Plastic Man, the sunglassed pink guy who can stretch his body to any shape, also happened to be the first and probably most famous cartoonist for *Playboy* magazine. All that pink stretching wasn't for nothing, you know.[65] Or that the psychologist William Mouton Marston, who, as we have seen, invented Wonder Woman after the Greek Amazon myths (under the penname of Charles Moulton), got into trouble with his editor, Sheldon Mayer, mostly because he was always trying to get Wonder Woman (or any other woman, for that matter) tied up. One of his stories involved a contest to see who could rope up the most girls, and another illustrated some form of bondage in seventy-five panels! Mayer did his best to edit out Marston's fantasies, but the original bondage fetish remained coded in Wonder Woman's truth-telling golden lasso.[66] The lie detector again.

The more recent film versions of the Marvel stories handle this ever-present eroticism very differently. Consider the blockbuster films *Spider-Man 2* and *X2*. The central narrative of the former film revolves around Peter Parker's love life and his troubling inability to, well, shoot his white stuff—in this case, gooey webs out of his wrists.[67] As Peter's love life collapses, so too does his superpower to spin webs and leap from tall buildings. As he learns to love, he simultaneously regains his confidence and his mystical powers, white stuff and all. The message could not be any clearer: the two powers are the same power on some deeper metaphysical level. Similarly, when a young mutant boy finally breaks the news to his parents about his own supernormal gifts in *X2: X-Men United*, the event is framed around a classical "coming out of the closet" scenario: to be a mutant and to be gay are more or less interchangeable here.[68]

This most recent motif—sexual expression *as* superpower—witnesses in turn to the indubitable fact that it is around early adolescence, that is, around puberty and the onslaught of the "secret" and largely misunderstood powers of sexuality, that the American superhero comic book has always revolved. Hence it has been the pubescent male that has always overwhelmingly defined the main audience of the American superhero comic book. And what simultaneously gifts and curses the boy or young man as reader/hero is the mysterious X-factor of sexual maturation, understood (quite correctly) by the myths not simply as a biological instinct, but also as a potential occult energy or "superpower."

Whether framed most recently in a heteroerotic or a homoerotic code, these latter examples make a rather transparent linkage between the erotic and the super-human and work at the same time against *both* the asexual norm as manifested in the archetypal Golden Age character of Superman *and* the sublimation techniques of the Silver Age. Very much against the celibacy and sublimation models, now sexual expression and superpowers manifest *together*, suggesting in the process, once again, that their energies are in fact linked on some profound metaphysical level. This new erotics, I would suggest, is precisely what heralds what we might call the Next Age superhero.

*O*RIENTING THE NEXT AGE BODY: THE PRACTICE OF TANTRIC YOGA

I suspect, but can hardly prove, that the libidinal organization of the Next Age su-perhero is deeply indebted to the mytheme of Orientation, and that this particular superbody is at least partly shaped by Tantric yoga models of sexual energy and its hydraulic transformations through the chakra system of the subtle body. We saw this quite explicitly with Alan Moore and Grant Morrison in our opening salvo. A few more words are in order here now.

The chakras or "energy centers" of various Hindu, Buddhist, and Taoist systems of yoga were a central feature of the American counterculture and are now staples of the New Age and metaphysical scenes. In what is probably the most historically influential version of these in the West, the Hindu Tantric system set out in Sir John Woodroffe's *The Serpent Power*, an occult feminine "Energy" or Shakti called the "Coiled One" or Kundalini is imagined as a sleeping serpent coiled up at the base of the spine. Once aroused, the serpent power spirals up from the anal and genital centers through the stomach, heart, and throat regions into the "third eye" and core of the brain, the *brahmarandhra* or "portal of cosmic being," and then explodes out the top of the skull through the "crown chakra," through which the mystic realizes his or her true nature as an immortal energetic superconsciousness. Shakti and Shiva, Energy and Conscious-ness, are now realized, and erotically united, as One.

All of this is quite relevant to the Next Age superhero, since Woodroffe's books were widely read in the human potential movement and the American countercultural embrace of Asian religions in the 1960s and '70s, as well as in the New Age movement of the 1980s and '90s, that is, in the exact decades that produced our contemporary comic-book writers and readers, including superwriters like Alan Moore and Grant Morrison.

Hence Morrison's portrayal of the beautiful Phoenix in his famous *New X-Men* run (2001–4). Phoenix is an omnipotent supergoddess who possesses the human body of Jean Grey in order to do things like blip out the entire universe for a second or effortlessly bend space and time to her whim. In terms of cosmic scope and pure power, Phoenix has few, if any, peers. Now consider how writer Morrison explains to his readers how Phoenix takes over Jean's body: "the Phoenix consciousness accesses its human host via the so-called Crown Chakra port at the top of the skull" (NXM 154.6). In other words, the Phoenix consciousness manifests in Jean's body through Tantric yoga.

Hence as we move toward the end of the second millennium and beyond, more and more superheroes begin to speak and act like Hindu or Buddhist mystics, and numerous figures (far too many to list here) are portrayed in the lotus posture of yoga. Figures like Kirby's Eternals, Sharkosh the Shaman in *Conan the Barbarian* (C 1.19), Wolverine, Phoenix, Doctor Manhattan, Aleister Crowley in *Promethea*, and Magneto all take on this classic meditating pose, often with waves of metaphysical energy, plasma, or fire emanating from their subtle superbodies.

A concrete historical example, again from the influential 1960s, may help here. Consider Gopi Krishna's classic *Kundalini: The Evolutionary Energy in Man* (1967). A humble Kashmiri civil servant, Krishna was meditating on Christmas Day of 1937 when he found himself overwhelmed with a fantastic energy stream erupting through his spinal column and out the top of his head in a classic experience of the kundalini. What makes Krishna so interesting and so relevant for our purposes here are the very explicit ways he understood these occult energies as the secret force of evolution itself (Radiation to Mutation). For Krishna, at least, the kundalini was "the evolutionary energy in man" or the secret "mechanism of evolution." Indeed, he described it as a "superintelligent energy" or "living electricity" that intends to transform our very flesh until we become veritable gods on earth (Divinization).[69]

Krishna was very clear, moreover, that these occult energies, at once divine and dangerous, are the deepest metaphysical catalyst of both sexual desire *and* spiritual transcendence, that is, he insisted on a deep link between sex and spirit. Hence his teachings that the reproductive system is "reversible," and that its spinal streams of energy can be transformed into a kind of "radiation"—yes, he actually uses the word, and often—that activates the cosmic portal in the brain core.[70] He also taught that celibacy, although necessary at a certain stage of practice, is a real mistake as a general rule, since it deprives the next generation of the transmission of the biological, cellular, even atomic transformations that the occult energies effect in the body-mind of the empowered mystic. In our own present terms, although he can be understood in all three, Gopi Krishna was in the Next Age X-Men mutant camp, not the Superman celibacy ideal or the Silver Age sublimation school.

Krishna also insisted that these evolutionary energies are "the biological basis" of genius, and that they can produce a whole host of supernormal capacities. These are the *siddhis* or "superpowers" of Indian yogic lore. How does the kundalini grant such things? By opening up the spinal channel and physically transforming the body-brain in order to make it a more translucent "filter" of the ocean of consciousness and energy that constitutes our true supernature. The manifestation of the Phoenix consciousness, we might say.

This Ocean of Mind, Krishna explains, is "a boundless world of knowledge, embracing the present, past, and future, commanding all the sciences, philosophies, and arts ever known or that will be known in the ages to come . . . a formless, measureless ocean of wisdom from which, drop by drop, knowledge has filtered and will continue to filter into the human brain."[71] I cannot help but recall here Ray Palmer's experience of a "universal record or storehouse of meaning" and his conviction that "somewhere, somehow, the total sum of all knowledge exists." Recall also that it was a broken back, that is, an accidentally opened spinal column that initiated Palmer into a world of paranormal powers, psychical experiences, and flying saucers. As with Gopi Krishna's evolutionary energy, Cosmic Mind could filter in now.

And so the Golden Age handled the superpower of human sexuality in one way, the Silver Age in another, the Next Age in still another—through transcendent celibacy, radioactive sublimation, and yogic mutation. Each era produced a different superbody through its own unique cultural repressions and sublimations. But they all had to deal with what John Keel called the superspectrum, which, like the human spine, was sexual on one end and spiritual on the other. Put more mythically, they all had to deal with the age-old truth that a hero or god-man is born not from a radioactive accident, but from an erotic union at once human and divine. Now *that's* a libido.

4 *MUTATION*

X-MEN BEFORE THEIR TIME

*YOU ARE A MUTANT, KURT. I CAN HELP YOU FIND
YOUR TRUE POTENTIAL.*

*PROFESSOR XAVIER TO KURT WAGNER
(NIGHTCRAWLER) IN **GIANT-SIZE X-MEN** #1,
1975*

et's put the date at 1960. If Einstein's mathematical demonstration that matter, including the matter of the human body, is really frozen energy and the subsequent dropping of the atomic bomb in 1945 inspired the mytheme of Radiation, it was the appearance of Darwin's *Origin of Species* in 1859 and the discovery of the double-helix structure of DNA in 1953 by Francis Crick and James Watson around which the mytheme of Mutation was about to develop. It had been a full century since individuals began to realize with the force of a religious revelation that life is transhuman, that the human being as we know it (as we presently *are* it) is a transitional phenomenon on the way to either extinction or something else. But popular culture still lacked public ways to express this familiar, disturbing, liberating, uncanny truth. That was about to change.

RADIATION TO MUTATION: THE MANHATTAN PROJECT AND THE BIRTH OF PROFESSOR X

In an elegant essay about "Growing Up Mutant," Lawrence Watt-Evans described how purchasing a copy of *X-Men* #1 in Bedford, Massachusetts, in the summer of 1963 changed his life. At eight going on nine, he was not particularly fond of Marvel Comics. Indeed, he found them odd, even a bit stupid: "the Hulk and the Thing never did anything clever, they just kept hitting the bad guys until they fell down. . . . Iron Man always seemed to have exactly the gadget he needed, and Dr. Strange didn't make any

4.1   THE COMING OF THE X-MEN

sense at all."[1] Not that the DC standards were much better: "Most superheroes—well, who'd want to be Batman, really?"

But the X-Men were different. Watt-Evans explains: "These weren't aliens or super-scientists or magicians. They were mutants. I knew about mutants. I suspected I *was* a mutant. Seriously, I did. My parents had worked on the Manhattan Project, building atomic bombs, during the Second World War—who could say I *wasn't* a mutant?"[2]

The kid had a point. After all, in that same *X-Men* #1 comic book, Professor Xavier, the wheelchair-bound leader of the X-Men, leads his new recruits to make the exact same connection between Radiation and Mutation when he tells his new recruits how he became a mutant: his parents had worked on the first atomic bomb, that is, on the Manhattan Project. He even wonders out loud if he may be the *first* such radiated mutant, thereby explicitly suggesting a causal link between the earlier mytheme of Radiation and the later one of Mutation. Later, we learn that the Beast, a member of the first X-Men team, possesses a similar Radiation-to-Mutation genesis: his father was "an ordinary laborer" at an atomic site (XM 357). Eventually, the motif became nearly universal, as, for example, when Roy Thomas, who took over the series with issue #20, observed in a recent commentary that *all* of the parents of the original X-Men had worked on the Manhattan Project.[3]

Perhaps this notion is a carryover from an earlier mutant story that Stan Lee wrote the year before the X-Men debuted, "The Man in the Sky" (1962). Here Lee could only imagine a mutant superpower (the man could fly) in an atomic scientist who had absorbed small doses of radiation in his work.[4] We can almost track, then, the process through which the mytheme of Radiation evolved into the mytheme of Mutation.

Such patterns would continue apace. Responding to a generation that feared the possibility of genetic mutations as a result of atomic radiation (or, interestingly enough, LSD), the comic-book writers would eventually revision the X-Men along similar atomic lines. In December of 1975, the X-Men thus became "Children of the atom, students of Charles Xavier, MUTANTS." Mutation and Radiation were now inseparable parts of the same basic mythos. Which is all to say that the early mutant fantasies of Watt-Evans, the son of two atomic scientists, fit seamlessly into the origins of the new Marvel Universe.

And there was another shared dynamic behind this gradual morphing of Radiation into Mutation. There was *eros* again. If the mytheme of Radiation was a kind of pop sublimation of the graphic "sex and violence" of the 1950s comics into the respectable radioactive "superpowers" of the 1960s superhero, the mytheme of Mutation carried very similar morphing metaphysical energies, and this in at least three ways.

First, within the X-Men mythology itself, there is the already noted observation that a mutant potential first actualizes around puberty, that is, with the onset of sexual maturity. This is as true in the earliest story arcs as it is in the latest. Hence the rather matter-of-fact observation of geneticist Dr. Kavita Rao in *Astonishing X-Men* #2 that a "child's mutant power usually manifests at puberty." The mutant power and human sexuality are thus explicitly and consistently linked *by the standard narrative*.

Second, biologically speaking, mutations and the evolutionary process are carried through sex, sex, and more sex. It takes a whole lot of sex for evolution to happen. Mutation, then, whether articulated as such or not, is a thoroughly erotic mytheme. In the *New X-Men* series, writer Grant Morrison makes this quite explicit in the voice of Angel, whom he has reimagined as a tough but insecure black teenage girl. As Angel is trying to convince another mutant named Beak to have sex with her in the forest, she explains the facts to her unwilling partner: "Even the *birds* and *bees* managed to figure *this* out, you moron . . . it's genetic evolution. It's the whole *point* of the X-Men School!" (NXM 136.7).

Third, the writing itself becomes erotic. In the Morrison story arc, for example, Emma, "the X-Men's only qualified sex-therapist" (NXM 131.15), controls an entire angry crowd by psychically hitting their "bliss button," that is, by inducing them to orgasm (never named as such, of course) (NXM 118.11). Morrison also explicitly linked the motif of mutation with that of sexual orientation, and especially homosexuality (this, by the way, is the probable source for the *X2* "coming out" scene discussed in our previous chapter). Hence a protest sign proclaiming that "God Hates Mutants" (as opposed to "fags") appears in one issue (NXM 117.5), and "LEV 20:15" (the biblical passage forbidding men to lay down with men) is sprayed over the sign of Professor Xavier's school for the gifted in the next (NXM 118.8). The Beast, moreover, will fake being gay simply to attract tabloid attention and make a social point (NXM 131.8, 134.11). Morrison is certainly making *his* point. Gathered around a campfire, the vaguely Buddhist character of Xorn is teaching his students what it is like to be a mutant: "Like you, my difference made me a *target* of ignorance and fear." A student wryly responds: "Different. Hyuk. You mean, like 'gay,' right?" (NXM 135.20). Right.

And the erotic themes go on and on. Emma and Scott have a telepathic affair (NXM 136.17), one effect of which will be Jean Grey-Summers, Scott's wife, manifesting her cosmic alter ego, the Phoenix, out of erotic jealousy (NXM 139.6). Scott castrates a statue of David with an errant blast from his eyes (NXM 118.6). And this is before we even get to a figure like Mystique, who is basically a naked blue woman with, in some versions, a skin-tight covering—is that a covering?—drawn in every possible suggestive pose.

And then there is all the sex and erotic humor behind the scenes, like artist David Cockrum's advice to future artists attempting to draw Nightcrawler: do *not* position his devil's tail in such a way that it emerges between his legs. The results, he warned, will not be productive.[5]

Obviously, then, the X-Men became both sexy and "in"; they were dealing with some of the most potent social issues of the day; and mutation had become an effective fantasy code for social and sexual difference. So why, then, did the series barely survive throughout the 1960s? This is the question to which my chapter title alludes. Why *did* the basic concept of the X-Men remain a minor one after it was first introduced in 1963, but then become a megahit in 1975, when it was relaunched in *Giant Size X-Men* #1? Why did a series that never really caught on in its initial version become the very bedrock of the later Marvel Universe?

Watt-Evans has an answer for us, and it is as simple as it is convincing: the X-Men caught on in 1975 and exploded in popularity from there not because the basic concept had changed that much, *but because American culture had*. Basically, the counterculture of the 1960s and early '70s had laid a very solid foundation for the mutant mythology to build on—a foundation that simply was not widely available in 1963 when the team first appeared (the counterculture did not definitively begin until around 1964). "The comic book I fell in love with in 1963 had just been a dozen years ahead of its time," Watt-Evans writes. "The world caught up with it eventually, but *X-Men* was there first."[6]

I am in complete agreement with Watt-Evans that it was the American counterculture that laid the social foundation for the plausibility and popularity of the X-Men mythology. I would, however, like to qualify his suggestion that the X-Men were there first. If we stick to the immediate history of comic books, he is correct enough. If, however, we expand our historical view to the larger Super-Story we are telling in these pages, we must conclude that the X-Men were definitely not there first—not even close.

Whatever immediate sources Stan Lee and Jack Kirby drew on in the spring of 1963, they were in fact tapping into a set of Western biological, occult, and psychical research traditions that had already been interacting with each other for almost ex-actly a century and, moreover, would continue to interact with one another well after the X-Men made their not-so-successful debut. That full X-history extended from the public dawn of evolutionary theory in 1859, with the appearance of Darwin's *Origin of Species*; through the countless séance rooms, Spiritualist circles, and highest echelons of European and American intellectual culture in the nineteenth and early twentieth centuries; into the birth of the human potential movement and the French, British, and American countercultures in the 1960s and '70s; and, from there, into the paranormal espionage projects on both sides of the Iron Curtain during the Cold War. Through the complicated, always controversial histories of these latter secret programs, this X-history would even make its way into the inner halls of the Pentagon, Red Square, the KGB, the CIA, Congress, and the White House in the 1970s, '80s, and early '90s.

Nightcrawler, the occult X-Man par excellence, was not attacking the president of the United States in his own Oval Office, as we have it in the opening scene of the film *X-Men 2*, but the superhero "mutants" had indeed come to Washington (and Moscow). Here is how.

THE MORNING OF THE MAGICIANS

It was the morning of the magicians, otherwise known as 1960. Two men, Louis Pauwels, an editor, publisher, and self-confessed mystic, and Jacques Bergier, a chemical engineer, former Resistance fighter, and practicing alchemist, had just published *Le Matin des Magiciens* in France. The book came out in England as *The Dawn of Magic* in 1963, and a year later in the U.S. as *The Morning of the Magicians*.[7] The result was a veritable occult explosion with echoes that would reverberate for decades through the French, British, and American countercultures. Gary Lachman, who participated in the later 1970s versions of this counterhistory as a founding member of the rock band Blondie, describes the cultural effect of the book in stark and humorous terms:

FRANCE HAD A HISTORY OF INTEREST IN THE OCCULT . . . BUT PARIS IN 1960 WAS THE
CAPITAL OF FUTILITY, NIHILISM AND DREARY "AUTHENTICITY." IT WAS THE PARIS OF
JEAN PAUL SARTRE AND ALBERT CAMUS, OF "NAUSEA" AND "THE ABSURD," OF ALIEN-
ATION AND OF BEING ***ENGAGÉ***, OF BLACK TURTLENECKS AND ***WAITING FOR GODOT***.
IN SUCH AN ATMOSPHERE, A BOOK ON MAGIC WOULD BE THE LAST THING ONE WOULD
THINK WOULD DO WELL. BUT WITHIN WEEKS OF ITS PUBLICATION, ***LE MATIN DES***

MAGICIENS HAD BOTH BANKS OF THE SEINE TALKING ABOUT ALCHEMY, EXTRATERRES-

TRIALS, LOST CIVILIZATIONS, ESOTERICISM, CHARLES FORT, SECRET SOCIETIES, HIGHER

STATES OF CONSCIOUSNESS, AND THE HERMETIC ORDER OF THE GOLDEN DAWN. . . .

[THE BOOK] HAD THE EFFECT OF A FLYING SAUCER LANDING AT CAFÉ DEUX MAGOTS.[8]

It was Jacques Bergier's alchemy and his enthusiasm for quantum physics that made Pauwels finally realize that traditional mystical ideas could be married to modern science, that modern physics *is* modern magic—in short, the mytheme of Radiation. It was physics again that convinced him that the fantastic was not "out there" in some other transcendent world, but right here, in the very heart of matter and the world as it evolved toward a future superconsciousness and what the two authors called, rather beautifully, "That Infinity Called Man."

Significantly, *The Morning of the Magicians* was rooted in the authors' own mystical experiences of the fantastic as real, or, better, the real as fantastic. Pauwels thus freely confesses that the book would not likely have been written "if Bergier and I had not on more than one occasion had an impression of being in contact—actually, physically—with another world."[9] This certainly helps explain their attraction to such impossible ideas as contact with alien intelligences and the existence of parallel universes. This also explains their obvious affection for Charles Fort, science fiction, and Superman allusions. The book positively swims with traditional Fortean, sci-fi, and superheroic themes.

Here are just a few impossible things gleaned from one of those wonderful old-fashioned tables of contents:

- "ALCHEMY AND MODERN PHYSICS"
- "IN WHICH BERGIER BREAKS A SAFE WITH A BLOW-LAMP AND CARRIES OFF A BOTTLE OF URANIUM UNDER HIS ARM" (BERGIER WAS A SECRET AGENT WHO, ACCORDING TO THE BACK COVER FLAP, "WAS INVOLVED IN THE DESTRUCTION OF THE GERMAN ATOMIC PLANT AT PEENEMUNDE")
- "ATOMIC BOMBARDMENTS AND INTERPLANETARY VESSELS IN 'SACRED TEXTS'"
- "THE GERMANS AND ATLANTIS"
- "THE 'UNKNOWN SUPERMAN'"
- "MARTIANS AT NUREMBURG"
- "IT IS DARKER THAN YOU THOUGHT"
- "PARAPSYCHOLOGY AND PSYCHOANALYSIS"
- "AN INVISIBLE SOCIETY OF MUTANTS?"

The goal here, it seems, was not to believe this or that, but to put everything and anything on the table until the reader's sense of reality was thoroughly shaken, or deeply offended, or oddly inspired—or all three at once. Read literally, the book is perfectly outrageous. Read fantastically, that is, as an act of imagination in touch with some deeper stream of physical and cultural reality, the book is perfectly prescient.

The book's last chapter, "Some Reflections on the Mutants," is especially striking for the way it seems to predict the various evolutionary visions of the countercultures and human potential spiritualities that were about to explode on the scene in such astonishing numbers. Hence Lachman begins his study of "the mystic sixties and the dark side of the Age of Aquarius" in the France of 1960 with this book and these two authors, whom he credits as the central creators of the mutant-myth that would become so central to the hippie movement.

Lachman explicitly invokes *The X-Men* as an immediate influence here. Its 1963 vision of "mutant teenagers with weird powers who band together for support in a world that won't accept them" uncannily predicted (or helped produce) the events of 1966, when a large group of teenagers banded together in a place called Haight-Ashbury for very similar reasons. These hippies, as they came to be known, also called themselves mutants. Lachman notes that the *San Francisco Oracle* for January of 1967 even published a "Manifesto for Mutants," which went like this:

> Mutants! Know now that you exist!
> They have hid you in cities
> And clothed you in fools clothes
> Know now that you are free.[10]

The rest is, as we say, history. Whether, of course, one happens to think that this is a history to forget and repress or one to remember and develop further depends largely on whether or not one experiences oneself as such a mutant.

COSMOS, CONSCIOUSNESS, AND COUNTERCULTURE: ESALEN AND THE X-MEN

There were in fact multiple precursors of this mutant myth and both high and low versions of its cultural expression.[11] There were Fort's books, of course, especially his *Wild Talents*, which reads like a playful but serious study of real-world mutants. There was also the pulp science fiction of the 1940s and '50s, which through editors and magazines like Ray Palmer's *Amazing Stories* and John W. Campbell's *Astounding Science Fiction* made the theme of paranormal powers, imagined as either evolving buds of our future supernature or as reemerging potentials long lost through the pampering of civilization, a standard of the genre. Indeed, sci-fi writer, science writer, and paranormal theorist Damien Broderick goes so far as to call the theme of evolved paranormal powers a "fetish" of this period.[12]

There were also institutional, cultural, and intellectual experiments along these same "mutant" lines. One of the best known, most influential, and certainly most sophisticated of these found expression at the Esalen Institute in Big Sur, California, just three and a half hours down the coast from the San Francisco Bay Area, where the young mutants would eventually gather at places like Berkeley and at the corner of Haight and Ashbury.

Down in Big Sur, well before the mutant hippies, in the fall of 1962, two young Stanford graduates, Michael Murphy (b. 1930) and Richard Price (1930–86), cofounded a little community of visionaries in a transformed spa motel on a cliff. They soon named their little enterprise the Esalen Institute, after a Native American tribal group (the Esselen) that once populated the area. The place quickly became both the original home of the human potential movement and a countercultural mecca.

Murphy and Price adapted the key idea of "human potential" from the British American writer Aldous Huxley, who had spoken of something he called "human potentialities." Much indebted to his famous experiments with psychedelics (another keyword that he helped coin and another countercultural subject that was quickly linked to Mutation, in both highly negative and highly positive ways[13]), Huxley used the expression "human potentialities" to argue that human consciousness and the human body possess vast untapped resources of Mind and energy. Consciousness, Huxley thought, is not something produced without remainder by the brain. It is something more likely *filtered through* and *reduced by* the brain, much as a television set or radio receives a distant signal that is not really in the box (or the brain). Think Ray Palmer's storehouse of knowledge or Gopi Krishna's Cosmic Mind filtering into the brain. Consciousness in its true nature, then, is something to capitalize for Huxley. It is essentially transcendent and ultimately cosmic in nature and scope. He called it Mind at Large.

Drawing on such altered states and altered words (and Frederic Myers), Murphy would go on to suggest that the human potential includes all sorts of extraordinary powers that are "supernormal," from psychical abilities like clairvoyance and telepathy, to extraordinary physical phenomena like dramatic healings, to, in a few rare cases (like Teresa of Avila, Joseph of Copertino, and Daniel D. Home), apparent levitation or flight. All of these things, of course, have been exaggerated in religious literature, folklore, and modern fantasy as supernatural, but, according to authors like Murphy, they are better understood as foreshadowings or intuitions of the hidden potentials of evolution. Seen in this light, pop-cultural genres are essentially human-potential genres in disguise, genres that "might prefigure luminous knowings and powers that can be realized by the human race," as Murphy put it in his 1992 magnum opus, *The Future of the Body*.[14]

So, too, Murphy sees modern sports as a kind of paranormal theater in which supernormal capacities and altered states of energy are commonly evoked and ex-perienced "in the zone." Here he echoes the ancient martial arts traditions of East Asia (tai' chi, karate, aikido, chi kung, kung fu, etc.), in which sport, subtle energies, and paranormal powers are profoundly linked. These, I must add, played a major role in the various 1970s martial arts titles of the superhero comics, thus constituting yet another line of Orientation. Hence one of my own favorites, the Iron Fist story arc of Roy Thomas and Gil Kane. Some of the stranger moments of sports lore that Murphy has documented in great detail also bear a distant relationship to one of the crazier genres of comic books that I adored as a kid: the occult sports genre.

Much like the martial art masters and the athletes, Murphy most of all wanted a *practice* to actualize the evolutionary potentials. So too did the institute. Esalen imag-ined itself from the very beginning as a kind of alternative private academy for this evolving future of the body, that is, as a place where the human potentialities hinted at in psychedelic, psychical, and mystical experiences could be supported, nurtured, and developed further through consistent transformative practices and a stable in-stitutional structure.

Consider, for example, the case of George Leonard, *Look* journalist, education reformer, and later aikido master who coined the phrase "the human potential move-ment" with Murphy in 1965. Leonard was well known in the late 1960s for his radical models of education reform. One of the opening scenes of his wildly popular *Education and Ecstasy* (1968) has Leonard entering a classroom and sensing a young witch whose psychic powers, he realizes, are laced with an obvious and dangerous eroticism. He can feel his skin tingling as he exits the room and wonders about the young girl's fate in a superficial and uncomprehending world. In Leonard's model of ecstatic education,

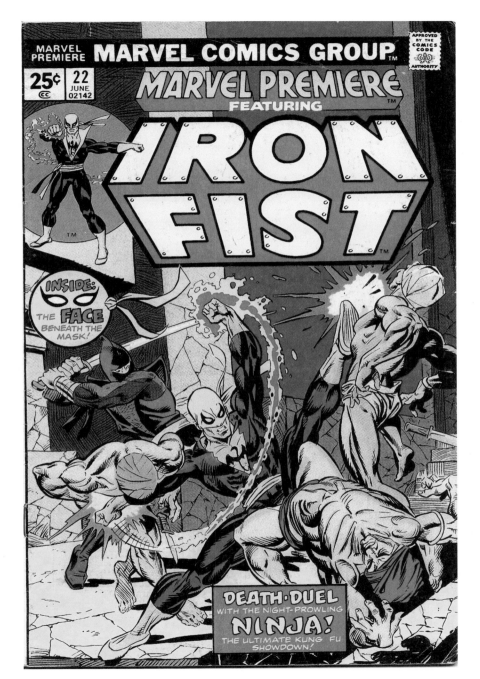

4.3   THE OCCULT SPORTS COMIC

the typical American high school classroom is a place where occult talents are first manifested (often around puberty and the appearance of the sexual powers) and then cruelly crushed under the weight of social control, disbelief, and pure neglect.[15] The young woman will forget about her own human potential, about her own magico-erotic superpowers. She *must* forget them to survive in this particular social world.

If this is beginning to sound like the base mythology of the X-Men, that is, if Esalen sounds more than a little like Professor Xavier's school for mutants, well, then you have some idea of where this is all going. If you also already know that the language of actualizing human potential is omnipresent in the X-Men stories, as my opening epigraph makes clear, you are even closer. If you imagine, however, that our story goes back to New York City in 1963 with Lee and Kirby, or even to Big Sur in 1962 with Murphy and Price, you are quite mistaken. As we have seen already with the my-themes of Alienation and Radiation, it is my central intention to demonstrate that the mytheme of Mutation possesses a "secret life," that is, that the superhero mythologies involving mutation are deeply indebted to the earlier Spiritualist, psychical research, and metaphysical traditions.

In terms of the present, one only need point to Michael Murphy's *The Future of the Body*, an eight-hundred-page masterwork that is without peer in the history of the literature on the mystical and occult potentials of evolution. Put mythically, this is something that Professor Xavier could have written for his private school for the gifted—a kind of textbook for educating mutants in the theory, history, and practice of their Fortean wild talents. Murphy, however, was hardly the first to propose that evolution may hide within its mysterious processes much more than pure chance and nonmeaning. Indeed, Murphy's own primary inspiration was none other than the Indian philosopher and spiritual teacher Sri Aurobindo, who, as we noted in chapter 2, developed an elaborate visionary metaphysics pointing toward a highly evolved spiritual Superman in the second decade of the twentieth century. But there were others still.

We have already seen, with respect to both the ancient-astronaut thesis and Carl Sagan (Alienation) and the mystical implications of quantum physics and Niels Bohr (Radiation), how the lines between "popular" and "elite" theories are not always so clear, and how what many assume to be popular or "pseudoscientific" ideas in fact have deep and distinguished prehistories. We can see the same patterns here again in Mutation, and with no less a scientist than Francis Crick, the codiscoverer of the DNA molecule. In 1973, Crick wrote a paper with Leslie Orgel on directed panspermia, "the theory that organisms were deliberately transmitted to the earth by intelligent beings on another planet." What they actually had in mind here was early life as a kind of "infection" of microorganisms stabilized and carried for millions of years in a "special long-range unmanned spaceship." After recognizing just how similar this sounds to science fiction, the two authors even cite another scientist who had speculated that "we might have evolved from the microorganisms inadvertently left behind by some previous visitors from another planet (for example, in their garbage)."[16]

Now there's a twist.

Closer to Murphy's own evolutionary vision was the famous biologist and science activist Julian Huxley, who happened to be both the grandson of T. H. Huxley (who gave us the word "agnosticism"), and the brother of Aldous Huxley (who gave us the word "neurotheologian" and answered his distinguished grandfather's agnosticism with his own search for a new Gnosticism). In 1942, in his classic *Evolution: The Modern Synthesis*, Julian encouraged his readers to own their own role in determining the "purpose of the future of man" and to cease putting human responsibilities "on to the shoulders of mythical gods or metaphysical absolutes." In short, in a stunning example of Authorization, he suggested that we must now evolve ourselves. More radically still, well within the mytheme of Mutation this time, he wrote openly about how "there are other faculties, the bare existence of which is as yet scarcely established: and these too might be developed until they were as commonly distributed as, say, musical or mathematical gifts are today. I refer to telepathy and other extra-sensory activities of mind."[17]

Closer still was the great French philosopher, Henri Bergson. Bergson held a prestigious chair at the Ecole Normale Supérieure, worked with President Woodrow Wilson to help found the League of Nations, and won the Nobel Prize in Literature in 1928. During his prime, Bergson was as famous as Sigmund Freud and Albert Einstein. He was also the president of the London Society for Psychical Research in 1913. Mystics, for the philosopher, were forerunners of human evolution, and psychical powers were hints of what we might all still someday become in the future. Thus, in *Creative Evolution* (1907), he wrote beautifully of what he called the élan vital, a cosmic evolutionary force that reveals the universe to be, as he put it in 1932 in the very last lines of his very last book, "a machine for the making of gods."[18]

Well before Bergson, the Canadian doctor Richard Maurice Bucke (1837–1901) wrote an eccentric and rather erratic tome about evolution as a mystical force creating spiritual, cultural, and literary geniuses just before he died—his 1901 classic, *Cosmic Consciousness*. Despite its obvious flaws and historical naïveté, the book is just as obviously inspired. Accordingly, it would have a significant impact on later readers, including both of our case studies in chapter 6, fantasy artist Barry Windsor-Smith and sci-fi writer Philip K. Dick. Given this, and Bucke's obvious dissent from the essential randomness of accepted Darwinian biology, it seems wise to spend a bit more time on the author.

By birth, Bucke was a farm boy, by training an accomplished medical doctor and psychologist. The original inspiration for his mysticism was literary and, to be more precise, poetic. In 1867, a visitor read some Walt Whitman to him. He was stunned. Five years later, in the spring of 1872, this poetic inspiration resulted in a dramatic mystical opening in London. Bucke and two friends had just spent the evening reading the Romantic poets: Wordsworth, Shelley, Keats, Browning, and, above all, Whitman. On the carriage ride home just after midnight, it happened:

ALL AT ONCE, WITHOUT WARNING OF ANY KIND, HE FOUND HIMSELF WRAPPED AROUND, AS IT WERE, BY A FLAME-COLORED CLOUD. FOR AN INSTANT HE THOUGHT OF FIRE-- SOME SUDDEN CONFLAGRATION IN THE GREAT CITY. THE NEXT (INSTANT) HE KNEW THAT THE LIGHT WAS WITHIN HIMSELF. DIRECTLY AFTER THERE CAME UPON HIM A SENSE OF EXULTATION, OF IMMENSE JOYOUSNESS, ACCOMPANIED OR IMMEDIATELY FOLLOWED BY AN INTELLECTUAL ILLUMINATION QUITE IMPOSSIBLE TO DESCRIBE. INTO HIS BRAIN STREAMED ONE MOMENTARY LIGHTNING-FLASH OF THE BRAHMIC SPLENDOR WHICH EVER SINCE LIGHTENED HIS LIFE. UPON HIS HEART FELL ONE DROP OF THE BRAHMIC BLISS, LEAVING THENCEFORWARD FOR ALWAYS AN AFTERTASTE OF HEAVEN.[19]

Here we see immediately our mytheme of Orientation ("Brahmic Bliss") and at least a hint of Radiation ("a flame-colored cloud," like a "sudden conflagration"). But it was the mytheme of Mutation that would carry the "intellectual illumination quite impossible to describe" for him and finally result in the appearance of *Cosmic Consciousness* almost thirty years later.

Cosmic Consciousness, as its name implies, is defined as "a consciousness of the cosmos, that is, of the life and order of the universe." It is not some vague emotional experience. It comes with a definite intellectual enlightenment or illumination—*it teaches things*, even if these things far exceed the present cognitive development of the brain (hence the "quite impossible to describe" part). Cosmic Consciousness also transforms the human being, whom it wraps in living flame, rendering him or her "almost a member of a new species." The experience also morally elevates the individual, providing a "sense of immortality, a consciousness of eternal life, not a conviction that he shall have this, but the consciousness that he has it already."[20]

Bucke is convinced the human race as a whole will eventually evolve into this Cosmic Consciousness, that "this step in evolution is even now being made," and that such individuals are becoming more and more common (this is where his argument gets really dicey, and statistically wacky).[21] In any case, he clearly understands studying the history of such experiences as a key component to this awakening, and he approaches the writing of his book as a means to "aid men and women in making the almost infinitely important step" of making conscious contact with this Cosmic Consciousness. Which is all to say that *Bucke understands his book as itself a force of mystical mutation*: in essence, *Cosmic Consciousness* can catalyze Cosmic Consciousness.[22] And why not? Had Bucke himself not been changed, in an instant, after reading the Romantic poets?

Writing such a book-as-mutation involved hard intellectual labor. Thus Bucke reports how in correspondence with the British writer and interpreter of Hinduism Edward Carpenter (yet another early evolutionary mystic), his speculations were deepened and disciplined until he arrived at his "germinal concept," namely, the idea "that there exists a family springing from, living among, but scarcely forming a part of ordinary humanity, whose members are spread abroad throughout the advanced races of mankind and throughout the last forty centuries of the world's history."[23] In short, the X-Men before the X-Men.

But even Bucke at the turn of the century was hardly the origin point of the mytheme of Mutation. In chapter 1, we looked, for example, at John Uri Lloyd's 1895 novel *Etidorhpa*, whose hollow-earth themes, particularly in the mouth of the gray, alienlike guide, are positively *filled* with references to superhuman powers and latent faculties that "further evolutions" will actualize in the race as telepathy or "mind language," telekinesis, cosmic spirit, and so on.

We have also already encountered the real historical origins of two absolutely key terms in the X-Men mythology: magnetism and telepathy. It is not much of an exaggeration to suggest that, without these two key concepts, there could be no recognizable X-Men series. These, after all, are the superpowers of the mythology's main villain (Magneto) and its founding teacher (Professor Xavier), respectively, both of which, moreover, appeared in that very first issue.

As the sensitive reader may now guess, Magneto's magnetic powers stem back to the late eighteenth- and early nineteenth-century movement of animal magnetism around the figure of Anton Mesmer. The same reader might also now realize that Professor X's central superpower of telepathy can be definitively traced back to the London Society for Psychical Research (the S.P.R.) and a single man whom we have already met numerous times, Frederic Myers. Recall that Myers coined the term "telepathy" in 1882 and linked it directly to the spiritual forces of evolution, that is, he saw it as evidence of our evolving "extraterrene" supernormal nature.

Attending the first official meeting of the Society for Psychical Research that same winter of 1882 was none other than Alfred Russel Wallace, the co-originator with Charles Darwin of the theory of biological evolution. Fame aside, Wallace cared little for the orthodoxies of religion or science. He attended séances, performed Mesmeric experiments on his students, asserted the postmortem survival of our mental and spiritual natures, and speculated, with his S.P.R. colleagues, that "there yet seems to be evidence of a Power which has guided the action of those [evolutionary] laws in definite directions and for special ends."[24]

In other words, the mytheme of Mutation, the idea of mystical mutations that produce various supernormal powers, is not a countercultural invention or some superficial fancy, and it certainly did not begin with the Lee and Kirby's X-Men in 1963. It has been in the air for 150 years now and has flourished among some of Western culture's most distinguished intellectuals, philosophers, and scientists. Indeed, it goes back to the very origins, and to one of the two historical founders, of evolutionary biology itself.

THE X-QUESTIONS

If one reads the early issues of The X-Men in light of this secret life of Mutation, one thing becomes patently obvious: there would be no X-Men mythology without the ideas and terminology generated by the British and American psychical research traditions centered at Cambridge and Harvard (the latter around the American psychologist, philosopher, and theorist of mysticism William James) and the later laboratory parapsychology of J. B. Rhine centered at Duke University. Once again, the elite inspired the popular here.

Indeed, the first thirty issues, written by Stan Lee and Roy Thomas, read like a veritable glossary of technical terms taken directly from these academic traditions (it is *Professor* X, after all). These technical terms include: telepathy (coined, again, by Myers in 1882), telekinesis, teleportation (coined by Fort in 1931), levitation, extrasensory perception or ESP (coined by Rudolf Tischner but popularized by Rhine at Duke), the sixth sense, counterego (what was called a "double personality" in the nineteenth-century literature), trance, and, perhaps most obvious of all, magnetism (from the earlier "animal magnetism"). Indeed, in one delightful *X-Men* panel, Jean is even seen telekinetically pulling some books on "telekinetic research" off the shelves of Professor Xavier's library in order to borrow them so that she can "continue to study ways to utilize my mutant power" (XM 555). Here the debt is openly acknowledged.

Lee is clearly still learning the terms himself in the early pages of the first few *X-Men* issues, even as he is doing his best to teach his young readers some very big words with some even bigger meanings. In the first issue, for example, Lee mistakenly calls Jean Grey's telekinetic ability to mentally pick up and put back a book "teleportation" (XM 17). He confuses the two terms again in other places (XM 34, 39, 301), but already back in the second issue, he uses "teleportation" correctly, this time for the Vanisher's ability to "pop" out of one place and into another (XM 43). As Lee gets a handle on his terminology, the storylines explode with a flurry of references to telekinesis or telekinetic powers, often with multiple appearances in each issue.

One can also detect the presence of the nineteenth-century occult traditions that we examined in chapter 1. While Professor X is "in a trance," for example, he meets Magneto "on a mental plane" (XM 90). Like two Theosophists, Magneto and Professor X both astral travel in a later issue (XM 134–35), during which time Magneto is "guided by the extra-sensory perception of his mutant brain." Later, we encounter Professor X's "invisible *astral image*" (XM 361) and learn of a new skill called "thought projection" (XM 423). We also encounter a European witch by the name of Wanda, who, of course, is now refigured through the paranormal register as a mutant (XM 88).

It is not all Mutation, though. The mytheme of Orientation makes a number of appearances in the X-Men mythology. We learn, for example, that Professor Xavier, "fascinated by tales I had heard of a mysterious walled city in the shadow of the Himalayas," journeyed to Tibet as a young man. Nor was this some minor pilgrimage or tourist jaunt: "It's as though my entire life, my ultimate destiny, were somehow bound up behind those grim, grey walls!" (XM 473). It was there that he met the villain Lucifer and lost the use of his legs. But Lucifer, it turns out, is an alien, a menace

from the stars, "an agent of some alien, star-spawned race" (XM 493). Orientation to Alienation once again.

Announced early on, the mytheme of Alienation never leaves. It returns again, when a man mistakes a Mayan sun god for "one of them *flyin' saucers*" (XM 605), or when Xavier begins to have nightmares of an alien craft and its insectoid pilot (UXM 100), who turns out to be his lover and telepathic partner Lilandra, princess of the Shi'ar space empire. The human species is put in its cosmic place when it is described as "sentient hominid life forms—level 4.7 on the Varakis scale" and a space cruiser detects multiple races now active on the planet: "Kree, Skrull, Badoon, even Celestial activity" (UXM 261). The earth, it turns out, is a "*cross-roads* planet for half the star-faring races in the *Milky Way*" (UXM 303). Charles Fort, by the way, had written the same thing.

More complex Orientation themes will also appear much later in the series, when we learn, for example, that Wolverine spent some time in Japan as a boy, speaks fluent Japanese, and practices Zazen or "seated meditation" to calm his nerves and restore his body and mind. Numerous issues show the buffed hairy man in a perfect lotus posture. The later Grant Morrison run will also have Wolverine practicing both "Za Zen sitting meditation" (NXM 117.9) and the martial art of tai chi (NXM 152.10–12). Perhaps most complexly of all, however, Morrison will create a fascinating figure named Xorn, who is supposed to have a star or tiny black hole for a brain (really no head at all) and who ends up, at one point, in Lhasa, in a Tibetan Buddhist monastery, where he is being treated as a living Buddha.

I cannot help but think here of *On Having No Head*, a stunning little manifesto written by a British gentleman named D. E. Harding, who discovered while hiking in the Himalayas that consciousness was not at all the same thing as the brain, and *that he had no head*. Rather like Xorn. Headlessness is also a common mystical trope in Indo-Tibetan Hindu and Buddhist Tantra, where decapitated heads are pretty much everywhere in the iconography and art. To lose one's head, that is, to know that one is not one's brain, is to be enlightened. The Next Age superbody is, once again, a Tantric body.

Professor Xavier's telepathy, Jean's telekinetic abilities, Xorn's apparent headlessness—all of this raises a deep philosophical issue. What, exactly, *is* consciousness? The different X-Men story arcs offer no single answer, although the question is often central to the paranormal action that grounds the mythology.

In the early issues, Lee seems to be working with a fairly typical materialism that equates consciousness and brain. Hence Lee's constant references to Professor Xavier's "mutant brain." Things would change radically, however, as the mythology developed and the consciousness of the counterculture set in and matured. By the late 1970s, with the beginning of the Chris Claremont *Uncanny X-Men* run (1975–91), and continuing at the turn of the millennium with Morrison's *New X-Men* revisioning, all of that brain talk is gone. Claremont gives his readers the series' ultimate mystical cipher—Phoenix, a kind of Cosmic Consciousness as goddess. He also drops a hint about his own understanding of the splitting of consciousness through the two hemispheres of the brain: he has the Beast reading Julian Jaynes's *The Origin of Consciousness in the Breakdown of the Bicameral Mind* in issue #134. "Good book," the Beast quips. "Can't wait to see the movie" (DP 104). So, too, Morrison informs his readers that Xavier is "the world's premier super-consciousness" and treats us to any number of stories that only work because the forms of consciousness of the characters are not equated with or restricted by their brains and bodies (NXM 122.12).

Indeed, both Claremont and Morrison's story arcs *depend* on various occult forms of consciousness leaving and entering different bodies, "possessing" them, to use an old-fashioned word. Morrison's famous villainess Nova Cassandra, for example, is described as "a bodiless lifeform" who, when she takes over Charles Xavier's body, is described as "wearing the professor like a glove" (NXM 125.7–8). Similarly, Emma Frost is described as a "disembodied consciousnesses" or as simply "disembodied" (NXM 140.6, 141.16). And when a young X-Man goes bad and is killed, Professor Xavier gives the following speech at his funeral: "Quentin Quire was liberated from his physical cocoon and born into a higher world at exactly 4:32 this afternoon. I know how ridiculous that sounds, but in this case we believe it to be the literal truth" (NXM 138.14).

I will return to these themes at the end of the chapter, where I discuss the implicit, really explicit, mysticism of the X-Men mythology. For now, it is enough to mention that such scenes and their philosophical implications point to some of the deepest and most consistent questions behind the X-Men mythology: What is the nature of consciousness? How is consciousness related to matter and energy? What are its limits? *Are* there any limits? As the series has developed over the decades, the answers to these questions have morphed and mutated with the characters themselves. As we move further and further along that story arc, however, we might catch glimpses of three sorts of answers coming into sharper and sharper view: "Consciousness is not the brain," "Consciousness and Energy are One," and "There are no limits."

In other words, Xavier, Magneto, and Phoenix are the answers, and X has become a kind of sign for mind, energy, consciousness, and God, which are more or less (mostly more) interchangeable now. The counterculture has worked its real magic, the culture has mutated as a result, and the X-Men are no longer "before their time."

THE SECRET LIVES OF THE SUPERPOWERS: REMOTE VIEWING

However fantastic such a mysticism might at first appear, there were some very plausible real-world reasons for exploring it. Perhaps none of these reasons, however, came closer to a true X-scenario than the secret paranormal programs of the Russians and Americans during the Cold War. The secret life of superpowers—*literally*.

On the American side of things, a number of the military and intelligence branches were funding the training of an elite corps of psychic spies or "remote viewers."[25] The practice of remote viewing involved a small team of carefully selected individuals who were trained to locate and describe targets around the world that were otherwise hidden, secret, or simply unknown (for example, the location of a Soviet bomber crashed in an African jungle), very much like police departments are said to use psychics to help crack particularly difficult cases or locate bodies.

For over two decades, from 1972 to 1995, the CIA, the Defense Intelligence Agency, the army, and the navy together invested over twenty million dollars in research and development. Most of the work was done at just three locations: (1) a private think tank called SRI (formerly Stanford Research Institute); (2) an army base in Maryland called Fort Meade; and (3) another think tank called Science Applications International in Palo Alto, California. Since many of the files were declassified in 1996 under the Freedom of Information Act, the details of this particular plotline of our Super-Story have been elaborately documented and analyzed from a variety of perspectives, including a number of firsthand accounts from those who took part in the paranormal programs, programs with evocative names like Gondola Wish, Grill Flame, Center Lane, Sun Streak, and Star Gate.

The American story begins in 1972 with a young laser physicist by the name of Harold Puthoff. Puthoff had just finished some postdoctoral research at Stanford University. He had already also done a stint in the navy as an intelligence officer and had worked as a civilian for the National Security Agency. He was now working in laser research for SRI, California, but his real interest was the interface between quantum and biological processes, or quantum biology. He was especially interested in parapsychological phenomena and how they might throw some much-needed light on the strange interface between physics and consciousness (Radiation again).

As Puthoff was settling into his research at SRI in California, an artist by the name of Ingo Swann was working with some parapsychologists in the Department of Psychology of the City College of New York. They were working with Swann in some highly unusual tasks, like psychically detecting weather patterns in randomly chosen cities. At about this time, a research proposal of Puthoff's came to Swann's attention through his City College colleagues. He decided to write the physicist on March 30, 1972, outlining his experiments in the psychology department and suggesting that he may be able to help Puthoff investigate quantum biological effects. Three months later, on June 4, 1972, Swann stepped off the plane in California to meet Puthoff.

What happened two days later, on June 6, is as legendary in the annals of remote viewing as it is controversial outside them. Puthoff and his SRI colleagues were interested in Swann's alleged psychokinetic powers. More practically (or impractically), they wanted to see if he could manipulate the recorded output of a superconducting magnetometer or quark detector, a kind of supersensitive compass used to register very subtle magnetic fields that was located in a vault below the building under a three-feet-thick concrete floor. Beyond the concrete, the apparatus was also protected by "a mu-metal magnetic shield, an aluminum container, copper shielding, and most important, a superconducting shield."[26] To the great puzzlement of the physicists, Swann successfully and dramatically altered the output of the magnetometer in their presence. He also "saw it," that is, he described a gold alloy plate that was part of the apparatus. To say that the physicists were impressed would be a gross understatement. According to Swann, one researcher was so freaked out by what he witnessed that, in his haste to get out of there, he walked into an orange support pillar.[27]

During that same June and soon after the Swann affair with the magnetometer, Puthoff delivered a public lecture at Stanford. Afterward, another laser physicist by the name of Russell Targ, then working for Sylvania, approached Puthoff and proposed that they work together at SRI. Targ was hired on. The collaboration between these two men would last for ten years, from 1972 to 1982. It would also come to define much of the early history of remote viewing.

Shortly after the Stanford lecture, two CIA officials showed up at Puthoff's door, asking about a privately circulated report that he had written on the Swann magnetometer incident. After speaking to him about the paper, they were sufficiently intrigued to leave the physicist some money in order to get Swann back to Palo Alto to see if they could find a psychical capacity that was replicable and therefore useable. Swann returned in December.

Paul Smith, who would himself become a remote viewer later in the program's history, explains why Puthoff and Targ were initially interested in psychokinesis: "If PK skills could be developed and controlled, one could use them to manipulate the physical world, including the enemy's weapons. Using 'mind over matter' to melt tank barrels or stop bombers in mid-flight was the stuff of comic books. Far more likely, given the subtlety of typical PK effects, was the possibility of mucking up the intricate guts of military computers, electronic equipment, or missile guidance systems."[28] The "stuff of comic books" indeed. Magneto makes yet another appearance.

Almost, anyway. Alas, after thousands of experiments, the researchers had to conclude that, although they had witnessed some very suggestive evidence for the phenomenon, controlling psychokinesis was not possible or, as they put it in more technical language, "willed perturbation effects appear to be intrinsically spontane-ous."[29] In short, the stuff is probably real, but fundamentally unpredictable. Exit Mag-neto. Enter Professor X.

Swann quickly grew bored with the standard parapsychological tests that fol-lowed and suggested that he be allowed to view distant places and objects, anywhere in the world. "There was an awkward silence."[30] Finally, they decided to give in to Swann's request as a diversionary game, if nothing else. The results were no game, though. On too many occasions to dismiss, the results were simply stunning.

The results of Targ and Puthoff's experiments with Ingo Swann and another man named Pat Price at SRI were published in the prestigious British science journal *Nature*. A second essay followed two years later in the *Proceedings of the IEEE* (Institute of Electrical and Electronic Engineers). A year later, these two technical essays grew into the first published book on remote viewing, Targ and Puthoff's influential *Mind-Reach: Scientists Look at Psychic Ability* (1977).[31] Well-known anthropologist Margaret Mead wrote the introduction. Richard Bach, author of the megahit *Jonathan Livingston Seagull* (which *totally* confused me as a kid), wrote a foreword and donated forty thou-sand dollars toward the research behind it. Swann provided the cover art, a striking painting called *Salt Flats Vision*.

Gradually, Swann and Puthoff developed an elaborate six-stage protocol that used coordinates (at first longitude and latitude and later random numbers) to "locate" the desired target. This mind-bending method (with a random number inexplicably providing a workable coordinate for the viewer to find an object anywhere on the planet) became known as coordinate remote viewing (CRV).[32] Intriguingly, the protocol drew intimately on concepts from the British and American psychical research traditions, psychoanalysis, and split-brain research. These included the most basic categories of the preconscious and the unconscious, the "limen" or threshold between the conscious and the unconscious (Frederic Myers again), the notion of analytical overlay or AOL (more or less equivalent to what Freud had called "secondary revision"), and the central role of right-brain processing, that is, intuition, symbol-making, and sketching.

Even more intriguingly, the protocol also drew on something Swann called the Matrix, which was basically a kind of hyperspace containing all of the universe's information whether from the past, present, or future (something akin to Alan Moore's Immateria, Ray Palmer's conviction in "heavenly libraries," and Gopi Krishna's "boundless world of knowledge"). In his own technical language, Swann believed that the remote viewer receives a "signal line" from the Matrix through an "aperture" or opening in the subconscious, which is then transmitted through the right brain and "objectified" via the feedback "loops" of sketching "ideograms" and writing descriptors.

Easily the most storied remote viewer out at Fort Meade was a man named Joseph McMoneagle. Known as RV Agent 001, McMoneagle became a remote viewer after a dramatic near-death experience in 1970 convinced him that consciousness was not restricted to the biological boundaries of the skin and skull—not even close. The subtle body McMoneagle used in that out-of-body experience, for example, looks *a lot* like Superman: McMoneagle describes himself "cruising just above the car, zipping up, down, and through the overhanging telephone and electric wires" as he followed the Volkswagen Beetle that was taking his body to the hospital. And the total experience climaxed in an erotic encounter with God that McMoneagle himself compares to a "sexual peak" or "normal climax" times twelve times ten to the thirty-third power.[33] Now *that's* a libido.

And McMoneagle goes further still, describing the human mind as "the ultimate time machine" and writing of what he calls "the Verne effect." The latter is named after Jules Verne, who appears to have accurately predicted in his novels everything from the submarine to the American lunar shot. In *From the Earth to the Moon* (1865), for example, Verne "not only anticipated that the launch would take place from Florida, but he also foresaw a three man crew traveling in a capsule with approximately the same dimensions as the Apollo Command Module, and he had already worked out the necessary launch velocity required to escape the earth's gravity."[34] The Verne effect, then, refers to what McMoneagle suggests is our innate ability to paranormally predict and create—or, in my own terms, *author*—our own futures.[35] Science fiction as prophecy.

McMoneagle would become known for feats like accurately remote viewing the interior of a still experimental, highly secret XM-1 or Abrams tank. Or describing, in great detail, the interior of an immense Soviet naval structure in northern Russia, including a weird submarine that fit no known type. McMoneagle was angered when he learned that the analysts scoffed at his work for many reasons, including the fact that the building was far from the water. McMoneagle had his "I told you so" moment, though. A few months later, American spy satellites showed the never-before-seen *Typhoon* submarine (560 feet long) being floated out to sea through a channel the Soviets had recently dug from the building to the icy waters.

Fellow remote viewer Paul Smith notes that almost all of the thirty-three real-world assignments performed at Fort Meade by 1984 were the work of McMoneagle. Physicist Edwin May, who worked closely with McMoneagle for years, adds to this already impressive resume by describing his friend and colleague as "the most certified psychic in the country."[36] The intelligence community seems to agree. In 1984, it awarded him its prestigious *Legion of Merit* for "producing crucial and vital intelligence unavailable from any other source."[37] So much for the nonexistence of paranormal powers.

For our own purposes, it is also important to know that McMoneagle was closely involved with the consciousness laboratory of Robert Monroe, the business entrepreneur who, after he began spontaneously and regularly leaving his body at age forty-two, developed an elaborate "Hemi-Sync" technology (involving interfering sound waves designed to integrate the two sides of the brain) for inducing various altered states of consciousness, from "Focus 10" (the "mind awake, body asleep" state) to full-blown out-of-body experiences and astral-like travels. Monroe wrote three important books on his experiences, including the classic *Journeys Out of the Body* (1971).

Like the secret life of any superpower, there are competing narratives here, claims and counterclaims, much debate about what actually happened, and even more debate about what whatever happened really means. Consider, for example, a key player in this story, Edwin May. May, an accomplished and published expert on low-energy, experimental nuclear physics, joined the SRI team in 1975. He directed the research program there from 1985 until 1991, after which he shifted his affiliation to another U.S. defense contractor, where he continued his involvement with government-sponsored parapsychology until 1995, when the Star Gate program at Fort Meade was finally shut down. May's importance is signaled by the fact that he presided over an astonishing 70 percent of the total funding and a full 85 percent of the data collection for the government's twenty-two-year involvement in parapsychological research.

The key point here with respect to May is that he is extremely dubious about most of the more extreme claims, *and* he is convinced that at least some of the parapsychological phenomena (particularly those displayed by McMoneagle) are very real. The phenomena, he argues, will eventually be explained through the principles of physics, that is, through the nature and behavior of matter and the structure of space-time. May describes his final conclusions as "materialist," that is, he is convinced that the final and fundamental nature of reality is matter.

Another physicist, Russell Targ, sees things differently. He is convinced that his former espionage activities hid profound metaphysical truths, and that they essentially constitute scientific proof of what he likes to call "nonlocal mind." Nonlocal mind is a form of consciousness "that connects us to each other and to the world at large" and "allows us to describe, experience, and influence activities occurring anywhere in space and time."[38] Accordingly, Targ has been deeply drawn to nondual Asian philosophies, like Advaita Vedanta and Tibetan Buddhism (Orientation again). His final conclusions can be described as "idealist," that is, he is convinced that the final and fundamental nature of reality is mind.

As a civilian with no military or scientific background, I cannot make any claims about the details of the remote-viewing narrative, much less the fundamental principles of quantum physics. So I won't. However, as a historian of religions who specializes in the interpretation of unusual, extreme, or anomalous states of consciousness in both the West and South Asia, many of which bear a rather obvious relationship to the perennial debates around materialism and idealism, I can make two related observations here.

First, it seems important to point out that any scientific explanation of something like remote viewing must, in principle, remain an abstract, third-order account of what are, in the end, deeply personal, often fantastically meaningful states of consciousness. Yes, there is an objective scientific perspective here, but there is also a subjective human perspective, a perspective, moreover, without which this history could not have taken place. May's materialism and Targ's idealism, then, need not be read as mutually exclusive options. Both may capture a key part of the larger picture. Indeed, *both* may be right, as we will see in a moment via *Apollo* astronaut Edgar Mitchell's "dyadic" vision of matter and mind.

Second, I am struck by how, if we focus on the deeply personal descriptions of those who actually experienced these things, what we encounter is a rich spectrum of mythical, sci-fi, and superhero allusions. Following Frederic Myers, I would like to call this *the imaginal dimension* of the remote-viewing history. Such mythical patterns appear to be nearly irresistible.

Consider the following. Science writer Jim Schnabel has described McMoneagle's psychic abilities to detect radioactive material as green and glowing as "the kinds of talents one might imagine in comic book superheroes."[39] Historically speaking, the superhero allusion is deeper than Schnabel probably realized, since it was McMoneagle's friend and teacher of the out-of-body experience, Robert Monroe, who produced the early radio shows of *The Shadow*, a clear and unambiguous precursor of the later superhero comics, as we already noted.[40] Nor is it an accident that McMoneagle has used expressions like "the Verne effect" and titled one of his books *Mind Trek*, an obvious allusion to *Star Trek*. And this is in addition to the fact that in the early years of remote viewing both Puthoff and Swann were members of Scientology, a new religion founded by a very well-known science fiction writer, Ron L. Hubbard. Both men would leave Scientology, but Swann has been quite clear that his early psychical feats would have been impossible "had there been in me an absence of the transcendental structural ideas presented by Hubbard."[41] In another sci-fi spirit, *Washington Post* journalist Jack Anderson, once a harsh skeptic but now a self-described "firm believer" ("my initial reports were wide of the mark"), opens his foreword to Paul Smith's history of remote viewing with the phrases "psychic warfare" and "straight from the pages of pulp-fantasy magazines."[42]

Indeed. Smith himself opens up his own story a few pages later by explaining the unofficial but affectionate acronym that he encountered early in his own journey: TZO, or Twilight Zone officer.[43] Smith entered the story of remote viewing a little less than halfway through its twenty-two-year run. His initial exposure to what he describes as the army's "secret paranormal espionage program" involved a certain Major Stubblebine. In early 1983, Major General Albert Stubblebine III was the commanding general of INSCOM, the U.S. Army Intelligence and Security Command. He had created his own staff agency called the Advanced Human Technology Office, whose chief was a man named John Alexander.

Alexander had a Ph.D. in education, had been a Green Beret, and had a long-standing interest in near-death experiences. Even more significantly, he was the author of "The New Mental Battlefield," an essay on the possible military uses of psychotronics or bioenenergetics, which, "to the astonishment of many of the Army's brass," Smith explains, "became the cover story for the normally staid *Military Review*, the official journal of Fort Leavenworth's Command and General Staff College." The army major who edited the review, it turns out, had had a near-death experience of his own and "as a result was open to possibilities that most of his peers would likely have rejected."[44] As with most things mystical, it is ultimately extreme experience that finally convinces. In any case, "Be all that you can be" was probably much more than a catchy army slogan thrown up on hundreds of millions of television screens, posters, and T-shirts. It was also likely a kind of public echo of an early 1980s dream of a "New Age Army," a human potential special ops team with deep connections to the very paranormal research program that we are tracing here.[45]

Hence the "New Earth Army" of the movie *The Men Who Stare at Goats* (2009). This humorous, heartfelt film contains numerous allusions to historical figures and events treated here, as well as a manual (which you have to pause the movie in order to read) that sports a comic-book style sketch of a meditating soldier sitting in the lotus posture and listed sections on things like "The Warrior Monk's Vision," "Evolutionary Teamwork," and "First Earth Batallion"—perhaps coded references to the psychic warrior monks discussed in Ron McRae's *Mind Wars*.[46] The film also ends with a little speech of disgust on what the media inevitably does with such a secret life. It distorts and censors these experiences until the story comes out the other end as ridiculous and twisted.

Smith explains how he became a remote viewer. Major Stubblebine was inspecting the intelligence school at Fort Huachuca, Arizona, where he was stationed. Sitting in a gathered crowd, Smith listened to the major as he described how the technological advances in intelligence gathering "cannot compare to the power that lies within our own minds. We only have to learn to tap it." The major then did something very odd: he threw tangled pieces of clanking silverware into the audience. Weirder still, each fork or spoon was contorted in unfamiliar, seemingly impossible ways. Smith, a trained linguist capable in German, Hebrew, and Arabic, picked up one. "An eerie feeling washed through me, dredging up from somewhere deep in my subconscious the German word *unheimlich* [usually translated "uncanny"]. What I was holding in my hands was *creepy*."[47] The major explained that these had all been bent and twisted by himself and his staff with nothing but the power of their minds.

Enter the Israeli superpsychic Uri Geller. After a stint in the Israeli military during the Six-Day War, Geller was famous for doing things like bending spoons, fixing watches during television broadcasts, photographing UFOs, and, in one bizarre scene right out of the movie *Jumper*, spontaneously teleporting from a street in the East Side of Manhattan through the porch screen window of his colleague Andrija Puharich's house in Ossining, almost an hour away. Good luck with the spoons, the UFOs, and the porch crash. The fixed-watch scene, at least, is a trick, since if you can get hundreds of thousands of people to hold up their "broken" watches in front of their warm television sets, it is extremely likely that many of the watches will suddenly be "fixed" by the movement and heat of the hand and screen.

From the perspective of the SRI scientists, Geller was an artful mixture of stage magician and the real deal—the trick and truth, or tricky truth, again. They studied him at SRI for six weeks toward the end of 1972. He never managed to demonstrate his psychokinetic powers under the controlled laboratory conditions of SRI, but he did produce some fantastic effects outside the lab, including one really weird instance of teleportation with *Apollo* astronaut Edgar Mitchell.

As Geller reports the story, the two men were having lunch with Russell Targ in the SRI cafeteria when Geller almost broke a tooth on something in his ice cream. It turned out to be half of a miniature arrowhead. Mitchell thought it looked familiar. Back in the laboratory after lunch, everyone suddenly saw something fall on the carpet. "We picked it up, and it was the rest of the arrow. Together, the two pieces made a tie pin."[48] Mitchell was shocked, as he now recognized the arrowhead tie pin for what it was: *his* tie pin, which he had lost years ago. Somehow it had now returned to him, in two parts, from God only knows where.

A trick? Not at least from Mitchell's perspective, which differs in a number of details but not in substance. From Mitchell, for example, we learn that that same day the American astronaut had just challenged the Israeli psychic to produce a camera he had left on the moon. Mitchell knew that the camera had its own NASA serial number, which he did not know. So he had a kind of perfect experiment dreamed up here. Except for the fact that, as usual, the psychical event refused to follow the experimental design.

Mitchell also explains that he had lost the tie pin, along with a whole box of pins and cuff links, during one of his frequent trips to and from Cape Kennedy, well before he had even heard of Uri Geller. He also explains that there were actually *three* pieces, not two, that fell that day, as if out of nowhere: "a silver miniature hunting arrow mounted over the silver image of a longhorn sheep"; a tie bar that fell on a tile hallway floor and perfectly matched the hunting arrow emblem down to the broken solder joint (the two halves of Geller's story); and, finally, another pearl tie pin that his brother had given him and that he had lost with the same box of jewelry. The astronaut concludes: "Three of Edgar Mitchell's lost articles recovered telekinetically within the span of thirty minutes. But no camera. Startling phenomena, but accepted science still remained just outside the door."[49] As it always would, almost as if the phenomena themselves were keeping it out, intentionally, mischievously.

It was no accident that Mitchell and Geller were together at SRI. Mitchell had helped raise the funds to get him there. Edgar Mitchell became the sixth man in human history to walk on the moon on February 5, 1971. On his trip back home in the *Kitty Hawk* command module, he became absorbed in a weightless contemplative mood before the beauty of a blue jewel planet suspended in black space and had an overwhelming experience of the universal connectedness of all things within an intelligent, evolving, self-aware universe. This "grand epiphany," as he described it, led him the following year to found the Institute of Noetic Sciences (the same one featured in Dan Brown's 2009 novel *The Lost Symbol*) in order to pursue the study of psychical phenomena and what he would eventually call the "dyadic" relationship between the material and the mystical worlds.

Such a vision is the key to assuring the survival of the species for Mitchell, who envisions a future in almost perfect sync with the humane wisdom of Professor Xavier. After rejecting the usual misplaced trust in "bionic computers" and artificial intelligence, the wise astronaut writes:

I FIND IT MORE PROMISING WERE WE TO ALLOW THE NATURAL PROCESS OF EVOLU-
TION TO CONTINUE, AIDED AND AUGMENTED BY AN INFORMED, KINDLY, AND INTEN-
TIONAL SCIENCE THAT FULLY UNDERSTANDS THE PROCESSES OF CONSCIOUSNESS.
IN A DYADIC SCENARIO, THE BIONIC PROCESSES REMAIN THE ASSISTANT, NOT THE
DESTINY. . . . A DYADIC MODEL [WHICH POSITS THE FUNDAMENTAL UNITY OF MIND AND
MATTER] PREDICTS THAT EVOLUTION IS ONGOING BUT COMING UNDER CONSCIOUS

CONTROL. TO SUGGEST THAT EVOLUTION IS COMING UNDER CONSCIOUS CONTROL ALSO
IMPLIES THAT IT HAS BEEN UNDER SUBCONSCIOUS OR UNCONSCIOUS CONTROL . . .
THE INDIVIDUAL WHO EXHIBITS STARTLING CONSCIOUS CONTROL WITH MIND-OVER-
MATTER PROCESSES REPRESENTS ONLY THE TIP OF AN ICEBERG IN AN AWARE AND
INTENTIONAL SEA. THE UNTAPPED POTENTIAL THAT LIES JUST UNDER THE SURFACE IS
ALMOST INCOMPREHENSIBLE AT OUR CURRENT STAGE OF EVOLUTION.[50]

What he has in mind here are individuals like Uri Geller and Ted Owens, "the PK Man," whom we will meet in our next chapter and with whom Mitchell also worked. In other words, what Mitchell has in mind is another evolutionary mysticism—more X-Men.

In the context of our Super-Story, the patterns around Mitchell are quite extraordinary. After all, the astronaut's Fantastic Four–like initiatory experience in outer space (which he later referred to as his *samadhi*, a Sanskrit term meaning "yogic union" and, according to our opening epigraph for chapter 1, one of the ancient sources of supernormal powers); his unambiguous openness to the possible reality of UFOs and human-alien encounters; his dyadic or "nondual" universe in which matter and mind are two sides of the same cosmic coin; and his insistence—no doubt based again on his mystical experience in outer space—that evolution is a fundamentally meaningful process that is gradually coming under the control of consciousness are *all* precise expressions of the mythemes of Orientation, Alienation, Radiation, and Mutation.

These mythical patterns, moreover, are just as bright and just as bold in the figure and writings of Ingo Swann. Jim Schnabel, for example, includes a chapter on Swann with a *Star Wars* title, "Obi-Swann," which appropriately quotes the seer to the effect that "the potential is there, just like Obi-Wan Kenobi said it was." Another author, John Wilhelm, wrote an early book on Swann, Geller, and remote viewer Pat Price with the title *The Search for Superman*.[51]

Swann himself has written extensively about what he calls the "superpowers of the human biomind." Of his many books, two are especially relevant here: an autobiography focusing on alien-human communication and NASA/moon conspiracy theories entitled *Penetration: The Question of Extraterrestrial and Human Telepathy* (1998), and a beautiful red book about what Swann calls "human energetics," which focuses on the submerged erotics of the psychical research tradition through autobiographical reflections and intuitive comparisons with Indian Tantra and Chinese Taoism (Orientation again) entitled *Psychic Sexuality: The Bio-Psychic "Anatomy" of Sexual Energies*

(1999). These two books, linked in their contiguous publishing dates, their erotically tinged titles, and their present status as rare collector's items, deserve a full study. Alas, I can only offer a few paragraphs here.

Penetration begins with some observations about the social mechanisms that have successfully rendered it impossible to acknowledge "the Psi potentials of the human species" and, more to Swann's point, to *develop* and *train* these superpowers in individuals. Such a project, Swann points out in perfect line with the X-Men mythos, would seriously disrupt our social institutions, which rely on all sorts of secrets being kept. "Psi," after all, "penetrates secrets."

But there may be more. Although he is very much aware that he is among "those unfortunates who experience what they can't prove," Swann suggests that if something like Psi or telepathy exists as a kind of universal language (a common claim in the occult and contactee literature, going back in the latter at least as far as George Adamski), such an ability to penetrate secrets would work both ways.[52] A space-opera sci-fi scenario immediately develops: "if developed Psi potentials would be an invasive threat to Earthside intelligences, then developed Earthside Psi would also be a threat to Spaceside intelligences."[53] It would thus be in the interests of the Spaceside intelligences to suppress Psi in the human species through all sorts of subliminal and covert means. This, I gather, is the "penetration" of the title. The problem, of course, is that the existence of the Spacesiders cannot be established. Hence Swann's book, which is clearly designed not so much to prove as to provoke.

Provoke indeed. The book is filled with fantastic stories that read as perfectly sincere accounts that are almost impossible to believe (and Swann is the first to point this out). In one story arc, for example, he is whisked away by some dark government operatives to the Far North, where he is shown an immense UFO hovering over an Alaskan lake (shades of the polar holes again?). A mysterious man named Axelrod then asks Swann to remote view the moon. In another scene, Swann sees two of the same operatives and meets a sensuous female ET wearing purple sunglasses (and very little else) in a Hollywood supermarket. After a wave of electricity shoots through his body, he *knows* that she is an alien. And this is before we get to the second section of the book, on such things as a hollow-moon theory (the moon as an artificial satellite), lunar lights, and immense dark shadows and glowing UFOs allegedly seen in front of and around the moon by amateur astronomers and silenced NASA scientists and astronauts.

In the third section, we are on more familiar, if still fantastic, ground. Swann

speculates here on the mechanisms of telepathy and the ultimate nature of consciousness "as a universal premise and life force." Put very simply, he suggests that telepathy
does not happen *between* minds or brains but *within* a shared universal consciousness.
Ever the artist, Swann notes that those squiggly lines drawn around telepaths, as if the
brain were some kind of radio, sender, or receiver, are almost certainly wrong. We may
all be biological islands, but we are all floating in a shared sea of cosmic consciousness.[54] Including, of course, the aliens.

Swann, like all self-reflexive authors of the fantastic, is of two minds about what
he is expressing in a book like *Penetration*. He presents the material as he experienced
it, but he is at the same time clear, particularly with respect to his remote viewing of
humanoids and structures on the moon, that, "as with all Psi experiments, there is a
100 per cent chance that I had been viewing my imagination and fantasies."[55] Toward
the very end of the book, he goes so far as to describe his pages as "a foray into gross
speculation."[56] In any case, certainly those pages—whether read as psychic ciphers
or as spontaneous fantasies—resonate deeply with our mytheme of Alienation and
its ancient-astronaut trope. As do Swann's references to Earthside and Spaceside
intelligences. Indeed, if we were to read these latter categories as a coded model of
double-brained consciousness rather than as a literal statement about earthly and
lunar humanoids, we are back to a familiar pattern: the Human as Two.

Psychic Sexuality, which appeared just a year later, is on the unity of what Swann
calls sexual, creative, and power energies. Its basic theme is the intuited conviction
that there is a profound (always censored and denied) connection between mystical and
erotic experience, and that the subtle but incredibly powerful energies that produce
both types of experience are not simply pious "metaphors" or social "discourses" relative to this or that culture, but *real forces* at work in every human being on the planet.
Randolph and Reich were right. Put in Swann's own unique language, such a force is
the morphing basis of all superpowers of the human biomind. The force might explode
in an orgasm, a creative work of art, a clairvoyant power-perception, or in a near-
death experience and erotically charged encounter with a loving God, but it is always
and everywhere the same cosmic Energy. We are back to the mytheme of Radiation.

 So what's my point about the remote-viewing literature, taken as a whole now,
instead of as this or that author or book? My point is this: if we are going to
understand—and I mean *really* understand—something like the history of re-

mote viewing and what it tells us about the secret life of the mytheme of Mutation, we need to acknowledge the subjective experiences and belief systems of the remote viewers themselves with as much unblinking honesty as we do the objective science of the physics, the mathematical models, and the laboratory protocols. If the world really is dyadic, we must take the subjective side of the coin as seriously as the objective side. And with respect to the subjective-mental side of the dyad, *the imaginal is key.* Put more bluntly, the simple truth is that you don't get Joseph McMoneagle without the supererotic mystical encounter with God, Edgar Mitchell without his samadhi in space, or Ingo Swann without the art, the lunar aliens, and the psychic sexuality. It's *all* part of the Super-Story.

Perhaps this is also why sketching and artistic "right-brain" skills are so central here. As Smith puts it with his usual clarity, "there is more art than science to this process."[57] And it helps to *be* an artist. The researchers recognized early on that what the remote viewer sketched through the kinesthetic right-brain wisdom of the hand was often much more accurate than what he or she said through the left-brain's rational and verbal modes. In essence, *sketching became a psychical technique.* Much of this seems more than a little relevant to some of the more extraordinary experiences of artists like Jack Kirby and, as we shall dramatically see later, Barry Windsor-Smith, both of whom appear to have accessed metaphysical realities *precisely* through a "right-brain" sketching practice.

This is certainly not a new insight. A number of writers have traced the origins of remote viewing back to the mysterious and essentially occult processes of artistic creativity and, in particular, to the art of telepathic drawing as it was explored in a 1946 Paris lecture at the Sorbonne—the same text, by the way, with which we began our own list of images.[58] Here we might also mention Upton Sinclair's *Mental Radio* (1930), which describes Sinclair's telepathic drawing experiments with his wife, Mary Craig. This, by the way, is probably the source of Wonder Woman's "mental radio." And on and on we go.

REAL-WORLD CEREBRO

To return to our superhero patrons of the present chapter, the X-Men, I am struck by how closely this real-world hidden history of remote viewing resembles the central figure of Professor Xavier and his technological creation called Cerebro. Professor X, after all, is basically a remote viewer with added superpsychokinetic gifts. He follows, guides, and instructs his X-Men telepathically, and much of his work involves finding and tracking new mutants around the globe with the help of Cerebro.

For my readers unfamiliar with the mythology, Cerebro is a piece of psychotronics developed by Professor Xavier in order to magnify a person's innate telepathic powers and so allow him or her to locate and track mutants anywhere in the world. Cerebro made its first appearance in 1964, in *X-Men* #7, where it appeared as a spider-like, Kirby-esque system of machines and wires that transmitted extrasensory data into Professor Xavier's private desk in another room. There it was described as "a complex E.S.P. machine" (XM 160).

It would then make multiple central appearances, including one when the X-Men were re-created in 1975 in *Giant-Size X-Men* #1; there Cerebro senses and locates a supermutant across the globe, which turns out to be a living island named Krakoa (almost certainly modeled on the real-world volcanic island of Krakatoa), whose every organism was transformed and refigured into a sinister community intelligence after the island was used for an atomic bomb test (what else?). By the time of the high-tech X-Men movies of the new millennium, Cerebro has morphed into a futuristic superroom into which Professor Xavier wheels over a bridge in order to don the helmet that would magnify his already extraordinary telepathic powers and project the results onto the skull-like internal walls of the room.

This mythical Cerebro can be seen in turn as a fantastic magnification of what was actually being attempted with government-sponsored human machines in the remote-viewing programs. Paul Smith certainly realized that he and his fellow remote viewers were basically equipment that could be "turned on" and "turned off" by the government.[59] Similarly, the standard practice and language in the early experiments at SRI involved a scientist or CIA agent traveling somewhere in the Palo Alto radius for the remote viewer to locate and describe, according to the theory that the outbound target acted as a kind of beacon for the remote viewer to home in on.[60]

Since these experiments did not begin until 1972 and the first book describing them in any detail did not appear until 1977 (Targ and Puthoff's *Mind-Reach*), it is obvious that the 1964 fantasy preceded the reality. But this hardly excludes the possibility that the historical reality later influenced the superhero fantasy, including the three X-Men movies of the new millennium. I could not help thinking exactly this during the second movie as I watched Storm and Jean Grey look for Nightcrawler in a Boston

4.5 *MIND-REACH* [1977] TO "PSI-WAR!" [1978]

church where Professor Xavier and Cerebro had homed in on him: "These are the coordinates," Storm says to Jean.

To take another, more personal example, when I invited both Rusell Targ and Roy Thomas out to Esalen for a 2008 symposium on the topic of this book, Thomas realized that he had in fact been familiar with *Mind-Reach* when he was working on a 1984 movie script for an X-Men film project.[61] The same is no doubt true of *X-Men* #117, which features on its January 1978 cover the phrase "Psi-War." *Mind-Reach* had appeared a few months earlier.

On a weirder note, it is also worth remembering that Cerebro has sometimes accidentally picked up mutant *aliens*. It is a difficult, and often happily overlooked, fact that UFOs and alien-human contact appear repeatedly in the remote-viewing story. Geller, for example, attributed his powers to a childhood UFO encounter in a Tel Aviv walled garden. Later in life, he would repeatedly speak of this Origins event. He would even grab a levitating camera on a Lufthansa jet to snap, seemingly without reason, a photo of an empty sky outside his cabin window only to discover, when the film was developed, three perfect flying discs.[62] Ingo Swann, as we have already seen, has written an entire book on alien-human communication and, according to Paul Smith, remote viewer Ed Dames was fascinated with the same subject and was constantly speaking of aliens and UFOs. The truth is that such subjects were constantly floating and spinning through the remote-viewing programs. Acknowledged or not, seen or not, they were, like the discs in Geller's photo, still there.

MYSTICAL MUTATIONS AND A SAN FRANCISCO EPILOGUE

As I have already noted, explicit metaphysical themes have long been part of the X-Men story arc. One might even argue that these *are* the story arc. A brief study of just a few of the numerous appearances and mutations of the adjective "mystical" is especially instructive here. These patterns start off as very minor riffs and passing references in the original Lee and Roy series and gradually enter the very heart of the story arcs in the Claremont and Morrison runs, primarily through the two (or three) characters of Professor Charles Xavier and Jean Grey and her cosmic alter ego, the Phoenix, but also through the blue figures of Nightcrawler and Mystique.

The first occurrence of the term "mystical" appears in issue #9, where Lee uses it in its adverbial form in order to refer to, of all things, Lucifer's atomic bomb (another clear example of the metaphysical energies of Radiation), whose fuse Professor Xavier is trying to telepathically locate so that Cyclops can zap it: "Then, suddenly, the bomb begins to throb, as though mystically endowed with a life of its own" (XM 221). Radiation again.

Chris Claremont, who was responsible for reimagining the team in the mid- and late 1970s, turns to the mystical in a much more explicit way. For example, he gives his Russian hero, Colossus, a surname with blatant occult connotations: Peter Rasputin. He also introduces the demonlike character of Nightcrawler, a pious German Catholic mystic named Kurt Wagner. Eventually, with other writers in other decades, we learn that Nightcrawler is the abandoned son of Mystique, the blue, sexy, shape-shifting, skull-wearing archvillainess who looks more than a little like the Hindu Tantric goddess Kali and whose name means, literally, "the Mystical"—as in the French *la mystique*. The mystical as the erotic again.

But it is another Claremont creation, the figure of Jean Grey become Phoenix, who becomes the fullest embodiment of the X-Men mysticism. Her own Origins story has Jean growing up the daughter of a professor of history at Bard College. When, as a girl, she witnesses a girlfriend struck by a car and watches her soul glow away in her little arms, something within Jean opens, "an agonizing snap within her brain" (DP 228)—trauma as initiation again. Much later, she becomes Marvel Girl, a member of the first X-Men team, and then finally Phoenix. In the latter role, she will become a cosmic goddess figure akin to those found throughout Hindu and Buddhist Asia. Perhaps this is why Claremont and Cockrum sometimes portray her seated in the classic lotus posture of yoga (UXM 729).

But Phoenix is not simply an Asian goddess. She is also a Jewish one. In one of his most striking and complex panels, Claremont imagines the X-Men in the metaphysical categories of Kabbalah, where each X-Man becomes one of the ten *sephirot* or "aspects of God," with Phoenix as the sixth central or heart aspect called Tiphareth or Beauty. Here is how Claremont puts it, as Phoenix spiritually unites with her friends to save all of reality from collapsing: "A new pattern forms—shaped like the mystic tree of life—with Xavier its lofty Crown and Colossus its base: each X-Man has a place, each a purpose greater than himself or herself. And the heart of the tree, the catalyst that binds these wayward souls together is Phoenix. Tiphareth. Child of the sun, child of life, the vision of the harmony of things" (UXM 327, DP 125, 200). I am not sure what teenage reader would have picked up on the complex kabbalistic references to the Tree of Life (I certainly would not have), but there it is, as clear as day for the knowing gnostic reader.

A writer like Grant Morrison takes these mystical patterns further still, although he seems to prefer a more Asian, often Buddhist, register, much of it focused on what he dubs "the Manifestation of the Phoenix," as it is called by the "neuro-mystical surgeons of the Shi'ar space empire" (NXM 128.13). The Manifestation of the Phoenix involves what amounts to the full actualization of an omniscient, omnipotent cosmic "Phoenix potential" in the human body of Jean Grey (NXM 127.15, 139.7). Hence, "if she ever taps into it again, she could become something akin to a god" (NXM 125.10). Indeed. Here is Wolverine counseling Jean about her Phoenix potential: "Last time you lit up like this, the whole universe peed its pants . . . Blind people saw it in Seattle, Jeannie" (NXM 120.22).

One of the most powerful panels expressive of this X-mysticism appears in issue #128 of the Morrison/Quitely *New X-Men* run. The Phoenix consciousness shines through the humanity of an entranced Jean. Silverware—that strangely quotidian

4.6   THE MANIFESTATION OF THE PHOENIX

conduit for paranormal powers—levitates around her head as Phoenix snarls a line that makes it very clear where Phoenix stands on the question of the true nature and scope of consciousness: "Jean is only the house where I live, Charles" (NXM 128.14). The explicit eroticism of this particular Manifestation of the Phoenix needs no comment.

In the end, of course, the full manifestation of divinity in a human person is too much for the fragile ego and the mortal coil. Hence when Jean exposes the villain Jason Wyngarde to a full-blown cosmic experience of "the infinite reaches of space and time," he is reduced to a babbling, drooling basket case. He is psychologically destroyed (PK 110). Neither is Jean immune to such destructions. She and Professor Xavier may have set up a "series of psychic circuit breakers" in her mind to cut the power back to a level she could endure (DP 87), but these finally blew. In the end, Jean was overwhelmed, and so she allowed herself—a "vessel," "form," or "avatar" of the Phoenix Force (DP 183, 218)—to be killed on the Watcher's alien base on the dark side of the moon. Back to Jack Kirby.

The message is clear enough. Claremont may be working within an evolutionary mysticism that sees the summit of human evolution as equivalent to "gaining in effect the powers and potentials of God," and Phoenix may have "symbolized the potential of the species," but we are not yet ready for such a Divinization. No one can be "bound irrevocably to the Divine" and survive, not at least on this plane (DP 206, 276, 207). The filter fries, and the human vessel dies.

Before we close this meditation on the mytheme of Mutation, it seems worth pointing out that in 2008, in order to commemorate the series as it moved to its landmark five hundredth issue, the X-Men moved to the Bay Area of San Francisco, confirming my initial X-intuition in that hot 2006 parking lot about the deep resonances that exist between this originally New York mythology and the California evolutionary mysticisms located largely around the Bay Area: mutants and mystics. One issue, #497, featured the X-Men decked out in classic hippie garb. A later cover from the summer of 2010 would go even further and feature Magneto in a classic lotus posture meditating a powerful electromagnetic field into existence on top of Mount Tamalpais, which overlooks the city from across the Golden Gate Bridge, as he tries to will back an immense missile-bullet shot at the earth by an alien race.

4.8   MAGNETO MEDITATES ON MOUNT TAM

It would be difficult to find a more iconic image of my thesis about the secret life of superpowers. The mutants have become practicing mystics. The X-Men are now living in San Francisco. Orientation (the yogic posture), Alienation (the missile-bullet), Radiation (the electromagnetic field), and Mutation (the X-Men) have become inseparable components of the story. The Super-Story.

5 *REALIZATION*

READING THE PARANORMAL WRITING US

Like Charles Fort's growing intuition that he was caught in some Martian-projected movie and that it was time to "step out of the screen," we too are now leaving our Super-Story. We are catching glimpses. We are awakening.

The superreader approaches this stage of Realization when he or she begins to suspect that paranormal processes are real. Realization is achieved when one comes to understand that such events are not only real, but also inherently *participatory*, that is, paranormal events often behave very much like texts: they appear for us and rely on our active engagement or "reading" to appear at all and achieve meaning. In some fundamental way that we do not yet understand, they *are* us, projected into the objective world of events and things, usually through some story, symbol, or sign. Realization is the insight that we are caught in such a story. Realization is the insight that we are being written.

Any model of the history of fantasy literature worth its salt should provide a certain payout. It should make sense of what was hitherto confusing and too often ignored. I suggested repeatedly in the previous chapters that the themes of the East and the Alien have played important, if not actually central, roles in the development of the Super-Story. I suggested that there is something foundational about the two first mythemes of Orientation and Alienation. If this is in fact true, we should expect to find these themes returning in surprising ways in figures central to the origins and development of the superhero genre.

And that is precisely what we find. Enter Otto Binder and Alvin Schwartz. Both men were key players in the Golden Age of superhero comics. Binder wrote many of the most memorable Captain Marvel stories for Fawcett and then performed similarly for DC with the Superman mythos, developing or introducing such central characters as Jimmy Olsen, Lois Lane, Superboy, and Supergirl. Schwartz wrote many of the Batman and Superman newspaper strips in the late 1940s and '50s and created one of the key Superman villains that Binder would also take up: Bizarro. Superman, Batman, and Captain Marvel are hardly minor characters. It would thus be difficult to underestimate either man's influence on the genre—or what they finally realized.

FROM ADAM LINK TO THE DESK OF CAPTAIN MARVEL

Otto Oscar Binder (1911–74) published his first fantastic tale with his brother Earl under a fused penname ("Eando Binder," for "E and O Binder") in the pulp magazine *Amazing Stories* (October 1932). "The First Martian" features an alien landing in Bessemer, Michigan, where the two authors had lived as young boys before they moved to Randolph, Nebraska, and then on to Chicago. Significant mostly for what it presciently signals about Otto's future fascinations, the story also happens to feature what would later be called a UFO scene, a topic that would come to absorb Binder's last years.[1]

Earl and Otto continued to write and publish in the pulps. As a result, they became humble celebrities of sorts among the early sci-fi fans, especially around Chicago, where they lived. The mid- to late 1930s saw Otto Binder actively pursuing a freelance writing career. His personal letters during this time are filled with references to "Mort" (Weisinger) and "Julie" (Julius Schwartz), two men who were or would become major forces in the fantasy and comic-book industries. Binder played bridge with both of them, dreaming up sci-fi plots amid the smoke and cards. Mort wrote him often. These letters make clear what the business was about on its most basic level: plot, plot, and more plot, and then length, character, and pennies per word.[2] The letters also reveal a single word that the authors and editors commonly used among themselves for their popular products: a story was called a "yarn."

Binder, as we shall soon see, had many different writing careers. By all accounts, including his own, the high point of his first pulp fiction career was a three-year series featuring a loveable sentient "thinking robot," the first of its kind, named Adam Link. Adam first appeared in a short story entitled "I, Robot" in *Amazing Stories* (January 1939), edited by an already very familiar figure—Ray Palmer. Palmer and Binder were close friends. In fact, Binder stayed with Palmer for a time just before his marriage.[3] Historian and archivist of sci-fi fan culture Sam Moskowitz (to whom Binder willed his papers and manuscripts) notes in his *The Coming of the Robots*, which he dedicates to Binder, that Adam Link single handedly changed "the pattern of robot stories so that the robots were treated sympathetically instead of as villains."[4] "Sam," as Binder knew him in his letters, would also discover another thing about Adam Link: he was the first robot in the literature to speak in the first person.

The idea of a humanlike robot would later be explored more famously by Isaac Asimov in an identically titled collection of short stories. To his credit, Asimov was all too aware of his debt to Binder and strongly objected to using Otto's title, preferring his own instead, *Mind and Iron*. But his editor would have none of it, and Binder did not in the end object. All he asked in return was a signed copy of Asimov's book.[5]

Late in 1939, Binder began writing comic strips. By 1941, he was writing scripts for Joe Simon and Jack Kirby's Captain America. But his real break would come with a different company, Fawcett. Fawcett became a major player in the industry after its introduction of Captain Marvel in *Whiz Comics* #2, in February of 1940. The character, essentially an answer to National's Superman, was written by Bill Parker (who coined the expression "holy moley" in the strip) and designed by Charles Clarence (or C. C.) Beck, who used film star Fred MacMurray as his original model for the superhero.

The mythos of Captain Marvel involves a homeless young boy named Billy Batson who encounters a phantom figure in the street as he sells papers at night in the rain. The mysterious man guides him down into a subway tunnel and onto a train sporting strange symbols. When the train comes to a stop, Billy finds himself in a subterranean hall. The two walk past statues of the seven deadly sins and finally encounter a white-haired wizard sitting on a throne. His name is Shazam, an acronym for Solomon, Hercules, Atlas, Zeus, Achilles, and Mercury. Shazam explains that he has been defending good and battling evil for three thousand years now. He is old, and it is time for him to go. He teaches Billy the magic word—*Shazam*. As he speaks it, a lightning bolt flashes down out of a dark cloud—Blam!—and transforms the young boy into a full-grown man, Captain Marvel. The wizard instructs him again to utter the word. Captain Marvel obeys, and a huge block of granite suspended from the ceiling falls on the wizard. The mystical vocation has passed on to a new generation. And with that, Billy finds himself back in the rain on the street, selling newspapers, as if it were all a dream.

But, of course, it is not a dream. Billy and Captain Marvel will spend hundreds of issues battling the evil Dr. Sivana, introduced in that very first issue, and other assorted villains. The Binder-Beck stories of Captain Marvel, or "the Big Red Cheese," as he became affectionately known (for his red-gold costume and trademark humor), were classic examples of comic books that worked on two levels—that of the child reader, who took it all very seriously, and that of the adult reader, who could laugh at all the puns and playful humor.

As comic-book lore goes, Captain Marvel bestowed two major symbols on the subculture: his magical cry of "Shazam!" and his signature lightning bolt emblazoned on his chest. The latter symbol would become virtually synonymous with the superhero genre. It would also play a key symbolic role in another American folk hero whom Binder would come to know and write about—Ted Owens, the "PK Man," whom we will meet in a moment.

Binder was assigned the writing duties for Captain Marvel in December of 1941. He never looked back. Binder's biographer Bill Schelly calls him the "most prolific writer of the Golden Age." It is difficult to argue with such a title. According to Binder, who kept studious records and careful files of his own work, between 1941 and 1960 he wrote no less than 2,465 scripts. In 1944 alone, he churned out 228 tales "on a smoking machine that I last remember melting away completely."[6] The majority of those 2,465 scripts were for Fawcett, but 24 of them were for EC, and he would come to write for DC as well. He probably identified with Captain Marvel more than any other superhero. I found, for example, some charming personal letterhead that Binder used to write Sam

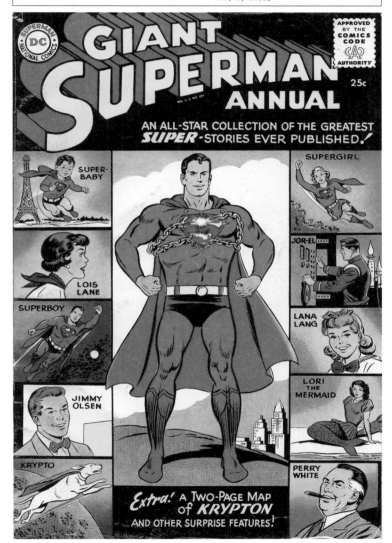

S.1   OTTO BINDER'S SECRET SHAZAM SELF AND SUPER WRITING

Moskowitz with the heading "A personal message from Captain Marvel." The hero, his trademark lightning bolt blazing, looks down on the reader.

By late 1953, after a Fawcett-DC Superman lawsuit was finally settled (DC successfully insisted that Captain Marvel was a knockoff and infringed on its rights), Binder was no longer legally blocked from writing for National or DC, as he had been during the suit. Hence his old friends, DC editors Mort Weisinger and Julius Schwartz, welcomed him on board. Binder wrote first for *Strange Adventures* and *Mystery in Space*, then *Jimmy Olsen* and *Superboy*. He introduced the character of Supergirl in *Action* #252 (May 1959) and penned numerous Superman stories as well. Schelly draws attention to Binder's accomplishments here by noting that when *Giant Superman Annual* #1 (1960) reprinted what were widely considered to be the best Superman stories from the 1950s, six of the nine were by Otto Binder.[7]

ON SPACE WORLDS AND THE SECRET OF THE SAUCERS

As the 1950s came to an end, *Sputnik* appeared in our skies, and President Kennedy began speaking of a moon shot, Binder became more and more interested in space exploration. He left comic writing and entered what amounted to a third writing career (after pulp fiction and superhero comics): popular science writing. In some sense, this was very much a return to origins, for science had always been his first love, even if the depression had frustrated his original dream to become a chemical engineer. Now in the 1960s, he would do things like contract with NASA to write school charts for the *Mercury*, *Gemini*, and *Apollo* programs, write an instructional comic book for Disney on space exploration, and join multiple science organizations. Basically, he became something of a space guru in the heyday of the space race.

He would also invest almost everything, and then lose it all, in a new magazine he cofounded and edited. *Space World* #1 appeared in May of 1960. The magazine ran for about five years and then collapsed. But not until it put him in touch with a new subject that would fascinate him for the rest of his life: the UFO. The flying saucer was not really new, of course. It had always been there in some form, from Otto's very first pulp story with his brother Earl. But now it was spinning into his own world and transforming him in the process. Here is how it floated in.

As the editor of a space science magazine, Binder participated in a radio show in April of 1961. During the course of the show, the conversation turned to the ever-present, ever-popular subject of UFOs. Binder expressed his doubts.[8] There just was

5.2   OTTO BINDER AS SPACE GURU

not enough convincing evidence. But as editor of *Space World*, he was also receiving a significant amount of correspondence on the subject, and he was gradually changing his mind behind the scenes and between the lines.

Schelly describes what would become Binder's UFO interest as the phoenix that rose out of the ashes of *Space World*.[9] The biographer also suggests that the skeptic-turned-believer Thane Smith, the central character of Binder's two saucer novels, *Menace of the Saucers* (1969) and *Night of the Saucers* (1971), is a stand-in for Binder himself.[10] Hence the opening line on the back cover of the first novel: "Smith was a writer of science fiction stories. Now, incredibly, he was witnessing the real thing." Like Thane Smith, Otto Binder was witnessing his science fiction fantasies coming true. Why and exactly how they were coming true, he was not so sure.[11]

The stories coming in, worthy of any pulp fiction magazine, were certainly delicious enough. Indeed, they were even better, since Binder was now writing them in nonfiction contexts. In a special UFO edition of the men's magazine *Saga*, for example, Binder wrote about the reports that he had received from amateur ham-radio operators, who told him that they had intercepted secret NASA signals during the lunar landing of July 11, 1969. In a scene worthy of a *Fantastic Four* comic, the Watcher and all, Binder reports that his sources allegedly heard Neil Armstrong exclaiming: "These babies were huge, sir. Enormous. Oh, God, you wouldn't believe it! I'm telling you there are other space-craft out there lined upon the far side of the crater edge. They're on the Moon watching us."[12]

It is not too difficult to know how Binder would have received such a tale. After all, by this time he had already published two nonfiction books on flying saucers, and he would soon publish a third just before he died. The first, *What We Really Know about Flying Saucers* (1967), was published by his old Captain Marvel publisher, Fawcett, thus linking, in the very act of physical production, the superhero fantasy and the real-world UFO encounter. The second contained in its very title a version of the line Armstrong would supposedly utter on the moon a year later, *Flying Saucers Are Watching Us* (1968). Then Binder pulled out all the stops and cowrote his boldest book on the subject with Max H. Flindt, *Mankind—Child of the Stars* (1974). This final book of the saucer trilogy, which we might read as a spiritual testament of sorts, makes explicit and speculatively real much that came before it in Binder's multifarious writing career, including and especially some of the key components of his science fiction and superhero writing. And why not? In Binder's mind at least, the imagined *had* become the real. Exactly like Thane Smith, Binder was "a writer of science fiction stories. Now, incredibly, he was witnessing the real thing."

What We Really Know about Flying Saucers was his first major attempt to come to terms with this personal evolution.[13] Of the three books, it is the most reserved, although it is not really very reserved, and most of Binder's ufological themes can already be found here. Significantly, the book is introduced by none other than John Keel.

Binder saw his project as a scientific one, if also an admittedly heterodox one. Claiming at the beginning of the book to have "pored over thousands of sightings," he states his conclusions as clear as they come: "That is all this book attempts to do— once and for all to take the UFO phenomenon out of the 'myth' category and place it firmly in the 'reality' category, despite all the brush-off machinations of the Air Force, the government, and orthodox science."[14] In this same spirit, he treats in the middle of the book such subjects as the famed cigar-shaped UFOs, widely believed to be mother ships; Ray Palmer's atmospherea theory of a civilization of nonmaterial energy beings existing in the upper atmosphere and interacting with us as deep-sea denizens living on the bottom of an atmospheric ocean; the hypothesis of time travel, which would explain why the aliens do not contact us ("they *can't* under this theory," Binder points out, since they are appearing to us not as physical objects but as "'projections' across the time barrier"); the earth as a kind of space colony, with humans either as descendants of the original space travelers or as hybrids of an alien-ape breeding program (well before von Däniken, by the way); and, finally and perhaps most interestingly, UFOs as "dimension faeries" appearing as "ghosts" in our dimension, as we would no doubt appear in theirs.[15]

Binder retains a certain rhetorical distance from each of these individual speculations, but he is also clear that the cumulative weight of the data, and particularly the *patterns* into which it all falls, is indeed conclusive: "The flying saucers are not myths but machines."[16] Or again, in his last line: "The flying saucers are here. The UFO's are real. The only thing unreal is earth's attitude toward these significant objects and their mysterious masters, who may well be here to tell us of a brotherhood of worlds in the universe."[17]

Flying Saucers Are Watching Us extends this project, radicalizing it further in the process.[18] Although it appeared just a year after the first book, it is a very different sort of text. For one thing, Binder now introduces a long list of affiliations to his resumé of ten science books (the pulp and comics writing are never mentioned), including the National Aerospace Education Council, the American Rocketry Association, and NICAP (the premiere American UFO research organization founded by marine corps pilot Donald E. Keyhoe).

In terms of content, he has also already clearly adopted a very familiar thesis by now, namely, the ancient-astronaut theory. Binder came to it through the writings of engineer and research scientist Max H. Flindt, who had sent Binder his manuscript *On Tiptoe beyond Darwin* while Binder was publishing *Space World*. This self-published text propounded, in Binder's words now, "that mankind is a hybrid product of prehistoric unions between spacemen and early tererrestrian primates or humanoids, deliberately bred ages ago in order to establish a future earth colony."[19] This is the core idea that will absorb Binder's last years and culminate in *Mankind—Child of the Stars*.

Flying Saucers Are Watching Us is deeply Fortean. "We are property," Binder announces at the end of chapter 1, employing, without reference, a famous Fortean gnomon. Then he softens the sinister undertones. "Family property, that is. Our extra-terrestrial and current cousins, stemming from the same long-ago sires we did, are today streaking through our skies in amazing vehicles. We call them flying saucers and UFO's."[20] According to Binder, what our extraterrestrial sires were really about is the speeding up of evolution. Basically, they were using their biotechnology to "con-dense evolutionary processes into brief periods of time." This is how the astonishing human brain evolved in such a short span of time. Binder thinks of the human brain as "imported," that is, as an evolutionary product inserted into an early primate species through an intentional hybrid breeding program. The implications? We carry the alien in us. We *are* the extraterrestrial. Alienation and Mutation are completely united here.

And sex is the secret that joins them. Hence Binder's elaborate discussions of "Sex and the Saucermen" (chapter 2); his fascination with the "star-borne" trait of the unusually large human penis (in the light of other primate penises, which are tiny in comparison); the sexual components of the contactee and abductee reports, which of-ten look more or less like instances of what Binder calls "space rape"; and the famous 1957 Villas Boas case, in which a Brazilian farmer named Antonio Villas Boas reported being taken on board a landed ship and bred with a beautiful, but growling alien woman.

We, of course, have already seen this alien erotics, many times. Still, it is worth noting that at least three mediums or channelers made very similar claims both just before and just after Flindt and Binder. William Dudley Pelley's *Star Guests* (1950), for example, had declared, as his title had it, that we are all "Star Guests," that is, alien spirits from interstellar space (more specifically, the star system Sirius) who entered the bodies of primates fifty to thirty million years ago to cohabit with animal forms and produce hybrid beings, like us. Three years later, George Hunt Williamson published— through Ray Palmer's press no less—*Other Tongues—Other Flesh* (1953), which claimed that the "Sons of God" of Genesis 6 constituted a spiritual migration from Sirius whose males co-habited with female primates in order to produce prehistoric or primitive humanity. Finally, in 1974 Phyllis Schlemmer, a trance medium from Ossinning, New York, began channeling a cosmic being named "Tom," who claimed to be part of "the Nine," a group of beings from "Deep Space" who oversee planet earth. Schlemmer's revelations, now recorded in *The Only Planet of Choice* (1993), include the Alteans, a species of unisexual, blue-eyed, voiceless humanoids who glow with a kind of silvery iridescence. It was the Alteans, Tom taught, who produced the Atlanteans through a hybrid seeding project, one of the accomplishments of which was the enlargement of the sexual organs toward more physical pleasure.[21] Why are such texts and teachings relevant here? Because they reveal in unmistakable ways the deep resonance, down to precise details, that exists between these channeled occult traditions and Binder's UFO writing.

And elite science fiction. Here's a whopper of a side-note. One of Schlemmer's auditors was none other than Gene Roddenberry, the legendary creator of *Star Trek*, who, Schlemmer's website claims, was visiting the medium as part of his research for the sci-fi series. Hence *Star Trek: Deep Space Nine*. Maybe. The truth, as usual, appears to be even stranger. Roddenberry, a humanist who was deeply critical of religion but who was fascinated by psi phenomena and altered states of consciousness (possibly stemming from a childhood out-of-body experience) and who accepted some measure of the "latent abilities" of telepathy, clairvoyance, and psychokinesis, appears to have been recruited by a paranormal organization called Lab Nine to help prepare the public, via a film-script that he would write, for an impending first contact event. Toward this end, he was given tours of parapsychological labs and introduced to Schlemmer and, through her, to Tom and the Nine. Neither the film nor the first contact panned out, although the script was written. Film or no film, landing or no landing, Roddenberry conversed with Tom through Schlemmer. It was Roddenberry, for example, who got the entity to affirm that some of us are "of Altean blood" and possess Altean "genetic features . . . mixed with our basic Earth features."[22] Human-alien hybrids again.

What is so extraordinary about Binder's particular version of this familiar alien erotic trope is how explicit he is. I suppose he has to be, though. After all, for Binder, cross-species sexual intercourse is *the* key to the central argument of this book (and the next). What he calls his Homo Hybrid thesis demands it, relies on it. Alien-simian sex is precisely what produces the human for Binder and Flindt. It is what makes us us. It is what gives us our dual nature, our sense of somehow being an angel and an animal at the same time. Binder and Flindt will even suggest in their later cowritten book that it this ancient sexual union that contributes to schizophrenia in some individuals: the uneasy union of the terrestrial and the extraterrestrial breaks apart in the schizophrenic "split mind" and produces all sorts of fantasies—fantasies, however, that often speak in distant and distorted ways of our true stellar origins.

Not surprisingly, then, Binder takes up the subject of religion itself at the very end of the book. Here he calls the saucermen "saintly" and imagines a "multi-million-year-old civilization" behind their advanced spiritual nature, which has developed a "universal super-religion more profound and meaningful than any [of] our fragmented and bickering sects on earth have ever reached." The skymen were not gods, though, despite the likelihood that "the awed primitives called them gods." They were only emissaries of "the God of the macro-cosmos from infinity to eternity." In other words, the history of religions as we normally think of it is a series of major mistakes. The basic mythology, found all over the world, of a sky-god bestowing culture and knowledge on human beings and then disappearing back into the sky is only partly true.

And partly false. Such local sky-gods are products of an ancient conflation of alien technology and divinity, which is to say that they are products of our own ignorance. Still, for Binder, much as we saw with Ray Palmer and Jack Kirby, there *is* a God beyond the gods, a superdivinity, a Being reflected in that "grander sense of ultimate Godhood implanted genetically in our hearts."[23] In the end, then, religion for Binder is a strange combination of naïvete and profundity, of fantasy and fact. More of Fort's truth-fiction.

◢ SI-FI: FROM PK MAN TO STARMAN AND BACK AGAIN

Finally, there is *Mankind—Child of the Stars*. Before we get to this last and most adventurous component of the Binder saucer trilogy, it is important to trace Binder's intellectual and philosophical development. We also need to take a brief detour and meet an apparent real-life superhero with whom Otto Binder corresponded between his second and third saucer books: Ted Owens, the self-proclaimed PK Man.

Like all thinking persons, Binder changed and developed his positions over the course of his life. His early philosophy is captured succinctly in an unsent postcard that I found in the Moskowitz Collection at Texas A&M University. There is no date, but the one-cent stamp puts it somewhere before 1952 (when the rate changed to two cents). In it, he thanks his correspondent for sending him some Rosicrucian booklets and confesses that his wide-ranging interests in different social movements or "Progressions" is mostly as a "spectator." He himself takes no stand, but rides the fence. In a similar fence-sitting spirit, he is suspicious of any "true believer," since no statement or doctrine can be absolutely true.[24] As the years and decades ticked on, Binder explored more and more of these "Progressions" and progressed himself into some quite extraordinary convictions. He finally got off that fence.

In his study of science fiction fandom, Harry Warner Jr. employs the catchy phrase "Psi-Fi" to discuss some groups of fans in the 1950s who turned to the scientific study of psychical phenomena.[25] These individuals did things like volunteer as subjects for J. B. Rhine's parapsychology lab at Duke University or form flying-saucer organizations. Palmer and Arnold are obvious icons here, but Binder too was clearly moving in a Psi-Fi direction. In February of 1960, he published a *Mechanix Illustrated* article on "Things You Didn't Know about Your Mind," which was about the state of parapsychology and psychical phenomena. The piece included classical moves, like this one that drew from writer Upton Sinclair's *Mental Radio* to make the following analogy: "If telepathy is mental radio, clairvoyance can be called mental television."[26] The article is balanced, but basically sympathetic. So too with another he published on reincarnation memories in the same popular magazine, "Have You Lived Before?"[27] This time, however, he wrote under a pseudonym, "C. J. Talbert." Given the two pen-names, one factual, one fictional, we might conclude that at this point the real Otto Binder drew the (public) line somewhere between telepathy and reincarnation. That line would move—a lot.

On October 31, 1963, Binder wrote the air force's Office of Aerospace Research, requesting copies of all the reports on a document entitled "Research in Extrasensory Perception." Happily, the chief of the Documentation Division sent Binder exactly what he requested, a bound copy of a research report entitled "Testing for Extrasensory Perception with a Machine."[28] The machine in question, an early random-number generator, was called the VERITAC.

By the late 1960s and early '70s, Binder's writing was making even the air force's ESP machine look tame and boring. There were all those saucers, of course. But there was also a man named Ted Owens, the self-proclaimed PK Man. PK Man, short for Psychokinetic Man, is already, of course, a very clear and obvious superhero allu-sion, a consciously chosen title designed to recall more familiar ones, like Superman and Batman. In a very similar but more respectable vein, Owen's biographer Jeffrey Mishlove described his subject as a real-life American folk hero, comparable to the likes of Paul Bunyan or Pecos Bill.[29]

Mishlove was not exaggerating. This, after all, was a man who claimed that he first realized his powers as a young man playing basketball when fellow players would find the ball in their hands without seeing him passing it: in short, a kind of athletic tele-portation from the pages of those occult sport comics.[30] More dramatically, the adult Owens claimed to be able to produce and direct lightning bolts at will using a specific technique involving mental visualization and the pointing of his finger. To underline the point, he used an abstract symbol in his correspondence that featured a Saturn-shaped UFO and a lightning bolt. He even inscribed this symbol on a little disc, which came with his book, that he claimed was "charged and coded" with PK power—much, I would add, like a saint's relic.[31] He also wanted to found his own religion, something he would call the Church of Sota (secrets of the ages).[32] Basically, Ted Owens was a real-life Captain Marvel or UFO mystic with his own *Shazam!* incantation and lightning-bolt insignia. If Binder had earlier witnessed his science fiction fantasies coming true through the UFO, now, more weirdly still, he was witnessing his superhero writing come to life through the PK Man.

And Owens' claimed power over lightning was just the beginning. He also claimed to correctly predict (or cause) the ending of major droughts, the assumed lightning strike of *Apollo 12* on November 14, 1969, and the near total ruination of the entire 1968 season of the Philadelphia Eagles professional football team. He had written over a dozen sports writers about the latter intention. Mishlove tells us that the Eagles suffered thirty injuries that season and lost eleven games in a row.[33]

On a darker note, Binder claims that Owens wrote government agencies on March 4, 1968, warning them of the "destruction of one or more highly-placed U.S. Government Officials—by assassination." Martin Luther King Jr. and Bobby Kennedy were both assassinated within the next twelve weeks.[34] The next summer, on July 30, 1969, Owens wrote President Nixon in order to warn him of a Cuban kidnapping attempt via the sea at his Key Biscayne residence in Florida. On August 24, 1969, the *Miami Herald* published a story with the headline "Spy Plot Shatters Prospects for Renewing U.S. Cuba Ties." It read eerily close to Owens's letter.

More bizarrely still, one could conclude that Owens "guided" Hurricane Inez with a map that he had drawn in October of 1966 (according to Binder, the hurricane did things that no one expected, as if it were following Owens's directions) and correctly predicted the appearance of three simultaneous hurricanes in September of 1967 (Beulah, Chloe, and Doris were all active on the same weekend).[35] Owens originally thought that such feats were worked through communicating with "the Intelligence behind Nature."[36] Later he concluded that these were actually UFO intelligences.[37] All in all, he claimed influence over or involvement in approximately two hundred predictions and events. And we're not talking spoons and wristwatches here. We're talking hurricanes, sports seasons, assassinations, and a U.S. president. He even claimed "to tap a reservoir of powers called the ODE forces," for "other dimensional effects."[38] Such

Fortean wild talents seem to be involved in scenes like the one in which Owens found himself parked on a narrow mountain road: a car allegedly appeared in the darkness, met him head on, and passed right through his car.[39]

This would all be easy to dismiss, except for the uncomfortable fact that Owens also had the foresight to collect signed affidavits from people who witnessed some of his predictions, which he then further documented with the later newspaper clippings. Indeed, he was obsessive about documenting everything and then sending the evidence to the proper individuals. Hence the back cover of his *How to Contact Space People* features a photograph of Owens holding a scroll, like Moses (to whom he often compared himself). When one looks closer, however, one notices that the scroll is in fact a scroll of address labels!

One can doubt (and that's probably much too weak a word here) all of these stories. What is more difficult to do is question Owens's sincerity. The man shows every sign of believing it all. He consistently sought out CIA and NASA officials, sports writers, team owners, government weather agencies, lawyers, and professional scientists. He *wanted* to be tested in the most rigorous manner. Most people, of course, completely ignored him.

Or simply made fun of him. Mishlove tells a heart-wrenching story of how Owens was laughed out of a scientific conference at the University of London in August of 1976 when he showed up with a toy wagon full of his newspaper clippings and claims. It was there that Mishlove first befriended the crestfallen psychic. Others, particularly the sports writers, but also at least one CIA official and one NASA official, also appear to have taken him more or less seriously. If nothing else, Ted Owens was a great story.

In terms of the evidence, the problem was not just that Owens claimed to control hurricanes, lightning strikes, and NFL seasons. The problem was that he claimed that he received these superpowers from a 1965 encounter with a cigar-shaped UFO spewing red, white, blue, and green flames near Fort Worth, Texas, before the thing just vanished, "like a light turned off," when it got close to his car.[40] And that was not all. More specifically, he attributed his powers to the SIs or space intelligences, "strange beings of pure energy" from "another eerie dimension," two of which he described as a cross between humans and grasshoppers (there is that damn insectoid theme again) and whom he affectionately named Tweeter and Twitter (it is at precisely this point that I begin to giggle).[41] The cover of the original edition of *How to Contact Space People* features a painting of an SI, presumably rendered by Owens himself.

HOW TO CONTACT
SPACE PEOPLE

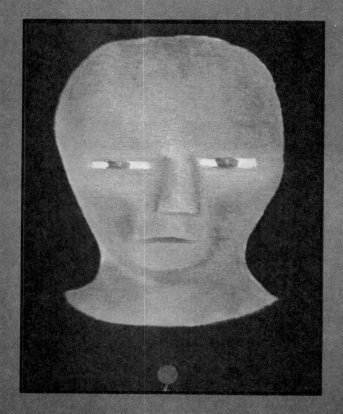

By TED OWENS

ILLUSTRATED

SAUCERIAN PUBLICATION/CLARKSBURG, W. VA.

Owens claimed that these space intelligences had performed "psychic surgery" on the right lobe of his brain in order to enhance his natural telepathic powers and make his brain a better receiver of their "high-voltage ESP messages." He also reported a "deep indentation" behind his right ear that his wife first noted and interpreted as some sort of insertion mark or, as some would say now, an implant.[42]

It is here that my own suspicions and intuitions kick in. Is it possible that such scenes constitute a sincerely believed but nevertheless coded story of some kind of right-brain trauma that opened Owens up to the altered states and empowered imagination of that myth-making hemisphere? There is certainly much to choose from here. Binder mentions not one, not two, but *four* brain traumas, what he calls "brain rattlings" or "brutal blows." Here he lists getting knocked fifteen feet when a car struck him at the age of five, an early boxing concussion, another childhood incident in which a boy rolled a log down on him and ripped open his scalp, and a high-speed teenage car crash. Later, Ted would interpret these early brain injuries as planned by the SIs. In my less mythical translation, he saw them as somehow related to his paranormal powers.[43] I suspect that he was right about that, since, as I have already noted, brain or spinal trauma is a common theme in the biographies of major psychics.[44]

In any case, Ted Owens honestly considered himself to be "the UFO Prophet" and constantly and sincerely compared himself to Moses for his ability to wreak havoc through the weather in order to prove his powers to his hard-hearted, unbelieving listeners (with the U.S. government as the new Egypt). He also understood his powers as "signs" that the SIs were using to get our attention, so that we could change our ways and avoid Nature's coming war on humankind for its disastrous polluting and nuclear foolishness.[45]

Mishlove, himself a psychotherapist, observes the obvious, namely, that much of this comes uncomfortably close to sounding like the symptoms of schizophrenia. When one encounters Owens describing how he communicates with the SIs through writing on a mental tablet or Men-Tel, one's suspicions only grow stronger. Mine do anyway, as I am powerfully reminded of Richard Shaver.

This hardly explains everything, though, since, if this was schizophrenia and *any* of the stories are true (and I suspect some of them are), it was a schizophrenia doing things like wreaking havoc on the weather and the poor Philadelphia Eagles. Moreover, these altered states of consciousness—whether rendered paranormal, pathological, or, most likely, both—were expressing themselves in a relatively uneducated man with a genius-level IQ (150) who happened to be a member of MENSA. On the wild side (as if it could get any wilder), we might recall that Otto Binder had his own explanation of the similarity between a figure like Ted Owens and a schizophrenic: for Binder, schizophrenia was *itself* a symptom of our ancient alien-simian "split mind."[46]

In many ways, Owens was a contactee, that is, a member of a small group of eccentric individuals who, since the late 1940s and early '50s, have claimed intimate contact with Martian, Venusian, and other assorted "space brothers," often on board various spaceships and usually toward some sort of utopian spiritual message or prophetic warning involving nuclear war and/or the environment. Most writers strenuously distance themselves from such people, as contactee claims, at least literally understood, are often obviously fraudulent and take on explicitly religious tones that raise eyebrows . . . high.

Interestingly, Binder did not distance himself from such people or their claims, as his constant reference to a galactic "brotherhood" and his ultrapositive reading of the saintly saucermen make crystal clear (although he does distance Owens from the earlier contactees, since, as he points out, Owens's communications were only "mental" and he never met the SIs face to face or traveled in their ships).[47] Such a qualified embrace of the contactee literature, I would suggest, is a natural outcome of both Binder's early superhero writing and his later Homo Hybrid thesis. After all, in the terms of the latter, we are *all* contactees, and this ancient contact is encoded in our DNA and our large brains and sexual organs.

Binder initiated contact with Owens in early 1970, when he wrote Owens about an essay that he wanted to publish in *Saga* magazine. This initial correspondence would result in a four-year collaboration (without a physical meeting), with Owens passing on hundreds of files, reports, and clippings to Binder, and Binder acting as a kind of unofficial biographer. For his own part, Owens was deeply appreciative of what Binder wrote about him. Indeed, he claimed that Binder's *Saga* essay, "Ted Owens—Flying Saucer Missionary," was the authoritative statement on the nature of his powers. He also stated flatly that he considered Otto Binder to be the only person alive who was capable of writing his biography.[48]

Binder never managed to write that biography. Mishlove did. But Binder, with Flindt (whom, like Owens, he never physically met), did write *Mankind—Child of the Stars*. I strongly suspect that he had Ted Owens in mind when he sat down to write this text. There is certainly nothing in the book that would deny Owens's claims, and there is much that would support them, or at least give them a worldview into which to plug. The book, after all, is filled with truly extraordinary claims of its own. Maybe it *is* Ted Owens's biography rendered in an implicit form.

All of Binder's claims in the book boil down to just two major theses, but they are whoppers: the idea that "Man may be a star-crossed hybrid of two worlds" and that "mankind is a colony."[49] These two basic ideas the authors call the Hybrid Man and Earth Colony theories. The book drives these two points home over and over again, with varying degrees of plausibility and outrageousness. In the end, though, their argument is carried most effectively not by a series of rational arguments or scientific proofs, but by a thought experiment involving an iconic figure named Starman.

Not too surprisingly, Starman was already the name of a superhero and had been appearing in comics since 1941. Binder would have definitely known about the Golden Age hero. But what he had in mind here was something altogether different. As this story is key to my own reading of Binder's entire body of work, it is perhaps with quoting at length. Here is how the authors begin their thought experiment, that is, their double thesis encoded in a conscious just-so story:

MANY MILLIONS AND PERHAPS BILLIONS OF YEARS AGO--AND NO HUMAN ON EARTH KNOWS HOW MANY LIGHT-YEARS AWAY--MAN EVOLVED ON A DISTANT PLANET. . . . THEN, IN TIME, HIS PLANET BECAME TOO SMALL, TOO COLD, OR TOO CROWDED FOR HIM, AND HE COLONIZED ONE OR MORE YOUNG NEARBY PLANETS. EVENTUALLY, PER-HAPS MILLIONS OF YEARS LATER, HE HAD TO MOVE AGAIN. . . . BUT THEN CAME THE SAVING DISCOVERY: STARMAN'S MIND WAS MARVELOUS AND HIGHLY DEVELOPED, FAR BEYOND THE CAPABILITIES OF OUR PRESENT-DAY EARTHLING MINDS. AT THE SAME TIME, UNFORTUNATELY, STARMAN'S BODY WAS TOTALLY INADEQUATE FOR PIONEERING JOBS ON OTHER PLANETS.

The solution? To divide the race into two branches: an ancestral race of wisdom and knowledge, and a hybrid colonial race that would be physically stronger but intel-lectually inferior. With this decision in place, other planets were colonized and scientific and spiritual progress continued apace. In the process, however, no colony was allowed to know that it was in fact a space colony. Until, that is, its population was sufficiently advanced to venture out into space on its own and was culturally and spiritually ready for the dazzling revelation. Then contact was initiated and the colony became aware of its true cosmic nature. "Thus, the colony fulfilled its destiny and became one more of the endless succession of planets chosen to be the home of the original interstellar Man. And there the tale ends."[50]

The moral of the story is clear enough: today, as one of those originally inferior colonies, we are almost ready ourselves to make contact with our interstellar coloniz- ers. And so our interstellar cousins swarm about in our skies. The time is near.

 So what should we make of all of this? Is there some way to make sense of the many lives of Otto Binder? What do pulp fiction, Captain Marvel, Superman, NASA, and Starman have in common?

I cannot help but note that much of Binder's history, archaeology, and espe- cially his knowledge of the history of religions, like that of his friend John Keel, is seriously flawed. For example, when he occasionally treats biblical texts or the his- tory of Indian religions (topics about which I know a good deal), he is either embar- rassingly literalistic or way, way off.[51] And, alas, this makes me worry about what he is saying when he writes about other subjects, about which I know little or nothing. Schelly has described Binder's science fantasies in his comic-writing days as "full of holes."[52] I suspect, strongly, that his saucer-trilogy science is similarly problematic, to say the least.

Which leads me to my main point, which is much more positive. Basically, I want to observe that *Otto Binder's final saucer trilogy is far more indebted to his pulp fiction, superhero, and contactee writing than it is to professional science*. What we finally have here, then, is not a new science, but a new *mythology* of science. In short, we are dealing with yet another framing of the paranormal (which is why Binder's saucer trilogy reso- nates so deeply with the channeled literature). The basic message of this paranormal mythology, moreover, boils down to a version of what I have called Realization. What Binder's myth suggests, to me anyway, is that we are being written, indeed that we have always been written in the deep biological sense that we are someone else's property or genetic experiment. We are, in effect, an unconscious colony of hybrid beings just now, barely, evolving into an awareness of who we are and where we sit in the cosmos. We have certainly not yet reached the stage of Authorization.

What does this have to do with Binder's superhero writing? A lot. After all, the elaborate Starman thought experiment involving an ancient species leaving a dying world, traveling across space, and finding an earth colony looks more than a little like the Superman mythos that originally initiated the superhero genre. Indeed, I suspect that Starman *is* Superman, filtered, translated, and transformed now through thirty-six years of pulp fiction, ufology, NASA lunar programs, and Ted Owens. Otto Binder's final UFO fascination, then, was not some fluke or late distraction. It was a "return to origins." O. O. Binder had lived up to his double name: he had come full circle.

WAKING UP INSIDE A STORY

Alvin Schwartz began writing comics in 1939 for *Fairy Tale Parade*, one of the earliest runs of the new genre. He wrote comic books to pay the bills, certainly not because he wanted to be writing cheap children's entertainment. At heart, he was a young intellectual, an aspiring novelist, and a friend of people like the writer Gertrude Stein, the poet William Carlos Williams, and the abstract painter Jackson Pollock, who famously wielded his splashing buckets of paint in a studio barn not far from where Schwartz lived. Schwartz would publish his first novel, *Blowtop*, in 1948. The *New York Times* described the book as the first conscious existentialist novel in America. Others considered it the first beat novel, influencing the likes of Allen Ginsberg and Jack Kerouac.

This, anyway, is what Alvin Schwartz wanted to be doing. In the 1940s and '50s, however, he was spending much of his time writing superhero stories. He wrote his first Batman story in 1942 and his first Batman and Superman strips in August and October of 1944, respectively. Between 1944 and 1952, he did most of the writing work for these two syndicated properties. Schwartz continued to work in the business until 1957, when he walked out after a sharp disagreement with Mort Weisinger over a storyline that he considered to be silly and unfaithful to the characters (Weisinger wanted Schwartz to have Superman transfer his powers to Lois Lane). One of his last creative acts was the invention of the reality-twisting villain Bizarro, "his own effort at deconstructing Superman," as he later put it.[53] He estimates that in the nineteen years of his career in the industry he wrote a total of some twenty thousand comics pages. After he left comics writing, Schwartz went on to other forms of the craft. He wrote three pseudonymous novels and two feature-film scripts and worked on thirty documentary dramas for the National Film Board of Canada as both a writer and researcher.

During these later careers, he did not think much (in both meanings of that expression) of his earlier superhero days. He tried not to anyway. Indeed, he told me flat-out that he had a "real distaste" for writing comics for a living. We saw this same pattern, of course, in Otto Binder, who, when he turned to science writing, space exploration, and ufology later in life consciously suppressed the fact, at least in his published bio pages, that he had spent most of his early career writing comic books. The point is a simple and understandable one: until very recently, comic books were considered childish, silly, escapist, or kitsch, if not actually subversive, dangerous, and obscene. Basically, they were considered a kind of "junk literature."

Otto Binder did not live to see the meteoric rise in popularity of all things super-heroic in the 1990s. Alvin Schwartz did. Partly because of this new cultural context (and a speaking invitation to the University of Connecticut that catalyzed his reflections), he began to look back on his career with a new eye. He also began to remember strange experiences that punctuated his life, magical moments that he had repressed or simply forgotten. "I realized that each of them had happened after I had gotten involved with Superman, as though my Superman experience had provoked them or had somehow been an initiating factor."[54] Stranger still, he began to realize that it was precisely these moments that had led him to write *Superman* in the first place.

He remembers the day in 1944 that he decided to accept the writing assignment. And the sandwich shop—Chock Full o' Nuts at 480 Lexington Avenue. A man walked in, as bland as they come, almost nonexistent in his indistinctness: "He was as vapid as the thin cheese-and-nut sandwich he was almost daintily munching on." Then it hit him. Clark Kent was just as bland, and he *had* to be—"in the ordinariness of each of us there had to be a place of rest, of relief. I didn't yet grasp all the implications of this, except that Superman seemed to highlight that common condition because in him the extremes were so much greater. . . . The sharp contrast between the self as nonentity and the self as all-powerful seemed to suggest a secret, private, but universal experience."

Then he began to remember all the ordinary "super" powers he had encoun-tered in his own life. Like the housewife who knew, regardless of distance, whenever a family member was in trouble; or the lithographer who could see people's auras and diagnose their health and emotional states on the spot; or the German refugee whose Nazi horrors rendered him incapable of holding down a job, but who could walk into a betting parlor and walk away a winner almost every time. That was the day he first realized, as the title of his University of Connecticut lecture and later published essay had it, "The Real Secret of Superman's Identity."[55]

Back in the 1990s, when he was writing his first metaphysical memoir, Schwartz noticed something more. He noticed that these sorts of paranormal experiences tended to appear in his own life only after he began writing comics, and that they worked in ways that led to his first novel, a process in turn that "had unveiled something within me that would speak of things I didn't know I knew" (UP 17–18). Hints of Ray Palmer.

Interestingly, this theme—quite common among artists and writers—found its most dramatic memory not in an authorial moment, but in a painterly one. Actually in two painterly moments. The first involved his first wife, Marjorie, and one of their more famous neighbors across the bay at Springs, East Hampton—Jackson Pollock. A little group of friends got to discussing what Marjorie, herself a painter, called ways of "uncovering that element in a canvas that went beyond what one knew." Alvin expressed frustration about not knowing how to do this in his own work. Pollock thought it easy and offered to show them how. He painted for them. Schwartz was stunned by what he witnessed in the barn that night: "the paint did not seem to obey the law of gravity. It poured in impossible directions . . . as if some other force were directing it." He concluded that "the circular forms already on the canvas were doing the influencing as though in their representations of pure acceleration they formed tiny gravitational fields of their own" (UP 20). It was as if the painting had taken on a life of its own.

A few months later, Alvin witnessed something similar happening through Marjorie. She was working on a semiabstract painting of flowers, fruit, and table when she felt blocked, then inspired. She began to paint over the flowers and fruit. Alvin was the first to realize what was emerging from the canvas: the Hindu elephant-headed god, Ganesha. Then Shiva appeared. And then the Buddha. Orientation everywhere.

Marjorie was amazed, fearful . . . and angry. "Take it away! That's not how I want to paint. There's nothing of mine in it." She then found herself picking up a pencil, which wrote out a command that they both become vegetarians. Not exactly a welcome message either. She was then commanded to bathe and meditate before the canvas. This she could do, and so she did it. After collecting herself through this method, she began to speak of "this force" and how it did not belong to her, how she belonged to it. She also spoke as if something was wrong or not quite right, as if the creative energies had somehow "short-circuited" in her.

Alvin remembered his reading of Tantric yoga and the chakras and how these sometimes become blocked or prematurely opened. Inspired by something himself now, he asked Marjorie to cross her wrists and hold his hands. She did. Alvin then held her hands and immediately felt "a swift surge of force rushing up my arms and through my body." It was exhilarating for Alvin. Marjorie quickly relaxed. She was breathing easier again (UP 22–23). Orientation to Radiation, again through the chakra system of Tantric yoga.

Schwartz tells us this story in the 1990s in order to explain why he decided to write *Superman*. Essentially, the story of the Manifestation of Ganesha and the mysterious creative force that gripped his wife, short-circuited in her body, and then "grounded out" through him acts as a gloss or commentary on his original decision to write the Man of Tomorrow. What do the two stories have to do with one other? What do they both mean or point to? "Precisely this: that there really had to be some sort of deeper hidden self of which our outward Clark Kent personality was but the dim reflection" (UP 25). Put mythically, each of us, whether we know it or not, is both a bumbling Clark Kent and a Secret Superman. We are persons. And we are portals.

And these memories of the telepathic housewife, the aura-seeing lithographer, and the empowered painters were just the beginning. There were many more. Now remembered and accepted as real, these anomalies began to fall into a consistent pattern. They seemed to connect to one another, to refer to each other in complex metaphorical ways across the decades. Sometime in the 1990s, Schwartz began to see in a new way that reality can be organized around meaning, story, and symbolism as well as matter, time, and cause. He began to realize in his own italicized terms that *"in the multilayered universe, as it really exists, there are clumps of events that belong together, that are related in a kind of noncausal grouping, their connection having to do with value and meaning rather than material events"* (GS 83).

Following C. G. Jung, he would call these patterns "deeper currents and vital synchronicities" (UP 14). In effect, these strange events were now making up their own story, as if they were taking on an independent life of their own. In my own terms, Alvin Schwartz was entering the stage of Realization, that is, he was beginning to realize that even as he wrote, and especially when he wrote, he was being written, and that the paranormal, like the person, is first and foremost *a story*.

SUPERMAN AND BATMAN IN TIBET: THE METAPHYSICAL MEMOIRS

Schwartz has expressed his own unique version of this idea in two metaphysical memoirs. The first, on the symbol or archetype of Superman, appeared in 1997 as *An Unlikely Prophet*. The second, on the dark forces embodied by Batman, appeared in 2007 as *A Gathering of Selves*.

Schwartz sees these two books as representing two distinct stages in his spiritual life. In the first stage and book, he comes to realize the most fundamental teaching of Tibetan Buddhism (which is in fact the fundamental teaching of Tantric traditions across all of Asia), namely, the deeper unity of form and formlessness, of the finite and the infinite, of the temporal and the eternal, of consciousness and energy, of mind and matter, and so on. This is precisely "the Path without Form" that Schwartz signaled in the subtitle of the book's first edition (*Revelations on the Path without Form*). It is also the universal wisdom he finds embodied in the mythical two-in-oneness of Superman and his fumbling alter ego, Clark Kent, who is a temporary form, a "superficial or temporal ego-accretion [of the real but invisible roots of consciousness] in the sense of his being at the center of the rational world of information—the newspaper."[56]

The plot of the first book revolves around a seven-foot Tibetan teacher named Thongden, who happens to be a *tulpa* or mind-created entity that materialized from the lifelong scholarship of a now-deceased scholar of Tibetan Buddhism named Everett Nelson. Thongden shows up at Alvin Schartz's house one day after reading the published version of Schwartz's lecture on Superman's identity at the University of Connecticut, a real-world text that I already cited. To Schwartz's considerable bafflement, Thongden begins to teach him that he has a "Superman phantasm" hanging over him, that Superman is, in effect, his own tulpa, his own mind-created entity that has taken on an independent life of its own. What is more, Thongden insists, Schwartz must work through this phantasm now. He must acknowledge its projected presence and power and, as we eventually learn, dematerialize its formed becoming back into his own formless being. This, of course, is the very same insight with which we began our own Super-Story in chapter 1, with Joscelyn Godwin's discussion of the imaginal status of Shambalah within the initiatory tradition of the *Kalachakra Tantra* and the need of the initiate to realize its illusory status, and hence the illusory status of every other mental and social construction (which is pretty much everything).

We could hardly ask for a more apt literary metaphor of what I have called Realization than a seven-foot tulpa teaching a baffled Alvin Schwartz about his Superman phantasm and the impossible imaginative powers that it might still actualize in him. Indeed, we are on target in an almost ridiculously precise way here. Thongden, after all, is a presence who has *literally* been written into being by the thoughts, meditations, and scholarship of a writer, in this case Everett Nelson. Very much like Schwartz's own life narrative seen now through the prism of synchronicities and paranormal events (or Binder's Captain Marvel "becoming real" in the person of Ted Owens), Nelson's scholarship has "taken on a life of its own" in the person and presence of Thongden. Thongden is Realization Incarnate.

Everett Nelson, Schwartz tells us, was a student of W. Y. Evans-Wentz, an historical figure who specialized in the comparative study of folklore (he was an expert on faerie folklore, among other things) and did much to popularize Tibetan Buddhism in the 1940s and '50s. We also learn that Nelson began his scholarly life working on early forms of Gnostic Christianity but then moved on to Tibetan Buddhism. As his choice of subjects suggests and as the story makes very clear, Nelson's knowledge was more than technical. It embodied an "understanding that goes beyond mere scholarship" (UP 56). Gnosis once again.

But Nelson is now dead and so Thongden, alas, is fading away. Like the ancient Greek gods, he will soon disappear if there is no human being to imagine him, to talk to him, to make him real. More specifically, he needs Alvin Schwartz if he is to survive as a form within the formless. So Thongden teaches Schwartz that he, very much like Everett Nelson, has played a major role in creating a different kind of tulpa—Superman. Thongden helps the author look back on his life and see the superconnections, the places where his own red, white, and blue tulpa took form.

As a result of all of this, Schwartz begins to weave around the pop figure of Superman any number of what he himself calls "philosophical glosses." Superman, for example, now appears alternately as "a sort of degenerated religious symbol—an avatar for the underprivileged and the dispossessed"; as "the image of something that [comes] into being in the individual in moments of extreme personal crisis" or in the midst of severe trauma; and, employing the language of quantum physics now, as "an archetype expressing the sense of nonlocality that is always present in the back of our minds—the capacity to be everywhere instantly."[57]

By "symbol" and "archetype," Schwartz intends something very specific, something in accordance with the depth psychology of C. G. Jung. A symbol is not a sign. The meaning of a sign is always known and is often arbitrary (for example, the English word "cat" or an octagonal red American stop sign). A symbol, on the other hand, arises from the depths of the unconscious and "acts as a means of release and transformation of psychic energy." A symbol, in other words, effects a kind of psychological or spiritual mutation, and this by virtue of its ability to open up the ego or conscious self to the archetypal depths and powers of the individual psyche and even the collective unconscious or World Soul. In the end, then, a symbol or archetype possesses a certain "living quality" or "autonomous functioning." This is precisely what Superman is for Schwartz. The writers and editors may have thought that they were manufacturing him, but in fact "we did no more than 'discover' Superman."[58]

Schwartz's invocation of quantum physics relates to his experience and understanding of telepathy. Telepathy, for Schwartz, is a function of the "nonlocal" nature of quantum processes (this, we might recall, was also the conclusion of Russell Targ, the laser physicist who helped originate the remote-viewing program at SRI). Just as Ingo Swann suggested in his own terms, for Schwartz, there are no "senders" or "receivers." Nor is telepathy a superpower that emanates in rays from our eyes or brains, or tingles around our skull, as in a Spider-Man comic book or a Jack Kirby drawing. Rather, telepathy is a human translation of the nonlocal nature of reality itself. "You don't have to go anywhere. You don't have to look for anything. It's there. Beyond the dimensions" (UP 131–32). This, of course, is where the mytheme of Orientation disappears, joins up with the mytheme of Radiation, and becomes the mytheme of Realization. This is where one realizes that the "Tibet" one desires is inside one, or, better yet, that the Somewhere Else one seeks is in fact Everywhere.

Toward the very end of the book, Schwartz explains to his wife, Kay, what he has learned through his various adventures and conversations with Thongden, namely, that Superman appears only in moments of crisis or trauma: "Don't you see—that's what Superman really is. The highest point of individual consciousness. He's totally fixed on a single point. His one defining act—his rescue mission. That's what he does. He's a being that converges totally, with all his mind and strength and energy, on a single demand arising out of a single moment. He's specialized, you might say, to live entirely in the *now*. . . . He's us—when we're truly impermeable, indestructible—totally concentrated" (UP 204–5).

Schwartz is particularly intrigued by why "Superman is silent." He is the Witness behind all that we do. One might say that Superman is pure consciousness streaming through the imaginative, language-less right brain that then becomes the chatty little rational ego or Clark Kent of the left brain. I think that Schwartz would have little difficulty with this reading. He points out, after all, that whereas speech and writing are always after the fact and represent acts of doing itself, being, in the Now, is always silent. "And that's why," he now explains to Kay, "you can't have a Superman without a Clark Kent—because no one can live all the time at that level of experience. There has to be a retreat to ordinariness, to self-recollection, to talk and planning and remembering" (UP 205). We *need* the ego. We *need* reason and language. We need that left brain.

We are back to the original 1944 insight in the sandwich shop. We are back to the central Schwartzian theme of the simultaneous reality of form and formlessness, of the finite and the infinite. This is the final lesson of Superman for Alvin Schwartz, and the final lesson of Clark Kent: "The Superman self, as you believed even then, was not something one could live in all the time. It's a far too heightened level of the personality. Sustaining it for too long could burn one out very quickly, and possibly do the same to those around one. So the Clark Kent everyday personality was a necessary safety valve—a retreat where one could live normally" (UP 96).

Schwartz also comes to understand the human imagination as a kind of near-omnipotent mystical organ that can act as a magical bridge between the poles of the formless and its forms—the "phone booth of consciousness," as he humorously dubs it. It is the imagination that creates our different experienced realities, including and especially our social and psychological realities. It is also that "chief organ of consciousness" that "particularizes" an identity or personality out of that "bedrock of ultimate self"—neither "I" nor "me"—that is watching it all, like a play or comedy, as if from "outside the whole thing" (GS 43, 177, 36). It is that place in our mind, from left to right or right to left, where we can switch back and forth between our different identities, as in a phone booth.

In his second metaphysical memoir, *A Gathering of Selves*, Schwartz descends from the heights of his hard-won Realization in *An Unlikely Prophet* and moves into a new stage of understanding, that is, into a conscious, active engagement with the world of forms, people, and even money.[59] As he explains his situation on the very first page, his was no longer a life of "higher understanding, promising peace or contentment," for this very understanding had become "a source of unrest and a strange new goad to pass beyond a state of passive awareness to one of action and participation" (GS 1). He was moving into Authorization. In his own terms, Schwartz was now uniting in his life, as he had in his vision, the forms of the temporal order and the formlessness of the eternal. What he once saw as polarized opposites he now was learning to see as two sides of the same fundamental reality.

Schwartz sees the very aesthetics of Batman in a similar Tantric light (and darkness). In a recent essay introducing a collection of the Batman Sunday strips, for example, he pointed out "the unique qualities of light and dark, of polarized contrast in the drawing style that Bob Kane introduced and that Tim Burton recaptured so effectively" in his classic 1989 *Batman* movie.[60] And he thinks that this "extreme polarity" is especially notable in the Sunday strips he wrote, one of which I have reproduced here. Indeed, "the whole strip is a study in polarity—an accurate simulacrum of the way the

5.4   A SCHWARTZ *BATMAN* STRIP

psyche works. As the bat on which the superhero founds his identity is a creature of the night, so also is Batman. The Batsignal that summons him to Commissioner Gordon's headquarters is only visible at night. And the underworld against which Batman's efforts are directed is also a night world. As anyone who has dabbled in psychology will recognize, the stage on which Batman appears is subliminal."[61] There is that word again—*subliminal*, under the *limen* or threshold—popularized early on by Frederic Myers of the London Society for Psychical Research.

This, of course, is all unconscious in popular culture. Artist Bob Kane or writer Bill Finger knew nothing of Fred Myers and did not set out to explore the psychical, subliminal psyche with their original art and scripting in the late 1930s and early '40s, anymore than Schwartz and his colleagues were aware of such psychological processes when they were writing, sketching, and publishing the *Superman* Sunday strips in the 1940s and '50s. As Schwartz explains, "it simply never would have occurred to us that we were, to put it bluntly, 'being directed.'"[62]

Late in life, Alvin Schwartz took up Batman's union of opposites, the darkness and the light, in both very practical and very metaphysical ways. Most dramatically, he confronted and employed the business savvy of Bruce Wayne and the raw strength of the dark figure of the Batman to carry him into the next stage of understanding, that is, into the interpersonal realization that what "we think of as 'self' is but one layer of an onion-like structure of multiple selves that coexist, representing the foundation of the fundamental unity of all being."[63]

Schwartz, like so many of our other authors and artists, also came to the understanding that there is only Now, and that linear time is an illusion. "Wherever you go, it is now. . . . Now is a point. Timeless, dimensionless. . . . Now is you. Now is—the observer. Do you understand? You are always and absolutely here and now." And our selves? Our egos? There are many of these, but they are really all happening at once: "You don't have any previous lives. But everyone has literally dozens of simultaneous selves" (GS 212–13, 46).

There is another way, a familiar way, to say this. In one of the more delightful exchanges of the second book, Thongden has just led the writer through a contemplative exercise with a mirror and shown him that he is not really "Alvin Schwartz," that his social ego is really "no more than a reflection in a mirror." When the teacher takes the experiment further and asks him to become his Bruce Wayne persona, Schwartz becomes puzzled:

"MY BRUCE WAYNE? HOW?"

"YOU MUST ASSUME THAT PERSONALITY. YOU WILL THEN SEE FOR YOURSELF."

"BUT I'M NOT BRUCE WAYNE. HOW CAN I--?"

"AS YOU JUST EXPERIENCED, YOU'RE NOT REALLY ALVIN SCHWARTZ EITHER. BUT IN
FACT, YOU CREATED BOTH. IF YOU CAN ASSUME YOUR ALVIN PERSONALITY, IT SHOULD
BE JUST AS SIMPLE TO TAKE ON THE BRUCE ONE." (GS 34)

Again, the message is a familiar one by now. And it is as simple as it is profound. The imagined figures of Batman and Superman are indeed fictions. But so too is the imagined figure of your ego. Egos are interchangeable, malleable, plastic, and finally related to every other in the ground of being. They are like the suits put on and taken off by superheroes. They are costumes. They are masks (personas). They are also dreams. "Our dreams are us," Thongden explains to a still unknowing student in the first book, "but we are not our dreams" (UP 142).

Such comparisons between the pop-cultural figure of Batman and the dizzying heights of Buddhist philosophy may strike some readers as forced and artificial. I mean, really, a Buddhist Batman? As it turns out, however, the Batman mythos, as if following Schwartz's own realizations, has recently turned in *exactly* this direction, and in at least one of the character's most celebrated and critically discussed appearances, no less.

We can catch glimpses of an Orientation mytheme already in Doug Moench's storyline for *Batman Annual* #21 (1997). There, the same year Schwartz published his *Unlikely Prophet* with Tibetan monks on the cover, we are introduced to the concept of the tulpa, "a Tibetan term meaning 'thought-form entity' and the ultimate explanation, some feel, for the Yeti or 'Abominable Snowman.'" In short, John Keel. The Yeti reference is hardly tangential here. Indeed, the tulpa Batman battles, in the golden city of Shambalah, *is* a Yeti.

Admittedly, this is a single story in a single comic. More recently, however, Grant Morrison explored a Buddhist Batman, very much in Schwartz's philosophical direction, in a multi-issue story arc that climaxed in *Batman R.I.P.* (2008). This same arc, by the way, also includes an allusion to Morrison's Kathmandu experience in the form of "an alien hyper-imp from the 5th dimension" who follows Batman around as a kind of comic genie-guide. Hyper-imp and all, here Morrison weaves his tale around Bruce Wayne's decision to undergo the Tibetan meditation ordeal known as Thögal in a cave in Nanda Parbat.

5.5   BATMAN'S HYPERDIMENSIONAL IMP

There really is such a practice as Thögal. It is a supersecret practice of the Dzogchen tradition, which is itself part of the Nyingma school of Tibetan Buddhism, which gave us texts like the *Bardo Thodal*, otherwise known as the Tibetan Book of the Dead (an instruction manual on how to negotiate the terrors and visions of the death process that is read to the disembodied soul as it hovers around its corpse). The successful practice of Thögal is said to be able to take the practitioner very quickly to the ultimate goal of complete enlightenment, which is accompanied by the attainment of something called the Rainbow Body—a consummate transformation, and dissolution, of the physical form into a Body of Light, often represented in Tibetan art as a huge rainbowlike energy field emanating from a Buddha (a theme we last encountered in Ezekiel's chariot vision of the fiery humanoid being on the divine throne, surrounded by a rainbow light). The mytheme of Radiation par excellence.

Nanda Parbat is another matter, that is, a fictional one. In the DC universe, Nanda Parbat is a Himalayan city overseen by the six-armed Hindu goddess Rama Kushna (a probable allusion either to the Hindu gods Rama and Krishna, or, more likely I think, to the nineteenth-century Hindu Tantric saint Ramakrishna, who was quite popular in the 1960s counterculture in which the DC goddess originally appeared). In a celebrated storyline initiated in 1967, the same Tantric goddess had transformed a faithless circus trapeze artist by the name of Boston Brand into Deadman, a superhero who looks a lot like a corpse and who is essentially a kind of superghost who can fly, become invisible, and possess any living body in order to take revenge on enemies and crooks alike. Corpses and possession, by the way, are both common features of the more radical Tantric traditions of India, Nepal, and Tibet. Which is all to say that Morrison's historical, fantastic, and mystical meditations around a "dead" Buddhist Batman in Tibet are rich and complex ones.

The Thögal practice itself is described on the first page of *Batman* #673: "The *Thögal Ritual* is one of the most highly advanced and dangerous forms of meditation. During a seven-week retreat know as Yangti, the practitioner undergoes an experience designed to simulate *death* and *after-death*. And *rebirth*, too." Alfred, now in the first pages of *Batman R.I.P.*, explains further: "Thögal is the *peak* meditative experience in the *Dzogchen* Tradition of Tibetan Buddhism. . . . Nothing *less*, as I understand it, than a complete rehearsal, while living, of the experience of *death*." Later in the story, Batman explains how through this practice he ultimately came to "a place that's *not* a place." His Tibetan interlocutor explains that this too "is customary. In

Thögal, the initiate learns what the dead know. The self is peeled back to its black radiant core." Like an onion.

CHANNELED WISDOM: THE PSYCHICAL BACKGROUND

Schwartz has described how he came to understand that his writing of the Superman and Batman adventures was finally "more like dictation than creation." He has also written about *An Unlikely Prophet* as a kind of "channeling" of Superman.[64] Both metaphors, it turns out, are more than metaphors.

When I spoke to Schwartz about his two metaphysical memoirs, I wanted to get some clarification about how he thought about these two books. Naïvely put, I wanted to know whether he thought of them as fiction or nonfiction. Or both. Or neither.

"I have to make it clear," he began almost immediately, "I don't write fiction, except when I wrote comics. I write narrative. The gospels, for example, are narratives, but they are not fiction." He then broke into a long discussion of a particularly powerful influence on his life that does not show up in either metaphysical memoir but that, I think, throws a great deal of light on his own intentions and authorial understanding of these two striking works. Much like Thongden had helped him to see that his original decision to write Superman was very much connected to his later experience with Marjorie being possessed by a greater force that painted through her brush and electrified him through her scared body, Alvin was now teaching me what he meant by "narrative" through another story.

This one stemmed back to the late 1940s, when he was involved in a long series of séance-like sessions with a disembodied entity named "Roy." Roy, it turns out, was being channeled through an acquaintance of Schwartz's, a psychically gifted man named Waldemar. But Roy had also been a historical, flesh-and-blood person. Roy was the deceased brother-in-law of Waldemar. He had died young. And now he was apparently communicating with the group through a traditional practice that bears directly, even literally, on my notion of "reading the paranormal writing us," that is, the practice of automatic writing. Very much like Thongden, Roy was literally written into being. Or at least into appearance.

The first session began with a single penciled line: "I am Roy the brother of Waldemar. . . . You are fun. Put out the lights." This was only the beginning. The communications soon became more explicit. "I have come to make Alvin my pupil." Schwartz asked the obvious: "Why?" The pencil responded: "A master needs a pupil." Roy then proceeded to speak of many things about which the young author was worrying at the time, including his career in comics.

The communications were sometimes didactic. At other times, they worked through parables or symbols. Schwartz described the reaction of one of his Freudian psychoanalyst friends, a man named Hans. Hans had studied with the great philosopher Ludwig Wittgenstein. Hans thought it was all projection. Schwartz was not so sure. For one thing, the pencil never lifted off the page. At one point, moreover, it wrote in a script that looked like Greek, though no one in the group could read Greek. They asked one of their neighbors, who happened to be the former president of Black Mountain College, to come in and give his opinion on the script. Yes, it was Greek, he confirmed: Attic Greek, to be precise. One of the penciled communications was in fact the well-known injunction that hung over the door at the famous Oracle of Delphi: *gnosthi seauton*, that is, "Know thyself."

This was what Alvin's later life would be all about—to know the self and the Self. One of Schwartz's central themes, after all, is the necessity of the Clark Kent alter ego. We cannot, and should not, live all the time in our secret Superman Self. Generally speaking (if one can speak generally about secretly being an omnipotent superhero), that other identity will only appear in times of grave crisis or severe trauma, such as a near-death experience. Otherwise, we are called to live in the ordinary, often humdrum world of family, profession, and business.

This same theme might already have been embedded in one of Roy's consistent teachings to Alvin and their little group, namely, that one does not have to meditate. "I've found that I can't meditate," Schwartz explained to me, and this despite the simple fact that both of his metaphysical memoirs rely heavily on Buddhist ideas and practices. "None of these books were deliberately Buddhist," he explained. "They came out the way they are because of what I am and what I experienced. I wouldn't allow my friends to become Buddhists. My knowledge of Buddhism is like my knowledge of the New Testament or the apocryphal books. I've always been drawn toward the metaphysical. As a kid, I read people like Poe and H.G. Wells. I also read a lot of Evans-Wentz."

This notion of a path that is not a path, this method that has no meditation, reminds me of any number of Asian contemplative traditions that teach more or less the same thing (and, ironically, a whole lot of meditation). Since the state of pure consciousness is always already there, there really is "nothing to do." There is certainly no way to *cause* this state of pure consciousness, as nothing in turn has caused or produced it. It simply *is*. It will appear when it appears. "If you see the Buddha on the road, kill him," that is, if you think that the Buddha is some sort of historical person outside yourself, someone you can meet "out there" in the world of cause and effect, you are gravely, wildly mistaken.

Alvin had obviously seen the Buddha and killed the guy. So I asked him about the clear Tantric undertones of the two books, "Tantric" here defined again as referring to the already-always fusion of the metaphysical and the physical realms—in short, the Path of Form within an ultimate and fundamental Formlessness. "I also read a bit about Tantrism," Alvin explained. "Roy got me into what I would call Tantric ideas, but they were not labeled as such."

It was not simply the fact that Roy could write in Attic Greek and knew about the Oracle of Delphi that impressed Schwartz and his friends (very similar things would later happen to Philip K. Dick [V 196–97]). Nor was it the fact that he taught seemingly surprising things, such as the nonnecessity of meditation. It was that he could also make the whole house shake. Literally. Such high strangeness went on for two and a half years.

Somewhere in there, the Hungarian-born psychoanalyst Nandor Fodor began to visit the group. Fodor was well known as a writer on parapsychological subjects.[65] He also practiced what he preached. Or better, he married it. His wife was a practicing psychic. Fodor was delighted with what he found in the group gathered around Roy and the pencil. He took particular pleasure in shaking up his skeptical psychoanalytic colleague, Hans, who somehow thought all of this could count as a standard symptom of projection. Projection, of course, it may well have been, but of an order that can shake a house. We are back to the problem of Ted Owens's seeming schizophrenic symptoms. Schizophrenic he may have been, but of an order that appeared to unite with the weather at its most awesome.

Schwartz described some of these events to me as "too grim, too serious." It was all about "getting your soul wrenched." Still, "that was an overwhelming event in my life. It impacted me in a much broader way than simply my writing career." And it continued to impact him. Years later, he was in a Canadian airport and came across *Seth Speaks*, one of the many books by Jane Roberts, the ESP teacher who became famous for her channeling of an "energy essence personality no longer focused in physical reality" named Seth, whose teachings included one of our next chapter's most radical themes, namely, the freedom from time and the Oversoul's ability to influence both future *and* past selves.[66] This particular book, Schwartz explained, "suddenly reminded me of my experience." He bought the book "because I felt that it was directed to me. It was like a continuation of my earlier experience, a stamp of authenticity." Seth, in other words, reminded him of Roy. And soon enough of Superman.

And that is how Alvin Schwartz explained to me how he channeled Superman and became Bruce Wayne on the Path without Form.

AUTHORIZATION

WRITING THE PARANORMAL WRITING US

OVER THE YEARS, I HAVE QUESTIONED THE MEAN-
ING OF SUCH MYSTICAL EXPERIENCES. NOT SO MUCH
THEIR INTEGRAL VALUE, WHICH STILL ELUDES ME,
AS WHAT IS MADE OF THEM BY THE PERCIPIENTS.
POTENTIALLY, EXTRAORDINARY EXPERIENCE CAN EN-
RICH AN OPEN MIND IMMEASURABLY. POTENTIALITY
IS WHAT YOU MAKE OF IT; YOU ARE PART OF ITS
VALUE, YOU COULD EVEN BE ITS ACTIVATOR.
BARRY WINDSOR-SMITH, **OPUS 2**

THE TIME YOU HAVE WAITED FOR HAS COME. THE
WORK IS COMPLETE; THE FINAL WORLD IS HERE. HE
HAS BEEN TRANSPLANTED AND IS ALIVE.
PHILIP K. DICK, **THE DIVINE INVASION**

uthorization begins when we decide to step out of the script we now know ourselves to be caught in and begin to write ourselves anew. If Realization is the
insight that we are being written, Authorization is the decision to do something
about it. If Realization involves the act of reading the paranormal writing us, Authorization involves the act of writing the paranormal writing us.

The period of time dating roughly from the summer of 1973 to the spring of 1974
was a truly remarkable one in the lore of our Super-Story, an *annus mirabilis* or
Year of Miracle. It was during this period of time, after all, that two exceptionally
gifted men experienced dramatic metaphysical openings that permanently transformed
their respective worlds and crafts. Living in New York, the young British fantasy artist
Barry Smith (now Barry Windsor-Smith) was in the midst of his famous work on *Conan*

the *Barbarian* for Marvel Comics. Living in California, the science fiction writer Philip K. Dick was about to write his most impossible story, which turned out to be his own.

I will not attempt to hide my sense of awe and confusion before what each man experienced, or my admiration for the self-critical honesty, humor, and social courage with which they expressed and analyzed their own extreme mystical experiences. Few artists have done it this openly, this explicitly, and, frankly, this well.

And by "this well," I mean something very specific. I mean the manner in which Windsor-Smith and Dick were able to fuse the critical powers of reason, the models of modern science, and the stunning visions of their own empowered imaginations into a whole series of insights that in the past would have certainly been projected into the sky and framed in traditional religious terms as "revelations." I mean their sophisticated employment of psychoanalysis, psychiatry, and neuroanatomy in order to understand their own altered states of mind. I mean their absolute refusal to surrender either self-reflective criticism ("Am I mad?" "Is this real?") *or* the patently obvious truth-value of their experiences ("I am not mad, and this is very, very real"). I mean their profound understanding that they had moved—or, better, had been moved—well outside the traditional boundaries of what we call reason and faith, that they were on new cognitive and spiritual ground. I mean their supermodern gnosis.

In their Twoness, in this double ability to think critically and imagine boldly through both sides of the brain, as it were, Barry Windsor-Smith and Philip K. Dick are models of what I have called the author of the impossible. Moreover, in their movement from bravely describing what is essentially a metaphysics of control and invasion to a self-conscious artistic transformation of all of this, these two men point us, their participating readers and visionaries, toward a new horizon, the horizon of Authorization. Enter the Endless Waves of Time and the Coming of Valis.

"*B*ENEATH THE PAGES"

"You might find this interesting," Jacques said, as he handed me a rather large, beautifully illustrated book. It was the spring of 2008, and I was in the library of Jacques Vallee, high over the hills of San Francisco. Vallee is something of a legend among ufologists. He transformed the still young and passionate conversation in the late 1960s with his *Passport to Magonia*, which essentially argues that many UFO encounters look a great deal like scenes from traditional folklore and comparative mystical literature. A few years later, he added psychical phenomena to the mix with his *The*

Invisible College. The punch line was as clear then as it is now: we will never really grasp the full range and meaning of these alien encounters, of this Alienation, unless we take these technomystical comparisons into account.

"The author sent it to me a few years ago. There is a letter with an address there, if you are interested." I looked at the book and then the letter. I was very interested, as I recognized the author immediately. He was in fact a hero of mine: Barry Windsor-Smith. Known as Barry Smith in the early 1970s, he had drawn the early run of the *Conan the Barbarian* series, #1 through #24, to be exact, for Marvel Comics. Based on the short stories of Robert E. Howard, beautifully adapted by Smith and writer Roy Thomas, these were among the most celebrated comics of their time. There was something vaguely familiar or countercultural about this Thomas-Smith Conan. Lithe and muscular, ultramasculine and yet somehow feminine too, long hair flowing, immense sword at hand, here was an eroticized barbarian battling sorcerers on almost every page, usually with a gorgeous, well-built, and often very strong woman not far from his side. To put it in the precise terms of a hormonally buzzed adolescent boy of the early 1970s, this was all *too cool* (see fig. 6.1)

Those were my distant memories anyway as I opened the book in Jacques' library. Two things became immediately clear. The first was why Barry Windsor-Smith had sent Jacques Vallee a copy of *OPUS*.[1] Much of the book, after all, treats mind-blowing cosmic perspectives that resonate deeply with those of Vallee. The second was the realization that the central narrative of *OPUS*, an essay called "Time Rise," represented something of a jackpot in terms of the working hunch that I had been pursuing ever since I found that little *X* in the movie parking lot, that is, the hunch that there is some sort of deep but still inarticulate connection between the paranormal and popular culture, between mystics and mutants. Here was a perfect, almost ridiculously precise, confirmation of that X-intuition. Here was a major fantasy artist and pop-cultural icon who, in 1999, was carefully documenting a metaphysical storm that raged just beneath the pages that he drew and inked in the early 1970s, the very pages, moreover, that garnered him his original fame among comic-book fans like me.

And by "beneath the pages," I mean *beneath the pages*. In the spring of 1970, Barry Smith was in his parents' home in east London, where he drew the first nine issues of *Conan*. He was working hard to make yet another Marvel deadline. He guesses it was early May. In any case, it was 1:30 or so in the afternoon. As one part of his attention focused on the art, another part looked toward the window. Standing in front of the bright sun-lit window, he saw a tall man with a mustache chatting with a woman to his right. *"They're gonna love it,"* the man said. And then the woman laughed, *"Oh, yeah."* And then Barry Smith went back to his drawing and thought nothing more of this odd vision. He likened the experience to a random daydream, and then promptly forgot about it.[2]

The next day he was working again on a Conan page: "I was leaning into the paper at close range when, in an instant, the off-white surface seemed to dissolve before my eyes, leaving only the wooden drawing board on my lap. Then the board itself also began to disappear, and in its place was a scene, full-color and movie-like, of a noisy traffic jam!" He saw the scene in great detail, as if he were just above it. He saw, for example, two white trucks, both stalled. All the yellow taxicabs told him that he was witnessing a New York City street scene. He even recognized that he was looking through a window above the traffic jam, as he could see his reflection in the glass as he peered through it. All this played out beneath the page before it faded away back into the whiteness of the paper on his drawing board. Back on the page. Back to Conan and his sexy costar, Jenna.[3]

Fast forward three years later, to New York City, June 8, 1973. Smith was now living in the States. Roy Thomas had suggested to him that they adapt Howard's short story "Red Nails" for the second issue of *Savage Tales*, one of Marvel's many magazine-format series. Smith was living in Brooklyn and working in the studio of an artist friend named Michael Doret. Doret was drawing advertisements for clients like *Time* magazine and Burger King and sharing studio space with another artist, Charles White III. So there were three artists, and an assistant named Carol, working in the studio that summer.

Charlie asked Barry for help with an ad he was working on for Levi Strauss and their "Original Fit" blue jeans. While the others were out to lunch, Smith dashed off a drawing, left it on Charlie's desk, and went back to work. A bit later, he heard his colleagues come back from lunch, so he got up to see what they thought of his drawing. As he entered the room, he saw Charlie and Carol standing in front of a sunny window discussing the drawing. Charlie's mustache seemed to blaze in the glare of the light as he exclaimed, *"They're gonna love it!"* Carol, all smiles, could only agree: *"Oh, yeah!"*

"In that instant," Windsor-Smith writes, "the present time winked out and I was back in my parents' home three years earlier," where of course he had seen the same scene in what he had thought was just a daydream. Back in 1973 now, he became dizzy from this realization. "I experienced a hard shove to my central perception of self, as if my awareness was pushed to the left of what I had hitherto not identified as

AN IVORY *DOOR* THAT SWINGS SILENTLY INWARD --FROM WITHIN, THE EXOTIC SCENT OF *INCENSE* ---

CONAN *ENTERS* CAUTIOUSLY, EYES DARTING ABOUT LIKE THOSE OF A *WOLF* IN STRANGE SURROUNDINGS, READY TO FIGHT OR FLEE ON THE INSTANT... AND THEN HE *SEES* IT...

AN *IDOL,* SEATED UPON A GREAT MARBLE COUCH--- AN IDOL WITH THE BODY OF A *MAN,* BUT *GREEN*--- WITH A HEAD TOO IN- HUMAN AND TOO LARGE... ITS EYES CLOSED AS IF IN *SLEEP*··

AND THEN ---

THOSE EYES ---

--OPEN!

PARALYZED WITH TERROR-- HELD FAST BY FEAR-- THE CIMMERIAN *FREEZES* IN HIS TRACKS. THIS IS NO IDOL, BUT A *LIVING THING*··

--AND HE IS *TRAPPED* WITHIN ITS CHAMBER!

JUST THEN, THE *TRUNK* OF THE HORROR IS LIFTED-- QUESTS ABOUT, AS TOPAZ EYES STARE *UNSEEING*-- AND THE CREATURE *SPEAKS* IN A STAMMERING VOICE, THRU JAWS NEVER MEANT FOR *HUMAN SPEECH*...

WHO IS *HERE?* HAVE YOU COME TO TORMENT ME *AGAIN,* YARA?

OH, YAG-KOSHA-- IS THERE NEVER TO BE AN *END* TO YOUR AGONY?

6.1   CONAN ENCOUNTERS THE ALIEN SPACE GOD YAG-KOSHA

my 'center of consciousness,' my oneness. A terrific rush of whirling, roaring sounds broke loose as if nonmaterial forces were slamming about in my previously centralized point of being: my dual-functioning mind." Then, like his drawing board three years earlier, the floor to his left just disappeared, and where it was supposed to be he now saw "a vast swirling mass of gases and billowing clouds of indistinguishable matter, all turning in a circular motion around new-forming globes burning like suns."[4] This crimson vision—"Red everywhere"—lasted thirty to forty seconds, he guesses. Then he was back, looking up at a confused and concerned Charlie and Carol.

"You okay?"

He wasn't. He was shaking. And he was in shock. He stumbled home (O 1.113–23).

The artist would analyze this double-event endlessly over the next years, indeed decades. He would finally conclude that the vision of the cosmos may have been an illusion, that is, an imaginative vision, but the uncanny connection of the two events from May of 1970 and June of 1973 definitely was not. Not even close. Time—which is the real subject of *OPUS*—had somehow looped back on itself.

Eventually, Windsor-Smith would come to realize that there are two sorts of time. There is linear, tick-tocking clock time, which has no real existence apart from our perceptual makeup. And there is TIME or big-*T* Time, which "alludes to eternity . . . as a conceptual continuum of partially interconnected dimensions," and that "implies continuing events of meaningfulness" (O 2.96, 1.154). Here we might recall Alan Moore's visionary distinction between a constructed and illusory linear time and the ever-present space-time, as well as Alvin Schwartz's "clumps of meaning" as temporal expressions of a nonlocal, timeless superconsciousness.

In 1973, through such interconnected dimensions, Windsor-Smith would now experience himself visiting himself as a child in his parent's London home somewhere around 1956. How sorry he felt for his younger self, who, of course, had no context for all the Hyborian architecture, dragons, and fantasy heroes that floated through his brain. How bad he felt for "scaring the crap out of myself from 17 years in the future" (O 2.198–200). In our own terms, we might say that in 1956 Barry Smith was having a mystical experience of himself from the future. He was his own metaphysical event.

That would be enough for anyone. But it was just the beginning for Barry Smith. The next morning, June 9, was a Saturday, and Smith was back in the studio working again when he heard a real mess outside the window—car horns, people yelling, that sort of thing. And it just kept on going and going. Disgusted, he got up and looked out the window to see what was destroying his concentration so effectively. Two white re-frigerator trucks had tried to run a light and stalled in the middle of the intersection. Taxi cabs, honking, dotted the streets.

It was happening again. "Circular formations of stars and planets" appeared, this time to his right. What he was seeing outside his studio he saw as if it were over-laid with the exact same scene that he had witnessed three years earlier beneath his Conan pages in his parents' home. He could even see their carpet superimposed on the present New York scene. Then he felt the same nudge in his perceptual center. "A separate presence seemed to slip into my central perception of self."

This time, however, the sense of being replaced had an immediate effect on the cosmic storm. The storm seemed to calm down, and he somehow began to perceive, precisely, unimaginable distances between the stars. "I knew I was experiencing a paradox, a mind-bending phenomenon that allowed me to be just where I was and yet be everywhere else as well." And there was more: "I felt and understood that I was a part of everything that I was seeing before me, that I and the stars were profoundly related as if by birth, but separated by some yet-to-be realized circumstance."

Then a final vista: "Just before this stunning vision dissolved into the normal-ness of a room in midtown Manhattan, a bright light soared from out of the nearest lower right void and fired upward. It then arced and came about to form an enormous circle, possibly light years in circumference, as its head met its tail. Then four bright pinpoints of white light fired in sequence along its path. In an utterly illuminated state of consciousness, I knew that these four lights represented the physical energy of the two future-sight/past-sight phenomena that I had experienced yesterday and today." In more traditional gnostic terms, Barry Smith had just seen a modern-day *ouroboros*, a cosmic snake biting its own tail in an expression of paradox, eternal unity, and cyclical process. Judging from the twilight that now reigned outside his studio window, Smith estimated that it had taken a full six hours for the entire event to transpire (O 1.130–32).

That was Saturday. Then there was Sunday, June 10. He was back in the studio working on the details of a wolf howling at the moon for Robert E. Howard's poem "Cimmeria" and preparing for lunch.[5] Suddenly, he became really, really tired, "as if the force of gravity had multiplied itself a hundred-fold." He fell into his couch unable to move, unable to resist whatever force was overtaking him, unable even to open his eyelids. He fell into a deep sleep.

Now Smith found himself lost in an utter and infinite blackness. There was no linear time in this "perfect nothingness." But there was "a supernatural calm" and "the completeness of forever." He eventually recognized all of this as a Presence, as an "embodiment of all Time and all Place." Once he accepted it as such, this Presence shifted dramatically and took a new form, that of Dimension. Smith is careful to explain at this point that our three dimensions of space cannot capture the sense of what he knew then, namely, that "a fourth and possibly a fifth or even more elements existed that all the words and grammatical tools in the English language could not describe."

Part of the language-smashing event was the perceived fact that he was no longer a body. "I had no heart, no lungs, no electrochemical systems pulsing in a red meat factory of materiality. My consciousness was my sole, prevailing existence." Pure transcendent Consciousness. Nor was there any clock time, no linear "before" and "after." That sense had been replaced by another kind of dimension, the dimension of "meaningfulness."

As the meaning grew, another form or movement appeared—Energy. This Energy appeared as an immense, black wave moving from a point of origin impossibly far away and expanding exponentially as it approached his sense of self. He understood that "in perceiving this movement, I had perceived light." As this black light "broke upon my shore of perception, just in front of me, perhaps a million miles away, I realized that the wave was actually *blacker* than the ultimate black of the surrounding infinity!"

And then, to his utter confusion, came a second wave, blacker than the first. And then a third, and then a fourth, each blacker than the previous, each bringing "uncountable experiences transmigrating Time and multi-dimensional space; the histories of trillions of otherwise unknowable events since this universe spawned consciousness. Each wave contained all the experiences of the previous waves, vested in the depths of all the knowing that exists everywhere, but is as yet unrecognized by the human race."

Barry Smith—if we can speak of such a person in such a state—could not long bear such a cosmic perspective, where endless waves of time flooded him with trillions of bits of experience and linear time was replaced by meaningfulness in an Everything All at Once. He certainly understood that his humanity "was immaterial to the cosmic everything that has always been, and shall always continue to be so." But he just wanted to be back in the city, preferably with his girlfriend in the bed he knew that she was curled up in at the moment. In the terms of Alvin Schwartz, Smith could no longer bear his nonlocal Superman Self that was everywhere all at once. He needed his Clark Kent ordinariness back. He wanted his precious finitude, the sense, even if illusory, that he was *not* everything everywhere always.

And so Smith panicked. In a kind of phantom body, he began to scream and throw himself about in a desperate rage. He wanted back to his goddamned three dimensions. Much like William Hurt in the 1980 movie *Altered States*, he points out, Smith tried to hold on to his humanity and shock himself back into this reality. In the movie, Hurt did it by throwing himself against walls. In reality, Smith did it by ranting and raving. The omnipotent intelligence that was the Presence responded by trying to correct his "disorder," but then sadly acknowledged what the frightened little earth creature willed: "I have never before or since experienced such a deeply palpable sense of regret as that which pervaded the Presence that had journeyed so determinedly to my door of self. First it was a momentary confusion about my actions, then an adjustment of sorts, then a profoundly pained retreat that accepted my free will to return to my existence as a flesh-bound being." And then it was over. Smith came back into this world and looked at his watch. It was 3:45, Monday morning. He had been in infinity for sixteen hours, earth-time. He stumbled back to his nearby apartment, narrowly escaping the threatening knife of two street thugs by running, screaming, and acting as if he were crazy. Yes, he was really back in this world (O 1.142–73).

INTERPRETING THE PSYCHIC SUMMER OF '73

As a kind of helpful shorthand, Windsor-Smith calls the four major events that he has just narrated for us in volume 1 of *OPUS* The Levi's Incident, The Traffic Jam, Time Cycles, and The Endless Black Waves. These four were the most dramatic of his metaphysical experiences, but by no means were they the last. Indeed, such paranormal events continued to swarm and swamp Barry Smith throughout the next few months in what he dubs The Psychic Summer of '73.

Volume 2 recounts many of these later events as the artist tries to come to terms with those three mind-blowing days of June 8–10, 1973. Such attempts, of course, had already begun in the first volume. There he had warned his readers off from one easy way out, which we might paraphrase this way: "Obviously, this man was smoking something." Barry Windsor-Smith has never used psychedelic drugs of any kind (O 1.139).

More to the point, he had also already identified in volume 1 the heart of the problem, that is, Western civilization's practical and efficient but hopelessly incomplete worldview. Committed as Western culture is to a metaphysically naïve vision defined by materialism (matter is all that exists) and contextualism (no human experience can transcend the limitations of place and time, of ethnic, racial, and religious background, of personal history, and so on), we are essentially locked in and chained down to a worldview that does not seriously question itself, that by definition *cannot* question itself. How, after all, can one have an experience beyond matter in a world that claims that there is nothing outside of matter? And how can one step out of a worldview that says one cannot step out of a worldview? Hence these sorts of paranormal experiences, which violate *both* our materialism ("my consciousness was my sole, prevailing existence") *and* our contextualism ("a paradox, a mind-bending phenomenon that allowed me to be just where I was and yet be everywhere else as well"), can only elude our grasp and frustrate our cognitively primitive attempts to understand them.

To illustrate this point, Windsor-Smith quotes one of his favorite authors, the Pulitzer prize–winning Harvard biographer and psychiatrist John E. Mack, whom we met briefly at the beginning of chapter 2. Mack, encouraged and supported by his friend Thomas Kuhn, the philosopher of science who introduced the notion of a "paradigm shift" in the 1970s, became very involved in ufology after he treated a number of abductees in his practice whose experiences he could not honestly dismiss. After surviving what was essentially a heresy trial at Harvard for his refusal to buy into the reigning materialist and contextualist paradigms, Mack persisted in his provocations until he was killed by a drunk driver in London in 2004.

Here is what Mack said in a lecture that he gave at MIT in 1992 during a conference on reported experiences of alien abduction: "You can't get there from here without a shift in our world-view—a world-view that contains a 'we're here and you're there' sense of separateness in which the physical world is all that exists. . . . In other words, you can't deal with something such as the [alien] abduction phenomenon that is so shattering to our literalist, materialist world-view and then try to understand it from a literalist, materialist world-view!" (O 1.140). Basically, what Mack was saying and what Windsor-Smith is saying (and certainly what I am saying) is this: you can't think yourself out of the story you are caught in with the rules and elements of the very story in which you are caught. You can't free yourself with the tools that the master provides you. You need a *new* story and *new* cognitive tools. You need an intervention from the outside (even if this outside turns out to be a deep inside).

At times, Windsor-Smith adopts the mytheme of Mutation to explain this situation. Inspired by Bucke's *Cosmic Consciousness*, he thus writes of his 1973 experiences as existing "in a plane of reality that our evolutionary stage of cognition does not allow us to experience" and refers to "our ambling, million-year stroll from barbarism to noeticism" (O 1.140, 2.45). He also believes that "our consciousness will eventually evolve to a stage of manifest presence," and he reports feeling that psychic summer "as if my perceptions had been accelerated beyond twentieth-century evolutionary parameters" (O 2.96, 153). In other places, actually in many other places, he employs the mytheme of Radiation to articulate a modern mystical code that is more adequate to his own paranormal experiences. Hence all those sentences about dimensions, space-time, waves, the quantum level, Energy, and so on.

But Bucke's 1901 *Cosmic Consciousness* holds a special place in Windsor-Smith's metaphysical library, that is, as the bookend that marks the beginning of the twentieth-century opening to this new world. The bookend that marks the end of the century for him is Mack's 1999 *Passport to the Cosmos*. It is to the library sitting between these two bookends, between this Mutation and this Alienation, as it were, that Windsor-Smith turns in the second volume of *OPUS* for guidance and analysis. Having thought for decades that his experiences were completely anomalous, that he was essentially alone in the high strangeness of 1973, he now realizes that these experiences are not so anomalous, and that he is in fact not alone. Essentially, in the second volume of *OPUS* Barry Windsor-Smith discovers the hidden history, the secret life of superpowers, that we have been tracing all along.

One of the most interesting aspects of these two volumes for our own purposes is the author's understanding of the writing process and the paranormal dimensions of language and communication. Windsor-Smith recounts numerous experiences of telepathy and psychometry (the reported ability to pick up information about a human being through an inanimate object, usually something he or she has owned, used, or simply touched). He describes, for example, a powerful auditory experience that was not an idea but a loud, perfectly audible "immaterial verbal projection" in his head (O 2.23). He also details psychometric experiences with furniture and various inanimate objects, including one with a secondhand couch that he had purchased at the Salvation Army. When he sat on it during that summer of 1973, he would empathically pick up distinct but completely unfamiliar memories and emotions, which he assumed were those of its previous owner (O 2.43–48). Late in the year, he would also receive "mild jolts, like electrostatic arcs" when he picked up his own artwork, in this case the pages of "Red Nails," which now vibrated with his own personal energies (O 2.168)—talk about the paranormal currents of popular culture!

Windsor-Smith goes further and theorizes what these sorts of communication experiences imply about the brain and the nature of language. At first, he posited that the human brain has some sort of built-in translation ability that can translate any telepathic message into one's native tongue. This implies some kind of "language that is perhaps universal or generic to us all." But then he discovered that "some telepathic data comes in what modern digispeak calls 'bundles,' with built-in conversion capacities" (O 2.75). This theme of telepathy as a kind of universal bundle language is worth flagging here. It is a stock theme in the contactee literature. We have seen a version of it in the remote viewer Ingo Swann. And a very similar notion will later appear in Grant Morrison's *The Invisibles*, where aliens are said to use a special "metalanguage" that works through single words that encode entire "emotional aggregates" (I 4.15–16).

Windsor-Smith will also reveal something else, something again already very familiar to us—the powerfully emotive, even erotic quality of some telepathic transmissions. Describing a particularly powerful and especially comforting communication that he received from the cosmic Presence as he struggled with the seeming madness of his experiences, he writes this: "Attempting an analogy, pallid thought it is, I will say that the sensation was not unlike sexual climax. Having likened it to an intense physical experience, I'm obliged to contradict myself and describe it as a sense of real passion transcendent of material reality. It was both intimate and universal. Magnanimous in a 'spiritually orgasmic' sense that I find very, very difficult to qualify in language." Such an event in turn had a profound effect on his reception of language. "Layers of information rippled through every otherwise casual word so that no further elaboration, nor any questions, were required" (O 2.158). In effect, language had *become* telepathy. As it will for all of us far in the future when, the artist believes, the human brain will evolve to a point where it can recover, in an advanced form, our now lost ability for telepathic communication.[6] Mystic mutants.

There are other conclusions. Foremost among them is Windsor-Smith's realization that Mind is not brain. Mind, that is, is not something that the brain produces. It is a presence, like Huxley's Mind at Large, that the brain filters or transmits. Hence Windsor-Smith affirms a kind of "transconscious" outside and beyond our "singular, space-time oriented ego[s]," which can and do vanish "as ephemeral as clouds" (O 2.156). As egos at least, we are all figments of our imaginations (O 2.97). At another point, Windsor-Smith perceives his Mind "to be outside of my physical body . . . suspended near my skull, about six inches or so away from my eyes. It was not a visible 'thing,' but, rather, an invisible *presence*."

The artist finally concludes that for Mind to be understood at all, consciousness must be accepted as an immaterial reality, that is, we must stop confusing Mind and brain. He recognizes, of course, that most professional neuroscientists would find such claims ludicrous, but then they have never known what he has known. As for the posthuman folks who think we can download consciousness onto computer chips, this all strikes the artist as patently confused and morally appalling, as a gross reduction of human consciousness "to digital codes in the control of cold-blooded mechanists" (O 2.50–55, 2.137). More hopeless brain-Mind confusion, here the confusion of cognition with consciousness.

I have written explicitly of the Human as Two, as brain and Mind, as contextual, historical social ego and nonlocal, nontemporal consciousness. There are innumerable ways to frame this insight. It seems very fruitful to do so, as the Human as Two is *both* a very strong pattern in the history of religions *and* a very rational way of synthesizing scientific and critical methods (that is, as relating to the brain and the social ego) and spiritual or paranormal claims (that is, as related to the transconscious Mind). It is in this same spirit that Windsor-Smith writes of humankind as "self-dissident" and of "our inborn schizophrenia" (sounding more than a little like Otto Binder). "Yes," he writes, "we do function in two cosmological planes simultaneously. No, it's not a problem." The human amphibian, as we saw in Alan Moore's occult world.

And here is Windsor-Smith's vision of what will happen when, more fully evolved, we finally crawl up on the beach for good: "Imagine the age of enlightenment. Quantum physics proves that mankind has the inbuilt potential to unite with the essence of our universe. Where everything that exists co-exists. Where our consciousness is absolute. . . . Physics and metaphysics would have to come together as one discipline. Then . . . an ultimate explication of our innermost selves could be made comprehensible to all, not just the specialized groups. Once it is comprehended, we would enter a new era of human potential. Knowledge of ourselves would defeat our fear of others—any others. All humanity would be profoundly, irrevocably changed" (O 2.56).

And then it departed. By the end of 1973, the artist's cosmic portals had closed. "Extracorporeality, psychometry, telepathy, precognition, super-memory, super-vision, and all my other comic book terms for advanced consciousness were about to get mothballed" (O 2.167). Superman put his civilian clothes back on and went back to work at the *Daily Planet*.

SOME FIVE HUNDRED FEET UP, AN ENORMOUS SHIP HOVERED IN MID-AIR. IT HAD ROWS OF TWINKLING YELLOW LIGHTS, AND A BLAZING WHITE CLUSTER IN THE CENTER.

I COULD JUST MAKE OUT THE FORMS OF ITS UNDERSIDE-- TUBING, DUCTS, AND PORTALS IN DEEP SHADOWS.

WHERE ONE WOULD EXPECT A DEAFENING ROAR OF ENGINES, ONLY A SLIGHT HUM COULD BE HEARD. THE GIANT CRAFT MOVED SLOWLY AND SILENTLY OVER OUR HEADS.

STEVE MUTTERED--

HOLY SHIT...

6.2 "UFO POV"

As the millennium turned over, Windsor-Smith would tell the world another story that preceded the events featured in *OPUS* by some seven years. With hindsight and what we have already learned about the common paranormal and psychic effects of UFO encounters, one might reasonably speculate that what we have in this earlier story is the paranormal key to the Psychic Summer of '73.

In 2000, Barry Windsor-Smith published a haunting short story called "UFO POV," with the subtitle "A True Story Dramatized for Comics," about an immense spaceship that he and a friend had watched float over their London neighborhood one summer evening in 1966. It was a mere five hundred feet above them. It was studded with complex lights, portals, ducts, and elaborate tubing. It made not a sound. "Coupled with its appalling size, the ship's uncanny silence created a strange, perhaps psychological, vacuum effect. . . . I tried to imagine the occupants of the craft. No visual impressions came, but I sensed they were not hostile. In fact, they seemed practically sublime. Utterly superior to us humans in every way."

A small piece in the next morning's paper on some UFOs sighted over London and the South Coast confirmed that what the two friends had seen the previous night was no dream, not at least a typical one. Smith tried to draw the event after the manner of artist legend Jack Kirby, but even this could not capture the technological majesty and spiritual awe of the actual encounter. But the paranormal event was now recorded as it often has been—in the form of a comic-book story.

The 2000 version of this comic-book short story ends with the next time the artist was reminded of that immense UFO over London that he had seen as a young man. The scene this time is a movie theatre. It is 1977, and Steven Spielberg's *Close Encounters of the Third Kind* is coming to a close as the gigantic mother ship rises over Devil's Tower. "Although fiction," Windsor-Smith notes, "much of Spielberg's story was based on real-life events."[7] Including the movie's central character of the French scientist Dr. Lacombe, whose figure was based on the life and work of Jacques Vallee, the man who first handed me Barry Windsor-Smith's *OPUS*.

*T*HE COMING OF VALIS

Just a few months after Barry Smith had undergone the altered states of the Psychic Summer of '73, another pop-cultural icon, Philip K. Dick (1928–82), underwent his own transformation before a similar cosmic Presence.[8] In his own precise terms, Dick was "resynthesized" or "reprogrammed" by a pink beam emanating from a vast superconsciousness that he called Valis, an acronym for vast active living intelligence system. Valis was no mere literary conceit for Dick. Nor was the pink light. Both were autobiographical facts of immense power and immeasurable, really infinite significance. This, after all, was a light that beamed the information-laden energies of entire books into him; hid itself in and as the material-virtual world; spoke Greek, Hebrew, and Sanskrit; and flooded him with information about the history of religions, particularly the ancient religions of Egypt, India, Persia, Greece, and Rome (PV xix, 5, 8; see also SR 295).

Dick's biographer, Lawrence Sutin, is clear that the writer's later work, and especially his final "Valis trilogy"—*VALIS* (1981), *Divine Invasion* (1981), and *The Transmigration of Timothy Archer* (1982)—flowed directly out of the author's metaphysical encounters with this superbeing or Sci-Fi Spirit. Indeed, in many places a novel like *VALIS* reads like a verbatim account of Dick's real-life paranormal experiences. That's because it is.

Sutin's biography, *Divine Invasions*, possesses the immense virtue of taking this metaphysical opening as the key to reading Dick's entire creative corpus. Dick certainly did. In the pink light, he reinterpreted his earlier novels, marveling at how they seemed to prepare the philosophical ground for this later metaphysical event and, in some places, even precisely describe it. *VALIS* thus became the "code book" to a ten-volume metanovel that had been building for years in him. They could all be understood now, but only *retroactively* (PV 200). It was finally the future that explained the past. Time had looped back on itself again.

Before he was a writer, Phil Dick was a reader, and he was reading on the ground floor, as it were, of the Super-Story that I have been telling. Dick, for example, fondly remembers reading as a kid Frank Baum's *Oz* books, which he considers to be "the beginning of my love for fantasy, and, by extension, science fiction" (SR 13). He probably didn't know that Baum held séances in his South Dakota home, wrote about the powers of clairvoyants for a newspaper there, joined a theosophical lodge in Chicago, and believed in reincarnation.[9]

Dick also read some of the very first comic books on the market, those of the 1930s (*Tip Top Comics*, *King Comics*, and *Popular Comics*), including "the lurid section of the Hearst newspapers which on Sunday told of mummies still alive in caves, and lost Atlantis, and the Sargasso Sea" (SR 12). Then there was Buck Rogers and, of course, the pulps. Dick read his first sci-fi pulp, *Stirring Science Stories*, at the age of twelve.

Around the same time, Phil had a secret drawer in his room, where he kept his

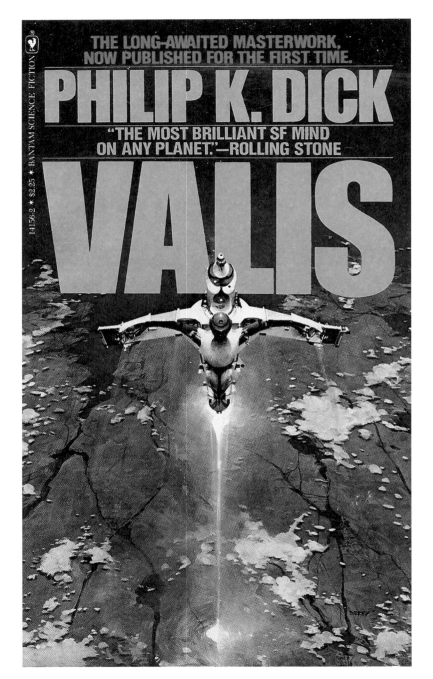

THE LONG-AWAITED MASTERWORK,
NOW PUBLISHED FOR THE FIRST TIME.

PHILIP K. DICK

"THE MOST BRILLIANT SF MIND
ON ANY PLANET."—ROLLING STONE

VALIS

BANTAM SCIENCE FICTION

14156-2 ★ $2.25

6.3 *VALIS*

men's magazines and something called "Captain Billy's Whiz Bang," one of the "Tijuana bibles" or porn comics of the era.[10] This secret drawer filled with adolescent sexual fantasies morphed in his adult years into a nine-hundred-pound, fireproof safe in which the author kept his precious pulp collection, which included complete runs of *Unknown*, *Unknown Worlds*, and *Astounding* back to 1933. Before Philip K. Dick became a great writer, then, he was an avid collector. Indeed, these pulps and comics remained his most cherished material possessions into adulthood.[11]

The fascinated, collecting boy would grow up to be a most unusual man whose strangeness was matched only by his tenderness, quirky humor, intellectual curiosity, and capacity to suffer. And suffer he would. It began shortly after birth, when his twin sister Jane perished from lack of proper medical care just a few weeks after both of them were born prematurely. He would long for his twin sister, his female half, for the rest of his life. He would also hate his mother for letting her die. His parents would divorce when he was just five, and he would grow up without his dad. As an adult, Phil Dick would go through five different marriages. He would die from a series of strokes and a final heart attack in a hospital at the age of fifty-three, his body exhausted from God only knows how much amphetamine, snuff, alcohol, and orange soda. These mind-altering chemicals had fueled his manic writing. Now they helped kill him.

Dick also suffered various psychological symptoms throughout his childhood and adult life, including, by his own count, three nervous breakdowns, numerous "schizo-phrenic" and "psychotic" episodes (his terms), various phobias (especially agoraphobia), an eating disorder that made it almost impossible for him to swallow in public (which one psychiatrist traced back to a possible childhood physical or sexual abuse scene with his grandmother's husband, Earl[12]), an adolescent existential crisis over his own existence (an existence that he found dubious at best), numerous suicide attempts and threats, a portfolio of drug addictions, and extremely debilitating episodes of vertigo that effectively demolished any hope of a normal education. It was certainly not for lack of intellectual talent or drive that the poor guy lasted only a few weeks at the University of California, Berkeley. He literally couldn't stand up.

Because Dick worked on all of this suffering through years of intense self-reflection, dream analysis, and psychotherapy, his self-descriptions are suffused with modern psychological insights. Sutin refers to him as a "well-versed Jungian," which is certainly true. But he was pretty damned good at the Freudian stuff too. Indeed, Dick's texts sparkle with both Jungian and Freudian ideas. It is also no doubt relevant here that one of his favorite books was William James's *The Varieties of Religious Experience* (1901), probably the most insightful and influential book on the psychology of mysticism ever written (and, as we have seen, the most famous passage of which was inspired by James's inhalation of nitrous oxide). In essence, we do not need to psychologize Philip K. Dick. He did this for us, spectacularly.

Consider, as a single example, how he traced his inability to form a lasting relationship with a single woman back to his difficult relationship with his mother, Dorothy, his oedipal desires for her, and his intense psychological struggles to break free from her smothering grasp. This is what he told his third wife, Anne: "When I was a teenager, I had 'the impossible dream.' I dreamt I slept with my mother." It was this "oedipal victory," he thought, that in turn resulted in his inability to stay married. "I am drawn to women who resemble my mother . . . in order to re-enact the primordial situation in which I fight my way loose at the end and divide off into autonomy" (DIS 56). What more is there to say here?

Actually, quite a bit, but there is no need (or space) to repeat Sutin's work on the details of Dick's complex emotional and personal life. We turn immediately, then, to Dick's metaphysical and mystical experiences, which, by all accounts, were as extraordinary as his writing—which late in life *were* his writing.

On February 20, 1974, the doorbell rang at Dick's apartment in Fullerton, California. The author was feeling a bit woozy from some sodium pentathol he had been given at the dentist's office for an oral surgery to remove two impacted wisdom teeth. A young woman was at the door. She was delivering a packet of Darvon for the pain. Dick was struck by her dark hair, her eyes, and her beauty. He was also attracted to her gold necklace, which featured the fish sign used by the early Christians as a symbol for Christ. This golden symbol that gleamed in the sun somehow triggered a two-month series of remarkable experiences in the author, including various memories of past lives (V 270–71).

Dick explains in terms that should now be more than familiar to the reader: "The (golden) fish sign causes you to remember. Remember what? This is Gnostic. Your celestial origins; this has to do with the DNA because the memory is located in the DNA (phylogenetic memory). . . . You remember your real *nature*. Which is to say, origins (from the stars). . . . The Gnostic Gnosis: You are here in this world in a thrown condition, but you are not *of* this world."[13] Consciousness, I might say, constructs a social ego on the left side of the brain, but it is not the ego or the brain. Consciousness thus really is "in this world, but not of it." Dick, as we shall soon see, would agree.

Here at least, though, he was much more interested in insisting that we are from the stars. Otto Binder would have cheered at this. But Phil Dick was not Otto Binder, and he was much more of a Platonist than an ufologist. Hence he commonly invoked the Platonic notion of *anamnesis*, "remembrance" or "re-cognition," in these contexts. Plato, we might recall, had used this category to explain how the soul progresses in wisdom—certainly not by learning something truly new, but by *remembering* something eternal, that is, the preexistent World of Ideas from which the soul descended and to which it will someday return after many births and many rememberings. Remembrance, re-cognition, and reincarnation, then, are the central techniques of the philosopher-writer's multilife, mystical path.[14]

Dick was on this path, and on that winter day he remembered one version of who he really was: a secret Christian living in fear of the Romans in the first century. This surprising fact was fired into his brain by "a transcendentally rational mind" (PV xvii). It did more than fire things at him, though. It killed and resurrected him so that he could now also know *what* he really was: "an immortal being" (PV 81).

Dick's remembrances circled around first-century Rome, a space-time dimension that was somehow layered over his own space-time dimension in California of 1974, as if they somehow existed simultaneously. It was this sort of experience that led him to write of two kinds of time, more or less exactly like Barry Windsor-Smith. There is "linear time," which we all know and experience as moving in one direction by the tick of the clock, mostly because this is the way our brains organize it for us. And there is "orthogonal time" or "rotary time" or "Real Time," the outer time flow of the universe that moves perpendicular or at right angles to the straight arrow of linear time, containing in its dimension everything that has come before, "just as the grooves on an LP contain the part of the music that has already been played" (SR 215–16).

If space-time was two, though, so was he. Dick thus remembered himself as Simon Magus, the great first-century gnostic teacher and archetype of Christian heresy. He also identified himself as a persecuted first-century Christian named Thomas, whose divine nature was an entity named Firebright. Such fantastic identities were multiple and varied in confusing ways in his visions and memories, but the important thing was that Dick dramatically experienced himself as a kind of historical hybrid. He was, in his own term, a "homoplasmate," which Sutin defines as "a bonding of a human and an information-rich 'plasmate' form," the latter having been "programmed" into Dick at around four years of age (DIS 211; see also PV 79).

We might say that, for Dick and the homoplasmate, the human mind consists of two basic levels or dimensions. There is the surface ego that comes to be and withers away and understands very little. And there is the "divine infinitude of absolute mind" that lies behind the little ego and is always already awake. "Behind the human mind lies God. Behind the counterfeit universe lies God" (SR 294–95). The real, as Dick explained in one of his more charmingly shocking metaphors, can thus be imagined as a ham sandwich, with the two pieces of bread as the divine and the human, and the ham as all the fake ego-world in between: what we have to do, or have done for us, is remove the ham so that the two pieces of bread can come together and realize their identity beyond their temporary meaty separation (SR 302). Within this same Twoness, Dick now felt that both hemispheres of his brain had come on line for the first time, and that they were firing together, *fast*. God speaks to us, Dick concludes, through our right hemisphere (PV 89).

The visions started in March. For eight solid hours, he witnessed energy-paintings of light that looked remarkably like Kandinskys, Klees, or Picassos (note the role of painting or *art* again). He believed that his right brain was picking these signals up, perhaps because he knew from his reading that telepathic signals are said to be best carried through right-brained images, not left-brained words or numbers.[15] He also believed that he had been the object of an ESP experiment from Moscow. He wrote a lab in Leningrad and flat out asked them if they were sending images of modern art in their experiments. Then he began to think that this attempt at contact was coming not from Russia, but from space (Orientation to Alienation again). "I was sure it came from above—maybe from the sky. Especially the stars" (DIS 213–14).

Not that his home life was any more normal. His cat Pinky (this is where I start to giggle) suddenly seemed smarter, and, perhaps eeriest of all, the radio would play music even after it was unplugged. The easy explanation here is made less easy by the alleged fact that his wife, Tessa, also heard the unplugged radio.

Then a series of what Sutin calls "tutelary dreams" began. Almost every night for three months, Dick was having what he thought were precognitive dreams. They were in the form of literal texts: printouts, words, sentences, letters, names, numbers, "sometimes whole pages, sometimes in the form of writing paper and holographic writing. . . . and during the last two weeks a huge book, again and again, with page after page of printed lines" (DIS 219). Dick was so impressed that he posited the existence of a kind of Logos (the Cosmic Christ, or the universe as preexistent ideas in the mind of God), a Logos, moreover, that could somehow communicate from the future back into the past.[16] He also concluded that this metalevel of the cosmos does not involve space, time, and causation, but rather "pure, absolute consciousness" possessing volition and using material things as language or information (JV 201).

Dick wondered whether such time-transcending experiences could be explained by tachyons, subatomic particles that, theoretically, can move from the future to the present or past. The mystical languages of Radiation are everywhere here. He experienced Valis, for example, as "electrostatic and alive," as "a form similar to radiation," and, invoking Reich now, he described a "bio-plasmatic orgone-like energy" that entered and transformed him: "From within me, as part of me, it looked out and saw itself" (PV 64, 66–67). Or again and most explicitly: "I knew I was dealing with field theory and quanta when I dealt with Valis" (SR 342). Most of all, though, he pondered the Pink: "The beam of pink light fired at my head . . . is, I have always believed deep down underneath, not God but technology, and technology from the future at that" (DIS 226).

Dick referred to this future technology and what it wrought in him as "2-3-74," for February and March of 1974. The mathematical brevity of the numbers is deceptive, for it hides even as it encodes what these events meant to him. Indeed, the meaning of these events was, for all practical purposes, inexhaustible. Dick wrote *eight thousand pages* and over two million words of interpretation in his private notebook, most of which he hand wrote, thus setting it apart from his novels, which he always typed. He entitled the Valis journal *The Dialectic: God vs. Satan or God's Final Victory Foretold and Shown, Exegesis, Apologia Pro Mea Vita*, but called it—thankfully—simply the *Exegesis*, an old Christian Greek term for the "reading out" or "deep interpretation" of a revealed or sacred scriptural text.

For eight years, deep into the nights, Dick labored on these pages in order to explain the paranormal events to himself, only to find that every path of interpretation led him finally to an infinite loop of paradox and self-reference (PV 45–51). As hard as he tried to get the Pink on the page, he found that meaning, as transmitted to him through Valis, was literally infinite. It just kept looping back, and back, and back. His ruthlessly honest interpretations ranged widely, from the "minimum hypothesis" that he was being deluded (by what or whom was not at all clear), to the conviction that

Valis was his beloved dead sister Jane speaking to him from beyond the grave through the right hemisphere of his brain, to the possibility that he had encountered the living God, Christ, the Logos, or Jung's collective unconscious.

Then there were all the various psychical effects that Valis wrought in the author. Sutin points out that Dick's fascination with the technology of psychical powers, or what the sci-fi literature called psionics, was a standard feature of his writing that peaked in the sixties—more Psi-Fi. Here we have such novels as *Martian Time-Slip*, which revolves around an anomalous boy on a Mars colony named Manfred Steiner, whose schizophrenic disorder appears to be a "window into the future" of the human species; *The Three Stigmata of Palmer Eldritch*, based on a 1963 hallucinatory vision Dick experienced of a nonhuman, metal-masked evil presence in the sky; and *Ubik*, a novel about, in Dick's own words now, "salvific information penetrating through the 'walls' of our world by an entity with personality representing a life- and reality-supporting quasi-living force," a force, by the way, that sounds remarkably like both Valis and the Yahweh of the Hebrew Bible: "I am the word and my name is never spoken, the name which no one knows. I am called Ubik, but that is not my name. I am. I shall always be."[17] During the same sixties, Dick had also been very close to Bishop James Pike, a radical Episcopalian bishop in the diocese of California who proclaimed various ultraliberal views on the historical person of Jesus and the nature of Christianity (for which he was put on heresy trial) before he died in the Judean desert from exposure after his jeep broke down. Pike was a crucial figure for Dick. Indeed, Sutin believes that Dick received some of his gnostic convictions from the bishop. A quick look at Pike's writing bears out such a suspicion—and then some.

Pike's *If This Be Heresy* (1967), for example, rails against what the bishop called "the thralldom of overbelief" and positively assesses both psychical phenomena and early Christian Gnosticism, which "until recently," he notes in what looks like an ironic self-allusion, "has been seen as a Christian heresy."[18] So, for example, Pike observes that the Resurrection accounts recorded in the New Testament may point to genuine psychical communications with a postmortem Jesus on the part of his disciples, which were then refashioned by oral memory over the decades and finally framed as a literal, physical resurrection by a later orthodoxy, that is, by a set of overbeliefs.[19]

Gnosticism, moreover, is closely aligned with psychical phenomena for Pike to the extent that he defines Gnosticism as that strand of ancient Christian practice that regards the consummation of Christian hope symbolized in a doctrine like the Resurrection as "already accomplished" and available "for present fulfillment by those individuals who *know* the realities."[20] Pike in fact concludes his book with a call to synthesize these ancient gnostic or psychical sensibilities with the more future-oriented social activism of the mainline liberal churches.[21]

Pike wrote about psychical phenomena again a year later, and in much greater detail, in *The Other Side* (1968), a double-edged title alluding to both Pike's heartfelt attempts to communicate with his dead son, Jim, who had committed suicide in February of 1966, and his desire to correct the gross media distortions and skeptical manipulations of these same intimate family events. "Mr. and Mrs. Phil Dick" are thanked in the foreword.[22] These events would help inspire Dick to write *Ubik* and, years later, he would base much of *The Transmigration of Timothy Archer* on his old friend and teacher, who is, more or less, "Bishop Timothy Archer" (PV 4, 202).

The latter novel, the final one of the Valis trilogy, treats Pike's deep commitment to psychical phenomena mostly in sarcastic and largely despairing ways. Whatever he told the bishop in real life, Dick was expressing a deep, deep skepticism in the novel (TTA 698–706). Still, it is also true that the story ends with what its title suggests, that is, Timothy Archer (or Jim Pike) alive again, as a kind of possessing spirit in a man who knows a lot about cars and has a history of mental illness. "I am Tim Archer," the man explains to the narrator of the story. "'I have come back from the other side. To those I love.' He smiled a vast and secret smile" (TTA 798).

This climactic scene, which alludes to one of Pike's books ("the other side"), appears to be more than a fictional thought experiment. Dick, after all, would also speculate in his *Exegesis* that the events of 2-3-74 look a lot like the teachings of Pike and may in fact *be* Pike. That is, Dick suggested that Valis may be a symbolic manifestation of the soul of Bishop Pike cross-bonding with his own from beyond the grave, from that other side (DIS 151). In one place, for example, after observing that "I seem to be living in my own novels more and more," Dick goes on to note that, in *Ubik*, "certain anomalies occur to the characters that prove to them that their environment is not real. Those same anomalies are now happening to me." In the novel, these anomalies involved a dead man named Runciter communicating with the living, who turn out to be dead. In his own life, Dick now explains to himself how Bishop Pike "has been breaking through in ways so similar to that of Runciter in *Ubik* that I am beginning to conclude that I and everyone else is either dead and he is alive, or—well, as in the novel I can't figure it out. It makes no sense" (PV 2–3).

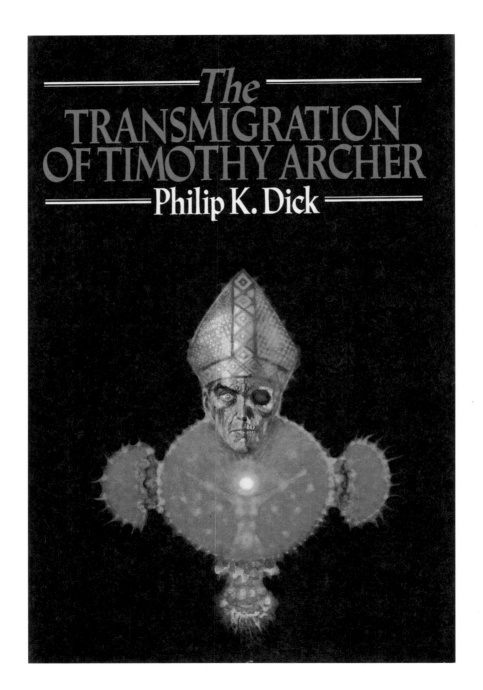

6.4   *THE TRANSMIGRATION OF TIMOTHY ARCHER*

What did make sense to Dick is the idea that Jim Pike, who while living had be-come convinced of communications from the other side, would now try such a thing. Dick could also now make sense of all his newfound mannerisms. They were Pike's. For example, he now remembered completely unfamiliar phone numbers. He drove his car and looked for mechanisms on the dashboard that were not there, as if it were another car (i.e., Pike's). He read books that Pike would have read. And he drank beer instead of wine, chugging it like the bishop did. Phil Dick was channeling Jim Pike. Which is all to say that, once again, Phil Dick had himself in mind when he wrote about "the Transmigration of Timothy Archer" into a man with a history of mental illness (TTA 800).

However one makes sense of Dick's psychical experiences, it is difficult to deny that sometimes these anomalous cognitions were incredibly useful, if not actually lifesaving. Like the time Dick allegedly diagnosed an invisible internal hernia in his little boy, Christopher, through a pop song, a pun, and the pink light. It was the early fall of 1974 and Dick was listening to the Beatles song "Strawberry Fields Forever." He looked toward the window. "My eyes close & I see that strange strawberry ice cream pink. At the same instant knowledge is transferred to me" (PV 32). That "instant knowl-edge" or "theophanic disclosure" (V 265) involved the realization that his son had an undiagnosed birth defect, an inguinal hernia.[23] The diagnosis turned out to be correct. Surgery was scheduled and the hernia was fixed.

Other sorts of paranormal experiences would continue for years. Accordingly, in a 1977 interview, Dick reported a series of dreams that bear a remarkable similarity to Windsor-Smith's time-loop experience of his future self visiting his fifteen-year-old self in a dream. For two years, Dick explained, he had been having the same dream of being back in a house he was living in around 1951: "I have a strange feeling that back then in 1951–52 I saw my future self . . . that I crashed backwards as my future self through one of my dreams now of that house, going back there and seeing myself again." "That," he continues, "would be the kind of stuff I would write as a fantasy in the early Fifties" (DIS 79–80). And the time-slip is a common occurrence in superhero comics (DP 33–34). But Phil Dick, much like Otto Binder's fictional character of Thane Smith, was experiencing it as *real*.

Like Windsor-Smith again, Dick understood such powers as expressions of evo-lution, which progresses by actualizing latent powers in us. The mytheme of Mutation once again. The ultimate goal of evolution, though, is not occult powers. It is the real-ization of one's own divinity, of which the superpowers are simply a natural expression.

Thus, in his late essay "Cosmogony and Cosmology" (1978), Dick states that the purpose of evolution is to create an "isomorphism" between the cosmic Ground of being and the Divine Spark that exists in us as our deepest secret nature. His experience of Valis is now reread as representing not a stage in evolution, but as the ultimate goal of evolution, that is, the moment in which the separation between human and divine consciousness is abolished and God comes to know itself through the temporary terminal of a human brain (SR 311).

He writes the same thing in his journals that year, and in even brighter colors. He confesses his belief in "the Great Blasphemy" hinted at in the biblical story of the Garden of Eden and the serpent's gift of gnosis, namely, the knowledge that "we are pluriforms of God voluntarily descended to this prison world, voluntarily losing our memory, identity, and supernatural powers (faculties), all of which can be regained through anamnesis." This regained isomorphism between the divine and the human, this remembrance of our own essential divinity, is "the replication of the original sin" (SR 333). It is our destiny. And it is true.

This, I take, to be the final message of Philip K. Dick. It is a mystical humanism and a modern Gnosticism on the grandest scale. It is also a vision of the Divine Man deeply rooted in the history of Western esotericism. Hence Dick's final line of *VALIS*: "From Ikhnaton [the Egyptian pharaoh who initiated monotheism] this knowledge passed to Moses, and from Moses to Elijah, the Immortal Man, who became Christ. But underneath all the names there is only one Immortal Man; *and we are that man.*"[24]

*I*NTERPRETING VALIS

What was it, exactly, that Valis beamed into him through the pink light? There are many, *way* too many ways to answer this question. Dick, we must remember, spent eight years and eight thousand pages attempting the same—and failed. We're hardly going to do it in eight pages, then, and we must finally agree with Sutin that any stable label (philosopher, mystic, Gnostic, monotheist, Jungian, Freudian, etc.) attached to this questioning, questing author can only be used for specific passages and novels.

There is a very good reason for this chameleon-like nature of Dick's self-interpretations, I would suggest, and that reason boils down to the fact that Dick understood himself to be a kind of gnostic comparativist, that is, he saw the deepest truth of things as being available to us in the history of religions, but also as "splintered up over thousands of miles and years." There are sparks and bits, for example, in Neoplatonism,

Zoroastrianism, Gnosticism, Taoism, Brahmanism, Buddhism, Orthodox Christianity, Judaism, Orphism, and so on, but *no* single system taken alone is true, hence "none is to be accepted at the expense of all the others." Rather, like the Soul or the Self, the truth must be recollected from its dispersal in history and culture. "This is my task," Dick declares.[25]

Having admitted all of that, it is also true that Dick was profoundly drawn to systems of thought that he himself identified as both "Christian" and "gnostic." Dick understood Gnosticism to be an accessible, "already accomplished" truth that was best reflected in a set of early Christian communities and texts that saw the world of matter as corrupt or even evil and that understood the biblical creator-god to be a kind of dumb demiurge or lower creator god. As we have already had many occasions to note, the true gnostic Godhead, who was entirely beyond this material world, could be reached not through the violent and finally ignorant beliefs and rituals of the orthodox churches, but through a personal *gnosis*, that is, a mystical experience that revealed to one the ultimately illusory nature of the material, social, and religious worlds and the essential divinity of the soul-spark. In other word—Valis.

This is a dangerous truth. Hence the simplest summary of Dick's gnosis is probably Sutin's potent observation that one of the most common and consistent features of the *Exegesis* is the author's sense of himself as "a frightened 'knower' of a secret" (DIS 117). He certainly believed that the only sure way to knowledge and salvation was "disobedience"—disobedience, that is, to the ruler of this world of civility and church.

This sense of fear and forbidden knowledge, of course, was already encoded in his science fiction before he came around to a conscious gnostic worldview. Science fiction, for Dick, was a kind of natural Gnosticism without revelation, which we might frame for our own purposes in its simplest terms as a refusal to yield to the social reality in which one happens to find oneself. Here is how Dick put the same insight:

> OKAY, SO I SHOULD REVISE MY STANDARDS; I'M OUT OF STEP. I SHOULD YIELD TO REALITY. I HAVE NEVER YIELDED TO REALITY. THAT'S WHAT SF IS ALL ABOUT. IF YOU WISH TO YIELD TO REALITY, GO READ PHILIP ROTH; READ THE NEW YORK LITERARY ESTABLISHMENT MAINSTREAM BESTSELLING WRITERS. . . . THIS IS WHY I LOVE SF. I LOVE TO READ IT; I LOVE TO WRITE IT. THE SF WRITER SEES NOT JUST POSSIBILITIES BUT WILD POSSIBILITIES. IT'S NOT JUST, "WHAT IF--." IT'S *"MY GOD*; WHAT IF--." IN FRENZY AND HYSTERIA. THE MARTIANS ARE ALWAYS COMING. (DIS 4)

In the pink light of Valis, he also came to see that many of his earlier sci-fi novels, and especially *Ubik*, encoded the later revelation. He came to see that these earlier novels were, in effect, messages from the future.[26] They thus "have a strange ring of (revealed) truth about them." This leads him to ask a question. Is "something writing *through* us?" (PV 77–78). In another place in his journals, Dick answers his own question and in the process articulates, perfectly, my own metathesis about the paranormal speaking through popular culture: "First for years I did it in my writing, & then in 2-74 I did it in real life, showing that my writing is *not* fiction but a form . . . of revelation expressed not *by* me but through me" (PV 135).

In terms of sources, Dick's Gnosticism displays numerous deep roots, but one remains unexplored here: Dick's reading and practice of C. G. Jung's depth psychology. Dick read Jung for most of his life and was in Jungian therapy for two years. It is certainly of significance here that Jung himself considered ancient Gnosticism, along with medieval and early modern alchemy, to be the most significant precedents of his depth psychology. Also relevant in this context is Jung's similar appreciation for particular forms of Asian religion, especially Tantric yoga and Chinese Taoism. Jung was drawn to their bipolar theologies and the central place they give to the *coincidentia oppositorum* or "coincidence of opposites," which was also central to his depth psychology. Dick was perfectly aware of all of this in Jung (V 335).

And in Asia. Indeed, Dick consulted the famous Chinese divinatory text, the *I Ching*, about which Jung had written appreciatively, for much of his life. He even used it to create the plot structure for *The Man in the High Castle* (1962), the novel for which he won sci-fi's highest honor, the Hugo Award. As is often noted, many of the countercultural actors of the 1960s and '70s who turned to the *I Ching* for their own varied projects did so after they had read Dick. Dick also consistently used Taoism and its *yin-yang* philosophy to explain that the apparent world is a fake copy of seeming opposites that have been projected from a deeper unity of "complementary bipolarities" (PV 73). In a similar spirit, he compared his observation that reality does not honor the logic of the excluded middle to Zen and Taoist thinking.[27] He also equated the event of his ego "crumbling away" in 2-3-74 with Buddhist enlightenment, indeed with becoming a Buddha (PV 158).

Dick also did not hesitate to employ the Hindu philosophical concepts of Atman and Brahman, the immortal witness Self (*atman*) and universal ground of Being, Consciousness, and Bliss that are identical or "nondual." Thus he compares the godlike

Logos of his novel *Ubik* to the Atman.[28] And he compares Valis to the Brahman, which hides itself in and as the trash of the material world and the kitsch of pop culture— "Zebra," as Dick liked to call this Being, with the suggestion that we are being deceived by a higher power, just as animals are deceived by mimicry and deception in the animal kingdom. "Zebra, if it can be said to resemble the contents of any religion," Dick wrote, "resembles the Hindu concept of Brahman."[29] God, it turns out, shows stripes in the high grass not to help us, but to hide from us and to trick us. Or to eat us, for tigers have stripes too.

Dick's specific use of Asian religious ideas displays, moreover, the exact same morphing that I traced above, that is, the transformation of the mytheme of Orientation into that of the alien or Alienation. Hence he can write: "I saw the world dissolve into Brahman. . . . I saw it as it really is: I saw with the *ajna* eye." This is a reference to the chakra just above and between the eyebrows, often called "the third eye" (PV 44–45), or what Dick in one place calls "our prime evolutionary attribute . . . which VALIS re-opens" (V 345). What is so alien about this? Dick writes elsewhere of the "'*ajna*-eyed' humanoid," and when he draws one in his journals, it looks remarkably like an alien (PV 74, 77).

Dick's Gnosticism, like his vision of time, was fundamentally Two. In some of his novels, it is also the case that there are two gods. There is a lower sinister or stupid creator-god, who has trapped us in matter and is worshipped by the orthodox systems through the sacraments; this is "the arrogant one, the Blind God (i.e. the artifact) which supposes itself to be the one true God," as Dick glossed his own character of Palmer Eldritch.[30] And there is the transcendent Godhead, Yahweh, Ubik, or Yah (in *The Divine Invasion*), whose absolute nature we share by virtue of our deepest divine spirit, the "wise, benign, powerful true God from 'outside,'" who has "invaded our *spurious* reality & is transforming it ontologically into the good and real," as he hides in the trash of pop culture (PV 70, 193).

Then there is the World as Two. Sutin calls this "Two Source Cosmogony" the most consistent starting point in the *Exegesis* entries (DIS 264). There is the cardboard fake of consensus reality, the world of particulars. And there is the hyperworld, the deeper, profoundly liberating dimension of the real, an Ürgrund or primordial ground of "fundamental Being." Things are more complicated than that, however, for this fundamental Being projected a fake world in order to come to know itself, and reality for Dick is actually always a combination or interference pattern of "two coaxial worlds" created by the real *and* the unreal: "Thus the spiritual realm *is here*, commingled with the Lower Realm: our universe is not the Lower Realm but the mixture of the two" (PV 121–22).

In *VALIS*, this Two World doctrine is expressed by the character of Horselover Fat ("Philip" is Greek for "horse-lover" and "Dick" is German for "thick" or "fat") in the form of a dream and the claim that we are all imprisoned without knowing it. Note in particular how a pulp fiction magazine plays the central role of revelation or scripture here:

> "THE EMPIRE NEVER ENDED," FAT QUOTED TO HIMSELF . . . ORIGINALLY THE SENTENCE HAD BEEN REVEALED TO HIM IN A GREAT DREAM. IN THE DREAM HE AGAIN WAS A CHILD, SEARCHING DUSTY USED-BOOK STORES FOR RARE OLD SCIENCE FICTION MAGAZINES, IN PARTICULAR *ASTOUNDINGS*. IN THE DREAM HE HAD LOOKED THROUGH COUNTLESS TATTERED ISSUES, STACKS UPON STACKS, FOR THE PRICELESS SERIAL ENTITLED "THE EMPIRE NEVER ENDED." IF HE COULD FIND IT AND READ IT HE WOULD KNOW EVERYTHING; THAT HAD BEEN THE BURDEN OF THE DREAM. . . . A BLACK IRON PRISON. THIS IS WHAT THE DREAM REFERRED TO AS "THE EMPIRE." EVERYONE WHO HAD EVER LIVED WAS LITERALLY SURROUNDED BY THE IRON WALLS OF THE PRISON; THEY WERE ALL INSIDE IT AND NONE OF THEM KNEW IT--EXCEPT FOR THE GRAY-ROBED SECRET CHRISTIANS. (V 212--13)

"Do we collectively dwell in a kind of laser hologram," Dick asked, "real creatures in a manufactured quasi-world, a stage set within whose artifacts and creatures a mind moves that is determined to remain unknown?"[31] Dick called this a "two-source hologram" or "the false work that's blended with the real world" (V 319, 342). Note that such an image implies both an illusion *and* a reality behind the illusion. That's the paradox. That's the fundamental twoness of his thought.

An experience like Dick's Valis, we might say, is a kind of subjective hologram created from the fusion or superimposition of these two dimensions: the real as an utterly transcendent "alien" Consciousness beamed through and projected by the fake imaginings and social fictions of the (left side of the) human brain. This is not something to "believe." This is something to learn from and then *see through*. Enlightenment for Dick, at least, is all about distinguishing the fake from the real, or, as we might say, the brain's projections from the universal truths of the Mind of pure Consciousness, which is God. As long as we conflate and confuse these two levels of human experience, we are doomed to delusion. We are doomed to confuse our social fictions, our material brains, and our religious myths with the deeper truth of things.[32] We are caught—whether we know it or not—in the Black Iron Prison, that is, in the police state of materialism and ignorance of our true immortal nature.

Dick goes further still and, in a strong echo of Charles Fort, repeatedly worries that the mind behind the universe, that is, the creator deity, is "totally irrational," even "insane" (V 201, 204, 226). This is precisely why the Logos or the Divine Reason comes into the world, to "invade" it, to "eat" it, and so transform it from within into something rational and salvific. This "divine invasion" of the rational into our irrational world is the "bottom line" of Fat's (and Dick's) worldview (V 274).

What we need now are more gray-robed secret Christians. Or maybe just more time to escape this Black Iron Prison. *Lots* of time. One of the late, and most radical, conclusions of the *Exegesis* involved the conviction that 2-3-74 was indeed real and directly accessible, but that any full understanding of it was impossible at this point in our species' cognitive evolution. The passage dealing with this most gnostic of ideas, dated September 11, 1981, is well worth quoting at length:

THUS WE MAY STAND AT THE THRESHOLD OF DISCOVERIES . . . WHICH MAY REQUIRE A LITERAL EVOLUTION OF OUR SPECIES--AND THIS MAY INDEED BE TAKING PLACE. THUS EVEN TO KNOW THIS HYPER-STRUCTURE IS TO CEASE TO BE HUMAN, AND YET SUCH KNOWLEDGE--NOT FAITH, NOT REVELATIONS, BUT THE UTILIZATION OF PURE INTELLECT--IS POSSIBLE. I ARGUE, THEN, THAT MAN AS A SPECIES MAY BE COMING TO AN END, SUBSUMED INTO A HIGHER LEVEL OF ORGANIZATIONAL COMPLEXITY; AND A NEW SPECIES MAY BE EVOLVING OUT OF HIM. I ARGUE, FINALLY, THAT THE HYPER-STRUCTURE IS TO SOME DEGREE ACTIVELY INVOLVED IN PROMOTING THIS, SINCE IT IS AN EVOLUTIONARY PROCESS IN WHICH IT IS INVOLVED.[33]

Such mutant thoughts are perhaps never more apparent, and nowhere more spectacularly owned, than in Dick's tongue-in-cheek, but seriously titled private essay "The Ultra Hidden (Cryptic) Doctrine: The Secret Meaning of the Great System of Theosophy of the World, Openly Revealed for the First Time (March 2, 1980)." Dick explains here that, although he has drawn on Tibetan Buddhism, Orphism, Gnosticism, Neoplatonism, and esoteric Christianity in order to interpret Valis, what he has *also* done is employ his experience of Valis in order to reread these historical traditions and derive from them "a single sensationally revolutionary occult doctrine."

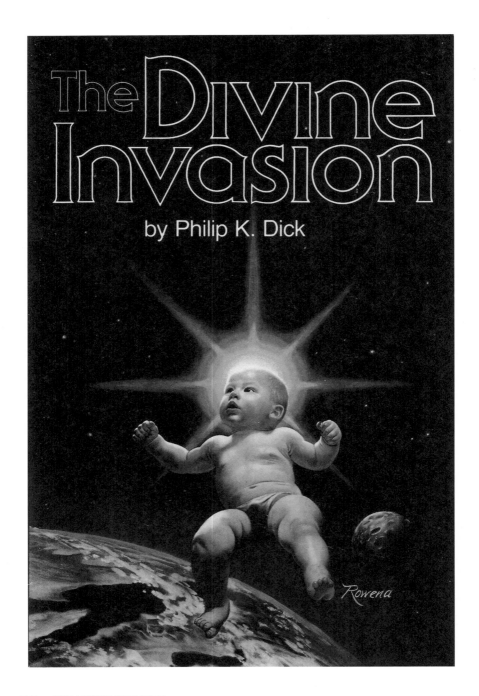

The Divine Invasion

by Philip K. Dick

Rowena

This is what he calls his *sophia summa*, that is, his final and highest wisdom (SR 337–38).

And what is this final wisdom? The claim that there exists in the human being a particular "paranormal talent" that is capable of altering the past from the future through a warping of space, time, and causality. Here Dick seriously suggests that in Valis his mind fused with a mind from the future (which may have been his own). He thus now believes that "I may have actually literally caused time to run backward." This is the only way he can make sense of Valis and explain to himself why he knew things in 3-74 that could not have been known until much later. It was not simple precognition, however (as if that is simple). It was much more: it was the future altering the present toward itself. It was "the future of the past."

Such mind-bending thoughts help Dick explain both the ultimate nature of human freedom and the deeper mechanisms of evolution. The ability to step out of the temporal groove and affect our own past (particularly when we have made mistakes in that past) represents a radical sort of freedom, to say the least. This, moreover, would be incredibly useful as a "new survival talent" or evolutionary ability. After all, if one can influence the past, one can influence or reinfluence the present, and presumably as many times as necessary.[34] Moreover, if one can access future information, one can "problem-solve like a crazy thing" (SR 345).

Dick draws from this an even grander possibility, namely, that there exists "a vast meta-mind . . . who is encouraging the development of this time-disruption faculty in order to evolve the human species further." Here he is thinking of the three-eyed people whom he has seen in his visions, evolved superhumans, perhaps, who are using this faculty to guide our present evolution: "us" from the future.

We are not DNA robots, then (Dick despised mechanistic materialisms of all sorts). We are DNA memory coils extending over multiple lives with access to vast amounts of information from both the past and the future. Essentially, we are conscious time-loops influencing our own evolution from the future in a never-ending dialectic of experiment and correction. What Fat then really encountered in Valis, at least in this reading, was "himself from the far future. Himself so evolved, so changed, that he had become no longer a human being" (V 282). This freedom to transcend time and influence the past from the future is the cryptic doctrine toward which the great esoteric systems of history are striving. Seen in this esoteric pink light, *we are evolving ourselves.*

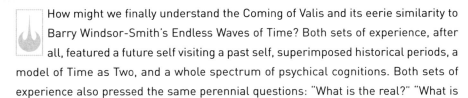

How might we finally understand the Coming of Valis and its eerie similarity to Barry Windsor-Smith's Endless Waves of Time? Both sets of experience, after all, featured a future self visiting a past self, superimposed historical periods, a model of Time as Two, and a whole spectrum of psychical cognitions. Both sets of experience also pressed the same perennial questions: "What is the real?" "What is the human?" And, perhaps most mysteriously of all, "What is time?"

Reductionism and dismissal are always the easiest ways out of the profound challenge that an author like Dick or Windsor-Smith poses to us. It would be easy, of course, to assert that a sci-fi author like Dick is not "really" religious, that he is pretending a revelation that he does not in fact possess, that his vast *Exegesis* was the result of a schizophrenic episode or a temporal lobe epilepsy and a subsequent paranoia and hypergraphia or "manic writing." In some ways, such diagnoses fit the bill, as Sutin has shown in detail. And indeed, Dick was obviously suffering, seriously and deeply. In other ways, however, they miss the mark, and widely. Dick, after all, experienced 2-3-74 as profoundly healing, as an ending of the gulf that separated him from the world, as a "repair" (PV 130).

Easy phrases, then, like "schizophrenic episode" or "temporal lobe epilepsy," finally mislead in their false sense of full explanation. In truth, there is no full explanation here, as such neurological states could be the necessary biological conditions or catalysts, as opposed to the materialist causes, of such spiritual inrushes. In short, a correlation is not a cause and may in the end be a catalyst of something entirely different.

There is also, of course, the very common "drug reading" of Philip K. Dick. Sutin deals admirably and at great length with Dick's well-known drug habits, but he finally dismisses this explanation as too easy. I can only agree. More specifically, I would suggest in the spirit of my remarks above that Dick's drug-taking habits, like his possible temporal lobe seizures, may have indeed played key psychological roles in his creativity and mystical experiences, and this precisely to the extent that they rendered his psyche more porous to the metaphysical dimensions he entered so dramatically in 2-3-74. Put differently, the drugs may have well dissolved his ego here and there, and this may have been precisely what let Valis in, but it does not follow that Valis was a product of the drugs.

In other words, I think we must distinguish between the psychological conditions of a mystical inrush—be they, for example, psychedelic, psychosexual, bipolar, schizophrenic, or traumatic—and the inrush itself. Let me put it bluntly: it is one thing to acknowledge that John Doe left his body because his Toyota Camry slammed into an oak tree at seventy miles an hour in a blizzard. It is quite another to claim that the immortality of the soul he *knew* with certainty in that state can be reduced to the oak tree, the smashed Camry, the blizzard, or even his traumatized brain. So too with "mental illness" or "madness." Mad people suffer horribly, and I have absolutely no desire to romanticize mental illness. But, as we have known at least since the time of Plato, mad people are sometimes also gifted people with exceptionally porous egos and so very special powers of seeing and being.

Dick explicitly invoked what I have called the brain-filter thesis to make the same points. In commenting on his terrifying vision of Palmer Eldritch in the sky of 1963, for example, he admits that we must have our own idiosyncratic world (*idios kosmos*) to stay sane. We simply cannot handle reality as it is, the world "out there," the universal or real world (*koinos kosmos*). Reality as such "has to filter through, carefully controlled by the mechanisms by which our brains operate" (DIS 127). He also stated explicitly that *anamnesis* or the mystical recognition of one's true immortal nature comes about "when certain inhibited neural circuits in the human brain are disinhibited," that is, when the brain filter is temporarily suppressed (SR 293; V 269, 271, 283; DI 440–41, 544). Dick reasoned in this same spirit again that drug-induced hallucinations may simply be aspects of genuine reality that are, in daily life, filtered out by our Kantian *a priori* neural organizing categories (such as space and time) (SR 171–72).

Sutin is referring here to a potent little 1964 essay entitled "Drugs, Hallucinations, and the Quest for Reality," in which Dick took this idea very far indeed, extending it into the realm of extrasensory perceptions and abilities, LSD experiences, and mysticism. He noted, for example, that numerous psychiatrists from Freud on have taken telepathic cognitions very seriously, and that Jan Ehrenwald developed a theory of severe mental illness from the idea that such patients are "experiencing involuntary telepathic linkage" with people around them. In another essay, Dick similarly suggested that the schizophrenic has fallen outside of time and causality into a state in which what the physicist Wolfgang Pauli called synchronicity has taken over and engulfed the individual "in an endless now."[35]

In other words, individuals fall ill and become paranoid or schizophrenic not because they are misperceiving, but because they are overperceiving: their brain filter is not functioning properly, *but there is a "what" there that they are perceiving.*

Paul Williams made the same point in his 1974 interview with Dick in *Rolling Stone*. Here is how Williams described reading Dick's novels: "It's all marvelous fun, especially if you've ever suspected that the world is an unreal construct built solely to keep you from knowing who you really are. Which it is, of course. Paranoia is true perception."[36]

Drugs—or temporal lobes or car wrecks or sexual trauma or schizophrenia—do not necessarily cause telepathic or mystical experiences, then. They may also *let them in*. And as soon as these alien states come in, they are, of course, immediately filtered, translated, and shaped by the cognitive and perceptual apparatus of the human brain, including and especially its cultural fantasies. Dick's double conclusion is stunning: "The sane man does not know that everything is possible," and "the mentally ill person at one time or another *knew too much*" (SRI 174). Stated from another angle, the "veil" of reality serves a benign purpose (SRI 214). This, of course, is another way of stating, yet again, the secret of Superman. We *need* Clark Kent. We *need* the brain filter to keep absolute Consciousness at bay.

These brain-Mind distinctions, it seems to me, are even more relevant to a case like that of Barry Windsor-Smith, since he himself has invoked exactly the same distinction, and in clearer and more explicit terms, in order to make sense of his own metaphysical experiences. It should also be emphasized, and then underlined, that the simplistic drug reading does not and cannot work here in any sense, since the artist took none.

In his own mind, it was the "double work of art" that functioned as the real catalyst of his remarkable experiences, that is, it was "the layered complexities of my thought processes whilst I work" that was "the key that opened my doors of perception to mystical experiences."[37] The allusion here is to Aldous Huxley tripping on mescaline in his justly famous tract *The Doors of Perception*. But again, Windsor-Smith needed no mescaline. That's the point. There are many ways into mystical states.

Including art. Time, after all, looped back for the artist *in the very act of drawing*. We have as yet no real way of understanding this, much less explaining it. We might say that such a time loop had something to do with the unique ways that the creative process draws on both the rational and intuitive powers of the double human brain, the way the words work with the images and the images work with the words. But this hardly captures the mystical arts of Barry Windsor-Smith, which, after these events, moved far beyond the graphic scenes of action and violence that still dominate the superhero comic and moved into what he calls "a knowingness" that finally transcended the usual rules and tropes of the genre. Barry Windsor-Smith—like Alan Moore, Grant Morrison, Ray Palmer, Jack Kirby, and Alvin Schwartz—had become a modern Gnostic.

A neuroscientist may want to invoke something like temporal lobe seizures, and Windsor-Smith himself may or may not find these sorts of descriptions appropriate as neuroscientific labels of what his brain was doing at the time. But again, what do such "explanations" really explain? Is the filter really the filtered? And how do such easy labels explain the objective fact that the artist saw, in precise detail, two events in 1970 that did not occur until three years later in 1973? Just how much of these men's courage and honesty do we need to savage (or just politely ignore) in order to protect our little materialist worlds? Must the Black Iron Prison be *that* fricking thick?

THE THIRD KIND

THE VISITOR CORPUS OF WHITLEY STRIEBER

THE SECRET SCHOOL SUGGESTS THAT WE ARE THE AUTHORS OF OURSELVES, ENGAGED IN SOME EXTRAORDINARY EFFORT THAT WE ARE ONLY JUST NOW BEGINNING TO SEE WITH OUR ORDINARY MINDS. . . . WE ARE REACHING TOWARD A NEW KIND OF MIND, ONE THAT CAN WALK THE PAST, READ THE FUTURE, AND USE PSYCHIC POWER WITH KNOWLEDGE AND SKILL.

WHITLEY STRIEBER, *THE SECRET SCHOOL*

HUMANITY IS NOT A FRIGHTENED INFANT BUT MORE A GIANT IN BONDAGE, AND THE CHAINS THAT BEAR US DOWN ARE FASHIONED FROM THESE SECRETS.

WHITLEY STRIEBER, *CONFIRMATION*

One of the central purposes of the present project has been to suggest that there is a kind of metanarrative or Super-Story developing in these various sci-fi and superhero mini-mythologies. One way we might begin to conclude, then, would be to take a single contemporary case study and see whether the model works, whether we can "walk the talk" or, if you will, "store the Story." After all, the real test of the mythical patterns and paranormal currents that I have sketched out in these pages—and, alas, these can only be sketches—is simply this: whether or not they help bring some measure of order and meaning to real-world, lived stories, that is, to those selves-as-stories we call "people."

Although a very strong case could be made for Charles Fort, Ray Palmer, Alvin Schwartz, Barry Windsor-Smith, or Philip K. Dick, there is probably no author more illustrative of our mythemes and the experiential paranormal currents that they fictionalize within American popular culture than the novelist Whitley Strieber. The facts that Strieber is a contemporary author and so brings our Super-Story into the present, and that he has related his traumatically transformative experiences with such psychological detail, obvious honesty, and philosophical subtlety, while "keeping the question open," that is, while refusing the easy pacts of both the true believer (it's all literally true or objective) and the dogmatic denier (it's all completely illusory or subjective), make him an ideal figure with which to close *Mutants and Mystics*. That I have had the opportunity to converse and correspond with the author at some length makes him an even more appropriate figure.[1]

STRIEBER AND THE SUPER-STORY

It is difficult to know where to begin, as Strieber's writings explore and express, often in astonishing detail, each of our seven mythemes. Here is a hopelessly bare outline.

1. DIVINIZATION/DEMONIZATION. ALTHOUGH STRIEBER INSISTS THAT WHAT WE HAVE BEEN WITNESSING AND EXPERIENCING THROUGH THE POP MOTIF OF THE ALIEN FOR THE LAST SIXTY YEARS IS "STUNNINGLY NEW" (CON 87--88), HE ALSO LOCATES THESE EXPERIENCES IN THE GENERAL HISTORY OF RELIGIONS AND CLEARLY UNDERSTANDS THE SACRED AS AN AWE-FULL REALITY THAT CAN BE EXPERIENCED AS EITHER POSITIVE OR NEGATIVE, AS DIVINE OR DEMONIC, DEPENDING ON THE INDIVIDUAL'S OWN PSYCHOLOGICAL CONDITIONING AND SPIRITUAL MAKEUP. IN MY OWN TERMS NOW, WE MIGHT SPECULATE THAT ANY DEEP ENCOUNTER WITH THE SACRED INVOLVES A TEMPORARY DISSOLUTION OF THE EGO. IF THE PSYCHE IS READY FOR SUCH AN EGO DEATH, THE ENCOUNTER WILL TEND TO BE EXPERIENCED POSITIVELY, EVEN ECSTATICALLY. IF THE PSYCHE IS NOT READY, HOWEVER, THE ENCOUNTER WILL TEND TO BE EXPERIENCED NEGATIVELY, EVEN DEMONICALLY. THE ANGEL CAN QUICKLY BECOME THE DEMON, AND THE DEMON CAN JUST AS QUICKLY TURN INTO AN ANGEL. PERFECTLY FAITHFUL TO THIS DOUBLE-EDGED, BOTH-AND NATURE OF THE SACRED, STRIEBER, AS AN EGO WITH EXTENSIVE SPIRITUAL TRAINING, HAS KNOWN WHAT HE NEUTRALLY CALLS "THE VISITORS" AS **BOTH**.

2. ORIENTATION. STRIEBER HAS READ DEEPLY INTO COMPARATIVE MYSTICAL LITERATURE, INCLUDING INTO THE ASIAN CONTEMPLATIVE TRADITIONS OF ZEN BUDDHISM, CHINESE TAOISM, AND INDO-TIBETAN TANTRA (B 68, 70). LIKE OUR OTHER AUTHORS AND ARTISTS, HE OFTEN INVOKES CATEGORIES LIKE THE **KOAN** OF ZEN PRACTICE OR THE KUNDALINI AND "THIRD EYE" OF INDIAN TANTRIC YOGA. HE HAS DESCRIBED TO ME HOW, AS HE BECAME MORE FAMILIAR WITH THE VISITORS, HE NOTICED THAT THEY SMELLED OF SOIL AND HE THOUGHT OF THEM

AS MINERS. HE WOULD EVEN SOMETIMES HEAR DRILLING BELOW THE HOUSE—A KIND OF PERSONAL HOLLOW EARTH. HE ALSO DESCRIBES HIS EARLY FASCINATION WITH EGYPT (SS 179) AND HIS PERSONAL INVOLVEMENT IN THE EARLY DISCUSSIONS ABOUT THE *VIKING* DISCOVERY AND 1982 PHOTOGRAPHIC RESOLUTION OF THE "FACE ON MARS," WHICH HE INSTINCTIVELY ASSOCIATED WITH THE ANCIENT IMAGE OF THE SPHINX (SS XVIII—XIX, 4—17). THE HAWK-HEADED EGYPTIAN GOD HORUS, OR A VISITOR POSING AS THE GOD, EVEN SHOWED UP IN HIS CABIN ONE NIGHT BEFORE A STUNNED HOUSEGUEST.

3. **ALIENATION.** ALTHOUGH STRIEBER CONSISTENTLY REJECTS AND AVOIDS THE LANGUAGE OF "THE ALIEN" (FOR ITS BAD SCI-FI B-MOVIE ALLUSIONS), HE HAS WRITTEN FIVE PROVOCA-TIVE NONFICTION BOOKS ON HIS ENCOUNTERS WITH THE VISITORS, WHICH CLEARLY INVOKE, EVEN AS THEY RESIST, SUBVERT, AND COMPLICATE, THE EARLIER SYMBOLIC FRAMES OF THE ALIEN AND THE UFO. ALL OF THIS, MOREOVER, WAS FIRST SIGNALED IN A BESTSELLING BOOK, *COMMUNION*, WHICH FEATURED ON ITS COVER A FEMALE BEING, WHOM STRIEBER DESCRIBES AS "SPIDER-LIKE." TED JACOBS WOULD MAKE THIS BEING'S HUGE, BLACK, WRAP-AROUND EYES IMMEDIATELY RECOGNIZABLE THROUGH HIS ICONIC PAINTING OF HER ON THE BOOK'S FAMOUS COVER. WHETHER UNDERSTOOD AS "OTHER" OR AS SOME DEEPER ASPECT OF "US," CLEARLY ALIENATION IS THE CENTRAL MYTHEME OF STRIEBER'S VISITOR CORPUS.

4. **RADIATION.** BUT STRIEBER ALSO CONSTANTLY RETURNS TO THE EARLIER MESMERIST, SPIRITUALIST, AND THEOSOPHICAL REGISTERS OF AN INFLUX OR "ENERGY" AND ESPECIALLY THE LATER LANGUAGE OF QUANTUM PHYSICS AS THE MOST ADEQUATE FRAMES IN WHICH TO UNDERSTAND HIS MULTIDIMENSIONAL MYSTICAL EXPERIENCES. HERE, FOR EXAMPLE, STRIEBER SPECULATES THAT THE SOUL IS OF AN ELECTROMAGNETIC NATURE, A KIND OF CONSCIOUS ENERGY OR PLASMA. LIKE THE EARLIER LITERATURE ON THE OD AND THE OR-GONE, HIS TEXTS ARE FILLED WITH AN ELECTRIC BLUE LIGHT (B 69—70; T 57, 73, 179). THERE ARE EVEN SOME BRIGHT PINK SCENES REMINISCENT OF PHILIP K. DICK (T 81—82, 179). IN PERSON, HE RELATES STORIES OF HOW HIS POST-ENCOUNTER PRESENCE WOULD OFTEN PUT OUT STREETLIGHTS AND, MUCH LIKE WOLFGANG PAULI, FIZZLE OR EVEN BLOW UP ELECTRONIC EQUIPMENT. HE ALSO DESCRIBES BOTH THE NEGATIVE AND POSITIVE, REALLY EXPLOSIVE EROTIC DIMENSIONS OF HIS EXPERIENCES WITH AN ALIEN "HER" AND RELATES A PLEASUR-ABLE VIBRATORY SENSATION THAT PRECEDES HIS SEEMING EXPERIENCES OF TELEPORTA-TION, LEVITATION, OR OUT-OF-BODY TRAVEL (B 69, 139). HIS TEXTS, RADIATED WITH SUCH METAPHYSICAL ENERGIES, GLOW FOR THE READY READER.

5. **MUTATION.** THIS IS ANOTHER MAJOR MYTHEME FOR STRIEBER. HE WRITES EXPLICITLY OF THE FURTHER EVOLUTION OF HUMAN NATURE AS INTUITED IN THE ICONIC IMAGE OF THE ALIEN

COMMUNION

A TRUE STORY BY

WHITLEY STRIEBER

Co-author of WARDAY

(CON 93) AND ASKS, EXACTLY LIKE PHILIP K. DICK, WHETHER HUMAN CONSCIOUSNESS "HAS LITERALLY BOOT-STRAPPED ITSELF, REACHING BACKWARD ACROSS THE AGES TO INITIATE ITS OWN HISTORY" (B 148). HE WONDERS, WITH WRITERS LIKE JACQUES VALLEE AND DICK AGAIN, IF THE VISITORS ARE NOT IN FACT US FROM THE FUTURE COMING BACK TO GUIDE AND COR-RECT OUR OWN EVOLUTIONARY DEVELOPMENT.[2] AND HE SEEMS CONVINCED THAT EVOLUTION IS NO MEANINGLESS RANDOM PROCESS, BUT "THE OUTCOME OF A DESIGN," AN IMMENSE QUANTUM PROCESS PERHAPS BROUGHT INTO BEING VIA "A LARGE-SCALE PERCEIVING FORCE THAT GOVERNS THE STRUCTURE OF THE UNIVERSE" (SS 115--16). CLEARLY, WHITLEY STRIEBER IS AN X-MAN, A MUTANT MYSTIC.

6 § 7. REALIZATION AND AUTHORIZATION. MOST RADICALLY OF ALL, THOUGH, STRIEBER'S CENTRAL MYSTICAL NOTION OF "COMMUNION" IS ALL ABOUT MOVING FROM AN AWARENESS THAT WE ARE BEING WRITTEN OR MANIPULATED (CON 221), EVEN SOMETIMES SEEMINGLY RAPED OR MIND CONTROLLED (REALIZATION), TO AN ACTIVE, SHARED, FULLY RE-CIPROCAL, EVEN LOVING COAUTHORSHIP WITH THE ALIEN OTHER OF A SHARED SUPERNATURE (AUTHORIZATION). IN THIS SAME REALIZED AND NOW AUTHORIZING SPIRIT, HE INVOKES QUAN-TUM PHYSICS AGAIN IN ORDER TO MAKE SENSE OF THE RADICAL PARTICIPATORY NATURE OF HIS VISITOR EXPERIENCES, THAT IS, THE MYSTERIOUS WAYS THAT THE OBSERVATION OF AN ENCOUNTER EVENT IN THE EXTERNAL ENVIRONMENT IS IN SOME SENSE DEPENDENT ON THE SUBJECTIVE STATE OF THE OBSERVER. NOT UNLIKE JOHN KEEL, WHITLEY STRIEBER UNDER-STANDS DEEPLY THAT *THE OBSERVER SOMEHOW HELPS CREATE, LITERALLY BRINGS INTO BEING, THE OBSERVED*. IN OUR SECRET LIVES, STRIEBER SUGGESTS, WE ARE RE-ALLY AND TRULY PARTICIPATING IN THE AUTHORIZATION OF REALITY ITSELF, AND IN WAYS THAT REMAIN LARGELY UNCONSCIOUS AT OUR PRESENT LEVEL OF EVOLUTIONARY DEVELOPMENT. AS HE HAS IT IN OUR OPENING EPIGRAPH, WE ARE, TOGETHER, A GIANT AWAKENING INTO OUR OWN UNBELIEVABLE POWERS.

That is the vision in the proverbial nutshell. Here are the barest outlines of Whitley Strieber's life and nonfiction work.

From 1977 to 1983, the author wrote bestselling horror novels like *The Wolfen* (1978) and *The Hunger* (1981). Horror, of course, with all of its depictions of the dead and the monstrous, is a profoundly religious genre, even when it is not explicitly religious, since terror, a close cousin of trauma, can also catalyze transcendence. Strieber then col-laborated with James Kunetka and wrote two works of social criticism, one about limited nuclear war, *Warday* (1984), and one about environmental collapse, *Nature's End* (1986).

Then, on December 26, 1985, the author's world turned upside down. On that night, he experienced a dramatic abduction by a group of transphysical beings in upstate New York in his own forest cabin-home. In *Communion* (1986), he recreates that night, its foreshadowing that earlier October, and its various deep threads back into his childhood through conscious memory, journal entries, and, eventually, some hypnosis sessions with a professional psychiatrist by the name of Dr. Donald F. Klein, who verifies Strieber's psychological health in an appendix to the book. Strieber in fact had no coherent understanding of what happened to him that night until he sought out medical attention for his intense psychological sufferings and physical symptoms, which included, he learned to his shock and horror, clear physiological evidence that he had been raped. According to Strieber, Dr. Klein originally approached his symptoms, which had developed into PTSD or posttraumatic stress disorder, as signs of a crime.

An early short story entitled simply "Pain" (1986) represents an immediate, largely indirect or unconscious attempt to work through the experience before he began to articulate it through hypnosis, the UFO phenomenon, and his own double-concept of the visitors. Strieber wrote this short story in the days immediately after his abduction in what he describes as "a state of extreme terror and excitement that somehow involved a provocative, even devastating, female figure. The story reflects my first attempt to cope with the explosive, profoundly confusing combination of ecstasy and terror that the experience inspired."

On the surface, "Pain" is about a prostitute named Janet O'Reilly who teaches the protagonist, a married man named Alex, that he is not the body, that "the cup is not the wine." Through Janet's instruction and tortures, Alex learns that pain "breaks down the barriers of ego, of personality, of false self. It separates us from ourselves and allows us to see deep." It enables us to see the whole world "as a single, coherent entity, an enormous living organism."[3]

Enter the image of the spider again, this time through the sexuality of death: "For death is connected to sexuality—witness the spider. Who hasn't wondered what the male spider feels, submitting at the same time to the ecstasy of coitus and the agony of death?"[4] A few pages down, Strieber speculates that there is "something that feeds on human suffering," that this suffering frees the soul from ego and so leads it to genuine wisdom, and that this is the real meaning of sacrifice in the history of religions. This is no "nebulous spiritual presence," though. It is rather "a real civilization, albeit with higher goals, motives and understanding than our own."[5]

Then, still groping toward what happened to him a few days earlier in real life, Strieber manages to invoke within the story both the UFO and, through the allusion of the earth as a kind of farm, the figure of Charles Fort: "the fantastic notion that [UFOs] are the artifacts of an intelligent civilization so far in advance of our own that we literally cannot see its manifestations except on rare occasions when they probe into our temporal space, much as the farmer enters the pigsty to check the health of his animals. The underlying thesis of the paper is that this higher species is native to earth, and that—by their own lights—they use us just as we use the pigs. I know that this is true because Janet has shown me that it is true."[6] The story ends with Alex realizing that "Janet" comes to us all in the form of death, that it is only a matter of the ticking clock and the declining calendar until we all will watch our burdensome identities dissolve in the ecstasy and agony, the rapture and oblivion that is physical death.

Communion, via the altered states of the recorded hypnosis sessions, took up this "Pain" and worked it through more systematically and consciously. Here Strieber tells the story of how in the middle of the night on that day after Christmas, that Feast of the Divine-Human Hybrid, he woke up suddenly to "a peculiar whooshing, swirling noise" in the living room, as if a large number of people were moving around the room. The visitors.

Most were three and a half feet tall, with two dark holes for eyes and "a black downturning line of a mouth that later became an O" (COM 11–12). They carried him out of his bedroom, naked and paralyzed. Strieber sensed that one of the creatures was a woman, "with extremely prominent and mesmerizing black slanted eyes." Her voice, like those that Philip K. Dick heard, had "a subtly electronic tone to it," though hers also possessed "accents flat and startlingly Midwestern" (COM 19). Later, he would describe another visitor's voice as "radiolike" (T 88), and his correspondents would report metallic echoes, as if a technology was involved (B 84–85)—again, more echoes of Fort's Martian X and Dick's Valis.

There followed eleven years of further contact with the visitors, a long series of spiritual teachings and metaphysical speculations, and four more nonfiction books on these same events: *Transformation* (1989), *Breakthrough* (1996), *The Secret School* (1997), and *Confirmation* (1998). Two smaller books followed, both originally self-published metaphysical testaments of sorts: *The Key* (2001) and *The Path* (2002).

RECEIVING COMMUNION

Both the content of this visitor corpus and the reception of *Communion* bear out perfectly Fort's model of the three Dominants. We will get to the content of Strieber's communion soon enough. In terms of the reception history, both official religion (Fort's first Dominant) and official science (Fort's second Dominant) derided and demeaned the book. Strieber explains in a new foreword to the 2008 edition: "This was probably the only time that the religious right and the intellectual left have been united on much of anything, but they were united on this: Whitley Strieber had to go. In the case of the intellectual left and the media, that meant methodical and persistent public derision. The religious right was more sinister: we began to receive death threats" (COM xiii–xiv).

Strieber is very clear that, whether derisive or dangerous, the basic worldview of the dogmatic scoffers worked in the exact same way as that of the dogmatic believers. Each excluded—"damned," Fort would say—what did not, what *could not* fit into its particular system and assumptions. The official critics "were promoting a religion of skepticism that was as belief-based as the demonization of me that was going on among fundamentalist Christians" (COM xvi). Both damned him.

Strieber's mature thoughts about the nature of the visitor experience are also eerily close to those of Fort. "But the visitors are not only real and here," he writes. "In fact, I don't think they are visitors at all. I think that the truth is that we are embedded in their world in the same way that animal species are embedded in ours" (COM xv). We are property. Hence when Strieber complained to the taller female that they had no right to do this to him, she snapped back emphatically: "*We do have a right.*" In essence, they were not just studying him. They were changing him, taming him. Like a wild animal.

Another key component of the reception history was the phenomenon of what came to be called "the Communion letters." From the publication of *Communion* in 1986 until 2008, Strieber received over half a million letters from people around the world who had encountered similar little humanoids—often the letter writers recognized the iconic face on the cover of the book—and were seeking him out for advice and moral support (COM xiii). In the early years, the letters would arrive in large gray bags hauled directly to the Strieber home when the mail service they had employed could no longer handle them. There were so many that the Striebers had to hire someone to open them all. We might recall that something similar, if on a much smaller scale, occurred with writer-editor Ray Palmer and the Shaver mystery in the pages of *Amazing Stories*.

Anne Strieber, who read or at least skimmed all of these letters, responded to as many of them as she could, kept tens of thousands of them, and published a selection of the most remarkable samples in *The Communion Letters* (1997). Anne emphasizes the ordinary nature of the lives that such extraordinary experiences transformed: "The mailman, plumber, or teacher is not who you think he is," she said to a group of us. "He is a saint, a guru" in disguise. Whitley in his books and Anne in conversation often return to the data and details of the Communion letters, usually to point out the strongly individualist, democratic, or grassroots strategies that they believe the letters reveal. Whatever the phenomenon of the visitors is about, it is ignoring elite culture and going right to the base, to the "ordinary" man or woman on the street (or, more likely, in the bed).[7]

It is as if the visitors, Strieber suggests, have decided that the U.S. government (which, since the late 1940s, has treated them as targets to shoot down), our religious institutions (which, with precious few exceptions, have treated them as "demons"), and our media (which has chosen, with the professional scoffers, a strategy of public ridicule) are more or less incompetent. In such a situation, Strieber speculates, direct one-on-one intervention would become a reasonable strategy to effect specieswide change. This is why, Strieber suggests, the visitors quickly ceased to rely exclusively on their "theatre in the sky" and began to interact with the human unconscious via the deposits of dream, myth, and out-of-body experience. Put in my own terms, the visitors (which, again, may be us) are ignoring our left-brain reason and working instead on our right-brain mythmaking, that is, on our Super-Story. They are not "convincing" us. They are rewriting and retelling us.

Such esoteric techniques more or less guarantee that human beings will have to work for what they get out of the contact experience, that they will have to "make it their own" through the active interpretation of symbolic material and conscious cultural constructions that are themselves hybrid or synthesizing creations of the left and right brains, at once ego and Other. This, in turn, Strieber intuits, is a function of a wise and basically benign acclimatization strategy designed to prevent the usual scenario of colonial contact, whereby the much less advanced culture is almost immediately reduced to a state of complete nonmeaning (CON 252). "We know this," Strieber writes, "because of what happened here on Earth between 1550 and 1950" (CON 256). In other words, there may be a very good reason that the visitors do not land on the White House lawn, and it is a moral reason: they might fear that such a sudden, unambiguous contact would render our culture null and void. Charles Fort, by the way, had reasoned the same back in 1919: "It's probably for moral reason that they stay away," he wrote in *The Book of the Damned*. "But even so," he immediately added, "there must be some degraded ones among them" (BD 162).

For Strieber, in any case, what the visitors are probably about is not invasion, but a profound and sufficiently gradual change in our worldview and our souls. He is in some good company here. After corresponding with military officials and contactees in the States, no less an intellectual than Carl Jung had read the flying saucer craze of the 1950s in a very similar light in his classic and still prescient *Flying Saucers: A Modern Myth Seen in the Skies* (1958). Jung's conclusions were subtle, prescient, profound, and humble. He turned to parapsychology for suggestions—which were never any more than that—that these "things seen in the sky" might be planetary poltergeists manifesting a profound dis-ease or metaphysical imbalance in our present materialist worldview, that they may be, as it were, a manifestation of consciousness setting itself aright after a long night of materialism and mechanism. The crisis for Jung, in other words, was not yet environmental. It was primarily intellectual and spiritual.

The cover of the first run of the American edition of Jung's potent little book captures the psychologist's challenge beautifully. Two flying saucers become the eyes of an immense, looming, human figure, an early version of Strieber's humanity as "a giant in bondage" perhaps. Encountered in the context of Jung's words inside the covers, the dark monster on the outside challenges us to wake up from our hyperrational slumber before the technological, philosophical, and hyperreligious products of that slumber destroy both us and our fragile world. Need I point out that the same cover could have easily appeared on almost any pulp-fiction magazine, sci-fi paperback, or superhero comic of the same period?

Strieber, writing with sixty years of hindsight and a stunning array of personal experiences, adds further layers to Jung's original suggestions. He notes, for example, that a combination of the Cold War context of the original UFO sightings, the fact that fundamentalist Christians conditioned by simplistic Armageddon "cartoonlike" scenarios occupied many of the key positions in the military, and the production of dozens of really bad B-movies featuring evil invading aliens in the 1950s all came together to more or less guarantee that the situation would be seriously misunderstood and grossly misread (B 230–32, 278; CON 256). It is precisely these sorts of military and religious distortions that Strieber's visitor corpus attempts to address and correct.

C. G. Jung
Flying Saucers
A Modern Myth of Things
Seen in the Skies

It would be tempting to read this corpus as an extension of Strieber's horror writing and suggest that it was his fiction background that allowed him to have such remarkable experiences, that his fiction perhaps even produced such impossible events. There is no doubt some truth to this, but not in the simplistic way that I have just stated it. Strieber himself makes the deeper connection when he notes that his earlier fiction had been orbiting around a hidden purpose in his life that he did not yet understand. In other words, exactly like we saw Philip K. Dick doing in our previous chapter, with all those 1960s novels featuring psychical powers and Martians leading up to the metaphysical revelations of Valis in the winter of 1974, Strieber begins to read his life and work *backward*. He realizes, with more than a little concern, that "my whole life might have proceeded according to a hidden agenda," in effect a secret life that was leading up to *Communion* and all that it produced (COM 87). His entire corpus now appears as "some sort of attempt to cope with an enormous, hidden, and frightful reality" (B 125). Like Dick, he too was now a frightened knower of a secret. He too had become a Gnostic.

The works of fiction, Strieber now realized, were really about him struggling with repressed memories. *The Wolfen* was about "brilliant predators with huge, black visitor-like eyes." *The Hunger* was about "strange, immortal creatures that were very much like the tall, blond people I have occasionally glimpsed in my encounter experiences." And *Catmagic* was "about a fairy queen and a journey through the world of the dead and back again," another recurring theme of his visitor experiences. "In fact," Strieber confesses, "I believe my whole body of work—my whole life—has been an unconscious effort to somehow overcome my fears and reach back to the secret school" of his childhood occult encounters (SS xxi).

But the earlier horror fiction not only functioned as a kind of code for an emerging hidden agenda. It also functioned to *close down* the experience. Thus at one point Strieber comes face to face with the visitors and decides that he cannot cross over to their dimension. Why? "Because I remembered the horror stories and I could not cross that threshold" (COM xvii). The poignant cries of the visitors that Strieber heard echo precisely those that Barry Smith heard when he too said no to the Endless Waves of Time.

So popular culture can open up. But, as we saw with the B-movies, it can also shut down and take us down some very misguided paths. Hence one of the more interesting suggestions Strieber has made, this time in person to a group of us discussing metaphysical film, is that he is absolutely certain that his visitor experiences appeared the way they did because of the sci-fi movies that he watched as a kid and young adult, and that if we could create more accurate metaphysical films ("manipulations of light," as he poetically calls them), future generations might have more accurate visitor experiences. In short, if we could recreate "the actual energy of the close encounter" on film, this would definitely advance both consciousness and culture, but only if we are willing to abandon our rational denials and current cultural beliefs about invading space aliens.

This I take as a most remarkable confirmation of my present thesis about the magical correspondences between paranormal experience and popular culture. In this vision, at least, we are not only reading and writing ourselves. We are also viewing and projecting ourselves. What we need to do now is own this process, become more aware of it, and, most important, make it more mature. "Every time you go to the movies," Strieber noted, "your unconscious is convinced." So the work begins there.

There are many more things that can be said about the reception history of *Communion*. The book, for example, has generated a secondary literature of its own, including an extensive analysis by journalist Ed Conroy. *Communion* has even produced its own folklore, as exemplified in the widely distributed story of journalist Bruce Lee encountering two overdressed, very short people at the back rack of a bookstore in upper New York City in the winter of 1987. Lee watched as the couple walked directly to where *Communion* was displayed and began to giggle as they sped-read it: "Oh, he's got this wrong, he's got that wrong." When Lee, who at that point worked for the publisher of the book, asked them what they thought, he was stunned to see two huge almond eyes staring at him beneath the female figure's large sunglasses: "The hackles on the back of my neck just went up." They seemed profoundly angered by his presence. In his own precise terms, Lee "got the hell out of there."[8]

Personally speaking now, I read *Communion* as a most remarkable literary expression of a very honest, traumatized man, who also happens to be a gifted writer, struggling very publicly and very honestly with a set of impossible experiences that can find no home in our present worldview and official culture. I also see a deeply moral man attempting to speak a set of very difficult truths about the soul and about the environment. In short, I see a modern "ordinary mystic," who is really quite extraordinary.

I am also, frankly, drawn to his (and my own) Roman Catholicism. *Communion*, after all, can be read as a most unusual and most original Roman Catholic mystical text. His major abduction occurred just after Christmas, and there is no more Catholic a title than *Communion*. But if it is a Catholic mystical text, it is one that turns the orthodox sexual structures of traditional Roman Catholic mysticism on their head. How? Through an erotically charged communion with an alien "Her." Remarkably, there is no Christ as bridegroom of the feminized soul here, which is precisely what one would expect in a traditional Catholic mystical work. Nor is there a Blessed Virgin Mary, whose blessedness resides primarily in her immaculately white virginity.[9] But there is, as we shall soon see, an Ishtar and a long history of sacred sex with subtle beings, be they fairies, elves, or alien visitors.

It is this deep (hetero)sexual structure, I want to suggest, that constitutes Whitley Strieber's deepest heresy and his most original spiritual move. It is also, I suspect, why he originally turned to the ancient pre-Christian world of Mesopotamian religion, and to Asia, to find precedents for his remarkable experiences. There is, after all, no divine feminine in Catholicism with whom a male mystic can unite. None. Where else *could* he turn, then?

The Being with whom Strieber unites in *Communion* was essentially, in his own words now looking back, "a postindustrial vision of the mother goddess" (B 232). But he came to understand that even this was not the literal truth of things. Because the visitor experience is so incredibly strange, the imagination filters and forms it around whatever cultural materials are at hand, be these pulp fiction covers or ancient Mesopotamian goddesses. Strieber would eventually conclude, as we shall see, that this Being is as much "in here" as "out there," that the visitor is us, and yet not us. That is the paradox, the both-and of Whitley Strieber's alien gnosis.

I realize that that is not all entirely clear. Allow me, then, to explain through four major patterns that I find explored in the visitor corpus: (1) the explicitly religious nature of Strieber's texts and his self-described spiritual quest; (2) the role the erotic plays within his encounters as these are expressed, in a largely sublimated fashion, through his mystical "communion" with an alien goddess; and (3) Strieber's critical reflections on the origins and nature of religion in light of his abduction experiences. I also find two other themes that I would like at least to flag here: the insectoid trope that runs throughout the abduction experiences; and the playful presence of what I would call "superhero scenes" in the corpus. Finally, there is (4) Strieber's call for a "science of the soul," his bold vision of our species' immortal future beyond the parameters of space and time, and his mutant understanding of what we might call, following Michael Murphy now, the future of the body.

THE PATHLESS PATH

The first thing to note about Strieber's *Communion* is that it is an expression of a long and sophisticated spiritual quest. The author tells us, without reservation, that "my faith was a burning fire in me," and this despite the fact that he was deeply conflicted about his Catholicism. And had been so for some time, at least since his childhood, when an essay on the existence of God that he wrote for a catechism class was "declared to be a demonic inspiration" (COM 112). It is hardly surprising, then, that Strieber ranged widely in his spiritual quest, always looking for new resources, new insights, and less conflict. "For half my life," Strieber writes, "I have been engaged in a rigorous and detailed search for a finer state of consciousness" (COM 26). He notes that he was reading the fourteenth-century Dominican preacher and theologian Meister Eckhart at the time of his abduction (Eckhart's sermons are easily among the most sophisticated, and difficult, mystical texts one can read). He also repeatedly refers to Zen Buddhism and notes that he had made a meditation room in the upstairs of his cabin. Indeed, it was there, while he meditated, that the visitors would come as the encounters developed and deepened. He could hear them landing on the roof, like some sort of occult Santa Claus. He would go upstairs to meditate at around 11:00 each night: "A few minutes later, usually with a great clatter and thudding on the roof, they would arrive. . . . Night after night, I meditated with them." They entered his mind. They conjured memories. And they left him with two clear happy words: "have joy" (COM xxi).[10]

Strieber also describes a vision of a brilliant sphere in the sky just outside the cabin. Note the explicitly religious and vaguely sexual nature of his response: "This light had rays that I could feel penetrating my skin with gentle pinpricks. . . . I had something close to a seizure, a paroxysm as my body responded with fearsome, tingling pleasure to the most intimate touch I have ever felt, and I knew then utter compassion and an ancient love" (COM xxii).

Hence the title of the book, *Communion*. This was not the first title. Strieber wanted to call the book *Body Terror*, for that was the defining feature of his initial abduction: pure biological terror. But one night, while he and his wife were in bed, his wife spoke to him in a deep voice: "The book must not frighten people. You should call it *Communion*, because that's what it's about" (COM 216). He looked over to argue for his own title again. Anne was asleep. He now recognized the voice.

The channeled image-title of *Communion* functions on many levels in the book, not all of them perfectly apparent. Strieber, for example, tells a number of stories of the visitors, from his childhood on, force-feeding him with various substances, substances that he suggests are meant to transform him: "perhaps the very act of eating it has changed me," he reflects (COM 121). Both on the night of his first major abduction and, much later in life, on the night of a visit from a figure he calls the Master of the Key he was given a bitter white substance: "That could have changed me, for all I knew" (T 75). One cannot help seeing a eucharistic allusion here. That, after all, is precisely what "communion" signals to a Catholic reader: the devout Catholic consumes the flesh and fluids of a god-man to be transformed, to share in the divinity of Christ. So too here: as the abduction experiences advance and Whitley consumes this and that substance, he too is changed into something Other, something alien.

It is not clear to me how significant such eucharistic allusions are for Strieber. For him at least, the meanings and implications of a term like "communion" extend far beyond the boundaries of Catholicism, or any other religion for that matter. Contact often involves communication, Strieber explains, and it may sometimes look like a kind of conquest, even an act of colonialism. But ultimately, at least for Strieber, "it wants far more than that. It seems to me that it seeks the very depth of the soul; it seeks communion" (COM 5). Essentially, then, "communion" means "mystical union" and points to a kind of human-alien hybridization or, to employ more traditional Christian mystical terms, a divinization (*theosis*) or an incarnation (Christmas again). In short, the mytheme of Divinization.

THE MYSTICAL AND THE EROTIC

The path toward this communion, divinization, or incarnation, moreover, is often a deeply erotic process. And, again, by erotic I do not mean simply sexual. I mean what Plato meant—an explosive metaphysical force, a set of budding wings that can express themselves genitally, artistically, philosophically, or mystically. This too is a key.

Strieber himself certainly minces no words on the subject of the mystical as the erotic, as he confirms the commonly reported sexual components of abduction experiences and then tries to put these into the broader context of the history of religions: "It is terrifying, of course. But reflect also that mankind has had a sexual relationship with the fairies, the sylphs, the incubi, the succubi, and the denizens of the night from the very beginning of time." Particularly relevant for our present reflections on superhero mythologies, he also points out that the same sexual patterns commonly produced "the hero," that is, the classical divine-human hybrid. Hence Strieber reminds us that

Caesar Augustus was believed to be "the product of relations between his mother and an incubus"; Merlin the magician was believed to be "born of an incubus and one of the daughters of Charlemagne"; and so on (COM 247–48). Such conceptions may possess a conscious component as well, like that of Strieber himself, who, not unlike Ray Palmer, recalls a memory of his mother wearing a negligee in bed before his own conception and his entrance into her "whooshing, thudding, sloshing" womb (SS 139).

These mystico-erotic patterns spark and spike throughout all of Strieber's books, and they are just as transparent, if not more so, in conversation and correspondence. In *Transformation*, for example, he describes a four-fingered gray hand with black claw-like fingernails holding a gray box, two feet square. "For some reason this image had the effect of causing an explosive sexual reaction in me. My whole body was jolted by what I can only describe as a blast of pure sexual feeling," and this despite the utter nonsexual nature of the manifest image. The blast "seemed to loosen connections inside me. I rolled out of my body. It felt as if I had come unstuck from myself" (T 191). In other scenes, Strieber will feel his body, perhaps even his very electrons, vibrate or "spin" at incredible, and incredibly pleasurable, rates before he seems to leave his body and travel in some sort of hyperdimension. There is, in other words, a clear connection between the erotic and the out-of-body experience in the visitor-corpus, and all of this seems to be related to what he calls "contact with more energetic levels of being" (T 199).

Not that he has told everything in his books. No one does. No one can. He was clear with a group of us that the simultaneous "explosive power" of the eroticism and the sheer agony of the original visit was far greater than he wrote about in *Communion* (which is saying a lot), and he has since shared with me in correspondence that She left him "in a state of the most delectable emptiness that is possible for me to imagine." The original encounter, moreover, was not at all straight, although he is, and it resulted in what can only be called a profound oedipal anxiety. Explaining the latter, Strieber pointed out how the alien She, with whom he had a clear sexual relationship, told him that "I created you."

There is also Strieber's humor here. A mysterious Canadian, whom Strieber calls the Master of the Key, for example, once visited a pajama'd Strieber at 3:00 in the morning in his hotel room during a book tour. Amid a flurry of mind-blowing metaphysical teachings that may have been given in a dream (Strieber leaves the door open here), the Master jokes about a diamond commercial and calmly describes what the couple one floor up is doing: engaging in an act of fellatio (K 44). There is also a series of childhood memories, perhaps screen memories, of encounters with an alien "nun" whom little Whitley insisted on calling a "Sister of Mercy." The boy did not understand why his parents reacted the way they did to such innocent descriptions. He did not know that "Sister of Mercy" was a Texas euphemism for "prostitute" (SS 22, 175).

This sexual frankness—so incredibly refreshing in a mystical literature that is so often prudish, puritan, and prickly—was already present in Strieber's original abduction. Indeed, that post-Christmas night was dominated by a kind of raw sexuality that involved both his anus and his penis. His legs were drawn apart and "an enormous and extremely ugly object, gray and scaly, with a sort of network of wires on the end" was inserted into his rectum. Disturbingly, it seemed to "swarm" into him with a life of its own—probably, he speculates, to collect fecal samples. Whatever it was designed to do, it felt like a rape (later, he would have the courage to call it, without qualification, just that: "I was raped"[11]). Such a violation made him angry when he woke up the next morning, although he did not quite know why. He felt a profound unease as he remembered a barn owl staring at him through his window. He knew he had seen no barn owl that night and he had read his Freud, so he suspected that this was a kind of "screen memory," that is, a literally false but meaningfully true memory that encodes a real memory behind its symbolic face. A similar owl, which was not there, would peer at him through the window again as he began to write "Pain." Abductees, he notes, often remember animals in strange places when they attempt to recall the traumatic event.

From that day on, Strieber's personality changed, dramatically. He also developed an infection on his right forefinger and felt rectal pain whenever he sat down. Hypnosis offered more potential details about what had happened to him. Now he remembered a little room and a nonhuman female. What he really remembered, though, were her *eyes* (COM 75).

In this recovered memory, it is the same woman who "punches" the penislike organ into him. A Voice calls him "our chosen one." Bullshit, he responds. "Oh no, oh no," she hums back. Then follows this exchange, taken directly from the published hypnosis transcripts:

VOICE: "CAN YOU BE HARDER?"

"CAN I BE HARDER?" OH, LORD. DIDN'T KNOW I WAS HARD LIKE THAT. "NO, NOT WITH YOU AROUND I CAN'T BE HARDER."

VOICE: "WHAT WOULD YOU LIKE ME TO BE?"

"WHAT WOULD I LIKE YOU TO BE? I'D LIKE YOU TO BE A DREAM, IS WHAT I'D LIKE YOU TO BE."

VOICE: "I CAN'T BE THAT." (COM 77)

A bit later, he will describe the Voice and the nonhuman woman as old and bald with bulging eyes, floppy lips, and yellow-brown skin. Strieber confesses that he does not know if the being is even a woman, and yet he continues to call her a woman, sometimes, not always, even capitalizing her presence as "Her." A bit later in the book, now back in his cabin, he reflects before the fireplace on his hypnosis session and the memories of this female presence that the session called up in him. Seven hymn-like pages follow. She appears, staring at him with those astonishing eyes: "Sitting before me was the most astonishing being I have ever seen in my life, made the more astonishing by the fact that I knew her. I say *her*, but I don't know why. To me this is a woman, perhaps because her movements are so graceful, perhaps because she has created states of sexual arousal in me. . . . She had those amazing, electrifying eyes . . . the huge, staring eyes of the old gods" (COM 99–102).

Strieber wonders whether there are any connections between his experiences "and the mystic walk of the shaman, or the night ride of the witch" (COM 104). There are. The owl, he notes, was the personal symbol of the Greek goddess of wisdom, Athena. The owl's Latin designation, moreover, as *strix* is also related to later European words for "witch." Even further back, Strieber will associate the owl with the wisdom of Ishtar, the ancient Mesopotamian "Eye-Goddess" with the huge, staring eyes. He wonders out loud about what Ishtar really looked like, and if these ancient gods and goddesses were not similar to the semidivine beings imagined by the very modern visionaries who have formed the contactee cults (COM 121).

It is at this point that Strieber traces the origins of the alien and the UFO back not to contemporary pulp fiction, but into the furthest reaches of the history of religions, complete with possible memories of a past life (or lives); that is, in my own terms now, Strieber traces the mytheme of Alienation back to the mytheme of Orientation: "The closest thing I have been able to find to an unadorned image of these beings is not from some modern science-fiction movie, it is rather the age-old, glaring face of Ishtar. Paint her eyes entirely black, remove her hair, and there is my image as it hangs before me now in my mind's eye, the ancient and terrible one, the bringer of wisdom, the ruthless questioner. Do my memories come from my own life, or from other lives lived long ago, in the shadowy temples where the gray goddess reigned?" (COM 123). It is as if we have stepped into a Conan story here, worthy of Roy Thomas and Barry Windsor-Smith.

Eerily, Strieber often compares the old bald gray goddess who could both inspire and sexually arouse him to a bug, and, later in his work, to a spider. Enter the insectoid theme. There are far too many passages to treat here, but they are worth flagging as a group, since they connect so deeply to the insectoid theme in the histories of psychical research (a la Frederic Myers) and ufology.[12] Strieber has almost certainly read his Myers, as he reproduces Myers's larval allegory almost perfectly. Maybe, Strieber speculates, the visitors are our own dead. Maybe they are us in more perfect form: "Maybe we were a larval form, and the adults of our species were as incomprehensible to us, as totally unimaginable, as the butterfly must be to the caterpillar" (COM 90).

It is here, with the ancient gray goddess Ishtar who looked like a bug or a spider, that the iconic almond eyes of the alien find us again. Recall that we left them back in chapter 2, with our early discussion of the alien insectoid features of Spider-Man. For his part, Strieber traces the first appearance of the standard alien form back to June of 1957 and the cover of a sci-fi pulp digest, *Fantastic Universe*. His own mystico-erotic experiences of an ancient goddess, however, point much, much further back and recall, in striking detail, my own speculations linking the classic alien eyes to Indian art and Tantric goddesses. After all, much like Strieber's erotic union with an alien Ishtar, the Tantric aspirant in South Asia traditionally unites, sexually or symbolically, with a Tantric goddess like Kali to obtain spiritual insight, cosmic visions, and yogic superpowers.

I am hardly projecting here, as Strieber himself is clearly aware of these Tantric resonances. Indeed, he points them out himself to illustrate what he calls "the mystery of the triangle." Here Strieber turns explicitly to Indian Tantra and the goddess Kali, and especially to her *yantra* or down-turning triangle, an abstract symbol of her genitals with a *bindu* or "seed" in its center: "The object of the worship of the Yantra is to attain unity with the Mother of the Universe in Her forms as Mind, Life, and Matter." Strieber, in other words, imagines his visitor experiences as a kind of Tantric yoga or spiritual practice on the way to "union with Her as She is in herself as Pure Consciousness." Sexually uniting with the Mother of the Universe: the oedipal dimensions return again.

But he is also, at the same time, sexually uniting with his wife as Lover. This is how he put the matter to me in a letter: "In some way, she and Anne are the same person. She is with Anne and within Anne, but at the same time free in ways that no one of us have been free. My sensual relationship with her and my sensual relationship

REPORT ON
COMMUNION

An independent investigation of
and commentary on
Whitley Strieber's *Communion*
ED CONROY

with Anne are profoundly intertwined. This is why, when I tell Anne of my liaisons with her, she is never jealous, for they are also happening within her."

But, at least in *Communion*, it is finally not Kali but Ishtar to whom Strieber feels the most drawn. It is "Her," he senses, with whom he had really communed. He tells us that her name means "star" (COM 290–91). And what happens to a human being who unites with a star? He *becomes* that divinity. He takes on that stellar or astral nature. Hence the wonderful Ted Jacobs painting on the cover of Conroy's commentary and study, which imaginatively portrays the metaphysical effects of Strieber's erotic communion with Her. Those black cosmic eyes, slightly almond shaped and filled with stars, are now his. As in the Catholic eucharist, the author has been consumed by that which he has consumed.

Before we advance to Strieber's reflections on the ultimate nature of religion, there are a number of "superhero scenes" that are also worth noticing, and this in the light of our earlier observation that it was precisely out of horror comics that the silver age superhero largely arose, at least at Marvel. The energies of horror and the powers of the superhero share the same superspectrum again. Early in *Communion*, for example, Strieber describes having the impression that one of the visitors was wearing "a face mask" (COM 15). There is also that odd, never really explained moment in the book where Strieber sees a visitor rush by wearing a hat, a blue card on the chest, and a mask with eye holes and a round hole—in essence, a superhero costume (COM 72). Weirder still, there is what I would identify, inappropriately no doubt, as "the Ghost Rider scene." Strieber sees what he thinks is a skeleton on a motorcycle with "great big eyes that just scare the hell out of you." He realizes later that it is another buglike visitor, a visitor who resembles a praying mantis, which resembles a skeleton on a motorcycle. This is just a bit too close to the Marvel Ghost Rider character of the 1970s. All we are really missing is the flaming skull.

Except that we have that too—sort of. Strieber called his sister and asked her what her strangest childhood memory was. She told him about "the time we were sleeping out in the back lot and the fireball came across the lot." It was big and green. Strieber remembered no big green fireball. But he did remember Ghost Rider. "All of my life I have had a free-floating memory of a skeleton riding a motorcycle, a frightful effigy. Now I know the source of that image" (COM 156, 161).

Strieber also shared, in person this time, his vision of a Gray rushing through the forest behind his New York cabin. As he described the being zipping in and out of

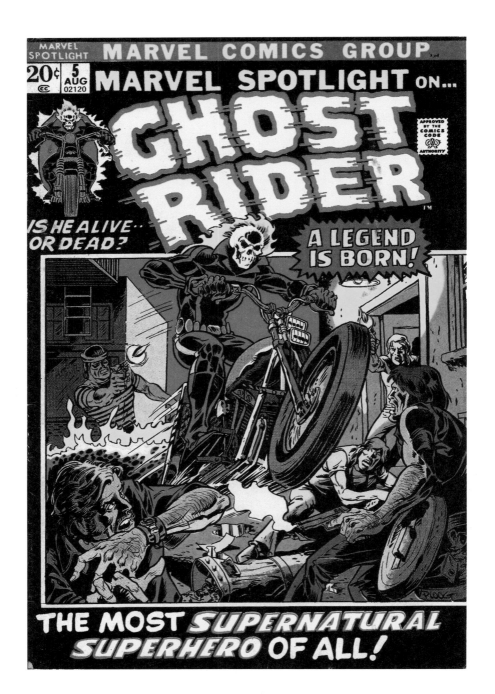

the trees, avoiding each tree trunk as if it too were physical, with "blinding speed," I could not help but think of all those drawings of the Flash I had seen as a kid doing, well, *exactly that*.

In this same superhero spirit, I might also mention the recurring metatheme of the alter ego, the secret identity that we all possess, that we all secretly *are*: "Not psychiatry, not religion, not biology could penetrate that depth," Strieber writes. "None of them had any real idea of what lives within. They only knew what little it had chosen to reveal of itself. Were human beings what we seemed to be? Or did we have another purpose in another world?" (COM 89). Strieber at least came to realize that his "conscious life was nothing more than a disguise for another reality, another secret life," that "we very well may be something different from what we believe ourselves to be" (COM 109, 250). Strieber's books are meant as catalysts, as triggers of awakening from this state of amnesia in which most all of us exist at the moment (SS xvi). They are meant, that is, to awaken us into our own secret lives.

So too with the Communion letters. A certain Dr. Colette Dowell, for example, had experienced a disappearing pregnancy with no obvious miscarriage at fifteen, and she had experienced UFO dreams since about the same time. During a camping trip in 1988, "a vibrating energy permeated my vehicle and continued through my body with the focus being my third eye or pituitary region." This resulted in "an even greater sense of clairvoyance." Since she was a teenager (the age of the Mutation, as we have seen), "I felt there were two Colettes, one from this planet and one up in the stars" (CON 166).

It is very difficult at such moments not to recall Otto Binder, who thought, of course, that the entire human species is a primate-alien hybrid. Or Frederic Myers, who wrote of our double "terrene" and "extraterrene" nature. Or Jacques Vallee, who wrote extensively about the paranormal effects of UFO encounters. Or Philip K. Dick, who knew himself as a homoplasmate. Or . . . well, you get the point by now.

THE NATURE OF RELIGION, THE OPEN DOOR, AND THE GNOSIS OF THE TRIANGLE

Perhaps most radical of all, however, are Strieber's speculations on the origin and nature of religion. These are no abstract speculations, no careful, endlessly qualified hypotheses designed for professional scholars. These are pained paradoxical thoughts quivering at the edge of a personal abyss. These are bold "What Ifs" that carry the energy of that green ball of fire that looked like Ghost Rider and shine with the soothing, sensual, pinpricking light of the immense crystal that hovered above his cabin and zapped him with its ancient erotic beams. These, if you will, are abductions-become-thoughts.

Strieber's writing is especially diverse and rich here, but it would not be too far from the truth to suggest that he moves through three different options, never quite settling on one, but leaning, always leaning, toward the third. We'll see why.

OPTION 1. Perhaps the visitors are gods. Maybe they created us. What he really has in mind here is some version of the ancient-astronaut thesis, which we encountered in the work of Doug Moench, Jack Kirby, and Otto Binder. After citing Francis Crick's panspermia or cosmic-seeding thesis, Strieber engages in a thought experiment that has a single woman, from whom we all emerged hundreds of thousands of years ago in North Africa, dashing across the plains of Mesopotamia (no doubt to put the fantasy in line with his own abduction experience and its Ishtar resonances). It's a sight worthy of Jack Kirby or Barry Windsor-Smith. "If we could slip back in time and find her dashing across the ancient Mesopotamian savanna, would we also find Ishtar gliding above in an enormous triangular spacecraft like the one that was seen over Westchester County in 1983, as elusive to her struggling little creation as flying disks are to the air force?" (COM 123–24).

OPTION 2. Or maybe we created them. Here he speculates that what he was experiencing in the abductions "amounted to some sort of deep and instinctive attempt to create a new deity for myself," even a personal religion. It is the physical-mythical nature of his experiences that really boggles the imagination, though. "It could be," he speculates, "that very real physical entities can emerge out of the unconscious" (COM 164). This is called projection theory in the study of religion, minus, of course, the idea that unconscious ideas can become quasi-physical beings that then have real effects in the material world. Here projection theory morphs into the bolder reaches of parapsychology. Thoughts become forces. The mythical become physical. Ideation becomes materialization.

OPTION 3. Or maybe they created us and we created them. This is the most sophisticated, and interesting, of the three options. It is also the most confusing. It is similar to option 2, except that the creation now goes both ways, at the same time.

Maybe belief becomes reality, which then creates new beliefs, which creates new realities, and so on. Here is the mind-blowing idea "that the gods we create would turn out to be real because we created them," that "in our universe their reality may depend on our belief. Thus the corridor into our world could in a very true sense be through our own minds" (COM 300).

This, it turns out, is an especially attractive, and especially scary, idea for Strieber. As he put it in person, these things "exist in another ideation of reality," that is, in a kind of parallel universe. Like the strange quasi-physical creatures of John Keel's cryptozoology (think the large humanoid apes and lake monsters of world lore), the visitors appear to "bleed over" from another dimension, always in a fleeting and unstable fashion. In such anomalous moments, we may be witnessing what amounts to a "process of discovery to penetrate our material world by another material world."

Strieber crystallized this idea in a most remarkable short story entitled "The Open Doors" (2003) about the last dying day of quantum physicist John von Neumann. The biographical background here is interesting. In correspondence, Strieber explained that through an uncle in the military who contacted him after *Communion* appeared, he met a general who shared with him the rumor that von Neumann, who was allegedly on a committee tasked with making sense of the Roswell recovery, had written a three-page paper on how the visitors might be able to enter our own dimension in large numbers: through the tripwire or trigger effect of our own acknowledgment of their existence. Strieber takes up this story to tell his own about, in the narrator's words now, "that last immortal day, where they speculated about the monsters in elegant phrases, where they used the language of physics to babble about the impossible that had become real."[13]

Such monster speculations boil down to the central idea that the world of experience is a kind of quanta, that is, a kind of indeterminate potentiality that "collapses" or becomes determinate through our individual decisions and beliefs (and, more so I presume, through our collective cultures and religions). The visitors, whose existence has recently been rendered definitive in the story through the recovered remains of the Roswell crash, are experienced as a kind of demon species within von Neumann's Jewish Catholic consciousness. The great physicist decided that the bomb, for whose creation he is partly responsible, has somehow attracted these demons into our world (Radiation). He is especially worried that the blue brilliance of the radioactive secret of the bomb, cobalt, has something to do with the glowing blue skin of some inner-earth beings or "kobolds" that he saw once in a mine back in 1914 (echoes of the hollow earth, Reichenbach's glowing blue Od, and Reich's blue orgone). In short, the Cobalt bomb loosed the inner-earth kobolds into our world (or, if you prefer, the kobolds are mythical expressions of the radioactive cobalt in the mine, with the entire story now read as a reflection on the horrors of atomic radiation). Most of all, though, von Neumann has discovered a most devastating secret, namely, that the burning blue demons "must use our belief in them as a bridge."[14]

Von Neumann struggles with whether to confess this greatest of sins to his priest (for how can one confess a sin whose very confession *is* the sin, whose very utterance would open the door yet wider?). Confession or no confession (in the end, he does not confess), the great physicist has decided that it is we who collapse the wave function of quantum indeterminacy and allow the other-dimensional beings to enter this one. It is humanity that functions as "a vast engine of doorways." Belief is now seen for what it is: "the alchemy that would dissolve the walls of the world."[15] And not always, I would add, for the good.

The early lineaments of such a vision can already be clearly seen in *Communion*. There, after all, Strieber speculated at length on the impossible physical-mythical nature of his experiences, that is, on the monsters that seemed to enter this dimension through the doorway of his own belief and empowered imagination. There, more specifically, in a chapter appropriately entitled "A Structure in the Air: Science, History, and Secret Knowledge," Strieber explored the various external correspondences that marked the environment around his deeply subjective experiences. In the first week of January, for example, a local newspaper published accounts of objects sighted in sky in the same area (COM 27). Strieber is left with two impossible conclusions: either the physical-mythical events are real, or the human mind is capable of producing something "that, incredibly, is close to a physical reality" (COM 4).

In the end, Strieber lands squarely with that both-and position that is the surest mark of what I have variously defined as the gnostic, the fantastic, and the paranormal. He understands perfectly well, for example, that what he perceived "may or may not have been what was actually there" (COM 51). And he is very familiar with the fantastic, that is, that place of hesitation that a text or experience produces in a person: "Every time one decides either that this is psychological or real, one soon finds a theory that forcefully reopens the case in favor of the opposite notion" (COM 105). This, of course, is what Philip K. Dick realized as well while writing his *Exegesis*: every line of thought led to a series of logical loops and self-reflexive paradoxes. For Strieber, such a realization amounted to a decision "to ride a sort of psychological razor, to accept and reject at the same time" (COM 278). A Third Kind.

Little wonder, then, that the deepest symbol of his alien gnosis is the triangle, the Three beyond the Two that is finally a One. Hence the visitors inscribed two little triangles in the flesh of his left forearm (COM 128), and another abductee was handed a crystal in the shape of two intersecting triangles, like a Star of David (or, I would add in the spirit of my earlier comments, a very famous Tantric yantra or "meditative diagram" consisting of two interlocking triangles, which is said to represent the union of the male and female or the transcendent and the immanent) (CON 129). Hence Strieber also notes that the trinity is "the most common symbolic structure of the visitors" (COM 117) and dedicates an entire section to "the inner meaning of the triangular shape," that is, on the symbolism of the triangle in the history of religions and in the work of the contemporary mystic Gurdjieff, with whose teachings, which include a clear, if bizarre synthesis of alien intervention and Tantric yoga, he had been involved for some time (COM 254–81).[16] These reflections climax in a vision another contactee reported of two shining discs in the sky that discharge an immense arc of energy between them before they fuse into one. Strieber takes the vision as symbolic, pointing again to the mystery of the triangle and the triadic structure of alien thought: "The fundamental idea of the triad as a creative energy is that two opposite forces coming into balance create a third force" (COM 281; see also T 104, 134, 139).

And so the sexual returns. For the ultimate human expression of two things becoming one thing that produces in turn a third thing is, of course, the sexual act between a man and a woman. Here Strieber invokes the famous *yin-yang* symbolism of Taoism and the common association of sexual climax with the "little death" of the ego: here, if only for a moment, the self enters pure being, "climax being a moment when the self is absorbed in ecstasy" (COM 282). So, it turns out, "communion" is no innocent coming together, no pious and simple feeling of being at one with something greater than oneself, no simple ritual consumption of a little white wafer. It is a sexual climax that is also a psychological destruction, an "instinctive awareness that our coming together may mean the creation of a third and greater form which will supplant us as the child does his parents" (COM 283).

"Are the visitors asking us to form a triad with them?" Strieber finally asks. This is a rhetorical question. I take its positive, erotic answer as the implicit message of the entire visitor corpus.

THE SCIENCE OF THE SOUL, THE TRANSCENDENCE OF TIME, AND THE FUTURE OF THE BODY

And so what would such a communion look like? What exactly would it entail? And where would it lead? Such questions can be answered through three of the most striking metathemes of Strieber's visitor corpus, what we might call the science of the soul, the transcendence of time, and the future of the body.

THE SCIENCE OF THE SOUL. Strieber believes that the soul is somehow material, a kind of conscious energy that has real effects in the physical world. In short, Radiation. He thus proposes in numerous places a future "science of the soul" (CON 116–17, 258–60), even a new psychotechnology that will someday be able to detect and account for souls and other subtle interdimensional beings. There is no "supernatural" for Strieber, nor does he care for the expression "paranormal," since both words for him suggest something beyond the physical world and its natural forces and something entirely outside our attempts to understand it (K 8, 40; B 77, 88; but see B 236).

And so Strieber proposes to use neurobiology in order to determine which memories are real and which are manufactured. He discusses the neurobiology of the temporal lobes. He had himself tested for temporal lobe epilepsy. He also submitted himself to an EEG, a CAT scan of his brain, and an MRI, as well as a battery of standard psychological tests too long to list here (T 245–47). He observes that the nasal passages, a common reported site in alien implant stories, would be the clearest way into the temporal lobes (CON 165). He gives examples of right-brain trauma and, like so many of our authors, comments on various right-brain/left-brain hemisphere issues (CON 195). He invokes childhood and sexual abuse as possible triggers of the visitor experience, something that the broader ufological literature would support (T 90; SS 83; CON 212). And he develops both a ten-point scale to organize his hundreds of thousands of letters (CON 199) and an elaborate protocol to handle the ultracontroversial issue of alien implants. The latter project included Strieber's Communion Foundation paying for MRI scans, the videotaping of surgeries, and the use of electron microscopes to determine the chemical composition and microstructures of the objects removed from the selected witnesses.[17] He also tested the water near his cabin for pesticides and the air in his basement for radon gas (T 245), and he wonders about the possible geomagnetic effects of the iron-laden subsurface of the area around his cabin. The latter thought has a downright Fortean subtext: according to both newspaper reports and local memory, some rocks in Stone Ridge, a town about thirty miles away, had levitated in 1803 (B 69), which recalls in turn the final landing scene of the sci-fi ancient-astronaut film *Knowing* (2009). And so we arrive at a neuroscience, a psychoanalysis, a chemistry, and a geology of the fantastic.

THE TRANSCENDENCE OF TIME. At the root of Strieber's final vision is the suggestion that mind is evolving toward a point where and when it will be able to manipulate both space and time, but, as we saw with Alan Moore, Alvin Schwartz, Barry Windsor-Smith, and Philip K. Dick, it is the deeper nature of time that really captures Strieber's attention. "The secret school is part of the process of revising reality," Strieber writes. It is a "clandestine meeting of minds struggling to restitch the fabric of the world. It is about getting free of time, about remembering ourselves in all our truth" (SS 190–91). This is not your typical secret society, though. It is not yet another power grab of the rich and the privileged. Rather, the secret school is "founded by the mind, and it lives in the mind." It is in all of us, as those half million ordinary letter writers give witness. And its greatest and most impossible teaching is that "time itself—even time—may become our servant" (SS 191).

Things can get particularly weird here. At one point, for example, Strieber became "an electric creature, a thing that seemed composed of pure ecstasy" (SS 140), until he experienced two very different time-worlds simultaneously, those of twentieth-century America and first-century Rome, where he was a slave tutor of the young Octavius (SS 122–27). The parallels—forgive the pun—with Dick are simply remarkable here. Dick, recall, experienced a very similar superimposition of late twentieth-century California and first-century Roman society, where he struggled and hid as a secret, gray-robed gnostic Christian.

It was through such time-bending experiences that Strieber came to realize that "Whitley Strieber" was "just one of many people whom I was inhabiting across a great turn of centuries. Far from being a little boy, I was an old, old creature on a mission toward ecstasy, who sought—and seeks—across history for some permanent connection to joy" (SS 124).[18] *The Transmigration of Whitley Strieber*, we might say.

It was in this way that the writer came to realize that one's past lives are not dead at all, that "it is possible to enter one's past lives in a completely unexpected way." "When you ascend above time, it isn't that everything seems like the past, but that the present expands to contain all events." "In this sense," he writes, "there is no time. We create the present. It's an invention. But we can reinvent it, and if we do that on a large enough scale, we may gain living contact with our past and future, and even become able to change them" (SS 134). And so this "wonderful mystery called humanity journeys across the ages creating itself" (SS 142).

This is a truly stunning, impossible vision. Still, Strieber claims that as we evolve into what he calls "the next age," "we will come to the prime moment of this species, when mankind gains complete mastery over time and space and lifts his physical aspect into eternity, inducing the ascension of the whole species into a higher, freer, and richer level of being" (SS 225–26). This he imagines as "a sort of singularity of consciousness where all moments, in effect, become one" (B 148). Such phrases strongly echo the Omega Point and evolutionary Catholic mysticism of Teilhard de Chardin. And, of course, our own mytheme of Mutation.

The closer we approach such a prime moment, singularity, or Omega Point, the more we will realize—with John Keel, I would add—that "the vague mythological beings of the past that have focused into the aliens of the present will soon become ourselves as we become the very time travelers whose shadows haunt all our history, including the present" (SS 227). In effect, we are haunting ourselves in the present from the past and the future via the ghost and the alien.

Indeed, whatever they are, the visitors are likely "responsible for much paranormal phenomena, ranging from the appearance of gods, angels, fairies, ghosts, and miraculous beings to the landing of UFOs in the backyards of America" (T 236). They may be extraterrestrials, "managing the evolution of the human mind," or they "may represent the presence of mind on another level of being" (T 236). The key for Strieber is that we cease being so passive and admit that we do not know what or who the visitors are. In other words, we must stop kneeling before the gods, quit "hiding in our beliefs," and begin actively, even aggressively exploring "a real relationship" with the visitors, whoever or whatever they are (T 237–38). Put a bit differently, we must "demythologize" them and evolve past "the level of superstition and confusion that has in the past blocked us from perceiving the visitors correctly" (T 241). How, after all, can we recognize ourselves if we keep projecting those selves into what are essentially religious cartoons? When will we realize that we ourselves are our own authors?

THE FUTURE OF THE BODY. Given Strieber's repeated insistence that the soul is part of nature and something physical, it should not surprise us that he also insists that the body will share in humanity's future evolution as much as the mind or soul, that, in the end, the body and the soul, matter and mind, share in the same conscious being. Such a future physical transformation is signaled in his texts in many ways. One of the eeriest is when the visitor experience is so extreme that the witness begins to experience his or her body morphing into that of an alien body.

One correspondent, for example, was told this: "My dear, one day you will look just like us" (CON 172–73). Another woke up in the night to find "that his arms were long and thin, and he felt light and seemed to be pulsing with the delicious electricity that eastern traditions identify as kundalini." The Tantra again. He could fly now. He flew up to see his son, who was happy to see him. The next morning, however, this shared occult experience was remembered by the son as a terrible nightmare, with his father as "a monster that had flown around his room like a giant bat"—a kind of paranormal Batman. Still another person, after physically touching a visitor in Strieber's own cabin and being left with "an electrical feeling," reported that she now knew herself as "a spiritual being solidified into physical form." She realized that, "physical and spiritual are not separated whatsoever" (B 86–89).

Strieber reflects on his own experiences to ask a series of questions. "What if the body is a quanta? What if its very shape depends upon the mind?" (B 139). Earlier in the same book, he had described a set of experiences meditating in a cave near his cabin. These experiences, he now believed, resonated with the teachings of Sri Aurobindo. Aurobindo, we might recall, was (after Nietzsche) the original Mystic of the Superman who developed an elaborate evolutionary mysticism in India in the early decades of the twentieth century. Strieber describes Aurobindo's teaching that humanity is "a transitional species, destined to literally be re-created physically in a new form." Such a Mutation, Strieber observes, "is embedded deeply in secret Tantric traditions and has emerged in the twentieth century as the notion that our bodies contain the potential for just the sort of reformation that seemed on the edge of happening to me in the cave." In short, and shockingly close to my own Tantric readings of the human potential movement, Strieber is suggesting that Aurobindo's evolutionary Indian Tantra became the American human potential movement. He is correct, uncannily correct, about that.[19]

Strieber knew something of this American Tantra in the cave amid an electric blue light (there it is again) and an experience of his body changing, "altering cell by cell." "I almost felt as if I'd taken on new physical properties, as if I was starting to become . . . something else" (B 69–70).

In a letter in response to this book, Strieber expanded on a similar moment, comparing it to the alchemical transformation of Cyrus Teed: "Once in, I believe, about 1991, I was lying on a couch in the living room while Anne was sitting nearby reading. I began to feel a sensation not unlike the one [Teed] describes. It was oceanic and also very electrical. I thought to myself, 'Well, now Anne is finally going to see a gray,' because I knew quite well that I was going to turn into one. It felt as if an inner body was going to reverse position with my outer body." But then one of the family cats jumped on Strieber's chest, got shocked by the electrical charge, and leapt off mewing. The transformation just stopped. Later that night, the metaphysical energies returned, and this time they carried through. Strieber left the bedroom and went upstairs, half-flying, to see his son. His son grinned when he saw him but could not understand his words. The next morning, the boy complained bitterly of seeing an alien in his room the previous night.

Such thoughts about the alien body are extended further in a more recent text, *The Key*, which purports to record the memories of a conversation Strieber had while on book tour with a stranger in a Canadian hotel, at 3:00 in the morning no less.[20] Humorously, the man describes himself as a Canadian who does not pay taxes and possesses no driver's license. Here we do not simply get speculative claims from the nondriving Canadian tax evader. We get the claims that the soul, which is a "part of the electromagnetic spectrum" (K 15), is "accessible to verifiable scientific exploration," and that our science "can part the curtain between the living and the dead" (K 9). More remarkably still, we get instructions on how to *practice* the future of the body and a lesson in the esoteric anatomy of the superbody.

What the instructions boil down to is the notion that one can build up a stable "radiant body" through meditation and intention so that this supersubtle body, composed of conscious energy with more and more "complexity" and "spin," can survive the dissolutions of death. The physical or "elemental body," of course, dies and disintegrates, but the potential radiant body, once actualized and stabilized through the authorizing intentions of meditation, survives and passes on to future births and lives. If it is not stabilized, it "goes into the light," that is, it is absorbed back "into the flux of conscious energy" (K 17). Or a bit more ominously: "Who does not meditate, disintegrates" (K 17).

In any case, whether or not an individual soul evolves or dissolves, "energy is eternal" (K 42), and in this sense we are all immortal. We are all the cosmos. We are all Radiation.

In terms of the esoteric anatomy, we learn that it is precisely this same radiant cosmic body that produces psychical and paranormal phenomena. Here the visitor explains: "A part of the electromagnetic field that fills the nervous system rests a few centimeters above the skin, outside of the body. This field is an organ just like the heart or the brain. It is in quantum superposition, the electrons effectively everywhere in the universe and nowhere specific. It may be imprinted by information from anywhere and anytime" (K 20). I am reminded here of Windsor-Smith's overwhelming sense that "I knew I was experiencing a paradox, a mind-bending phenomenon that allowed me to be just where I was and yet be everywhere else as well."

Once the electromagnetic field is imprinted, the nonlocal energy states—at once everywhere and nowhere—"collapse" and take on a specific experience or form of consciousness ("particularizes," Schwartz would say). A psychic, then, is someone who is able to keep the energy field in superposition, neither here nor there, and so acquire information from other places and times (Russell Targ, Alvin Schwartz, Barry Windsor-Smith again, and Philip K. Dick, we might recall, came to similar nonlocal conclusions). Meditation and contemplative concentration can do the same to the extent that such practices can shut down information from the external world, prevent the imprinting of a specific reality deposit, and allow the radiant body to remain in superposition and so expand (K 20–21). "You must be able to watch and to not watch at the same time," we are told (K 23). Such koan-like riddles, such questions "that can neither be borne nor answered," are the secret of spiritual advance. In "The Open Doors," this same kind of intellectual indeterminacy is also portrayed as the secret of all real creativity—it is what makes a truly great mind.[21] These superimposed paradoxes constitute what Strieber himself calls "evolutionary pressure" (K 34). They, of course, also hearken back to the mystery of the triangle and what I have elsewhere named, in very different contexts, the productive paradoxical structures of gnosis and "the religion of no religion."

Once detected locally through the nonlocal processes of this "organ of higher consciousness," psychical information is processed in the core of the brain, near the site of the pineal gland, which, we are told, is the neurophysiological base of the "third eye" of Asian and Western occultism (it was here as well, by the way, that Descartes located the seat of the soul).[22] The visitor tells Strieber that this is the "part of your brain that enables you to utilize electrons without drawing them into the particulate state." Most of us, of course, fail to do this through lack of training or genetic gift or just plain impatience. We seek certainty and clear structures. As a result, we become "time-bound." We sink "into the time stream" and become trapped like inmates in a prison named "earth" (K 56, 5). We confuse our particular cultural and personal imprinting of reality for the real itself. And so we return to the Black Iron Prison.

In correspondence, Strieber made it clear that although something like his childhood memories recounted in *The Secret School* cannot be handled uncritically, that is, they may be products of the later abductions and hypnosis sessions, there is nothing fuzzy or unreliable about his direct and immediate knowledge of his adult encounters between 1986 and 1997. These eleven years constituted, as he put it, a "narrative that is strange beyond anything you have ever heard." During this time, Strieber developed, as he put it, "a strong relationship with what appeared to me to be a very complex and little understood aspect of conscious being, in part including the visitors as I have known them, but also including, for example, spiritual beings, including the human dead, who were able to gather into physical form at times."

This is not quite as strange as Strieber imagines. It is in fact familiar territory for the historian of religions. C. G. Jung, for example, came to a very similar conclusion with respect to what he called his "confrontation with the unconscious," a long series of events that broke out into poltergeist phenomena (that is, visitors) in his house and resulted in him writing, in the channeled voice of a famous early Christian Gnostic no less, his *Septes Sermones ad Mortuos* or *Seven Sermons to the Dead*. Why? Because Jung realized that he had not just confronted the depths of the unconscious. He had also entered "the land of the dead."

Strieber stopped writing about the details of his own adult experiences after the late 1980s (that is, with *Transformation*), took his own "private counsel," and essentially retreated back into writing fiction for a number of reasons, but the main factor was the pure opprobrium and public disinterest with which his accounts were routinely met.

I can well understand Strieber's sense of the opprobrium and his frustration with the deafening noninterest. As someone who has experienced organized forms of harassment and censorship for my writings, I feel nothing but sympathy for and solidarity with Strieber's immeasurably more severe experiences here. He was branded a cult leader by the popular media and spat on in Washington National Airport. He suffered a period of clinical depression. He became the object of a fundamentalist per-secution campaign that would not go away. He witnessed multiple careers destroyed, intentionally and systematically. His own publishing career was virtually ruined when a famous animated television show lampooned the anal-sexual dimensions of his visitor experiences and so destroyed his credibility with his readers. He even experienced two home invasions, one of which appeared to involve a nasal implant (B 105; CON 176, 181, 190, 200, 201). Speaking secrets sometimes comes with a very heavy cost, and Whitley Strieber has paid it.

So I am anything but disinterested—which is not to say, however, that I know what to do with what Strieber himself very accurately describes as "four books full of one impossible story after another" (CON 146). And now there are more than four. I certainly do not know what to make of all of these impossible texts. But here are a few simple, painfully inadequate concluding thoughts.

At one point in *The Key*, as Strieber is struggling with his frustrations over trying to accurately recreate his conversation with his hotel visitor, he refers to his writing as a combination of "warmed over Catholicism and new-age mysticism" (K 79). He also worries out loud that his transcribed memories of his conversation are mostly just reflections of himself. There is much wisdom in such confessions, even though, in truth, there is nothing "warmed over" about Whitley Strieber's Catholicism. Quite the contrary, it is fiercely alive and wildly heretical. His rejection of the traditional God, that "old greybeard in the sky"; his understanding of Christ ("all are God, all are Christ. The difference was that he knew it"); and his rejection of belief ("belief is always a lie")—these are all thoroughly and completely gnostic in precisely the terms that I have defined the expression here and elsewhere (K 24–29, 38–39).

The "new-age mysticism" comment certainly hits the mark, though. Strieber's visitors, or, more precisely, Strieber's interpretations of his own visitor-experiences, sound remarkably like the authors and books in any good library on the history of Western esotericism, American metaphysical religion, the human potential movement, and the New Age. What the visitors finally are, in this reading anyway, are channeled Masters of the American Metaphysical Tradition. This, I would suggest, is the real key to the visitor corpus, and indeed to most everything that I have treated in the present volume.

Some might want to call this "New Age," but usually to demean and deride and, almost always, in total ignorance of the millennia-long sweep of sophisticated mystical, esoteric, and metaphysical thought (and experience) from which the New Age movement of the 1980s and '90s emerged and into which it disappeared again. Our Super-Story, visitors and all, it turns out, is not a few decades or even a few hundred years old, but a few, if not many, thousand. This total history is the *real* secret life of the superpowers, the real reason mutants look so much like mystics.

In the spirit of that astonishing tale, I must admit that I do not think that Strieber's message is simply a subjective one (although it is clearly that too), for the simple reason that I do not think that consciousness is simply subjective. The constant physical reflections of consciousness within paranormal experience (not to mention the half million letters that the Striebers received) render any purely subjective reading both absurd and ridiculous, as does the historical fact that similarly robust paranormal outbreaks have been reported and studied since, including a very recent one on a Utah ranch that resonates with Strieber's accounts in numerous ways, including the bizarre detail of hearing heavy machinery underground the haunted locale.[23] In my view, Strieber's visitor corpus is a highly complex, very sophisticated fusion—the mystery of the triangle again—of the subjective and the objective, of the trick and the truth, of the myth and the matter: in short, of the paranormal.

Strieber's texts also very clearly participate in what in *Authors of the Impossible* I have called the dialectic of Consciousness and Culture, that immensely rich historical process through which paranormal currents and mythical themes interact—through out-of-body ecstasies and metaphysical energies as much as through books and institutions—with specific individuals to shape and reshape the form and feel of the real from age to age. Whitley Strieber, in other words, is doing more or less exactly what Barry Windsor-Smith and Philip K. Dick claimed that they were also doing: evolving themselves and, through them, anyone who dares to pick up their impossible books and take seriously the Endless Waves of Time, the Coming of Valis, and the Secret School of the Visitors.

TOWARD A SOUL-SIZED STORY

[THE VISITORS] HAVE TAUGHT ME BY DEMONSTRA-
TION THAT I HAVE A SOUL SEPARATE FROM MY
BODY. MY OWN OBSERVATIONS WHILE DETACHED
FROM MY BODY SUGGEST THAT THE SOUL IS SOME
FORM OF CONSCIOUS ENERGY, POSSIBLY ELECTRO-
MAGNETIC IN NATURE.
WHITLEY STRIEBER, *TRANSFORMATION*

THE SOUL IS NOT IN THE BODY. THE BODY IS INSIDE
THE SOUL. DO YOU UNDERSTAND? LOOK. WE ARE
YOU. TRY TO REMEMBER.
HYPERDIMENSIONAL ALIENS IN GRANT MOR-
RISON'S *THE INVISIBLES*

So what are we supposed to make of all of this? What can we say, *really*, about the mythical patterns and paranormal currents that have absorbed us over the last seven chapters? An erotic transmission under a Tantric goddess in Calcutta, a magical conversion, a Goetic demon, a time-transcending DNA snake, shiny silver anti-bodies from the fifth dimension, and a god electrocution in Kathmandu; polar holes, conscious mythmaking, a mushroom-like manuscript in a book of love spelled backward, and a Martian in a Swiss silk shop; occult supermen, imaginal insects, flying saucers, a new American Bible, and ancient astronauts; an od and an id, a superspectrum, a Mothman, sex and violence become radioactive superheroes, and an evolutionary yoga; a morning of magicians, California mutants, Cold War psychic spies, military spoon benders, an Israeli magician-psychic initiated by a UFO, and a NASA astronaut's yogic union in outer space; a storm-raising contactee named PK Man, a thought experiment named Starman, Superman and Batman in Tantric Tibet, and a discarnate spirit named Roy; time loops, a summer of superpowers, a pink cosmic zapping, a sci-fi gnostic, a possessing bishop, and a divine humanity evolving itself backward and forward in time; an ancient Mesopotamian goddess showing up in a New York cabin, sunglass-wearing aliens in a bookstore, and a nondriving, Canadian tax evader bestowing secret teachings in a hotel room—if you are not *really* confused by now, you have not been paying very close attention. What can we say? How can we conclude?

I suppose the first thing to say is that all of this is completely impossible within our present mirrored cultures of religious fundamentalism and scientific materialism, which appear oddly united in their ferocious "damning" of the paranormal: Fort's two Dominants of Religion and Science again. A conservative social system, whether defined by the true believer or by the pure rationalist, protects itself from the dim awareness of the impossible nature of consciousness by defining those who know better as frauds, heretics, liars, selfish New Age floozies . . . mere promoters of popular culture . . . just anecdotes.

Here there are no Origins events or superpowers (pure fantasy). There can be no legitimate Orientations, no transforming pilgrimages to the East (just more romanticism or, worse yet, more colonialism in disguise). Nor can there be any experience of Alienation worth having, much less any empowering Radiations or evolving Mutations (so much pseudoscience, bunk). Nor liberating Realizations or creative Authorizations (obviously, narcissism run amok—you can't fricking write reality). And my little *X* in the parking lot, with which I began this book? It meant nothing. It was a cheap coincidence. Junk.

These are not my personal conclusions, of course. My conclusion is that American popular culture is suffused with these seven mythemes (and no doubt many more), which are forming a kind of Super-Story, a modern living mythology, right in front of our eyes. My conclusion is that American metaphysical currents—like *all* rich religious systems—are complexly indebted to other cultures, even as they profoundly transform that which they adopt and embrace from these other sources. My conclusion is that the *X* in the parking lot was functioning as a little piece of material magic, that is, as a sign that participates in that which it signifies. In Grant Morrison's terms, it was a synchronistic sigil. In Alvin Schwartz's terms, it was symbol that acted "as a means of release and transformation of psychic energy," a release and transformation of psychic energy that in turn produced this book.

Which you are still holding.

So how did you do?

I am reminded again of Dick's Valis. The whole experience was triggered by a shiny piece of Christian jewelry on a girl's neck in California that led Dick back to the gray-robed secret Christians of ancient Rome. At one point, Horselover Fat is even spiritually guided by "a beer can run over by a passing taxi" (V 318). I was guided by a shiny piece of jewelry run over by a moviegoer, which I originally mistook as a Christian cross, that led me back to the X-Men of California. As Dick famously concluded in the same novel, "the symbols of the divine show up in our world initially at the trash stratum" (V 384). No argument here.

Like Dick, of course, my authors and artists knew far more than beer cans and broken jewelry. Still, in the end, perhaps all *we* can know as readers and viewers of their material art is that such bodies of work are first and foremost, and maybe entirely, about the souls who first realized and then authorized them. Or can we know more?

Consider D. Scott Apel's *Philip K. Dick: The Dream Connection*. In this extraordinary book, Apel tells the story of how, after Dick died, Apel found himself caught in an intricate web of powerful synchronicities involving, in true Phildickian style, things like Dick's novels, *National Geographic* magazines, a tape recorder, television sitcoms, a passing truck, and hyperreal dreams in which his dead friend would appear to him in places like Disneyland or plot scenes of Apel's own writings. Overwhelmed, Apel contacted professional mediums and recorded two channeled sessions, the "dramatic harmony" of which deeply impressed him.

Apel eventually came to conclude that Dick was "energizing" or "turbo-boosting" his friends' writing practices from the other side, even commenting on his own books in order "to illuminate them with higher consciousness energy," as one of the séance session transcripts describes it in the familiar vibration-language of the channeling literature. Although he is perfectly aware that he lacks any final proof, Apel himself takes the final and logical step—almost unheard of in the ultrahip, postmodern world of Dick scholarship—and concludes from his own experiences that there is real *"evidence of a life beyond death*," and that "the spirit of Philip Kindred Dick lives on . . . not symbolically, through his writings, but *literally.*" Indeed, *"we all live on."*[1] Now there is a conclusion worth drawing.

But are we ready for such a conclusion? Many individual readers no doubt are, but as a public culture things seem less certain, and this for one simple reason: we still lack a story big enough for the soul. Alas, too often we seem torn, split in half between religious beliefs that are all too presuming about the scope and nature of the soul, and a materialistic scientism, which denies the presence of spirit altogether. As a result, I fear we are rather like the X-Men's Jean Grey—we cannot contain, cannot handle the full cosmic potential of the species. Our stories are too small, our visions of human nature much too puny.

Not so with the Super-Story. For all its confusions, here at least we have a vision of mythical proportions that can hold, handle, and sometimes even *express* such a Force. Is this not exactly what we have seen with our artists and authors? And to the extent that the self is a story and that we all share in this mysterious Force called life, are not we *all*, in our own ways, such artists and authors of the energy?

In "Man, Android, and Machine" (1976), Dick speculated that the right brain may be a "transducer or transformer of ultrasensorial informational input" that the left brain cannot process, and that all of our billions of right brains together make up a kind of collective unconscious or plasmic noosphere that in turn interacts with solar and even cosmic fields of energy and mind (SR 221–23). It is this Overmind, Dick believed, that primarily determines our reality, not our ego-centered, discrete left brains, which have far less to say than we suppose.

I am not promoting the exact specifics of Dick's metaphysical speculation here (and he would be the first to question them). But its general spirit—that we are not who we think we are, that we have not recognized the limits of reason, that we are individually Two, and that we are weaving, both together and plurally, some vast global reality-posit—rings true enough. As does Dick's constant call to us to become more aware of the vast reaches of the human psyche and so become our own authors, to step in and out of the storylines of our cultures and egos as we write ourselves toward the future (and maybe from the future!).

I would only warn us away from the too simple notion that the left-brain work of Culture and ego is merely filtering or only transducing the right-brain field of Consciousness and Mind. I think that such language, which I also used in *Authors of the Impossible*, is correct enough on one level, for the witness of the history of mystical literature strongly suggests that, yes, there really is Mind beyond brain or Self beyond self—the Human *is* Two. But the same language is much too dualistic and misleading on another level, for both brain and social self appear to have evolved to express Mind and Self, and most brain functioning operates globally, that is, across both hemispheres—the Human is *also* One. As I suggested in the very first pages of this book, I think that what we have here, what we *are*, is a nondual system of Consciousness and

Culture evolving itself in loop after loop; that Consciousness needs Culture to know itself as and in us, just as Culture needs Consciousness to exist at all; and that it is just as foolish to erase the universal (Consciousness) for the local (Culture) as it is to erase the local (Culture) for the universal (Consciousness). As Alvin Schwartz taught us on his Path without Form, form is formlessness and formlessness is form.

This central, paradoxical, "loopy" notion of the Human as Two—which, as we have seen, in turn spins out into the experience of Time as Two, the World as Two, God as Two, and so on—is about as conclusive as one can get at the moment—as conclusive as I can get, anyway. So here is my conclusion stated in its clearest terms: *the Human as Two (and One) is the neuroanatomical, cognitive, and spiritual bedrock of the paranormal and its fantastic both-and, physical-mythical, material-mental, real-unreal expressions in popular culture.*

This Two-in-One, this Third Kind, this impossible structure is why we have something profound to learn from the imaginative genres of science fiction and superhero comics. This is why the truth can sometimes only be spoken through the trick, and why the fantasy sometimes also expresses the fact. This is what makes both the words and the images necessary, and why the two together can feel (and work) like magic. Most of all, though, this is why we need to leave a door open to the human psyche in *all* its high strangeness, and, more radically still, why we need to see that high strangeness not as some delusion to damn and deny, but as part of the deepest message of who we are and what we may yet be.

In short, this is why we need to return anew to the question of the human soul not as it is naively imagined as some sort of stable thing or religious ego lasting through a never-ending linear time (for that would just be Two), but as our raging gnostic authors have understood and dramatically experienced it as a series of Thirds—as the Marvellous beyond mind and matter that sets up a "perpetual struggle" between "the creed of reason" and "the question" occult openings put to that reason (Bulwer-Lytton); as a subliminal Self that is evolving toward its own supernormal powers, imaginal potential, and godlike destiny (Lloyd, Myers, Murphy, Bergson, Bucke, and Wallace); as a subliminal romance or super-imagination that cannot possibly be captured by the "ostrich philosophy" of the materialists or the "puerile beliefs" of the spiritualists (Flournoy); as an Era of Witchcraft that can only be damned by the Dominants of Science and Religion (Fort); as a form of cosmic consciousness or Mind at Large that is transmitted into space and time through the portal of the brain-body but is finally contained by none of these (Moore, Morrison, Huxley, Targ, Swann, Schwartz, Windsor-Smith, and Dick); as a dialectical "metareasoning" or "infinite logic" that reflects our double experience of reality as a holographic projection or unreal-real interference pattern between two separate psychical systems—the finite, constructed, temporal ego and the infinite, immortal, eternal Logos or Divine Mind (Dick); and as an astonishing plasmic presence of giant form that intuits the mythical countenance of the alien as the force and future face of itself (Strieber).

These are astonishing claims. They are all also, every one of them, empirically, experientially grounded in real paranormal events. As are the colorful works of popular culture that we have celebrated and enjoyed in these pages. We dismiss these real events and cultural works, or uncritically believe them, at our own risk and loss. Much better to read them, as we have done here, in the light of gnostic, esoteric, and mystical literature, interpret them, and make them our own—to become our own authors and artists of the impossible.

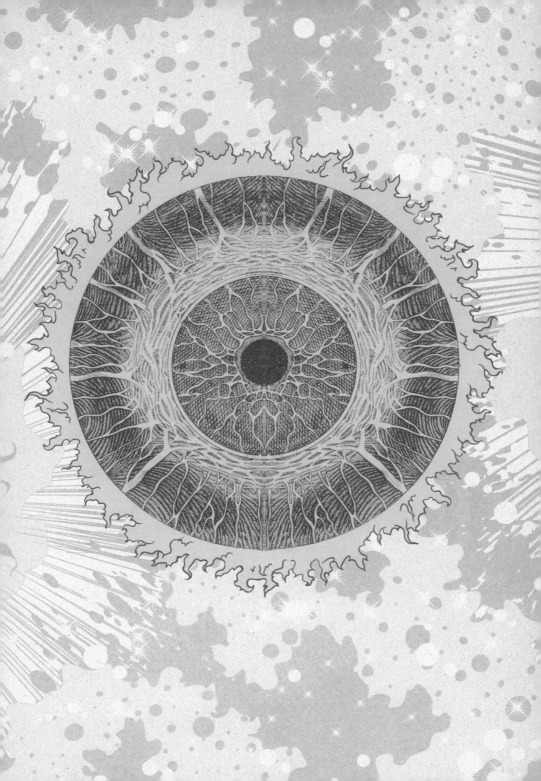

NOTES

ORIGINS

1. For two representative studies, see Bradford W. Wright, *Comic Book Nation: The Transformation of Youth Culture in America* (Baltimore: Johns Hopkins University Press, 2001); and Gerard Jones, *Men of Tomorrow: Geeks, Gangsters, and the Birth of the Comic Book* (New York: Basic Books, 2004).

2. Christopher Knowles, *Our Gods Wear Spandex: The Secret History of Comic Book Heroes* (San Francisco: Weiser Books, 2007), 221–22.

3. http://authorsoftheimpossible.com/webclip_doug_moench.html. For Moench's recounting of the full story, minus the paranormal dimension described here, see his essay "Victim," in the men's magazine *OUI*, July 1978, 79–80, 126–34.

4. Dan Aykroyd, foreword to Peter H. Aykroyd with Angela Narth, *A History of Ghosts: The True Story of Seances, Mediums, Ghosts, and Ghostbusters* (New York: Rodale, 2009), x.

5. Ibid., 183–84.

6. Ibid., 189.

7. John R. Johnston and David B. Sereda, producers, *Dan Aykroyd: Unplugged on UFOs* (Gravitton Productions, 2005), scene 13, "Men in Black."

8. For a fuller account, see my *Roads of Excess, Palaces of Wisdom: Eroticism and Reflexivity in the Study of Mysticism* (Chicago: University of Chicago Press, 2001), 199–206.

9. John E. Mack, "How the Alien Abduction Phenomenon Challenges the Boundaries of Our Reality," in *UFOs and Abductions: Challenging the Borders of Knowledge*, ed. David M. Jacobs (Lawrence: University Press of Kansas, 2000), 254.

10. The languages of a neural download through a portal or of an alien energetic transformation were not part of the original experience, although they capture the experience extremely well. They are interpretive frameworks adopted here to make my present point about the paranormal resonances of popular culture, about sci-fi as an eerily accurate mystical code.

11. I am relying here on Jay Babcock's *Arthur* magazine interview, "Magic Is Afoot," which was reprinted in *Alan Moore's Yuggoth Cultures and Other Growths* (Rantoul, IL: Avatar, 2007), 118.

12. George Khoury, *The Extraordinary Works of Alan Moore: Indispensable Edition* (Raleigh, NC: TwoMorrows Publishing, 2008), 186.

13. I am relying here on Christine Hoff Kraemer, "*Promethea*: Comics as Spiritual Tool," http://eroomnala.bravepages.com/Kraemer.html.

14. Jeremy Narby, *The Cosmic Serpent: DNA and the Origins of Knowledge* (New York: Tarcher/Putnam, 1998), 160.

15. Babcock, "Magic Is Afoot," 123–25.

16. Ibid., 131.

17. Ibid., 127.

18. Ibid., 126.

19. See Grant Morrison, "Pop Magic!" in *Book of Lies: The Disinformation Guide to Magick and the Occult*, ed. Richard Metzger (New York: The Disinformation Company, 2003).

20. Patrick Meaney, *Our Sentence Is Up: Seeing Grant Morrison's "The Invisibles"* (Edwardsville, IL: Sequart Research & Literacy Organization, 2010), 302. For more, see "Pop Magic!"

21. Andy Khouri, "Grant Morrison Talks with Fans at Meltdown Hollywood," *Comic Book Resources News* web magazine, posted April 1, 2005.

22. Meaney, *Our Sentence Is Up*, 293.

23. Ibid., 294–95.

24. This corresponds very closely to the gnostic vision of Philip K. Dick. See below, chapter 6.

25. Ibid., 290.

26. Ibid., 302.

27. Ibid., 344.

28. Ibid., 327.

29. Ibid., 330.

30. Hesiod outlined Five Ages: Golden, Silver, Bronze, Heroic, and Iron. The Heroic Age was the age of Greek civilization.

CHAPTER ONE

1. David Standish, *Hollow Earth* (Cambridge, MA: Da Capo Press, 2006), 13.

2. Quoted in Standish, *Hollow Earth*, 40.

3. Victoria Nelson, *The Secret Life of Puppets* (Cambridge, MA: Harvard University Press, 2001), 149.

4. Standish, *Hollow Earth*, 67.

5. Ibid., 93.

6. *The Illumination of Koresh: Marvelous Experiences of the Great Alchemist Thirty Years Ago, at Utica, NY* (Chicago: Guiding Star, n.d.), quoted in Standish, *Hollow Earth*, 145.

7. Quoted in ibid., 147.

8. Cyrus Teed, *The Cellular Cosmogony; or, the Earth, a Concave Sphere* (Chicago: Guiding Star, 1899/1870). I suspect this is where Charles Fort got his own cellular cosmology, but that is another story.

9. For a recent translation, see Saint-Yves d'Alveydre, *The Kingdom of Agarttha: A Journey into the Hollow Earth*, trans. John Graham (Rochester, VT: Inner Traditions, 2008).

10. Joscelyn Godwin, *Arktos: The Polar Myth in Science, Symbolism, and Nazi Survival* (Kempton, IL: Adventures Unlimited Press, 1996), 96.

11. See Nicholas Goodrick-Clarke, *The Occult Roots of Nazism: Secret Aryan Cults and Their Influence on Nazi Ideology* (New York: NYU Press, 1993), and chapter 5 of Godwin, *Arktos*. These Nazi-occult streams would in turn flow into comic-book writing through books like Mike Mignola's *Hellboy*.

12. Godwin, *Arktos*, 134.

13. The classic study is Ivan T. Sanderson, *Invisible Residents: A Disquisition upon Certain Matters Maritime, and the Possibility of Intelligent Life under the Waters of This Earth* (New York: World Publishing Company, 1970).

14. Godwin, *Arktos*, 37.

15. Christopher McIntosh, *The Rosicrucians: The History, Mythology, and Rituals of an Esoteric Order* (York Beach, ME: Samuel Weiser, 1997), xxi.

16. Christopher McIntosh, "A Theme to Conjure With: Rosicrucianism *in* Fiction—Rosicrucianism *as* Fiction" (unpublished manuscript delivered at the Esalen Institute, Big Sur, CA, May 14–19, 2006).

17. Godwin, *Arktos*, 86.

18. McIntosh, *The Rosicrucians*, xviii.

19. Quoted in ibid., 20.

20. For the dream inspiration, see Andrew Brown, "The 'Supplementary Chapter' to Bulwer Lytton's *A Strange Story*," *Victorian Literature and Culture* (1998): 157.

21. McIntosh, *The Rosicrucians*, 114.

22. Edward Bulwer-Lytton, *The Coming Race* (Middletown, CT: Wesleyan University Press, 2005), 27. The novel is dedicated to Max Müller, the preeminent scholar of comparative religion of the time.

23. Ibid., 40.

24. Ibid., 105.

25. Ibid., 135.

26. Ibid., 14.

27. Quoted in Brown, "The 'Supplementary Chapter,'" 170. The voice is that of the narrator of *A Strange Story*, but it is also clearly Bulwer-Lytton's.

28. Bulwer-Lytton, *The Coming Race*, 59.

29. Ibid., 38; the latter line is quoted in David Seed, introduction to ibid., xxxvi.

30. Quoted in Brown, "The 'Supplementary Chapter,'" 170–72.

31. Quoted in ibid., 173.

32. Quoted in ibid., 180n67.

33. Bulwer-Lytton, *The Coming Race*, xxxviii.

34. Jerry Snider and Michael Peter Langevin, eds., *A Magical Universe: The Best of "Magical Blend" Magazine* (Mill Spring, NC: Blue Water Publishing, 1996), 77.

35. Patrick Deveney, *Paschal Beverly Randolph: A Nineteenth-Century Black American Spiritualist, Rosicrucian, and Sex Magician* (Albany, NY: SUNY, 1997).

36. I am relying here on McIntosh, *The Rosicrucians*, 120–22.

37. The phrase "hidden under glyph and symbol" is taken from the Proem or preface of *The Secret Doctrine*.

38. For a sensitive discussion of this line of thought, see Catherine Albanese, *A Republic of Mind and Spirit: A Cultural History of American Metaphysical Religion* (New Haven, CT: Yale University Press, 2008).

39. "More about the Theosophists: An Interview with Madame Blavatsky," *Pall Mall Gazette* (April 26, 1884): 3–4. Cited in Seed, ed., *The Coming Race*, 159n63.

40. H. P. Blavatsky, *The Secret Doctrine*, abridged and annotated by Michael Gomes (New York: Tarcher Penguin, 2009), 110.

41. I am relying here on Joscelyn Godwin, *Atlantis and the Cycles of Time: Prophecies, Traditions, and Occult Revelations* (Rochester, Vermont: Inner Traditions, 2010), 83, 95.

42. Sumathi Ramaswamy, *The Lost Land of Lemuria: Fabulous Geographies, Catastrophic Histories* (Berkeley: University of California Press, 2004).

43. Ibid., 9.

44. There is a great deal of truth in this kind of social and materialistic determinism, hence my present reflections on how "we are written."

45. Quoted in Ramaswamy, *The Lost Land*, 22.

46. Quoted in ibid., 55.

47. Godwin, *Arktos*, 24.

48. Godwin, *Atlantis*, 100.

49. Quoted in Ramaswamy, *The Lost Land*, 67.

50. Ibid., 70.

51. Ibid., 75–76.

52. Wishar S. Cervé, *Lemuria—The Lost Continent of the Pacific* (Supreme Grand Lodge of the Ancient and Mystical Order Rosae Crucis, 1994), 259–61.

53. Godwin, *Atlantis*, 229. It is worth noting in this context that the channeled lore around Atlantis, so fully traced by Godwin, is *filled* with aerial vehicles of various kinds, including seamless glowing ones, a chariot from Venus, and others powered by Bulwer-Lytton's Vril (for representative discussions, see Godwin, *Atlantis*, 74–75, 82–83, 94–95, 96–97, 99–100, 217, 248). It is very difficult not to see this early occult material as somehow related to the later contactee literature and UFO encounter stories.

54. Frederic W. H. Myers, *Human Personality and Its Survival of Bodily Death*, 2 vols. (London: Longmans, Green, and Co., 1904/1903), 1:xviii.

55. Myers, *Human Personality*, 1:xx.

56. Peter H. Aykroyd with Angela Narth, *A History of Ghosts: The True Story of Seances, Mediums, Ghosts, and Ghostbusters* (New York: Rodale, 1999), 188.

57. Frederic W. H. Myers, *Science and the Future Life with Other Essays* (London: Macmillan and Co., 1901/1893), 37–38.

58. Brian Stableford, introduction to *H. G. Wells: Seven Novels* (New York: Barnes and Noble, 2006), ix.

59. Cited in Godwin, *Arktos*, 102.

60. I am working from the ninth edition. John Uri Lloyd, with illustrations by J. Augustus Knapp, *Etidorhpa: or, The End of the Earth: The Strange History of a Mysterious Being and The Account of a Remarkable Journey* (Cincinnati: Robert Clarke Company, 1998), 258.

61. Ibid., 364–65.

62. Michael A. Flannery, *John Uri Lloyd: The Great American Eclectic* (Carbondale, IL: Southern Illinois Press, 1998), 120–22.

63. Lloyd, *Etidorhpa*, 1.

64. Ibid., 203, 228, 296, 172.

65. Ibid., v–vi.

66. Standish, *Hollow Earth*, 218, 219.

67. Lloyd, *Etidorhpa*, 98.

68. Lloyd, *Etidorhpa*, 10. The extended forehead carries a submerged erotic meaning for this text, since as mind takes more and more control over matter, "an amorous soul will even protrude the anterior part of the skull" (ibid., 245).

69. Ibid., 24–25.

70. Ibid., 154.

71. Ibid., 171.

72. Ibid., 220. This is the "ether" of earlier parascientific and occult speculation.

73. Ibid., 65–66.

74. Ibid., 75, 274, 113, 13, 283 (for the last "mind and matter connection," see also 342–43).

75. Ibid., 159–60; see also 324.

76. Sonu Shamdasani, introduction to Théodore Flournoy, *From India to the Planet Mars: A Case of Multiple Personality and Imaginary Languages* (Princeton, NJ: Princeton University Press, 1994), xiii.

77. Ibid., 5.

78. Ibid., 9–10.

79. Ibid., 7.

80. Ibid., 26.

81. Shamdasani in ibid., xxxiii.

82. Ibid., 230.

83. Ibid., 233.

84. Ibid., 224; see also 230 for more on the "leftover" thesis.

85. Ibid., 231.

86. Ibid., 250.

87. See Jung's essay "Théodore Flournoy," which was used as a preface to ibid., ix–x.

88. This may also be an echo of Gustave Le Rouge's 1908 novel *Vampires of Mars*, in which the protagonist is dispatched to the planet by psychic Hindu Brahmins. I am indebted to Erik Davis for this connection.

89. Godwin, *Arktos*, 8.

90. Lloyd, *Etidorhpa*, 345–46.

CHAPTER TWO

1. Sam Moskowitz, *Seekers of Tomorrow: Masters of Modern Science Fiction* (New York: Ballantine, 1967), 119.

2. Greg Sadowski, ed., *Supermen! The First Wave of Comic Book Heroes: 1936–1941* (Seattle: Fantagraphics Books, 2009), 186.

3. Very technically, Superman is a landed alien, as the first issues had his spaceship landing.

4. Gerald Heard, *The Riddle of the Flying Saucers: Is Another World Watching?* (London: Carroll and Nicholson, 1950).

5. John G. Fuller, *Incident at Exeter, the Interrupted Journey: Two Landmark Investigations of UFO Encounters Together in One Volume* (New York: MJF Books, n.d.), 258, 100–101, 231, 125, 257.

6. http://www.talkingpix.co.uk/ArticleGaucheEncounters.html.

7. Fuller, *Incident at Exeter*, 144.

8. David J. Hufford, *The Terror That Comes in the Night: An Experience-Centered Study of Supernatural Assault Traditions* (Philadelphia: University of Pennsylvania Press, 1982); and "Awakening Paralyzed in the Presence of a Strange 'Visitor,'" in *Alien Discussions: Proceedings of the Abduction Study Conference held at MIT, Cambridge, MA*, ed. Andrea Pritchard, David E. Pritchard, John E. Mack, Pam Kasey, and Claudia Yapp (Cambridge, MA: North Cambridge Press, 1994).

9. Christopher Partridge, ed., *UFO Religions* (London: Routledge, 2003).

10. See Nick Redfern, *Contactees: A History of Alien-Human Interaction* (Franklin Lakes, NJ: Career Press, 2009).

11. I am citing *The Book of the Damned: The Collected Work of Charles Fort*, with a new introduction by Jim Steinmeyer (New York: Tarcher/Penguin, 2009), preceded by BD (*The Book of the Damned*), NL (*New Lands*), LO (*Lo!*), and WT (*Wild Talents*).

12. Fort's New Dominant bears all sorts of similarities to what later writers would call the New Age, and it is no accident that Fort's texts experienced a kind of renaissance in the 1960s and '70s. For more on this, see chapter 4.

13. Quoted in Jim Steinmeyer, *Charles Fort: The Man Who Invented the Supernatural* (New York: Tarcher/Penguin, 2008), 143. By "orthogenetically," Dreiser referred to a directed evolutionary process, a kind of occult intelligent design (without a designer, Fort would insist).

14. Sam Moskowitz, *Charles Fort: A Radical Corpuscle* (Newark, NJ, 1976), in the Moskowitz Collection of Texas A & M University.

15. *Astounding Stories* 13, no. 6 (August 1934), and 14, nos. 1 and 3 (September and November 1934).

16. Samuel Mines, "Charles Fort: The Disciple of Disbelief," *Fantastic Story* 3, no. 2 (Winter 1952): 9.

17. SW 20–21. Palmer does not specify whether this was in a dream or not.

18. Kenneth Arnold and Ray Palmer, *The Coming of the Saucers* (Amherst, MA: privately published, 1952), 163. Palmer does not specify that this was the Ziff-Davis office.

19. Palmer tells the story in *Amazing Stories* 21, no. 6 (June 1947): 8–9, 175–177.

20. *Amazing Stories* 18, no. 1 (January 1944): 206.

21. Jim Wentworth, *Giants in the Earth: The Amazing Story of Ray Palmer, Oahspe and the Shaver Mystery* (Amherst, WI: Palmer Publications, 1973), 23.

22. *Teros* was also the name for the protective psychic energy in *Agni Yoga* (1929) by Helena Roerich—the same Helena that witnessed with her esoterically inclined husband, Nicholas, a flying saucer in China. See Joscelyn Godwin, *Arktos: The Polar Myth in Science, Symbolism, and Nazi Survival* (Kempton, IL: Adventures Unlimited Press, 1996), 100, 104.

23. *Amazing Stories* 18, no. 1 (January 1944): 206.

24. *Amazing Stories* 19, no. 1 (March 1945): 71.

25. Wentworth, *Giants in the Earth*, 24.

26. *Amazing Stories* 19, no. 1 (March 1945): 14–15.

27. John A. Keel, "The Flying Saucer Subculture," *Journal of Popular Culture* 8, no. 4 (Spring 1975): 875.

28. Wentworth, *Giants in the Earth*, 31.

29. *Amazing Stories* 21, no. 6 (June 1947): 9.

30. Palmer explained past-life memories as the results of astral travel into the past (F 1.17.3), as messages from spirits who met traumatic ends (F B.1.32), as possession (F 1.21.21), or, worse yet, as an inappropriate hijacking of someone else's newborn body, which is "against the law" (F 1.22.26).

31. He is influenced here, as in so much else, by the *Oahspe* Bible (F 1.8.23, 28).

32. Wentworth, *Giants in the Earth*, 118; see also F 1.9.0–10.

33. Wentworth, *Giants in the Earth*, 66.

34. Ibid., 76–77.

35. Although he seriously entertained a literal hollow earth at the northern pole as late as 1970 (F 5.67.4).

36. Wentworth, *Giants in the Earth*, 82–83.

37. I am relying here on Keel, "The Flying Saucer Subculture," 881.

38. *Amazing Stories* 21, no. 6 (June 1947): 176.

39. Ibid., 104–5.

40. Ibid., 117. See also *Hidden World* (Winter 1961): 583; and *Forum* (July and November 1971). Shaver claimed it was a sanatorium and only a few weeks for a diagnosis of heatstroke (Wentworth, *Giants in the Earth*, 118).

41. *Amazing Stories* 21, no. 6 (June 1947): 8.

42. Wentworth, *Giants in the Earth*, 38–39.

43. Daniel Simundson, "John Ballou Newbrough and the Oahspe Bible" (Ph.D. diss., University of New Mexico, 1972); available through University Microfilms, Ann Arbor, MI.

44. I am relying here on Wentworth, *Giants in the Earth*, 102–3, who seems to be relying in turn on F 2.34.14–15.

45. Michael D. Swords, "Donald E. Keyhoe and the Pentagon," in *UFOs, 1947–1997: From Arnold to the Abductees: Fifty Years of Flying Saucers*, ed. Hilary Evans and Dennis Stacy (London: John Brown Publishing, 1997), 89.

46. Keel, "The Flying Saucer Subculture," 877.

47. See the three volumes Simon Welfare and John Fairley published as *Arthur C. Clarke's Mysterious World* (1980); *Arthur C. Clarke's World of Strange Powers* (1984); and *Arthur C. Clarke's Chronicles of*

the Strange and Mysterious (1987). For the essays, see Arthur C. Clarke, *Greetings Carbon-Based Bipeds!*, ed. Ian T. Macauley (London: Voyager, 1999).

48. I am relying here on the exceptional Wikipedia entry at http://en.wikipedia.org/wiki/2001:_A_Space_Odyssey_(film)

49. Mark Evanier, *Kirby: King of Comics* (New York: Abrams, 2008), 138.

50. *Marvel Premiere* #1 (New York: Marvel Comics, 1975), 61.

51. The situation is particularly inadmissible in the study of religion, since the vast majority of the history of any religion *is* a history of popularization.

52. See especially Joscelyn Godwin's discussion of the origins of the ancient astronaut theory in the British writers Brinsley le Poer Trench, Desmond Leslie, and John Michell in *Atlantis and the Cycles of Time: Prophecies, Traditions, and Occult Revelations* (Rochester, Vermont: Inner Traditions, 2010), 202-5, 273.

53. Consider Raymond W. Drake of England, Paul Misraki and Aimé Michel of France, and Morris K. Jessup and Jacques Vallee in the U.S.

54. I. S. Shklovskii and Carl Sagan, *Intelligent Life in the Universe* (San Francisco: Holden-Day, 1966), 448–62.

CHAPTER THREE

1. John E. Mack, *Passport to the Cosmos: Human Transformation and Alien Encounters* (Largo: Kunati, 2008), 68.

2. John Canaday, *The Nuclear Muse: Literature, Physics, and the First Atomic Bombs* (Madison: University of Wisconsin Press, 2000); and David Seed, *American Science Fiction and the Cold War: Literature and Film* (Edingburgh: Edinburgh University Press, 1999).

3. William Tsutsui, *Godzilla on My Mind: Fifty Years of the King of Monsters* (New York: Palgrave Macmillan, 2004), 13–14.

4. Eric Wilson, *Emerson's Sublime Science* (New York: St. Martin's Press, 1999), 5.

5. Karl von Reichenbach, *The Odic Force: Letters on Od and Magnetism* (New Hyde Park, NY: University Books, 1968), 93.

6. Trevor James Constable, *The Cosmic Pulse of Life: The Revolutionary Biological Power Behind UFOs* (Suffolk: Neville Spearman, 1976).

7. I am relying here on Robert Moss, *The Secret History of Dreaming* (Novato, CA: New World Library, 2009).

8. See Jeffrey J. Kripal, *Esalen: America and the Religion of No Religion* (Chicago: University of Chicago Press, 2007), chap. 13. Such "hippie physicists" have recently received some long-deserved expert attention from MIT historian of science David Kaiser, who shows in considerable detail how such theorists preserved, radicalized, and extended a strain of quantum speculation that was central to the founders of the field but was systematically squashed, even actively censored, through the militarization and professionalization of the discipline. For Kaiser, it was this Bay Area group that "saved physics" from the anti-philosophical "Shut Up and Calculate" mentality of professional science, particularly around something called Bell's Theorem, which appears to establish spooky, long-distance connections between elementary particles that many scientists have likened to teleportation or telepathy. See David Kaiser, *How the Hippies Saved Physics: Science, Counterculture, and the Quantum Revival* (New York: W. W. Norton, 2011).

9. Ronin Ro, *Tales to Astonish: Jack Kirby, Stan Lee, and the American Comic Book Revolution* (New York: Bloomsbury, 2004), 59.

10. Mark Evanier, *Kirby: King of Comics* (New York: Abrams, 2008), 50.

11. Ro, *Tales to Astonish*, 21.

12. Evanier, *Kirby*, 67.

13. Ro, *Tales to Astonish*, 36.

14. I am drawing here on Glen David Gold, who suggests posttraumatic stress disorder as a contributing, not defining, factor of Kirby's art: "This was a man who had actually fought Hitler. . . . Kirby was working out demons" (FW 3.9).

15. Evanier, *Kirby*, 109.

16. Bradford W. Wright, *Comic Book Nation: The Transformation of Youth Culture in America* (Baltimore: Johns Hopkins University Press, 2001), 213.

17. Neil Gaiman, introduction to Evanier, *Kirby*, 11, 13.

18. Quoted in ibid., 207.

19. Ibid., 132–33.

20. Ro, *Tales to Astonish*, 290–91.

21. Ibid., 75.

22. Ibid., 83, 214.

23. Evanier, *Kirby*, 163.

24. Ro, *Tales to Astonish*, 147.

25. Evanier, *Kirby*, 153.

26. Arlen Schumer, *The Silver Age of Comic Book Art* (Portland, OR: Collector's Press, 2003).

27. *The Mighty Thor* #138.

28. The two biblical "chariot" passages are 1 Chronicles 28:18 and Ecclesiasticus 48:8.

29. Michael Lieb, *Children of Ezekiel: Aliens, UFOs, the Crisis of Race, and the Advent of End Time* (Durham, NC: Duke University Press, 1998), 12–13.

30. For Ezekiel's psychopathology, see David J. Halperin, *Seeking Ezekiel: Text and Psychology* (University Park, PA: Penn State University Press, 1993). In another example of our elite/popular culture fusion theme, whereas Halperin's scholarly focus on heavenly ascents began with a very technical 1977 Ph.D. dissertation on the *merkabah* or "chariot" passages of the ancient rabbinic traditions, his latest book is the novel *Journal of a UFO Investigator* (New York: Viking, 2011), and he himself was a teenage UFO investigator.

31. Arlen Schumer, "The Graphic Designs of Jack Kirby," *Jack Kirby Collector* 50 (Spring 2008). Schumer identifies *Fantastic Four* #50 (May 1966) as the first obvious display of Kirby Krackle.

32. Evanier, *Kirby*, 185.

33. Ro, *Tales to Astonish*, 200.

34. For the speculative superhero allusions in the astral form and ordinary objects, see page 10 of the first story and pages 7 and 8 of the second.

35. For these images and other material discussed in my brief treatment of Knowles, see http://secretsun.blogspot.com, especially "Astronaut Theology: Jack Kirby, Astro-Gnostic" (October 28, 2008); "The Mindbomb: The Dreaming Mind and the Gate of the Gods" (June 11, 2009); and "Children of the Flaming Wheel," parts 1 and 2 (August 21 and 23, 2010).

36. The precognitive visions, dreams, telepathic communications, and "literary premonitions" surrounding this event far outstrip the coincidences with this single novel. The serious reader should consult Bertrand Méheust, *Histoires Paranormales du Titanic* (Paris: Collections J'ai lu, 2006), for a full description and analysis.

37. For much more on Keel, see my "On the Mothman, God, and Other Monsters: The Demonology of John A. Keel," in *Histories of the Hidden God*, ed. April DeConick and Grant Adamson (London: Equinox, forthcoming).

38. John A. Keel, *UFOs: Operation Trojan Horse* (New York: G. P. Putnam's Sons, 1970), 212.

39. Ibid., 274.

40. Ibid., 216.

41. John A. Keel, *The Eighth Tower: The Cosmic Force behind All Religious, Occult and UFO Phenomena* (New York: Saturday Review Press, 1975), 7.

42. Ibid., 59–60. For a similar, if more muted, framing in a scientific author, see Michael Persinger, "The UFO Experience: A Normal Correlate of Human Brain Function," in David M. Jacobs, ed., *UFOs and Abductions: Challenging the Borders of Knowledge* (Lawrence, KS: University Press of Kansas, 2000). Also relevant here are Persinger's early books on the statistical patterns of verbal reports of real-world psychical experiences and "space-time transients" (brief but robust paranormal events, such as telepathy and precognition, that violate our normal sense of reality): Michael A. Persinger, *The Paranormal: Part I, Patterns* (New York: MSS Information Corporation, 1974); and Michael A. Persinger and Gyslaine F. Lafreniere, *Space-Time Transients and Unusual Events* (Chicago: Nelson-Hall, 1977). In these early books, Persinger employed two major data sets: 592 cases drawn from the letters sent into *Fate* magazine and 6,060 reports taken largely from the four books of Charles Fort. In short, Persinger's data set was the paranormal as recorded and preserved in popular culture.

43. Keel, *UFOs*, 255.

44. Ibid., 276–78.

45. Alden P. Armagnac, "Our Worst Bridge Disaster: Why Did It Happen?" *Popular Science*, March 1968, 102–5, 188; reprinted in Jeff Wamsley, *Mothman: Beind the Red Eyes* (Point Pleasant, WV: Mothman Press, 2005), 113.

46. "'Strange plane turns out to be 'bird,'" reprinted in Wamsley, *Mothman*, 26. See also Donnie Sergent Jr. and Jeff Wamsley, *Mothman: The Facts Behind the Legend* (Point Pleasant, WV: Mothman Lives Publishing, 2002).

47. Wamsley, *Mothman*, 22, 38, 50, 72, 74.

48. Frederic Wertham, *Seduction of the Innocent* (New York: Rinehart, 1954).

49. Bradford W. Wright, *Comic Book Nation: The Transformation of Youth Culture in America* (Baltimore: Johns Hopkins University Press, 2001); Bart Beaty, *Frederic Wertham and the Critique of Mass Culture* (Jackson: University Press of Mississippi, 2005); David Hadju, *The Ten-Cent Plague: The Great Comic-Book Scare and How It Changed America* (New York: Farrar, Straus, and Giroux, 2008).

50. Wertham, *Seduction*, 257.

51. Ibid., 100–105.

52. Ibid., 175.

53. Ibid., 278.

54. Ibid., 244.

55. Mike Conroy, *500 Great Comic Book Action Heroes* (Hauppauge, NY: Barron's, 2002), 230.

56. Wertham, *Seduction*, 234.

57. Ibid., 236.

58. Ibid., 189–91.

59. See Bill Boichel, "Batman: Commodity as Myth," and Andy Medhurst, "Batman, Deviance and Camp," in *The Many Lives of the Batman: Critical Approaches to a Superhero and His Media*, ed. Robert A. Pearson and William Uricchio (New York: Routledge, 1991).

60. *The Rough Guide to Superheroes* (London: Haymarket Customer Publishing, 2004), 217.

61. Craig Yoe, *Secret Identity: The Fetish Art of Superman's Co-creator Joe Shuster* (New York: Abrams ComicArts, 2009).

62. Umberto Eco, "The Myth of the Superman," trans. Natalie Chilton, *Diacritics* 2, no. 1 (Spring 1972): 14–22.

63. Wright, *Comic Book Nation*, 297n43.

64. Gerard Jones, *Men of Tomorrow: Geeks, Gangsters and the Birth of the Comic Book* (New York: Basic Books, 2004).

65. Art Spiegelman and Chip Kidd, *Jack Cole and Plastic Man: Forms Stretched to Their Limits!* (New York: DC Comics, 2001).

66. *The Rough Guide to Superheroes*, 268.

67. The movie changes the original comic-book script, which has Peter Parker devising little web-spinning devices that he then wears around his wrists.

68. *X2: X-Men United*, Twentieth-Century Fox, 2003, scene 18, "The Drake Home."

69. Gopi Krishna, *Kundalini: The Evolutionary Energy in Man* (Berkeley: Shambala, 1971/1967); and Gopi Krishna, *The Biological Basis of Religion and Genius* (New York: NC Press, 1971). Frederic Spiegelberg correctly associates Gopi Krishna's writing with those of Sri Aurobindo and identifies the ultimate source of both systems of practice as "the world of Tantra" (introduction to Krishna, *Kundalini*, 9).

70. Tom Kay, "An Interview with Gopi Krishna," at http://www.ecomall.com/greenshopping/gopinterview.htm

71. Krishna, *Kundalini*, 213.

CHAPTER FOUR

1. Lawrence Watt-Evans, "Growing Up Mutant," in *The Unauthorized X-Men: SF and Comic Writers on Mutants, Prejudice and Adamantium*, ed. Len Wein with Leah Wilson (Dallas: Benbella Books, 2005), 155.

2. Ibid., 156.

3. Stan Lee, Jack Kirby, Roy Thomas, and Werner Roth, *The X-Men Omnibus* Vol. 1 (New York: Marvel Publishing, 2009), 507.

4. *Amazing Adult Fantasy* #14 (1962), reprinted in *X-Men Rarities* (New York: Marvel Comics, 1995).

5. See the back material to UXM.

6. Watt-Evans, "Growing up Mutant," 161.

7. Louis Pauwels and Jacques Bergier, *The Morning of the Magicians* (New York: Stein and Day, 1964).

8. Gary Lachman, *Turn Off Your Mind: The Mystic Sixties and the Dark Side of the Age of Aquarius* (New York: Disinformation Company, 2001), 15.

9. Pauwels and Bergier, *The Morning*, xi. Pauwels includes a brief description of his at the very end of the book (272–73).

10. Quoted in Lachman, *Turn Off Your Mind*, 29–30.

11. Parts of this section originally appeared as Jeffrey J. Kripal, "Esalen and the X-Men: The Human Potential Movement and Superhero Comics," *Alter Ego* 84 (March 2009): 50–59.

12. Damien Broderick, *Outside the Gates of Science* (New York: Thunder's Mouth Press, 2007), 219–20.

13. Whereas early scares around LSD circled around the damaging effects it supposedly had on chromosomes, Timothy Leary would later write explicitly about psychedelics and human evolution and pen a three-word invocation that would later focus a Spider-Man series: "Evolve or die!" See Timothy Leary, *Musings on Human Metamorphosis* (Berkeley: Ronin, 2003).

14. Michael Murphy, *The Future of the Body: Explorations into the Further Evolution of Human Nature* (New York: G. P. Putnam's Sons, 1992), 211–13. For more on the "superpowers" of the human potential movement, particularly as they historically emerged from the models of psychical research, physics, and evolutionary biology, on the Western side, and the traditions of Yoga and Tantra, on the Indian side, see Jeffrey J. Kripal, "The Evolving Siddhis: Yoga and Tantra in the Psychical Research Tradition and Beyond," in Knut A. Jacobsen, ed., *Yoga Powers* (Leiden: E. J. Brill, 2011). Radiation, Mutation, and Orientation again.

15. George B. Leonard, *Education and Ecstasy* (New York: Dell, 1968), 4.

16. F. H. Crick and L. E. Orgel, "Directed Panspermia," *Icarus* 19:341–48.

17. Julian Huxley, *Evolution: The Modern Synthesis* (New York: Harper & Brothers, 1942), 577–78, 575. My thanks to Istvan Csicsery-Ronay for this reference.

18. Henri Bergson, *The Two Sources of Morality and Religion* (London: Macmillan, 1935), 275.

19. Quoted in "The Man and the Book," preface to Richard Maurice Bucke, *Cosmic Consciousness: A Study in the Evolution of the Human Mind* (New York: Arkana, 1991), no page number.

20. Ibid., 3.

21. Bucke, for example, does not list a single woman in his list of highly evolved individuals.

22. Ibid., 4.

23. Ibid., 11.

24. Charles H. Smith, *Alfred Russel Wallace; An Anthology of His Shorter Writings* (Oxford: Oxford University Press, 1991), 33.

25. This section appears in a revised and expanded form as "Les vies secrètes des super-pouvoirs: la littérature de la vision à distance, et l'imaginal," in *Techniques du corps et de l'esprit dans les deux Ameriqués: Continuétes et discontinuetes culturelles*, ed. Antoine Faivre and Silvia Mancini (Paris: Éditions Imago, 2011).

26. Russell Targ and Harold Puthoff, *Mind-Reach: Scientists Look at Psychic Ability* (Delacorte Press, 1977), 21.

27. Paul H. Smith, *Reading the Enemy's Mind: Inside Star Gate, America's Psychic Espionage Program* (New York: Forge, 2005), 60.

28. Ibid., 70.

29. Quoted in ibid., 71.

30. Targ and Puthoff, *Mind-Reach*, 27.

31. See Charles T. Tart, Harold E. Puthoff, and Russell Targ, eds., *Mind at Large: Institute of Electrical and Electronic Engineers Symposia on the Nature of Extrasensory Perception* (New York: Praeger, 1979). The title is an allusion to Huxley.

32. For a precise description of CRV that privileges the metaphysics of nonlocal mind and humorously preserves the apparent impossibility of it all, see Smith, *Reading the Enemy's Mind*, 277–79.

33. Joseph McMoneagle, *Mind Trek: Exploring Consciousness, Time, and Space through Remote Viewing* (Charlottesville: Hampton Roads, 1997), 31–32.

34. Aaron Parrett, introduction to Jules Verne, *From the Earth to the Moon*, ed. Aaron Parrett (New York: Barnes and Noble Books, 2005), vii.

35. Joseph McMoneagle, *The Ultimate Time Machine: A Remote Viewer's Perception of Time, and Predictions for the New Millennium* (Charlottesville: Hampton Roads, 1999).

36. Personal communication, April 29, 2009.

37. "About the Author," in McMoneagle, *The Ultimate Time Machine*.

38. Russell Targ and Jane Katra, *Miracles of Mind: Exploring Nonlocal Consciousness and Spiritual Healing* (Novato, CA: New World Library, 1999), 27.

39. Jim Schnabel, *Remote Viewers: The Secret History of America's Psychic Spies* (New York: Dell, 1997), 35–36.

40. Charles Tart, foreword to Ronald Russell, *The Journey of Robert Monroe: Out-of-Body Explorer to Consciousness Pioneer* (Charlottesville: Hampton Roads, 2007), x.

41. Ingo Swann, *To Kiss Earth Good-Bye* (New York: Hawthorn Books, 1975), 196.

42. Jack Anderson, foreword to Smith, *Reading the Enemy's Mind*, 13. Anderson is alluding here to the investigative work of one of his reporters, Ron McRae, who wrote *Mind Wars*.

43. Smith, *Reading the Enemy's Mind*, 52.

44. Ibid., 32. The essay can easily be found online, cited as John B. Alexander, "The New Mental Battlefield: 'Beam Me Up, Spock,'" *Military Review* 60, no. 12 (December 1980).

45. Mitch Horowitz, *Occult America: The Secret History of How Mysticism Shaped Our Nation* (New York: Bantam Doubleday, 2009), 257.

46. Ron McRae, *Mind Wars: The True Story of Secret Government Research in the Military Potential of Psychic Weapons* (New York: St. Martin's Press, 1984).

47. Smith, *Reading the Enemy's Mind*, 20–22.

48. Uri Geller, *My Story* (New York: Praeger, 1975), 248–49. For a balanced study of the superpsychic, see Jonathan Margolis, *Uri Geller: Magician or Mystic?* (New York: Welcome Rain Publishers, 1999).

49. Edgar Mitchell, with Dwight Williams, *The Way of the Explorer: An Apollo Astronaut's Journey through the Material and Mystical Worlds* (New York: G. P. Putnam, 1996), 92–93.

50. Mitchell, *The Way of the Explorer*, 186–87.

51. John L. Wilhelm, *The Search for Superman* (New York: Pocket Books, 1976).

52. George Adamski, *Telepathy: The Cosmic or Universal Language, Parts I and II* (George Adamski, 1958).

53. Ingo Swann, *Penetration: The Question of Extraterrestrial and Human Telepathy* (Rapid City, SD: Ingo Swann Books, 1998), ix–xi, 175. Swann himself invokes the space opera or "the Telepathy War" analogies (83, 179).

54. Ibid., 174, 201.

55. Ibid., 63.

56. Ibid., 203.

57. Smith, *Reading the Enemy's Mind*, 252.

58. René Warcollier, *Mind to Mind* (New York: Creative Age Press, 1948).

59. Smith, *Reading the Enemy's Mind*, 205.

60. Ibid., 72.

61. See Roy Thomas's introduction to Kripal, "Esalen and the X-Men."

62. The photo can be seen in Geller, *My Story*, 186.

CHAPTER FIVE

1. I am relying here on Bill Schelly's *Words of Wonder: The Life and Times of Otto Binder* (Seattle: Hamster Press, 2003), 35.

2. Moskowitz Collection, files 428–29.

3. Schelly, *Words of Wonder*, 68.

4. Sam Moskowitz, *The Coming of the Robots* (New York: Collier Books, 1963), 23. See also Sam Moskowitz, *The Immortal Storm: A History of Science Fiction Fandom* (Westport, CT: Hyperion Press, 1974/1954).

5. Schelly, *Words of Wonder*, 121.

6. Ibid., 93.

7. Ibid., color insert section.

8. Ibid., 157.

9. Ibid., 192.

10. Ibid., 210.

11. Ibid., 221.

12. Quoted in ibid., 202. Schelly notes that Armstrong denied all such stories.

13. Otto Binder, *What We Really Know about Flying Saucers* (Greenwich, CT: Fawcett, 1967).

14. Ibid., 20, 210.

15. Ibid., 20, 154–55, 157, 159, 163–65.

16. Ibid., 88.

17. Ibid., 210.

18. Otto O. Binder, *Flying Saucers Are Watching Us* (New York: Belmont Books, 1968).

19. Ibid., 10.

20. Ibid., 22. Other Fortean scenes, references, or lines occur in ibid., 38, 43, 47, 103, 125, 129, 128–29, 140.

21. Joscelyn Godwin, *Atlantis and the Cycles of Time: Prophecies, Traditions, and Occult Revelations* (Rochester, Vermont, 2010), 262-3, 276-7.

22. For Roddenberry's questions and the channeled answers quoted here, see Phyllis V. Schlemmer and Palden Jenkins, *The Only Planet of Choice: Essential Briefings from Deep Space* (Bath, U.K.: Gateway Books, 1993), 95-100. For the publisher's claims regarding *Deep Space Nine*, see http://www.theonlyplanetofchoice.com/background.htm. For Godwin's commentary and note on the enlarged sexual organs, see Godwin, *Atlantis*, 285-288. For some critical discussion and background to the Roddenberry material, see David Sutton, "From Deep Space to the Nine: How Gene Roddenberry was hired to prepare Earth for an alien invasion," at http://www.forteantimes.com/specials/star-trek/1661/from_deep_space_to_the_nine.html.

23. Binder, *Flying Saucers*, 181.

24. Moskowitz Collection, file 427, addressed to Mr. K. Russell Miller.

25. Harry Warner Jr., *A Wealth of Fable: An Informal History of Science Fiction Fandom in the 1950s* (Van Nuys, CA: SCIFI Press, 1992/1976).

26. O. O. Binder, "Things You Didn't Know about Your Mind," *Mechanix Illustrated* 56, no. 2 (February 1960): 86–87, 181–83.

27. C. J. Talbert, "Have You Lived Before?" *Mechanix Illustrated*, 59–61, n.d. I found this undated essay in the Moskowitz Collection. Someone, I assume Binder himself, identifies "Talbert" as "Otto Binder" in the byline with an ink pen.

28. *Testing for Extrasensory Perception with a Machine* (Hanscom Field, MA: Air Force Cambridge Research Laboratories, Office of Aerospace Research, United States Air Force, May 1963), in the Moskowitz Collection, file 230.

29. I am relying here on three texts: Jeffrey Mishlove, *The PK Man: A True Story of Mind over Matter* (Charlottesville: Hampton Roads, 2000); Otto Binder, "'Spokesman' for the UFO's?" *SAGA*, August 1970; and Otto Binder, "Flying Saucer: Prophet of Doom," *SAGA*, April 1971.

30. Binder, "Flying Saucer," 24.

31. Ted Owens, *How to Contact Space People* (New Brunswick, NJ: Global Communications, 2008). The first edition of Owens's book was published by Gray Barker's Saucerian Press in 1969.

32. Binder, "Flying Saucer," 75.

33. Binder, "Spokesman," 92.

34. Ibid., 24.

35. Ibid., 25, 90.

36. Binder, "Flying Saucer," 25.

37. Binder, "Spokesman," 92.

38. Binder, "Flying Saucer," 70.

39. Ibid., 71.

40. Binder, "Spokesman," 25.

41. Binder, "Flying Saucer," 24.

42. Ibid., 25.

43. Ibid., 24–25.

44. I'm thinking of Edgar Cayce, Peter Hurkos, and Ray Palmer. Binder points out the same in ibid., 25.

45. Ibid., 22, 74.

46. As far as I can tell, Flindt and Binder first expressed this opinion in *Mankind—Child of the*

Stars (Greenwich, CT: Fawcett, 1974), 208–9, that is, well after Binder's extensive correspondence with Ted Owens. It is possible, then, that Binder came to this split-mind conclusion precisely because of his study of the Owens phenomenon.

47. Binder, "Spokesman," 92.

48. Mishlove, *The PK Man*, 140–45. Binder wrote four *SAGA* essays on Owens, which appeared in the August and September issues of 1970 and the March and April issues of 1971. I have only been able to locate two of these.

49. Flindt and Binder, *Mankind*, 37.

50. Ibid., 37–39.

51. I'm thinking here of scenes like the one in his *Mechanix Illustrated* essay on reincarnation in which he places the Buddha five thousand years ago, thereby missing the accepted dating by some 2,500 years.

52. Schelly, *Words of Wonder*, 148.

53. Alvin Schwartz, *A Gathering of Selves: The Spiritual Journey of the Legendary Writer of Superman and Batman* (Rochester, VT: Destiny Books, 2007), 216; hereafter GS.

54. Alvin Schwartz, *An Unlikely Prophet: A Metaphysical Memoir by the Legendary Writer of Superman and Batman* (Rochester, VT: Destiny Books, 2006/1997), 13; hereafter UP.

55. Alvin Schwartz, "The Real Secret of Superman's Identity," *Children's Literature* 5 (1976): 117–29.

56. Schwartz, "The Real Secret," 128n8.

57. GS 95, 95–96, 206. The last quote is from the back cover of the second edition.

58. Schwartz, "The Real Secret," 124.

59. This again is quite typical of many Tantric systems in Asia, which are explicitly designed for "the householder," that is, the man in the world.

60. Alvin Schwartz, "Batman—Backward Looking and Forward Leaning," in *Batman: The Sunday Classics 1943–1946* (New York: Sterling Publishing, 2007), 40.

61. Ibid., 43.

62. Schwartz, "The Real Secret," 117.

63. From the back cover of Schwartz, *A Gathering of Selves*.

64. Both expressions appear on the back cover of Schwartz, *A Gathering of Selves*.

65. See, for example, Nandor Fodor, *Between Two Worlds* (West Nyack, NY: Parker Publishing, 1964); and Nandor Fodor, *The Unaccountable* (New York: Award Books, 1968).

66. Godwin, *Atlantis*, 282–85.

CHAPTER SIX

1. Barry Windsor-Smith, *OPUS: Volume 1* (Seattle: Fantagraphics Books, 1999). *OPUS: Volume 2* would appear with the same publisher a year later, in 2000. Hereafter, I will cite these two works as O, followed by the volume and page number.

2. This description differs slightly from the one in OPUS after a personal communication from Windsor-Smith (September 2, 2010) offered more detail on the two figures' precise placement.

3. O 1.97–98. This would not be the last time he experienced the paranormal through the discipline of drawing Conan. For another "drawing the paranormal drawing us," see O 2.105–11.

4. The experience of the ego being pushed "to the left" is interesting in light of the evidence that pure consciousness may be filtered primarily through the right hemisphere of the brain (which controls the left side of the body), whereas the ego or the normal sense of awareness is primarily a left-brain function (which controls the right side of the body). Is the left-brained ego being temporarily "pushed out" here? The artist came to call these events the Reality Shift, which he compares to ufology's "the Oz factor," yet another pop-cultural paranormal reference (O 2.37).

5. This drawing can be seen on page 47 of *Savage Tales* 2 (October 1973).

6. Personal communication, August 22, 2010.

7. Jon B. Cooke and John Morrow, eds., *Streetwise: Autobiographical Stories by Comic Book Professionals* (Raleigh, NC: TwoMorrows Publishing, 2000), 148–58.

8. My treatment of Dick's metaphysical experiences would be impossible without two trilogies, one scholarly, one literary. In terms of the scholarship, I am relying primarily on Lawrence Sutin's labors, which include a biography and two important edited volumes: *Divine Invasions: A Life of Philip K. Dick* (New York: Citadel, 1991); *In Pursuit of Valis: Selections from the Exegesis* (Underwood Miller); and *The Shifting Realities of Philip K. Dick: Selected Literary and Philosophical Writings* (New York: Vintage Books, 1995); hereafter cited as DIS, IPV, and SR, respectively. In terms of the fiction itself, I am privileging what Dick himself called his "Valis trilogy," which consists of *VALIS* (1981), *The Divine Invasion* (1981), and *The Transmigration of Timothy Archer* (1982), as these appear in the American Library Edition, edited by Jonathan Lethem (New York: Library Classics of the United States, 2009); hereafter cited as V, DI, and TTA, respectively.

9. Patrick Hearn, introduction to *The Annotated Wizard of Oz: Centennial Edition* (New York: W. W. Norton, 2000), xc–xcv. See also Katharine M. Rogers, *L. Frank Baum: Creator of Oz* (New York: St. Martin's Press, 2002), 11–12, 96, 100–101.

10. DIS 38. The "Tijuana bibles" of the 1940s were underground publications in which cartoon-strip characters like Dick Tracy, Popeye, and Mary Marvel worked as pornographic tropes.

11. See "Notes Made Late at Night by a Weary SF Writer" (1968, 1972), in SR 19.

12. Dick remembers no such scene, though he spoke of being molested by a homosexual neighbor, which he relates to his feelings of inadequacy. For both readings, see DIS 25–26.

13. PV 102. For our stellar origins, see also PV 32, SR 332. Dick compared his awakening before the sun-lit golden fish to the seventeenth-century cobbler Jacob Boehme, who experienced his own enlightenment staring into a pewter dish reflecting the sunlight (SR 302). Their systems are certainly similar enough. Dick, for example, consistently employed Boehme's language of the **Ürgrund or "primordial ground,"** his notion that evil is something internal to the divine process, and his notion that the universe comes about "so that the maker can obtain thereby an objective standpoint to comprehend its own self" (SR 281).

14. For more on reincarnation, see PV 102.

15. D. Scott Apel, ed., *Philip K. Dick: The Dream Connection* (San Jose, CA: The Permanent Press, 1987), 101–2.

16. PV 123–24. *Logos* is Greek for "word" or "reason." In the opening of the Gospel of John (which Dick quotes in his journals), it is used to refer to the incarnate Christ, who is both "with God" and "is God." In later Christian tradition, it could also refer to the sacred scriptures as the linguistic incarnation of God. Such notions certainly shine behind Dick's constant references to the revelatory, channeled, or gnostic nature of his own writing practices. This is also what he means, I believe, by "rational." See also SR 277.

17. DIS 154. Dick traces the name "Ubik" back to *ubique*, the Latin for "everywhere," as in "ubiquitous" (PV 98)—the Everywhere of the unraveling of our Orientation mytheme.

18. James A. Pike, *If This Be Heresy* (New York: Harper and Row, 1967), 46.

19. Ibid., 145–46. The category of "overbelief" is from William James.

20. Ibid., 45.

21. Ibid., 197.

22. James A. Pike, with Diane Kennedy, *The Other Side: My Account of My Experiences with Psychic Phenomena* (New York: Doubleday, 1968), x.

23. The phrase "theophanic disclosure" is almost certainly derived from the historian of religions Mircea Eliade, whom we know Dick read. See note 25.

24. V 398. See also V 355–56, 358, 369, and DI 440–41.

25. PV 112. Hence he cites the work of Mircea Eliade throughout *VALIS* (V 202, 205, 211, 282). Given his own experiences of the same, Dick is especially drawn to Eliade's notion that "time can be overcome." Indeed, that, for Dick, is what the history of Western esotericism is "all about" (V 282).

26. *Ubik* is a special case for him, to which he repeatedly returns in his journal: "So in a way my exegesis of 2-3-74 says only, 'UBIK is true.' All I know today that I didn't know when I wrote UBIK is that UBIK isn't fiction. In all of history no system of thought applies as well to 2-3-74 as UBIK, my own earlier novel" (PV 160). Or: "It's obvious that the real author of UBIK was Ubik" (PV 185). And so on.

27. PV 79–80, 101, 103. Such passages point to Dick's concept of "metareasoning" as "the infinite logic of the dialectic" (PV 94).

28. For the Atman/Ubik comparison, see PV 63–64 and 98, where he connects it to the Jewish mystical notion of Adam Kadmon, "defined as man filling the whole universe."

29. DIS 244. See also SR 251–52. Dick also noted that the tenth and eleventh chapters of the *Bhagavad-Gita*, in which Krishna reveals his true and terrifying cosmic form to Arjuna, "remind me too much of Valis to be ignored" (PV 114).

30. DIS 133. For the equation of the Christian sacramental system with Satan or Palmer Eldritch, see PV 192–93. This, by the way, is an ancient gnostic move.

31. SR 253. See PV 98–99 for a Zoroastrian version of the same fake/real hologram.

32. For a related passage on the Human as Two doctrine via gnostic mythology, see PV 89–90. For another, this time via a Greek neologism received in a dream (*Ditheon*), see PV 119–20. The latter passage, which sees our experienced world as a kind of real-unreal interference pattern of set and ground created by two separate psychical systems, resonates deeply with the brain-Mind model that I set out in the conclusion of *Authors of the Impossible*.

33. PV 123. By "intellect" Dick is almost certainly alluding to something along the lines of the Johannine *logos*, the Plotinian *nous*, or the Western esoteric *mens*, that is, a "Divine Intellect."

34. This idea, however impossible, is widely entertained, including most recently by sci-fi and science writer Damien Broderick. Broderick makes the stunning suggestion that psi, as a kind of unconscious precognitive and psychokinetic capacity, has always been involved in human evolution, and that this same psi-capacity actually has the ability to manipulate and maintain the human genome. He also envisions all sorts of causal paradoxes and time-loops, with future-psi reaching back to inform and guide the past toward itself, always correcting and adapting as it scans its own future for possible disasters or major changes in the environment. See Damien Broderick, *Outside the Gates of Science: Why It's Time for the Paranormal to Come in from the Cold* (New York: Thunder's Mouth Press, 2007), 234.

35. "Schizophrenia and the Book of Changes" (1965), in SR 176. This is a hilarious essay.

36. Paul Williams, "The True Stories of Philip K. Dick," *Rolling Stone*, November 6, 1975, 45.

37. Personal communication, August 15, 2010.

CHAPTER SEVEN

1. Whitley and Anne Strieber attended a symposium on the paranormal and popular culture that I directed at the Esalen Institute, Big Sur, California, on May 16–20, 2010. I also corresponded with the Striebers from 2009 through 2011. Where I do not cite texts, I am drawing on these private exchanges and conversations.

2. The influence of Vallee's writings, especially *Passport to Magonia*, on Strieber are obvious enough (see, for example, COM 91, 227–28, 245–46).

3. Whitley Strieber, *Evenings with Demons: Stories from 30 Years* (Grantham, NH: Borderlands Press, 1997), 192, 176, 184.

4. Ibid., 171–72.

5. Ibid., 174.

6. Ibid., 175.

7. There is also the fascinating demographic fact that Irish surnames appear more often than others among the letter writers. Hints of a modern fairy lore, perhaps.

8. Ed Conroy, *Report on "Communion": An Independent Investigation of and Commentary on Whitley Strieber's "Communion"* (New York: William & Morrow Co., 1989), 39–42. Conroy interviewed Lee to confirm the details of his story.

9. Strieber sees Marian apparitions, with a host of other ufological writers, through the lens of the visitors. See Strieber's introduction to Michael Hesemann, *The Fatima Secret* (New York: Dell, 2000).

10. "Joy" is a technical term for Strieber. Like the Sanskrit *ananda* or "bliss," it refers to a state of being and consciousness that needs no object, a kind of "nondual eros," if you will.

11. See "Whitley's Journal: The Anguish and Pain of My Rape," August 5, 2009, at http://www.unknowncountry.com/journal/?id=375.

12. For select passages on the insectoid nature of the visitors, see COM 20, 142–43, 148, 151, 154, 155, 227, 230–31, 267, and so on.

13. Whitley Strieber, "The Open Doors" (privately distributed pdf), 35.

14. Ibid., 37, 5.

15. Ibid., 47, 6.

16. Joscelyn Godwin has pointed out that Gurdjieff's concept of the Kundabuffer, a special organ originally implanted at the base of the spine (and then removed) by a space commission to keep human beings ignorant of their use as a food source for the moon, reads like an alien implant via kundalini yoga. He also finds in Gurdjieff's *Beelzebub's Tales to His Grandson* early formations of alien "walk-ins" disguised as humans and notes that Gurdjieff's big-eyed, winged Martians resemble the Mothman. See Godwin, *Atlantis and the Cycles of Time: Prophecies, Traditions, and Occult Revelations* (Rochester, Vermont: Inner Traditions, 2010), 230-4.

17. See Dr. Roger Leir, *Casebook: Alien Implants*, edited and introduced by Whitley Strieber (New York: Dell, 2000).

18. One of Strieber's sources for his thoughts on reincarnation is the former University of Virginia psychiatrist Ian Stevenson (T 242). Another is his experience of the visitors, who claimed that the earth is a "school" and that "we recycle souls" (T 242).

19. This "Tantric transmission" is one of the four central theses of my *Esalen: America and the Religion of No Religion* (Chicago: University of Chicago Press, 2007).

20. This text's "fantastic" nature is signaled by the fact that Strieber originally could not bring himself to publish it as *either* fiction *or* nonfiction. It is now forthcoming from Tarcher/Penguin.

21. Strieber, "The Open Doors," 28–29.

22. Such teachings are clear allusions to Rick Strassman's *DMT: The Spirit Molecule*, which Strieber cites later in the book (K 95).

23. The brave can consult Colm A. Kelleher and George Knapp, *Hunt for the Skinwalker: Science Confronts the Unexplained at a Remote Ranch in Utah* (New York: Paraview Pocket Books, 2005). The underground reference is at 224.

TOWARD A SOUL-SIZED STORY

1. D. Scott Apel, ed., *Philip K. Dick: The Dream Connection* (San Jose: Permanent Press, 1987), 235–39, 189, 253, 234, 253; italics in original.